AF615466

American Sculpture at Yale University

A CHECKLIST OF

American Sculpture at Yale University

PAULA B. FREEDMAN

with the assistance of

ROBIN JAFFEE FRANK

Project photography by

MARIANNE BERNSTEIN

YALE UNIVERSITY ART GALLERY

New Haven, Connecticut · 1992

COVER ILLUSTRATIONS

Front: Chauncey Bradley Ives, *Undine,* between 1880–92
Back: Alexander Calder, *Gallows and Lollipops,* 1960

Printed in the United States of America

Library of Congress Cataloguing-in-Publication Data
Yale University.
A checklist of American sculpture at Yale University [compiled by] Paula B. Freedman with the assistance of Robin Jaffee Frank; project photography by Marianne Bernstein.
220 p.; 20.6 x 26.7 cm
Includes index.
ISBN 0–89467–058–1
1. Sculpture, American—Catalogs. 2. Sculpture—Connecticut—New Haven—Catalogs. 3. Yale University—Catalogs. I. Freedman, Paula B. II. Frank, Robin Jaffee. III. Bernstein, Marianne. IV. Yale University. Art Gallery. V. Title.
NB205. Y35 1992
730'.973'0747468—dc20

92–19928
CIP

This publication has been made possible by generous grants from

THE VIRGINIA AND LEONARD MARX PUBLICATION FUND

THE HENRY LUCE FOUNDATION, INC.

CONTENTS

PREFACE

Yale University's collection of American sculpture is remarkable for its scope and diversity. Housed in over forty separate locations are nearly five hundred objects by one hundred eighty-five artists. The works range in date from 1787 to 1990, embracing the entire history of American sculpture, from the carvings of colonial craftsmen to the metal fabrications of today. It is a collection that has grown in many ways—by anonymous gestures, memorial tributes, exceptional gifts, and selective purchases—yet always through the enthusiastic support of alumni, friends, and foundations.

One of the collection's greatest strengths lies in its nineteenth-century marbles. Among the artists represented are Hezekiah Augur, Horatio Greenough, Chauncey Bradley Ives, and Hiram Powers. Together they reveal a progression from Neoclassicism to Romanticism and touch upon subjects as grave as slavery or as fanciful as a fairytale. In addition to important Ideal works, many of Yale's most historic personalities have been depicted in marble, bronze, and plaster by artists as renowned as Augustus Saint-Gaudens and John Ferguson Weir.

The twentieth century is equally well represented. Works of avant-garde Modernists like Man Ray and Marcel Duchamp foreshadow the Abstract Expressionism of Herbert Ferber and Seymour Lipton, while Pop Art's Claes Oldenburg and Andy Warhol balance Minimalists like Ellsworth Kelly and conceptual artists like Richard Serra.

Indeed, this century proved particularly fertile as works of major significance entered the collection through the beneficence of important and enlightened collectors. Francis P. Garvan's magnificent gifts in the 1930s of the Mabel Brady Garvan Collections and the Whitney Collections of Sporting Art introduced elements as disparate as nineteenth-century genre and early classicized Modernism. Between 1941 and 1953 the gifts of Katherine S. Dreier and the Collection Société Anonyme altered dramatically the scope of Yale's holdings, making it a center for the study of modern art. In the following three decades, the gifts of

Katharine Ordway, Susan Morse Hilles, and Richard Brown Baker, passionate collectors and generous patrons, further enhanced Yale's collection of twentieth-century art. This tradition continues today as collections at the Yale Art Gallery and throughout the University comprise a comprehensive selection of American Sculpture.

Until now, lack of publication obscured Yale's works from general notice. This sculpture checklist addresses that omission by introducing the collection to an international community of artists, scholars, and collectors for the first time. By complementing a companion *Checklist of American Paintings at Yale University* published under the direction of Theodore E. Stebbins, Jr., and Galina Gorokhoff in 1982, it adds considerably to our appreciation of Yale's historic involvement in American art.

The Yale University Art Gallery is grateful to the Henry Luce Foundation, Inc. for funding the pre-publication stages of this project. Without their support the essential cataloguing, photography, and computerization of these objects could not have been undertaken. We are equally appreciative of Virginia and Leonard Marx, dedicated benefactors of American arts at Yale, for establishing The Virginia and Leonard Marx Publication Fund at the Yale University Art Gallery. Their generosity has made this handsome catalogue a reality.

Many years of diligent research went into the production of this checklist. Paula B. Freedman, the former assistant curator of American Paintings and Sculpture, coordinated the project with enthusiasm, paying close attention to every detail. She was assisted by an exceptional group of interns, graduate students, and talented colleagues whose collaboration proved invaluable. Their names are listed in Ms. Freedman's acknowledgments. I would also like to express sincere gratitude to Helen A. Cooper, curator of American Paintings and Sculpture, for her supervision and enthusiastic support of this project. We are indebted to everyone involved for bringing this collection to light, making it accessible, and thus furthering the study of American sculpture.

Mary Gardner Neill
The Henry J. Heinz II Director
Yale University Art Gallery

ACKNOWLEDGMENTS

This checklist was made possible by generous grants from The Henry Luce Foundation, Inc., and The Virginia and Leonard Marx Publication Fund. The Luce Foundation enabled us to focus on the University's diverse and important collections of American sculpture for the first time; Virginia and Leonard Marx made the publication of this significant body of material possible. To both, a sincere note of appreciation for their support in making this book a reality.

The knowledge and dedication of a great many people carried this project to fruition. I am grateful to all, but offer warm thanks to a roster of contributors from the Yale University Art Gallery. Foremost among these is Helen A. Cooper, curator, Department of American Paintings and Sculpture. Her consistently sound judgment and unwavering support ushered this long-term enterprise from conception to publication. Jeannine Falino Heath and Deborah Johnson, former interns, deserve praise for their resourcefulness in the early stages of checklist organization; Jennifer Hrabckak patiently read the proofs, and Miles P. Finley verified the final indices. Beverly Rogers kept communications flowing adeptly. I was also fortunate in having a most helpful group of graduate student Fellows. For research and cataloguing assistance I acknowledge Elizabeth Taft Armandroff, Jane Desmond, Diane Dillon, Sheryl Freedland, Kenneth Haltman, Laura Katzman, Susan Klein Landauer, Christopher Reed, Joanne Thompson, James Weiss, Amy Suzanne Weisser, and Christopher Yulo. Susan Matheson, curator, Department of Ancient Art, provided information about classical subjects, while Sasha Newman, associate curator, and her assistant, John Klein, Department of European and Contemporary Art, helped with contemporary works. The Operations Department willingly provided access to much of the Gallery's sculpture; my sincere thanks to Richard P. Moore, Robert M. Soule, Robert C. Soule, Fred D'Amico, V. Cayse Cheatham, Michael Stack, and Jonathan Lippincott for getting the job done. Susan Frankenbach, Diane Hart, Rosalie Reed, Sarah Cash, and Lisa Davis in the Registrar's Office smoothed my path considerably. Louisa Cunningham, Brigitte Meshako, and Carolyn Fitzgerald in the Business Office kept track of our labyrinthine finances. Joseph Szaszfai opened the Gallery's photography studio to us and was generous with his photographic expertise. William Cuffe was helpful in supplying hundreds of file photographs from the Gallery's Rights and Reproductions department.

My appreciation to Marianne Bernstein, the checklist's photographer, for bringing dedication, creativity, and a joyful energy to this project; and to Terence Falk, whose expert printing enriched the photographs. John Gambell, the checklist's designer, brought elegance, clarity, and vigor to a potentially cumbersome accumulation of data. Sincere thanks to Elise K. Kenney for editing the manuscript with wisdom and diligence, and to Lesley Baier for her insight on the Introduction.

A special note of gratitude to Robin Jaffee Frank, my successor as assistant curator of American Paintings and Sculpture; her generosity, warmth, and knowledge made the transition of departure easier on both the completion of this project and my spirits.

Despite the heavy demands and disruptions our requests entailed, my colleagues and I received patient support everywhere we went. My appreciation is extended to the staffs of the Historic Mount Vernon Association, Mount Vernon, VA; The State of Connecticut Governor's Residence, Hartford; and the Yale Club of New York; at Yale, to the Afro-American Cultural Center, Becton Engineering and Applied Science Center, Connecticut Hall, Connecticut Mental Health Center, Dwight Hall, the Elizabethan Club, Josiah Willard Gibbs Research Laboratories, the Hall of Graduate Studies, Kline Geology Laboratory, Osborn Memorial Laboratories, Payne-Whitney Gymnasium, Sheffield-Sterling-Strathcona Hall, Sterling Chemistry Laboratory, Woodbridge Hall, Woolsey Hall, the Wrexham Foundation, the Schools of Art and Architecture, the Divinity School, the School of Drama, and the Law School. I thank the staffs of Yale's Beinecke Rare Book and Manuscript Library, Kline Science Library, the School of Medicine Historical Library, the School of Music Library, and, in Sterling Memorial Library, the Arts of the Book Room, the Benjamin Franklin Collection, and Manuscripts and Archives. Finally, I appreciate being permitted access to works in Yale's residential colleges, Berkeley, Calhoun, Timothy Dwight, Jonathan Edwards, Morse, Pierson, Saybrook, and Trumbull.

I would also like to acknowledge the following people for their time and expertise: Lewis I. Sharp and Lauretta Dimmick, Denver Art Museum; Donna Hassler, Metropolitan Museum of Art; Eleanor Jones, Dallas Museum of Art; H. Nichols B. Clark, The Chrysler Museum; and Fernande Ross, Storm King Art Center.

A final note of warm appreciation to Thomas E. Curran III for his invaluable assistance and steadfast encouragement.

INTRODUCTION

The results of art depend so much on individual taste, that it is rarely found that the happiest efforts gain the favor of a general suffrage. A feature that is beautiful to the eye of one critic, is pronounced a blemish by another; and yet there is a standard of beauty, which, although undefinable by language, speaks to the senses of all.

"The Fine Arts," *The American Historical Magazine,* February 1836

Scattered throughout the more than forty locations represented in this checklist is a university collection of remarkable richness and diversity. It offers as many standards of "beauty" as three centuries of creativity can produce, and enough style and historic reflection to satisfy critical eyes from any period of our nation's past. Moving from the early flowering of artisanal carving to the conceptual treatment of contemporary art, encompassing media as different as wood and steel, and including subjects as varied as portraiture and abstract form, this collection effectively "speaks to the senses of all." It speaks, as well, of the sensibilities and aspirations that brought these works to Yale.

The University acquired its first American sculpture in 1804, a naturalistic portrait of Benjamin Franklin sculpted from life in 1787 by Philadelphia artist William Rush. It is a genial image of the new nation's eminent statesman, carved from indigenous white pine by its first native-born and trained professional sculptor. It is also a transitional work, grounded in the craft of wood carving yet aspiring towards a concern for pure sculpture. As such it reflects a pivotal period in the evolution of American sculpture when a rich and established tradition began to find expression in the fine arts.

Colonial Americans generated little support for formal sculpture. Instead, artisan-carvers satisfied a largely pragmatic clientele by producing such ornamental and utilitarian objects as furniture, tombstones, figureheads, and architectural details. Rush exemplified this tradition. The son of a ship's carpenter, he mastered his trade by assisting a wood-carver and went on to found a carving shop that attained international acclaim for the quality of its nautical work. It was this success, combined with post-Revolutionary America's growing interest in the arts, that allowed Rush to transcend his craftsman's background and embark on a career as a professional sculptor. From figureheads and ship's decoration he turned to private and civic commissions for portraits, allegorical subjects, and monumental figures in wood, clay, and terra cotta. In 1805, he became a co-founder of the Pennsylvania Academy of the Fine Arts and a member of its Board of Directors. American sculpture was in its infancy however, and the often practical requests of patrons and an inability to work in marble proved artistically limiting. *Benjamin Franklin,* executed early in Rush's career, exemplifies this dilemma. Carved for Isaac Beers, a New Haven publisher and bookseller, it was commissioned as an ornamental shop sign, not a formal bust. Minute traces of white paint still visible on its surface are remnants of an original coat employed to simulate marble, the demanding medium of Ideal sculpture that Americans had yet to master. Yale is fortunate to have this work as the cornerstone of its collection. Commissioned, carved, appreciated, and acquired well within its own historic period, *Benjamin Franklin* provides a valuable record of the era's maturing artistic outlook.

The earliest stylistic force to shape American sculpture was Neoclassicism. Initially an elite and intellectual movement born of mid-eighteenth century archaeological discovery and a taste for refined classicism, it disseminated broadly as the Western world emulated the architectural, artistic, and political glories of ancient Greece and Rome. Under this influence, art achieved a new esteem in the popular imagination, its ability to communicate the Ideal perceived as a means of absorbing virtuous and moral behavior. Marble, with its elegant purity and classical associations, was the preferred material for Neoclassical sculpture, but its costliness, difficult mastery, and an American predilection for functional and decorative carving left this country without a formal tradition in the medium. When it came time to celebrate the great leaders and events of the Revolution with monuments and memorials, Americans turned to French, Italian, and English artists to execute the commissions. Although these works were relatively few in number, they provided needed inspiration for America's first generation of professional sculptors.

Inspiration had to be augmented through training, however. For most, this meant study in Italy, specifically Rome and Florence, where a plentiful supply of fine marble, experienced stonecutters, and inspiring examples of ancient sculpture offered welcome sustenance. Many expatriated there, participating in a vibrant international arts community. By mid-century, American sculptors would establish their niche alongside European masters of the day. In achieving this remarkable transformation, they overcame their American patrons' somewhat circumscribed taste in subject matter. As had been the case with painting, America's initial demand for sculpture generally by-passed history, allegory, and the other themes of high art for the more commonplace portraiture. Although Rush and a small number of fellow carvers had successfully introduced a fresh perspective into their society, it was not until the second decade of the nineteenth century that a more liberal appreciation of the arts impressed itself upon the American consciousness. At the root of this transition lay an expanding base of patrons.

As an increasingly prosperous population became more supportive of its cultural needs, the establishment of academies, libraries, athenaeums, and museums greatly enhanced artistic exchange and patronage in America. In 1832 Yale College opened the doors of its Trumbull Gallery, the forerunner of today's Yale University Art Gallery and the first college or university art museum in America. Three years later, the Corporation of Yale College solicited subscriptions from the citizens of New Haven in order to purchase *Jephthah and His Daughter,* a pair of Ideal pendant figures quoted from a poignant Old Testament passage. Carved about 1828–32 by Hezekiah Augur, a self-taught New Haven sculptor who had never been abroad, the work was installed in the Trumbull Gallery in 1838 with the consent of its founder, the painter John Trumbull (1756–1843). Subscribers were charged an admission fee to view the figures, thereby raising scholarship money "to assist indigent and meritorious students in obtaining an education in Yale College." The same 1838 memoranda that set forth the terms of subscription also offered this note regarding the use of viewing tickets: "Said tickets to command access to the Gallery while the Statues remain there, and afterwards to the Museum of Sculpture, where it is proposed ultimately to deposit them." A separate Museum of Sculpture was never formed, but the community's enthusiastic support for Augur's work reflects America's changing attitude toward this once neglected field of art.

Yale acquired two additional Ideal sculptures in the nineteenth century: Samuel F. B. Morse's *Dying Hercules* in 1866, as the gift of the Rev. E. Goodrich Smith, and Joseph Mozier's *The Wept of Wish-ton-Wish* as the gift, in 1889, of the heirs of Mrs. Joseph E. Sheffield. Together they provide a glimpse of America's increasing sophistication in the classical idiom. Morse modelled the 1812 plaster, *Dying Hercules,* in London as a study for his heroic Royal Academy painting of the same title and date. He presented the oil to his alma mater, Yale, in 1866, the same year that Smith gave the plaster. Their consecutive accession numbers, 1866.3 for the painting, and 1866.4 for the sculpture, highlight the complementary nature of these two gifts. Both were conceived within the Neoclassical tradition of portraying intellectual, morally uplifting subject matter gleaned from history, literature, religion, or in this case, ancient mythology. That Morse executed these ambitious works in England rather than America is significant for, in 1812, appreciable patronage of history painting and Ideal sculpture was only available abroad. Mozier, a Vermont-born businessman turned sculptor, also chose the expatriate path, departing his native land for Italy in 1845 to settle first in Florence and then in Rome. There he enjoyed a successful career sculpting Ideal groups, among them an *Undine* and a *Jephthah's Daughter.* His 1859 marble, *The Wept of Wish-ton-Wish,* is based on the title character of James Fenimore Cooper's 1829 novel about a white woman who chooses the "primitive" but "pure" quality of life amongst the native Americans who abducted her over the "civilized" society she has left behind. The work is a microcosm of the forces that shaped mid-nineteenth century American sculpture: a classically conceived figure created by an American who, although living in Rome, depicted the heroine of a Romantic American novel that extolled the virtues of the nation's wilderness. Thirty years after its completion, *The Wept-of Wish-ton-Wish* became the first Ideal sculpture donated to Yale in memory of a family member.

Twenty-six of the twenty-nine sculpture acquisitions recorded between 1800 and 1899 were portraits, all but one with Yale connections. Most honored Yale worthies and were gifts from the subjects' families, classmates, and colleagues.[1] The acquisition of *Jephthah and His Daughter* was preceded by one of Augur's earliest marble busts, the 1825–27 portrait of Alexander Metcalf Fisher, a young Yale professor of mathematics and natural philosophy who died tragically in a shipwreck at sea. Fisher's classmates donated the classical, toga-clad work to Yale after the artist exhibited it at the National Academy of Design in 1827.[2] Although portrait busts provided an established form of homage, Yale proffered only one such tribute in the nineteenth century when, in 1851, it purchased a marble bust of John Trumbull carved about 1834 by Robert Ball Hughes. Hughes's strong, naturalistic image depicts the patriot/artist in an heroic mode, draped in a toga pinned with his coveted Order of the Cincinnati, thus drawing parallels between the nobility of the ancient Romans and Trumbull's own achievements.

Yale is notably rich in works by Chauncey Bradley Ives, the Hamden, Connecticut-born sculptor whose early career focused on portraiture. Of the sixteen works by Ives at Yale, fifteen are portrait busts. All but one, which remains unidentified, represent individuals with University affiliations. Those acquired in the nineteenth century depict Yale's long-term president, Jeremiah Day; Chauncey Allen Goodrich, the professor of rhetoric and theology who helped found Yale's theology department; the architect, Ithiel Town; Benjamin Silliman, Sr., the chemistry and natural history professor who secured John Trumbull's history paintings for Yale; and theology professor, Nathaniel William Taylor. All were gifts from the sitters' friends, students, or family.

After pursuing commissions in New Haven, Boston, and New York, Ives settled in Italy where executing portraits for tourists helped to finance his more ambitious production of Ideal subjects. The only Ideal work by Ives at Yale, his *Undine,* was given in 1926 by Mrs. Alice A. Allen in memory of Simon Sterne. Ives based the figure on Friedrich Heinrich Karl de la Motte-Fouqué's popular nineteenth-century novel about a water nymph who forsakes her profane, carefree life to marry a mortal and receive a soul. The heroine provided a vehicle for Ives's carving skills by allowing him to depict the transparent folds of the nymph's wet and clinging drapery. Undine's provocative sensuality was deemed acceptable by nineteenth-century audiences only because it was based upon a fantasy with uplifting moral overtones. In fact, the work proved so successful that, beginning in 1855, more than ten replicas were executed for the American market.

Sculpture evolved into a well-accepted component of America's artistic fabric during the second half of the nineteenth century. In 1866 Yale moved to the forefront of America's fine arts studies by founding a School of Fine Arts that incorporated studios, lecture halls, offices, and exhibition space into its specially built Street Hall. The school's first director, painter/sculptor John Ferguson Weir, created two of the three bronze sculptures that entered Yale's collections during this period. His monumental, full-figured portrait of Benjamin Silliman, Sr., was completed in 1884, and that of Theodore Dwight Woolsey, Yale's tenth president, was cast in 1896. Weir's *Woolsey* complements an 1875–79 marble by Augustus Saint-Gaudens that was given in 1880 by the Hon. Edwards Pierrepont. Although portraits continued to serve as symbols of honor during the closing decades of the century, the contemporary immediacy of Weir's and Saint-Gaudens's academically robed figures reflect a sensibility quite different from the remote, toga-draped, Neoclassical busts of former years.

The late-nineteenth and early-twentieth century decades witnessed an increase in the number of professional American women sculptors studying both at home and abroad. In 1973 the Yale Art Gallery purchased Bessie Potter Vonnoh's *Two Women (Daydreams)* of 1903 that reflects the rather lyrical aspects of Beaux-Arts style. The collection of works by women sculptors from the period was enhanced by Anna Vaughn Hyatt Huntington's powerful 1907 *Jaguar Eating,* Harriet Whitney Frishmuth's intimate *The Vine,* and Malvina Cornell Hoffman's sensuous *Pavlova and Novikoff in "La Péri,"* both from 1921.

The advent of the twentieth century brought subtle changes to the pattern of Yale's acquisitions. Of the sixty sculptures catalogued during the first three decades only fourteen were portraits. The vast majority of works recorded between 1900 and 1929 were created and acquired by their donors during the previous century.[3] Among them are some of the most important nineteenth-century marbles in Yale's collection. These include Ives's *Undine,* William

Henry Rinehart's *Sleeping Children,* and Horatio Greenough's *The Angel Abdiel* and *The Angel Warning St. John.* Both Greenoughs were commissioned by Edward Elbridge Salisbury, the first nineteenth-century patron and collector of American sculpture to present his collection to Yale. An orientalist and Yale professor of Arabic and Sanskrit, Salisbury spent many years studying in Europe. He also appears to have had an abiding interest in American Neoclassical sculpture. Ultimately, the University received seven marbles from him: three busts after the antique by Thomas Crawford presented in 1900, and three Greenoughs and one figure after Greenough bequeathed in 1919. Included in Salisbury's bequest were four letters he had received from the artist concerning the production of *The Angel Abdiel, The Angel Warning St. John,* and *Aeschines* (formerly known as *Aristides*). On April 28, 1839, Greenough wrote a letter from his home in Florence to Salisbury in London that expressed the artist's frustrations and his patron's sympathetic patience:

> *Accept my thanks for your delicacy in not hurrying me in the completion of these works. Believe that I shall be unremitting in my attention to them, and that they will be a sample of what I can do—Called on as we daily are to choose between speed and safety—an honest name hereafter, and the approval of our own conscience, or gain, and the temporary approval of our employers—it is a great comfort to be encouraged to obey rather the dictates of the art than the suggestions of a mere mercantile punctuality.... No man can state how long he will be employed in embodying poetry in marble....* [4]

In 1962 and 1968 the Yale Art Gallery augmented its holdings of nineteenth-century Ideal works by purchasing two additional masterpieces of American sculpture: Hiram Powers's 1851 *The Greek Slave,* possibly the most celebrated sculpture of its day, and a plaster after William Rimmer's stylistically advanced 1869 *Dying Centaur.*

Works by contemporary artists were beginning to enter Yale's collection as well. In 1900 Yale acquired *The Wounded Bunkie* of 1896, Frederic Remington's depiction of two cavalry soldiers caught in a skirmish on the Western frontier. It was contemporary in subject, and a brilliantly realized collaboration between the artist and the craftsmen-founders of the Henry-Bonnard Bronze Company. Remington had recently received an honorary Bachelor of Fine Arts degree from Yale, a tribute he repaid by donating both the sculpture and an oil, *The Scream of Shrapnel at San Juan Hill,* of 1898, the University's first American painting and sculpture acquisitions of the twentieth century. Remington was the first of many sculptors whose gifts now enrich collections throughout the campus. Some of the artists whose gifts followed were Anna Vaughn Hyatt Huntington, Malvina Cornell Hoffman, Harry Holtzman, Herbert Ferber, Thomas Wilfred, and David von Schlegell.

As the century progressed, the demand for documentary portraiture declined for cameras now offered less expensive alternatives to the chisel, and the pursuit of modern sculpture ascended. Donors continued to present portraits to Yale, but their appeal was often more historic than artistic. With universities, museums, galleries, and publications providing continuous exposure, American taste became more sophisticated, and national pride, sparked by the Philadelphia Centennial of 1876, burst into a colonial revival movement that encouraged the appreciation and exploration of America's heritage. It was this sensibility that Yale responded to when, at the instigation of George Dudley Seymour, it canvassed "graduates and friends" to support a memorial to Nathan Hale, the young patriot whose stirring last words, "I only regret that I have but one life to lose for my country," had become legendary. Hale graduated from Yale College in 1773 and received an M.A. in 1776, the year his execution as a spy made him a hero to both school and country. The sculptor selected for the commission was Yale graduate Bela Lyon Pratt, an assistant to Saint-Gaudens. Both had been students of the Ecole des Beaux-Arts, Paris having now succeeded Rome and Florence as artistic training centers. With no likeness of Hale to guide him, Pratt wisely elected to create a portrait that embodied, not an image of the man, but the noble, patriotic sentiments he personified. Completed in 1913, his monument now stands in front of Connecticut Hall, Hale's former dormitory and the only surviving eighteenth-century building at Yale.[5]

Private collecting increased during this period as individuals culled both the past and the present for representative expressions of a cherished American spirit. One of the most enlightened of these collectors, Francis P. Garvan, B.A. 1897, recognized the value that his comprehensive selection of fine and decorative arts held for future generations and, wishing to share and perpetuate this record of America's heritage, he offered them to Yale and established a study center. This extraordinary gift of more than one thousand objects arrived in 1930 and 1932 as two distinct collections: the Mabel Brady Garvan Collection, given in honor of his wife, and the Whitney Collections of Sporting Art, donated in memory of his college friends, Harry Payne Whitney and Payne Whitney.

A number of early American sculptures figure among the majority of eighteenth- and early nineteenth-century decorative arts that compose the Mabel Brady Garvan Collection. These include the allegorical forms of *Peace, Virtue, and Plenty,* carved in 1791 by the Skillins, John and Simeon, Jr., for the pediment of a Stephen Badlam chest-on-chest; an 1858 parianware figure of Henry Clay by Thomas Ball; three iron weathervanes; and a gilded bronze eagle. Garvan's appreciation for America's early artisanal sculpture is evident in the weathervanes whose bold silhouettes interpret their function, and the eagle whose form conveys a sense of power and national pride. The most sizeable component of this collection is its forty-two plaster genre groups by John Rogers whose depictions of historic personalities, Civil War incidents, literary and theatrical characters, and scenes from daily life provided embellishment for thousands of American homes during the second half of the nineteenth century.

The Whitney Collections of Sporting Art appealed to those who considered athletic endeavor and good sportsmanship to be the counterparts of successful intellectual achievement. It arose from a classical revival in the arts of the 1890s, exemplified by the re-establishment of the Olympics in 1896. Garvan avidly collected the sculpture of Robert Tait McKenzie whose bronze athletes embodied Greek ideals of form and achievement. Fourteen of these figures are installed in the environment Garvan intended for his sporting art, Yale's Payne Whitney Gymnasium. With few exceptions, Garvan's collection was contemporary and included Paul Manship's *Spear Thrower* as well as Elie Nadelman's *Classical Head* and posthumous portrait of Patricia Garvan.

While Garvan was concerned for the arts of America's past, another group of collectors rooted their concentration firmly in the present. The Armory Show of 1913 opened the way for Modernism in America and, although much of the country retained a conservative outlook, a small group of pioneers embraced the avant-garde. Yale was fortunate in receiving the attention of one of the most influential of these collectors, Katherine S. Dreier. Her friendship with Marcel Duchamp and May Ray led to the formation of the Collection Société Anonyme, an organization dedicated to the exhibition and promotion of modern art. Beginning in 1941 with the gift of Duchamp's 1920 *Rotary Glass Plates (Precision Optics)* and concluding in 1953 with the bequest of his 1943 readymade *Pocket Chess Set,* eleven modernist American sculptures representative of such movements as Dada, Cubism, Biomorphism, Constructivism, and Neoplasticism entered the Yale Art Gallery through Dreier and the Collection Société Anonyme. These included five works by Duchamp, two by Alexander Calder, and one each by Alexander Archipenko, Harry Holtzman, May Ray, and John Storrs.

Approximately two hundred American sculptures came to the Gallery between 1900 and 1953, more than six times the number acquired in the nineteenth century. Meanwhile, donors responded to specialized collections forming throughout the University. Today American sculpture can be found in locations as disparate as the Josiah Willard Gibbs Physics Laboratory, the Divinity School, Woolsey Hall, and virtually all of Yale's residential colleges. The greatest number, however, are housed in the Beinecke Rare Book and Manuscript Library, Sterling Memorial Library, and Payne Whitney Gymnasium. Edwin J. Beinecke, B.A. 1907, for example, presented six sculpted images of Robert Louis Stevenson, including four variations of Saint-Gaudens's popular bas-reliefs, to the Beinecke's Robert Louis Stevenson Collection; and Adrian Van Sinderen, B.A. 1910, provided the Collection of American Literature with eleven images of American writers ranging from a Grolier Club medallion of Edgar Allan Poe by Edith Woodman Burroughs to Samuel Aloysius Murray's plaster bust of Walt Whitman. At Sterling Memorial Library, the Department of Manuscripts and Archives received portraits of Yale worthies to complement its historical collections, and the Benjamin Franklin Collection has been endowed with numerous images of its namesake.

Beginning in the 1950s the Gallery's collections began to reflect increasing contemporary interest in such movements as Abstract Expressionism, Pop, and Minimalism. In 1954 Stephen Carlton Clark gave the Gallery its first Abstract Expressionist sculpture, Theodore J. Roszak's lyrical bronze *Skylark,* of about 1950. In subsequent years the Stephen Carlton Clark Fund enabled the purchase of such important works as David Smith's *Cubi XXII* of 1964, and Herk Van Tongeren's *Teatro IX* of 1982. Through the generosity of Susan Morse Hilles, the Gallery received Seymour Lipton's Abstract Expressionist *Jungle Bloom* in 1955, and David Smith's *Man and Woman in the Cathedral* in 1957. These gifts were followed in the 1970s and '80s by such contemporary pieces as H.C. Westerman's *One-Eyed Poet,* Ellsworth Kelly's *Untitled Curve XXIII,* and Marisol's *Dinner Date.* In 1971 the Seymour H. Knox Fund made possible the acquisition of Louise Nevelson's *Atmosphere and Environment,* and in 1980, Katharine Ordway's collection was supplemented with a fund for future purchases. Included in her gift were works by Harry Bertoia and Alexander Calder. Foundations have played a substantive role as well. Three genre works by Hugh Harrell depicting Afro-American life were given to the Afro-American Cultural Center at Yale by the Mildred Andrews Fund; and the Woodward Foundation presented the Gallery with three of Christopher Wilmarth's glass wall pieces.

Nearly two hundred years of generous patronage have brought Yale's collection of American sculpture to its present state. Under the directorship of Andrew C. Ritchie, major modern works by Elbert Weinberg, Seymour Lipton, Robert Engman, Herbert Ferber, Dimitri Hadzi, Alexander Calder, David Smith, Isamu Noguchi, and James Rosati entered the Gallery. Ritchie was fortunate in his association with curators Meyric Rogers, Jules D. Prown, and Charles F. Montgomery, as was his successor Alan Shestack, who worked with Theodore E. Stebbins, Jr., and Helen A. Cooper. Under the current director, Mary Gardner Neill, a formidable site-specific work, *Stacks* was commissioned from Richard Serra in 1990 for the Gallery's Sculpture Hall.

The impact of Yale's American sculpture collection on students, scholars, collectors, and the general public has been profound, but no discussion would be complete without acknowledging the effect it has had on generations of American sculptors. Since its inception, Yale has influenced or trained many whose work now appears in this checklist. A partial, chronological list includes Samuel F.B. Morse, Hezekiah Augur, John Ferguson Weir, Bela Lyon Pratt, Frederic Sackrider Remington, Augustus Saint-Gaudens, Lee Oscar Lawrie, Carl Milles, Claes Thure Oldenburg, Robert Engman, Josef Albers, and Richard Serra. The growth of this comprehensive collection will surely continue — teaching, inspiring, and giving pleasure for many generations to come.

Paula B. Freedman

Notes

1 In 1868, Larkin Goldsmith Mead's c. 1860 *Bust of a Young Boy* was given to Yale by James Jackson Jarves, author, critic, and far-sighted collector of early Italian art. In this same year, Jarves deposited his renowned collection of Italian paintings in Street Hall, Yale's new art gallery and School of Art; the college purchased these works three years later. In 1930 Jarves's daughter, Mrs. Walter Raleigh Kerr, continued the tradition her father had begun by memorializing his involvement with another work by Mead, a bronze bas-relief portrait sculpted during a visit Jarves had made to the expatriate artist's Florence studio in 1883.

2 Augur's classical bust complements a Romantic, posthumous portrait painted by Samuel F. B. Morse that was given to Yale by Fisher's colleagues the year of his death. The striking similarity between the features Augur carved in about 1825–27 and those Morse painted in 1822 is probably not coincidental, for it was at Morse's urging that the skilled New Haven woodcarver made his first assay into marble by copying a bust of the Apollo Belvedere in 1823. Ten years later Augur's achievements were acknowledged with an honorary Master of Arts degree from Yale.

3 The sixty sculptures acquired between 1900 and 1929 include thirty-five plaster bas-reliefs by John Singer Sargent given in 1929 by his sisters, Miss Emily Sargent and Mrs. Francis Ormond. Sargent prepared these studies between 1916 and 1918 as classical decorations for the dome of the Rotunda in the Museum of Fine Arts, Boston.

4 Greenough's letter also includes the following report, so indicative of the artistic process:

In answer to your inquiries respecting the actual state of the works I have on hand for you, I have the satisfaction to inform you that the Abdiel is entirely cut in the marble and that it is free from stain or vein or any blemish whatsoever... The bas relief waits only for the blocker to be free from the Abdiel to commence that also — ... You perhaps will be surprised when I tell you that the bas relief has cost me more time and a greater expense of models in short a greater outlay than the Abdiel—Yet I have done it willingly, and cheerfully and have twice modelled it entirely with a view of perfecting it as far as lay in my power—As you are the first American gentleman who has ever ordered a bas relief, it is but right that you should enjoy the benefit of taking the sharp edge off my curiosity and eagerness to sculpture one—The statue of Aristides is much admired it is also free from stain—

Correspondence from Horatio Greenough to Edward E. Salisbury. Original letters located in the Department of Manuscripts and Archives, Sterling Memorial Library, Yale University; copies found in the Horatio Greenough object files, American Arts Office, Yale University Art Gallery.

5 Seymour's fascination resulted in his 1945 bequest of three additional sculptures of Hale: a bronzed plaster study and a bronze reduction of Pratt's figure, and an 1890 bronze by William MacMonnies.

American Sculpture at Yale University

NOTES TO THE READER

This checklist is arranged alphabetically by artist with the works arranged chronologically. Works by unknown artists appear at the end.

DATING

The dates listed in this checklist reflect, as precisely as possible, each sculpture's date of completion. *Circa* (c.) designates a span of five years before or after the given date. *About* is used if a date is more certain than this ten-year range.

DIMENSIONS AND INSCRIPTIONS

Unless noted otherwise, height precedes width followed by depth (recession into space). The term length is used when the horizontal measurement exceeds height; maximum extension is defined as the greatest span of a mobile at rest. In all cases, inches precede centimeters. The designations, *proper left* and *proper right,* refer to the sculpture's left and right. All marks have been transcribed as they appear on the sculpture. Cursive script is rendered in italics; slashes indicate line breaks. The lack of any category denotes its absence from a sculpture.

BASES AND FRAMES

Material and dimensions are given for any base or frame separate from the actual sculpture if it is either designed by the artist, considered integral to an overall artistic conception, or has historical significance. If a base or frame is a physical part of the sculpture, it is included in the overall dimensions.

COMMENTS

We have included sculptures by non-American artists if their work proved significant to, or was executed in, America, the line of demarcation often being necessarily subtle.

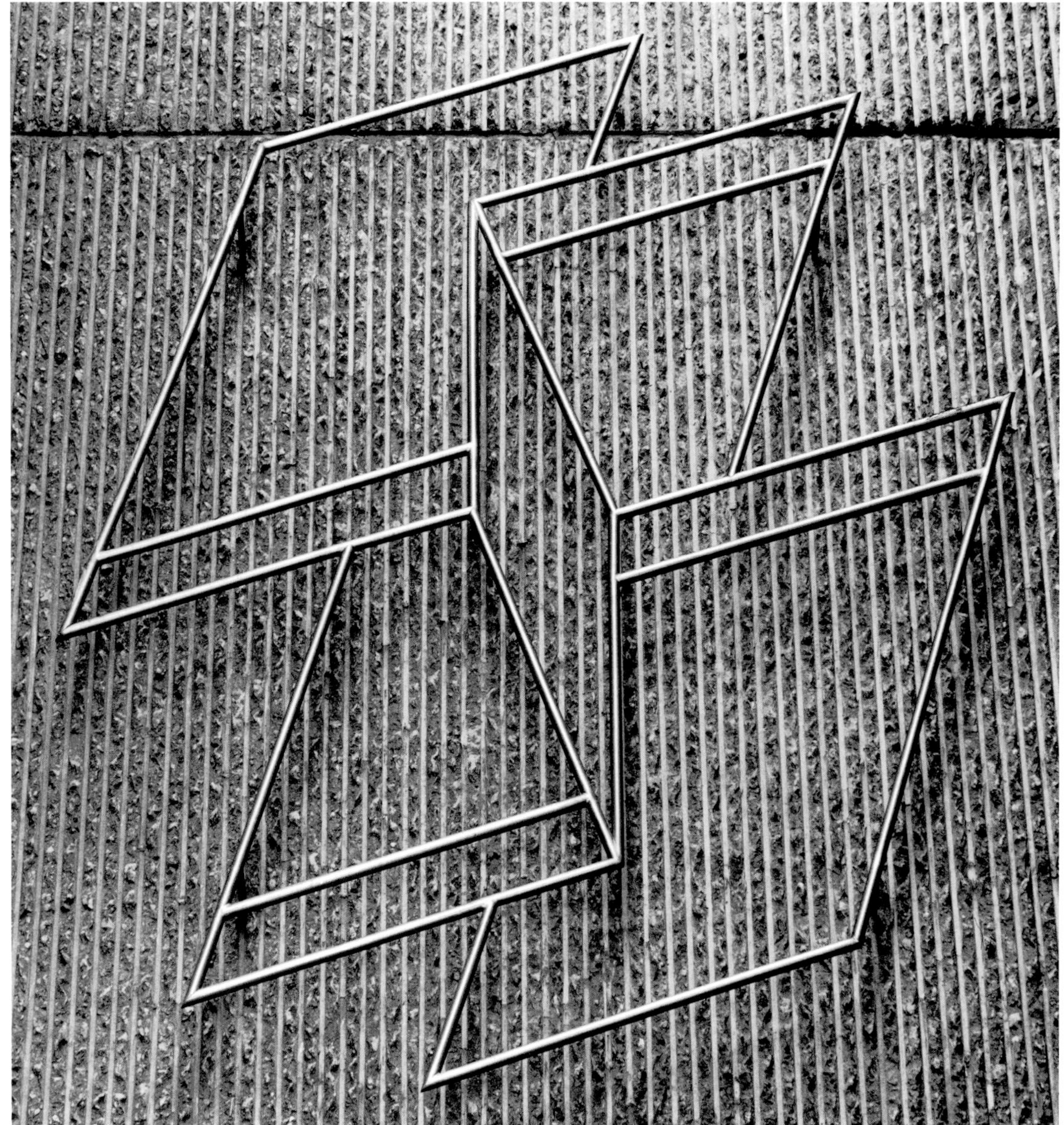

1

JOSEF ALBERS

1888 Bottrop, Germany –
1976 New Haven, Connecticut
Active U.S. 1933–76
M.A.(hon.) 1950, D.F.A.(hon.) 1962

1 *Repeat and Reverse*

1963
Stainless steel
72 x 36, width at narrowest point
(182.9 x 91.4)

Yale University Schools of Art
and Architecture

GERTRUDE AMIDAR

1907–1977

2 *George Bernard Shaw* 1856–1950

Probably 1963
Bronze, dark green patina
14½ x 8 x 6¼ (36.8 x 20.3 x 15.9)

Signed lower proper right on neck:
Amidar

Foundry: Modern Art Foundry, New York; mark, lower proper left on neck:
MODERN ART FDRY. N.Y.

Gift of the artist to the Yale School of Drama
1963.85

3 *Thomas Carlyle* 1795–1881

1969
Painted plaster and cloth
13½ x 9½ x 6¾ (34.3 x 24.1 x 16.5)

Signed and dated lower proper left side: *Amidar / '69*

Bequest of Gertrude Amidar to the Beinecke Rare Book and Manuscript Library
1980.367

4 *Robert Louis Stevenson* 1850–1894

c.1970
Bronze, golden bronze patina
17 x 9¾ x 6 (43.2 x 24.8 x 15.2)

Signed and dated on underside of hand: Amidar / 7[?]

Bequest of Gertrude Amidar to the Beinecke Rare Book and Manuscript Library
1980.368

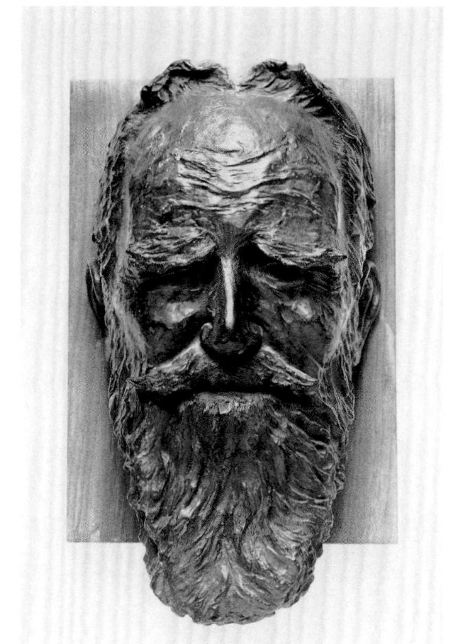

2

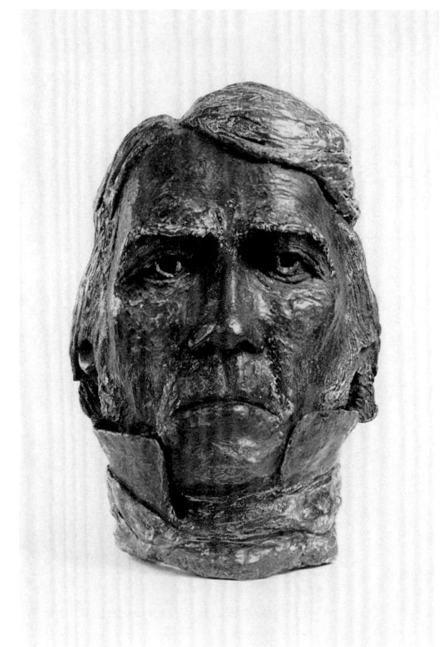

3

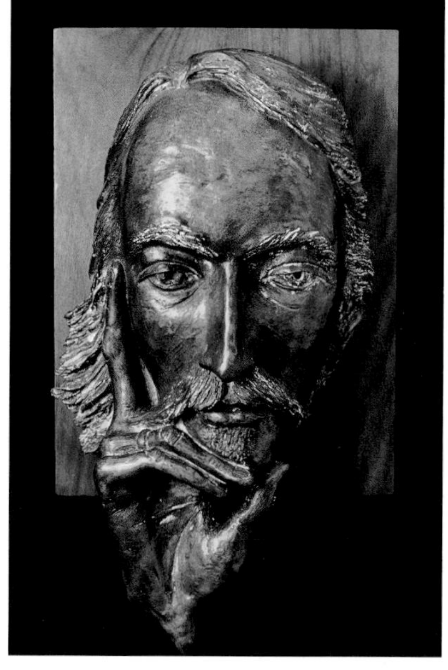

4

ALEXANDER ARCHIPENKO

1887 Kiev, Russia – 1964 New York City
Active U.S. 1923–64, citizen 1928

5 *Female Head*
(Angelica Archipenko) 1893–1957

Cast after 1964 from original marble of 1922
Bronze, green patina
16 x 5 x 5¾ (40.6 x 12.7 x 14.6)

Signed lower rear of proper left side:
Archipenko 8/8

Gift of Norman, Eleanor, Michael, and Elizabeth Solovay
1982.103

6 *Woman (Metal Lady)*
1923

Brass, copper, wood, new silver, paint
53 x 19¼ x 3 (134.6 x 48.9 x 7.6) sight

Wood frame
54¼ x 20¾ x 1½ (137.8 x 52.7 x 3.8)

Signed on plate attached to lower front of frame: A. Archipenko

Dated in paint lower left: 1923

Gift of Katherine S. Dreier to the Collection Société Anonyme
1948.207

7 *Thornton Niven Wilder* 1897–1975
B.A. 1920, LITT.D. 1947

1926
Bronze, black patina
21¾ x 18 x 11½ (55.2 x 45.7 x 29.2)

Signed center of proper left side:
Archipenko

Foundry: Kunst Foundry, New York; mark, rear lower center:
KUNST F'NDRY – N.Y.

Gift of Philip Neufeld and friends of the sitter to the Collection of American Literature, Beinecke Rare Book and Manuscript Library
1950.60

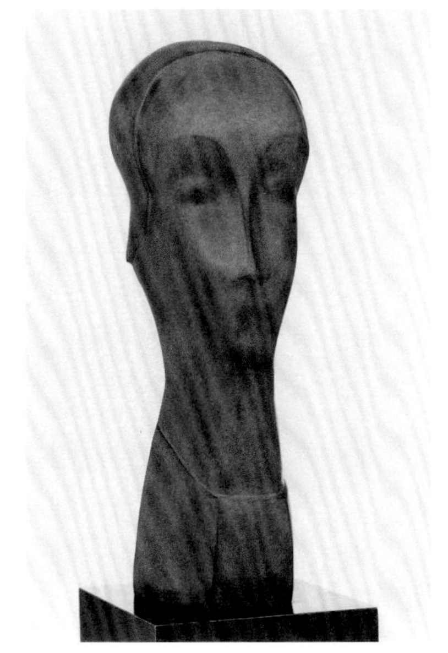

5

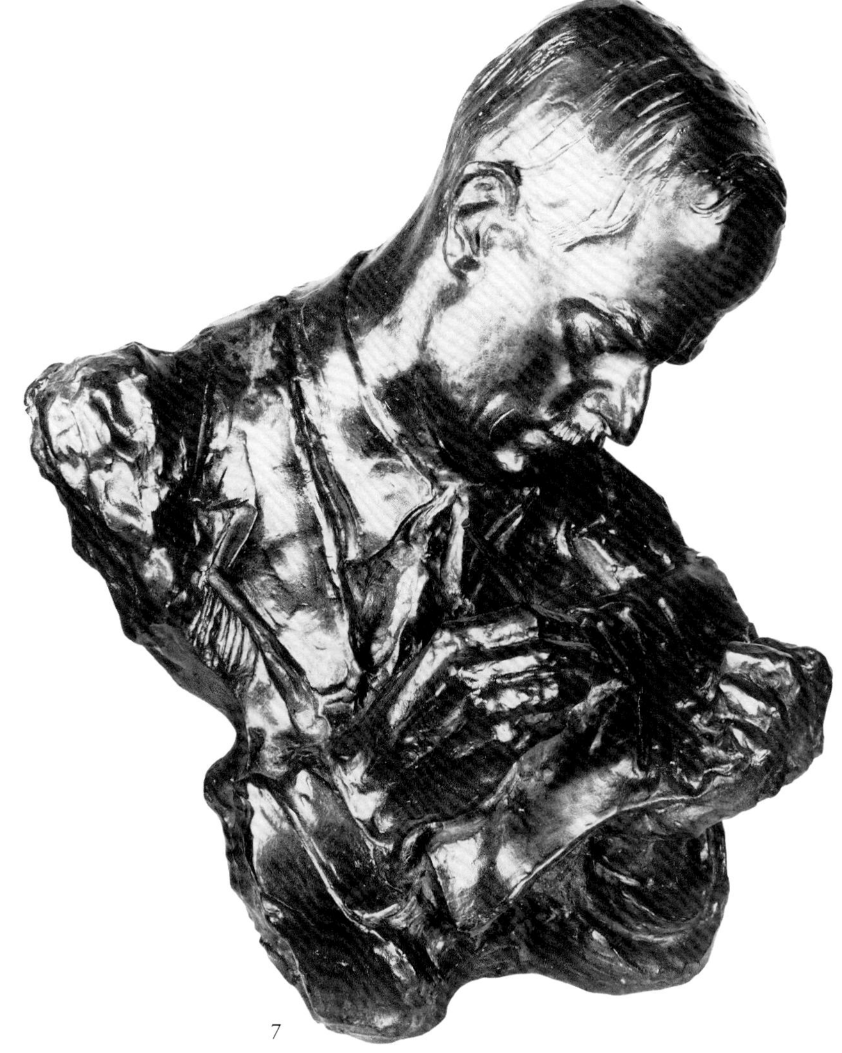

7

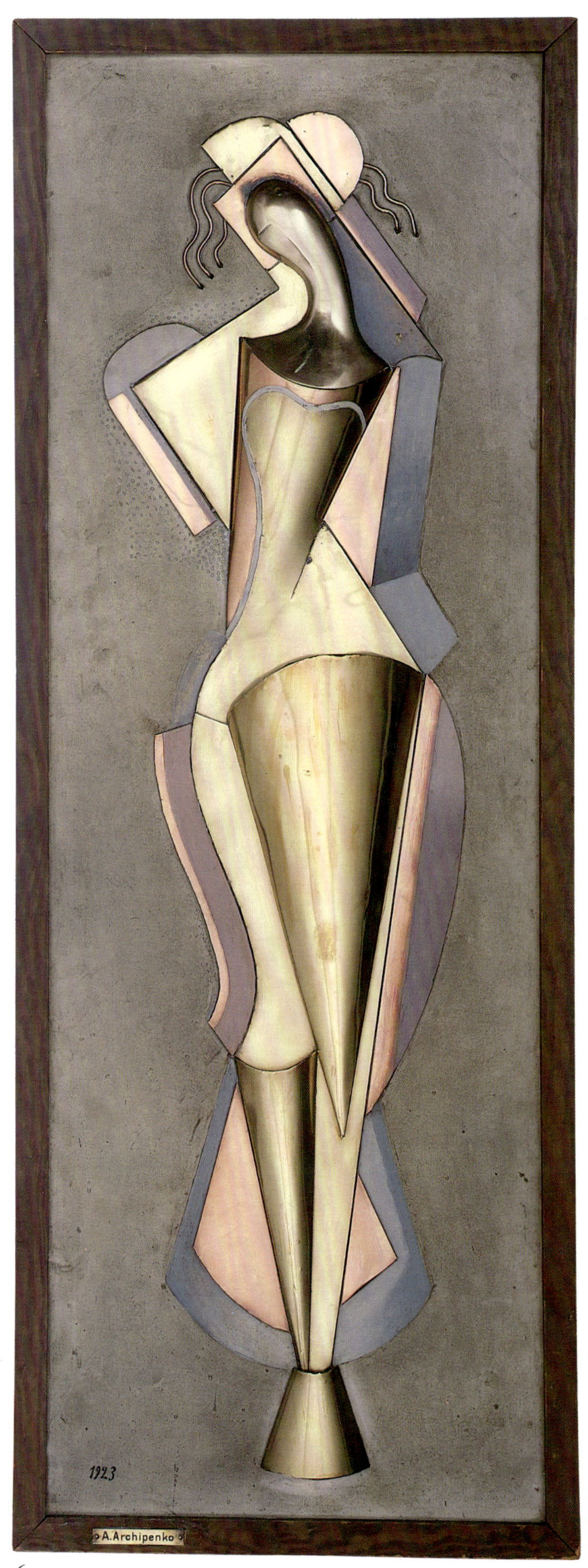
1923
A. Archipenko

HEZEKIAH AUGUR

1791 New Haven, Connecticut – 1858 New Haven, Connecticut
M.A.(hon.) 1833

8 *Alexander Metcalf Fisher*
1794–1822
B.A. 1813, M.A. 1816

About 1825–27
Marble
22¾ x 15¾ x 10½ (57.8 x 40 x 26.7)

Gift of the Class of 1813
1827.3

9, 10 *Jephthah and His Daughter*
About 1828–32
Marble
Jephthah: 44 x 18½ x 15½
(111.8 x 47 x 39.4)

Jephthah's Daughter: 36 x 17½ x 13½
(91.4 x 44.5 x 34.3)

Gift of the Citizens of New Haven
1835.11

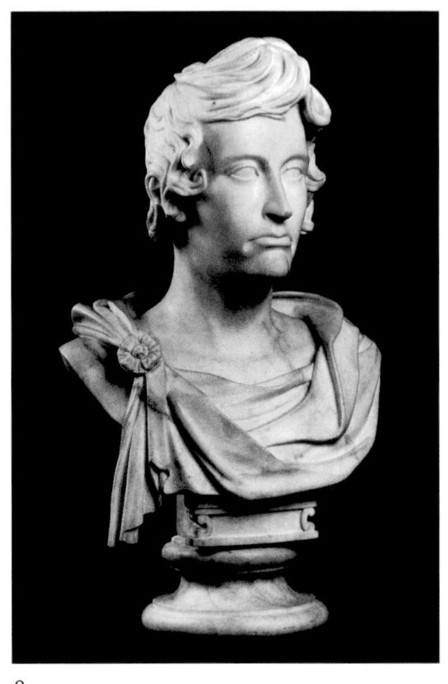

8

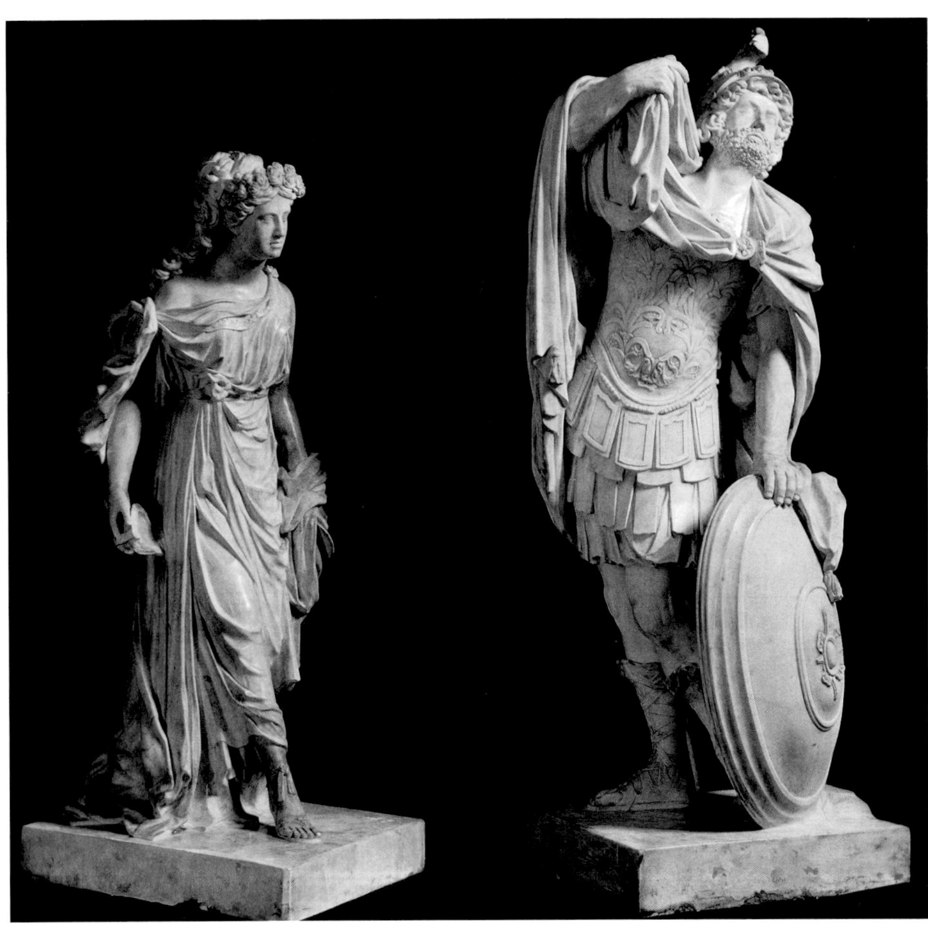

9, 10

PERCY BRYANT BAKER

1881 London – 1970 New York City
Active U.S. 1915–16

11 *President William Howard Taft*
1857–1930
B.A. 1878, LL.D. 1893

1922
Painted plaster
21½ x 13 x 10 (54.6 x 33 x 25.4)

Signed proper left side of base: *Bryant Baker / Sculptor*

Inscribed center rear of base: *William Howard Taft / modelled from life / in London. June + / July 1922.*

Gift of Charles P. Taft, B.A. 1918, LL.B. 1921, LL.D. 1952, and Helen Taft Manning, M.A. 1917
1943.354

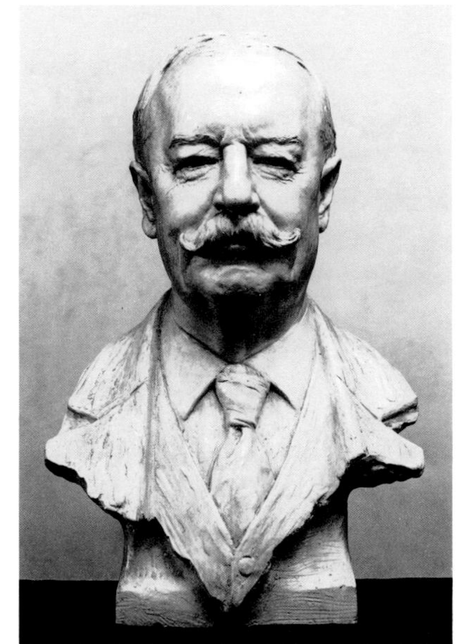

11

THOMAS BALL

1819 Charlestown, Massachusetts – 1911 Montclair, New Jersey

12 *Henry Clay* 1777–1852

1858
Parianware
25½ x 8¾ x 8½ (64.8 x 22.2 x 21.6)

Signed and dated rear edge of base: T BALL · Sculpt' · Boston Mass. 1858.

Inscribed rear edge of base: PATENT Assigned to G. W. NICHOLS.

Mabel Brady Garvan Collection
1930.830

13 *John Stoughton Newberry*
1826–1887

About 1860–65
Marble
22½ x 21¼ x 11½ (57.2 x 54 x 29.2)

Gift of John Stoughton Newberry, Jr.
1948.206

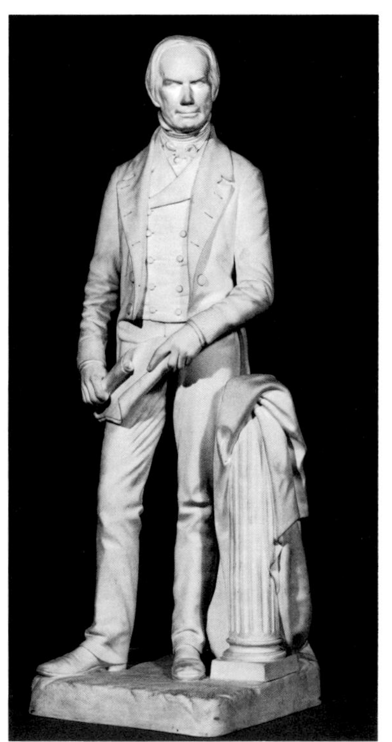

12

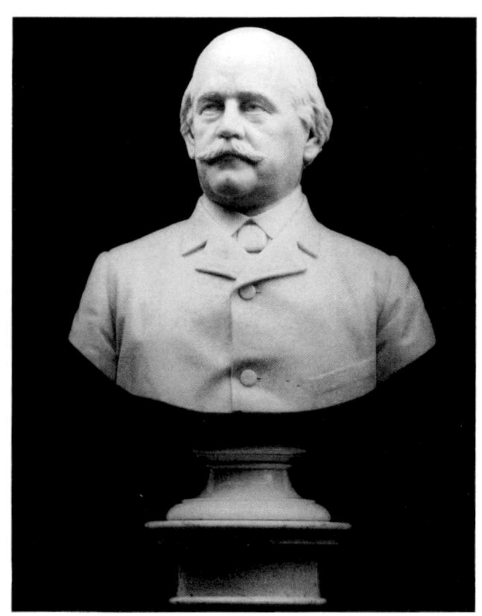

13

DR. BARBOUN

Dates unknown

14 *Face Cast of John Brocklesby*
1811–1889
B.A. 1835, M.A. 1838

1832
Plaster
9 x 6 x 3 (22.9 x 15.2 x 7.6)

Inscribed in ink on paper label adhered to verso: *Cast of the face of / John Brocklesby taken at the / age of 21 When he was in the Sophomore Class. in 1832 / in Yale College in the year 1832 / Taken by Dr. Barboun of / Boston Attest / John Brocklesby*

Gift of John Brocklesby, B.A. 1835, M.A. 1838, to the Yale University Library

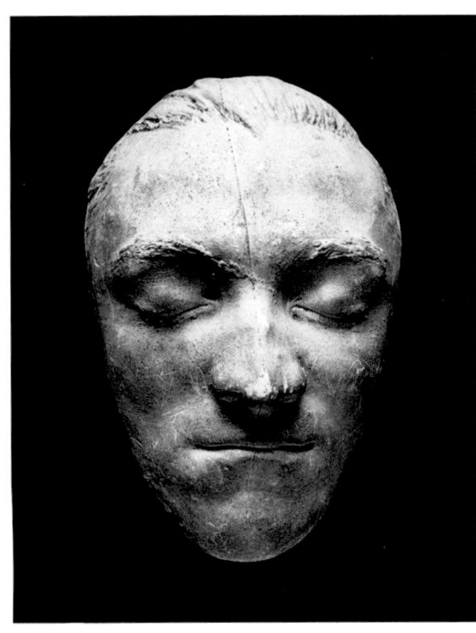

14

RICHMOND BARTHÉ

b. 1901 Bay St. Louis, Mississippi

15 *The Unknown Dancer*

c.1925
Bronze, dark brown and exposed bronze patina
20¼ x 6¼ x 5 (51.4 x 15.9 x 12.7)

Signed proper right top rear of base: BARTHE

Foundry: possibly Cellini Bronze Works, New York; mark, proper left rear edge of base: C.B.W.

Beinecke Rare Book and Manuscript Library

16 *Helen Mouat* b. 1896

1945
Bronze, light green patina
13 x 13¾ x 7¾ (33 x 34.9 x 19.7)

Marble base
1¾ x 15¼ x 6¾ (4.4 x 38.7 x 17.1)

Signed proper right lower rear edge: BARTHE

Metal label attached to front of marble base: E∀ENH / RICHMOND BARTHÉ

Gift of Mrs. Roswell Skeel, Jr., to the Collection of American Literature, Beinecke Rare Book and Manuscript Library
1948.310

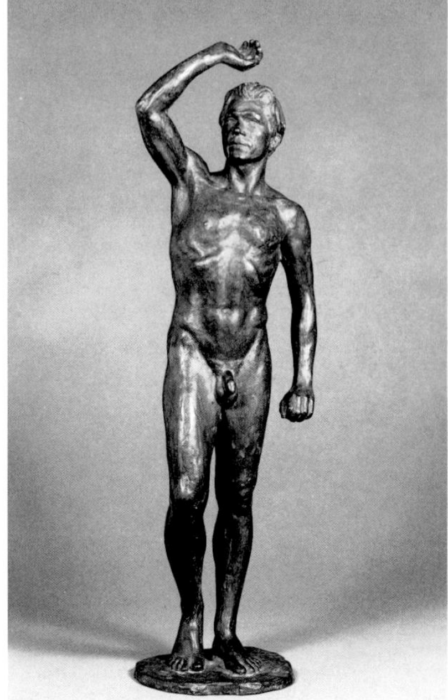

15

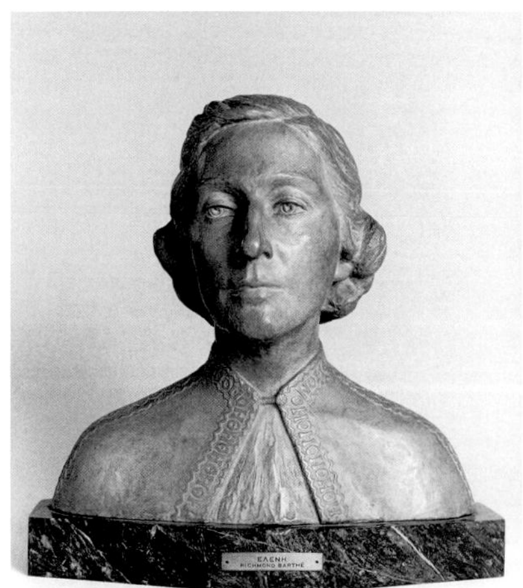

16

EDWARD SHEFFIELD BARTHOLOMEW

1822 Colchester, Connecticut – 1858 Naples, Italy

17 *Frederick Marquand* 1799–1882

1856
Marble
24¼ x 17¾ x 12 (61.6 x 45.1 x 30.5)

Signed and dated lower rear: E.S. BARTHOLOMEW. / ROME. 1856

Gift of Henry G. Marquand to the Yale Divinity School
1883.2

18 *Mrs. Frederick Marquand*
(Helty Perry) 1800–1859

1856
Marble
21¾ x 18¼ x 12¼ (55.2 x 46.4 x 31.1)

Signed and dated lower rear: E.S. BARTHOLOMEW. / ROME, 1856

Gift of Henry G. Marquand to the Yale Divinity School
1883.3

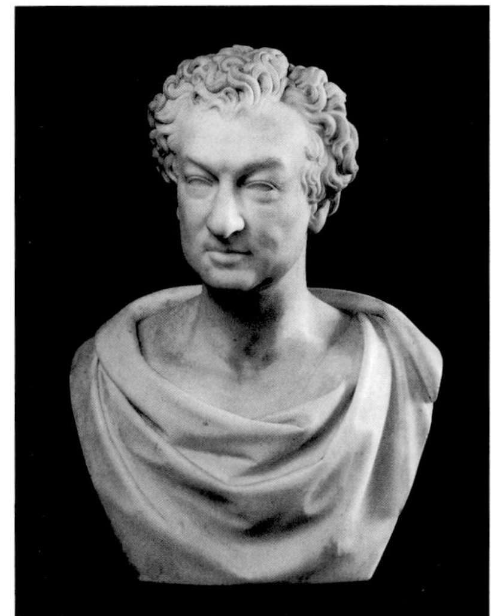

17

PAUL WAYLAND BARTLETT

1865 New Haven, Connecticut – 1925 Paris
M.A.(hon.) 1918

19 *Female Torso*

c.1895
Bronze, green patina
14¼ x 6 x 3¾ (36.2 x 15.2 x 9.5)

Marble base
4½ x 4½ x 4½ (11.4 x 11.4 x 11.4)

Gift of George Dudley Seymour, M.A.(hon.) 1913
1932.146

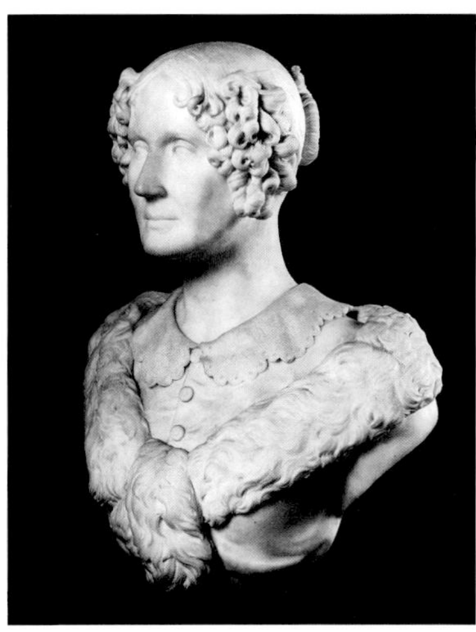

18

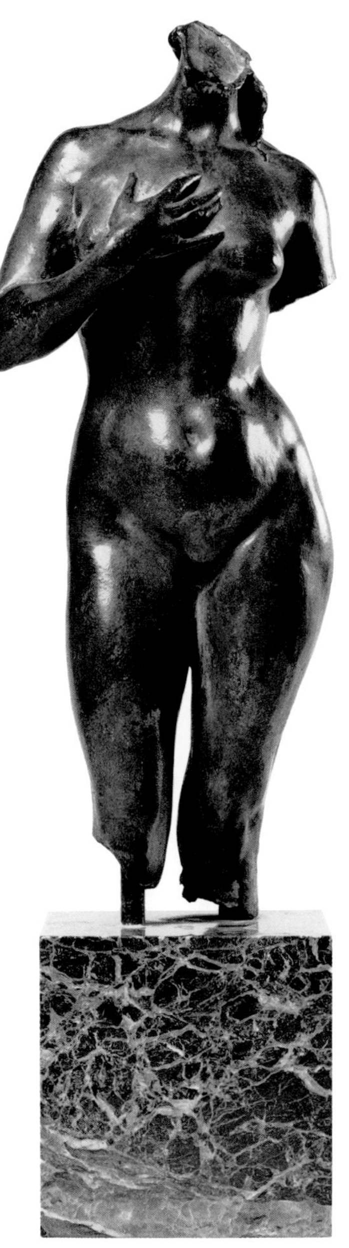

19

TRUMAN HOWE BARTLETT

1835 Dorset, Vermont – 1923

20 *Dr. Jonathan Knight* 1789–1864
B.A. 1808, M.A. 1811, M.D.(hon.) 1818

1865
Marble
22½ x 13½ x 10¼ (57.2 x 34.3 x 26)

Signed and dated upper proper left rear: B / 65

Inscribed lower center front: JONATHAN KNIGHT.

Gift of friends and students of the sitter to the Yale University School of Medicine
1865.1

21 *Dr. Jonathan Knight* 1789–1864
B.A. 1808, M.A. 1811, M.D.(hon.) 1818

1865
Plaster
22 x 14¼ x 11 (55.9 x 36.2 x 27.9)

Signed and dated center rear : THB (monogram) / MAY 16 '65

Gift of the friends of the sitter to the Yale University Library
1865.2

22 *Lowell Mason* 1792–1872

1866
Marble
22½ x 21 x 13½ (57.1 x 53.3 x 34.3)

Signed and dated center rear near bottom edge: T H B N Y 66

Provenance unknown
1875.5

23 *Charles Steele Thompson, M.D.*
1801–1890
M.D. 1822

1874
Bronze, dark brown patina
22 x 10½ x 12 (55.9 x 26.7 x 30.5)

Inscribed on base proper left side: MADE FROM / Photos by / Bartlett. / Paris / 74; front: Charles S. Thompson *M.D. / April 6, 1801 – August 15, 1890;* lower front: FOR FIFTY YEARS A PHYSICIAN OF THIS TOWN AND THE / FIRST PHYSICIAN OF THIS INSTITUTION; proper right side: Dr. Thompson / Fair Haven / Ct.

Founder's mark center rear of base: FRIE BOUÉ Paris

Yale University Library

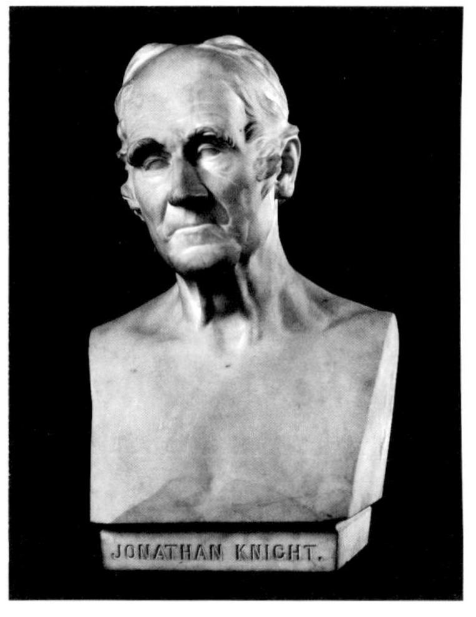

20

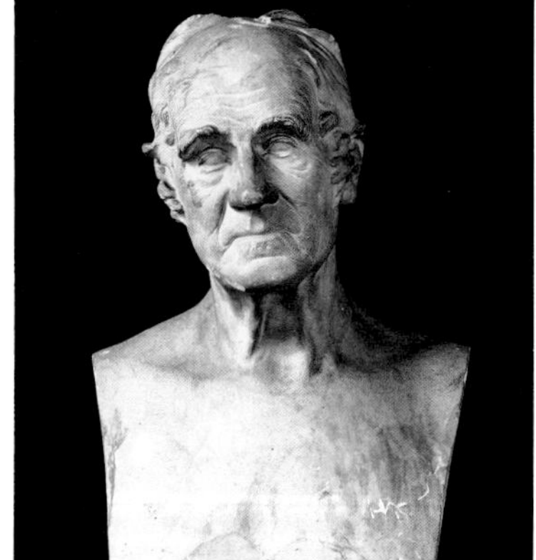
21

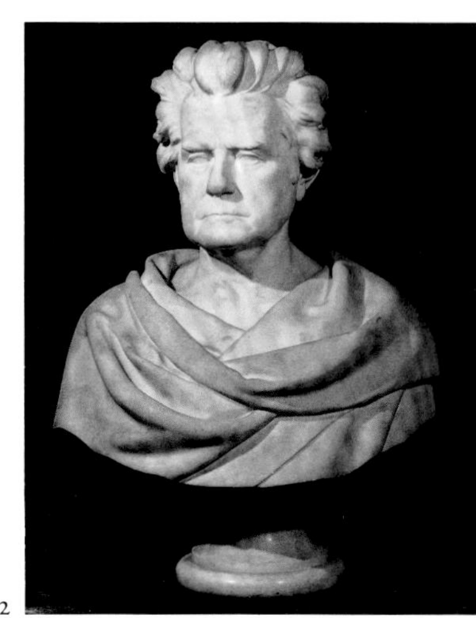
22

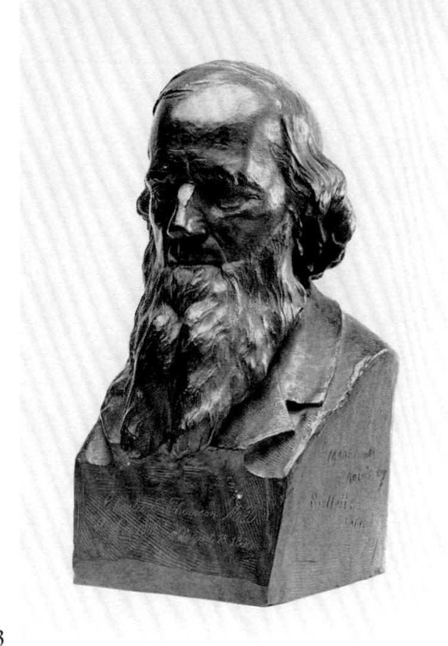
23

HARRY BERTOIA

1915 San Lorenzo, Italy –
1978 Bally, Pennsylvania
To U.S. 1930, citizen 1946

24 *Sculpture Screen*

1958
Welded metal, golden coloration
Three sections:
a) 107 x 46 x 13¾ (271.8 x 116.8 x 34.9)
b) 107 x 44¾ x 11¾ (271.8 x 113.7 x 29.8)
c) 107 x 45 x 11¾ (271.8 x 114.3 x 29.8)

Gift of the International Business Machines Corporation
1966.61

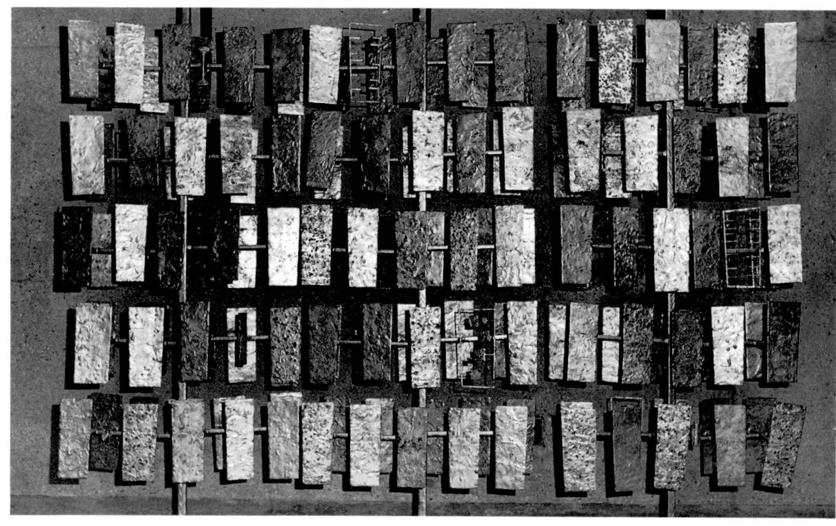

24

25 *Untitled*

About 1960–67
Manufactured bronze rods welded to bronze base, brown and green patina
37¼ x 17 x 15 (94.6 x 43.2 x 38.1)

Manufacturer's mark stamped on each rod: ANACONDA D PHOS BRZ I

The Katharine Ordway Collection
1980.13.43

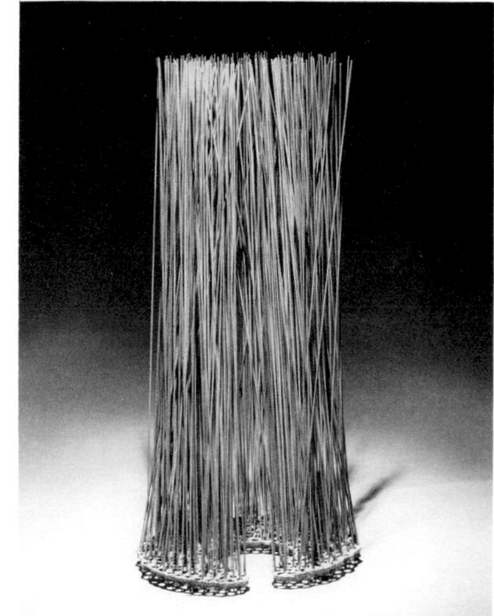

25

FRANK CRAWFORD BOARDMAN

1867 Hartford, Connecticut – 1938
B.F.A. 1901

26 *Theodore Thornton Munger*
1830–1910
B.A. 1851, M.DIV. 1855, D.D. 1908

1910
Bronze, dark brown patina
56½ x 33¼ x 4½ (143.5 x 84.5 x 11.4)

Signed lower proper left corner of figure:
BOARDMAN FECIT

Inscribed lower center in relief:
PREACHER AND AUTHOR / PROPHET OF THE FREEDOM OF FAITH / CLASS OF MDCCCLI / THEODORE THORNTON MUNGER DD / MDCCCXXX ANNO DOMINI MDCCCCX

Anonymous gift to the Yale Divinity School
1948.303

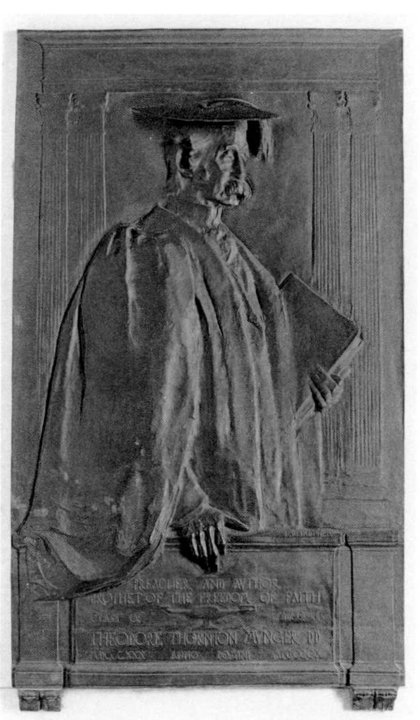

26

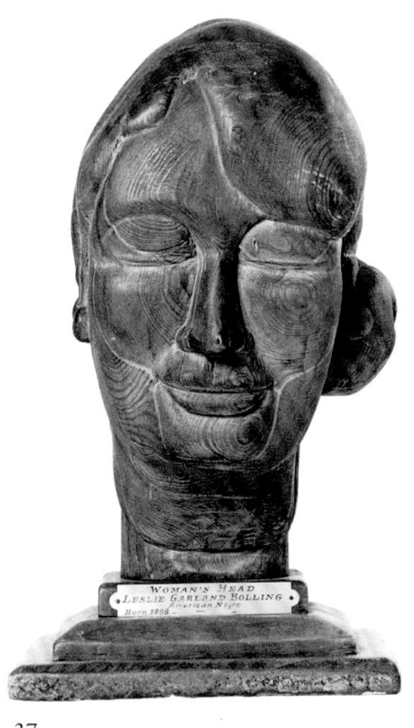

27

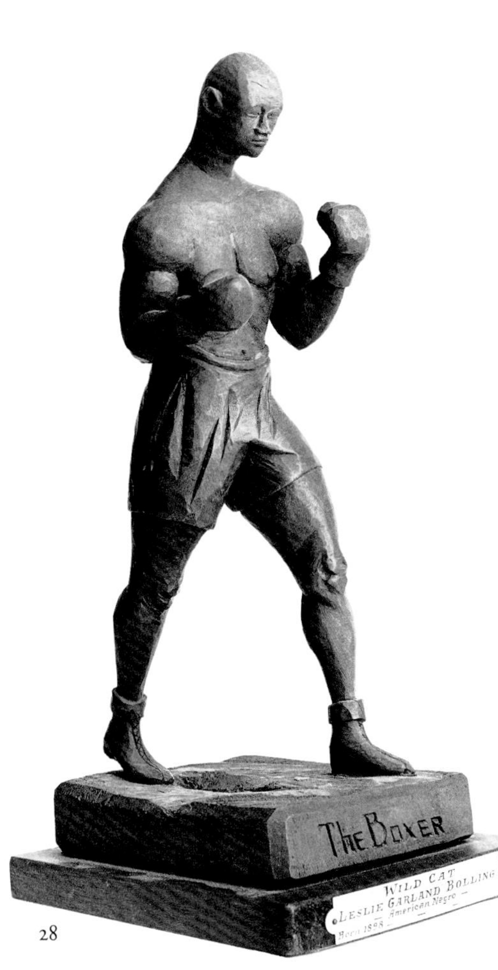

28

LESLIE GARLAND BOLLING

b. 1898 Dendrum, Virginia

27 *Woman's Head*

c.1930
Wood
13¼ x 7¾ x 7¾ (33.7 x 19.7 x 19.7)

Wood base
2½ x 9¼ x 7¾ (6.4 x 23.5 x 19.7)

Gift of Carl Van Vechten to the James Weldon Johnson Memorial Collection of Negro Arts and Letters, Beinecke Rare Book and Manuscript Library
1980.386

28 *Wild Cat (The Boxer)*

1933
Wood
14 x 6½ x 5¼ (35.6 x 16.5 x 13.3)

Signed and dated lower rear edge of base: LG Bolling / Sept. 13TH 33

Inscribed lower front edge of base: The Boxer

Gift of Carl Van Vechten to the Collection of American Literature, Beinecke Rare Book and Manuscript Library
1980.166

JOHN GUTZON BORGLUM

1867 near Bear Lake, Idaho – 1941 Chicago, Illinois

29 *Robert Louis Stevenson* 1850–1894

1915
Bronze, black and bronze patina
29 x 18¼ x ¾ (73.7 x 46.4 x 1.9)

Signed and dated lower proper left corner in relief: Gutzon Borglum / 1915

Foundry: John Williams, New York; mark, lower proper left corner: Jno. Williams Inc. N.Y.

Gift of Edwin J. Beinecke, B.A. 1907, to the Robert Louis Stevenson Collection, Beinecke Rare Book and Manuscript Library
1980.387

30 *Nude (Angna Enters)*

1916
Bronze, golden bronze patina
8½ x 6½ x 2½ (21.6 x 16.5 x 6.4)

Signed on proper left leg: Gutzon Borglum

Gift of Mr. and Mrs. Jason Berger
1982.16.3

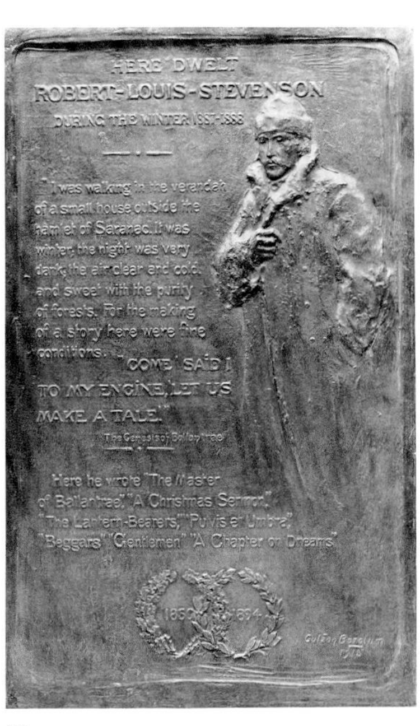

29

31 *Swimmer*

c.1920
Bronze, red patina
23 x 13¾ x 12½ (58.4 x 34.9 x 31.8)

Signed proper right top of base:
Gutzon Borglum

Gift of Edwin Binney and Alice Stead Binney, 1933, in honor of Edwin Binney, Jr. (1899–1928), B.A. 1921, to the Payne Whitney Gymnasium

32 *Archibald Henderson* 1877–1963

1924 or 1925
Bronze, brownish-bronze patina
28¼ x 19¼ x 2 (71.8 x 48.9 x 5.1)

Signed and dated center left front:
Gutzon Borglum / Raleigh / 192[*4* or *5*]

Inscribed on front in relief, upper left: ARS ET / SCIENTIA; lower center: ARCHIBALD HENDERSON

Foundry: American Art Foundry, New York; mark, lower right front corner: *Amer. Art Fdry N.Y.*

Gift of the sitter to the Yale University Library
1926.115

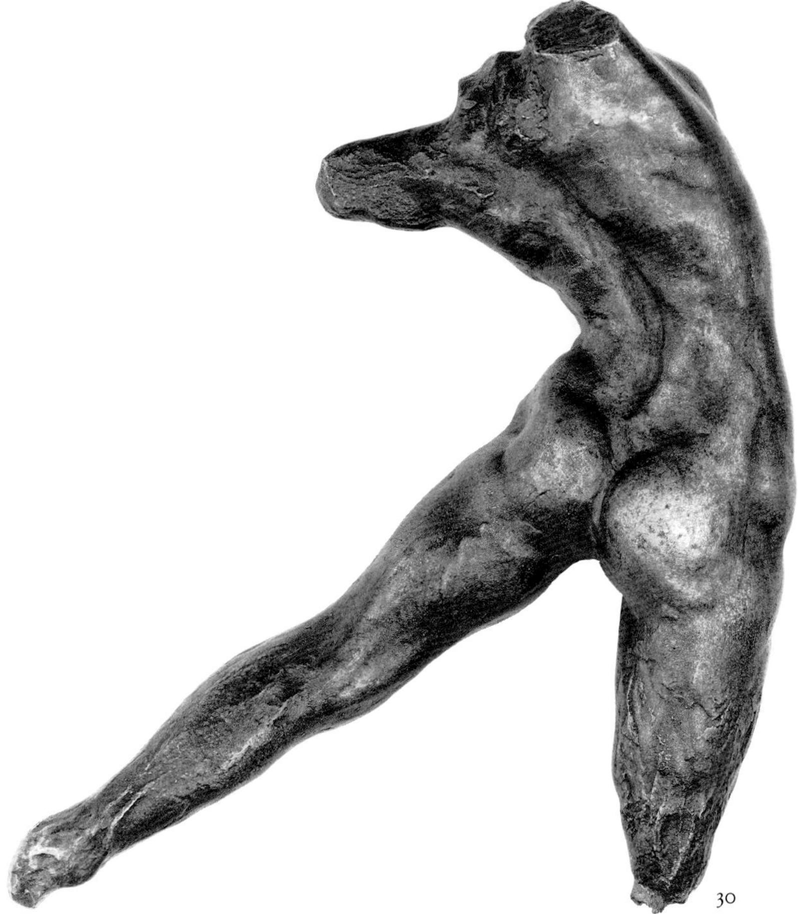

30

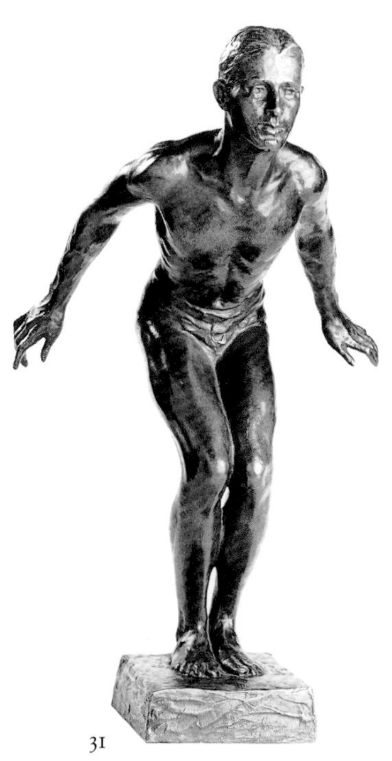

31

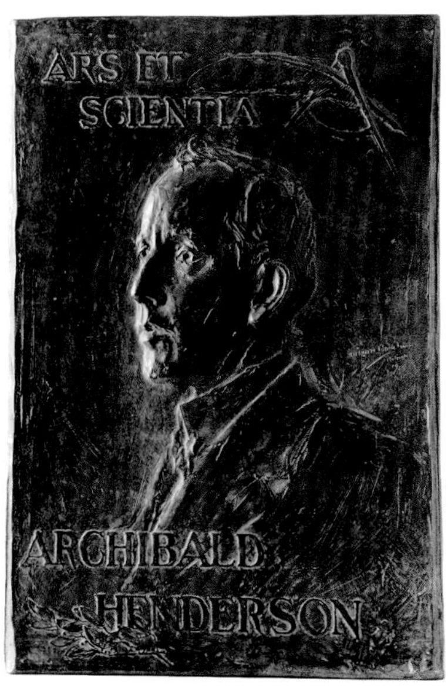

32

VICTOR DAVID BRENNER

1871 Siauliai, Lithuania –
1924 New York City
Active U.S. 1890–98, 1901–24

33 *Simon Sterne* 1839–1901

1903
Painted plaster
24 x 16¼ x 13½ (61 x 41.3 x 34.3)

Signed and dated center rear: V.D. BRENNER / 1903

Given by Mrs. Alice A. Allen in memory of Simon Sterne
1926.117

34 *Ralph Waldo Emerson* 1803–1882

n.d.
Bronze, gold patina
DIAM. 7¼ x D. ½ (18.4 x 1.3)

Signed along lower left front: V D BRENNER Sc

Inscribed on front in relief, along upper edge: RALPH WALDO EMERSON; lower left: Grolier Club seal; lower right: MDCCCIII / MDCCCLXXXII

Gift of Adrian Van Sinderen, B.A. 1910, to the Collection of American Literature, Beinecke Rare Book and Manuscript Library
1980.319

35 *Ralph Waldo Emerson*

Same as cat. 34
1980.320

GEORGE THOMAS BREWSTER

1862 Kingston, Massachusetts –
1943

36 *Horace Tracy Pitkin* 1869–1900

B.A. 1892

c.1904
Bronze, black patina, mounted on marble
29¼ x 28¾ x 2¼ (74.3 x 73 x 5.7)

Signed lower right: G.T. BREWSTER Sc.

Inscribed on front of marble mount: IN MEMORY OF / HORACE TRACY PITKIN / BORN IN 1869 AT PHILADELPHIA / GRADUATED / IN 1888 AT EXETER ACADEMY / AT YALE COLLEGE IN 1892 / AND AT UNION THEOLOGICAL / SEMINARY IN 1896 / THREE YEARS MISSIONARY / IN CHINA / KILLED AT HIS POST / IN PAO TING FU / BY THE BOXERS I JULY 1900. / WHOSOEVER SHALL LOSE HIS LIFE / FOR MY SAKE AND THE GOSPEL'S / THE SAME SHALL SAVE IT.

Gift of the Classes of 1892 Yale College and 1891 Sheffield Scientific School

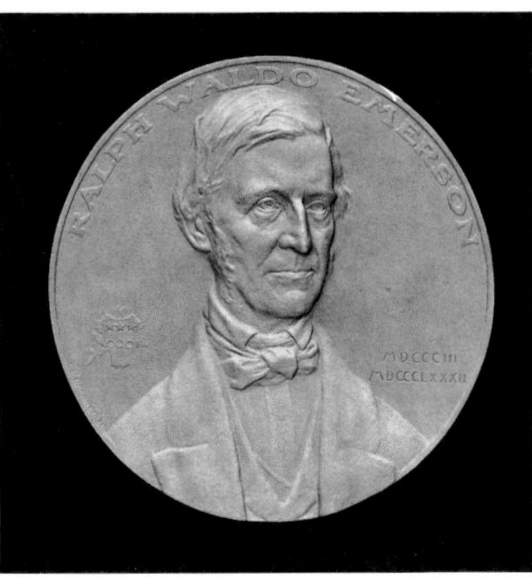

34

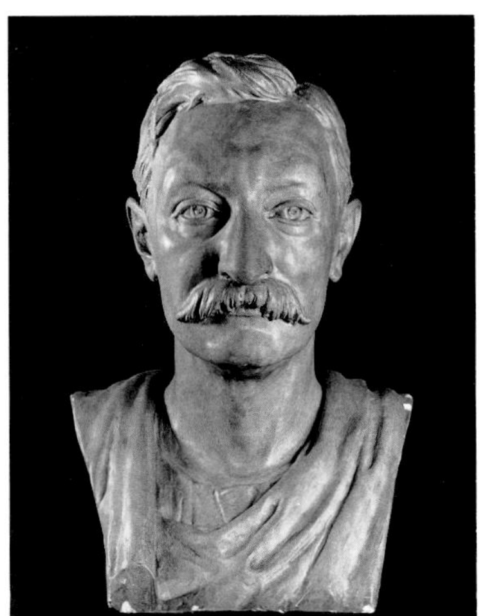

33

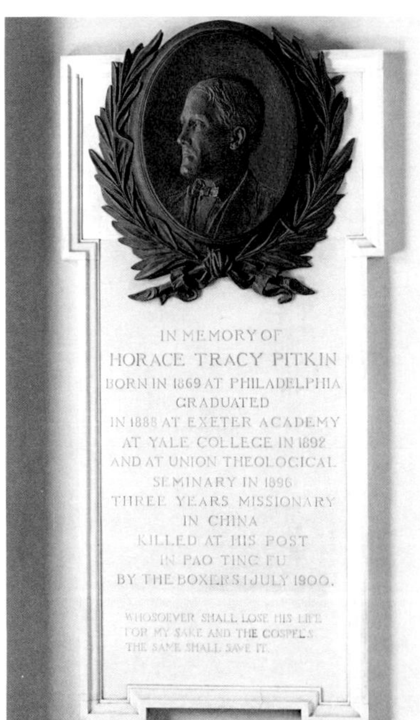

36

HENRY KIRKE BROWN

1814 Leyden, Massachusetts –
1886 Newburgh, New York

37 *General George Washington on Horseback* 1732–1799
LL.D. 1781

Cast 1932, after the plaster model of 1851
Bronze, green, yellow, and orange-brown patina
42½ x 37¾ x 16 (108 x 95.9 x 40.6)

Given by Miss Marion Terry in memory of Edmund Terry, B.A. 1837, Edmund Roderick Terry, B.A. 1878, and Eliphalet Bradford Terry, B.A. 1888
1932.1183

38 *William Augustus Larned*
1806–1862
B.A. 1826, M.A. 1829, Divinity School 1834

c.1855
Marble
24 x 22½ x 11½ (61 x 57.1 x 29.2)

Signed lower center rear: H K B

Bequest of Mrs. William Augustus Larned to the Yale University Library
1877.11

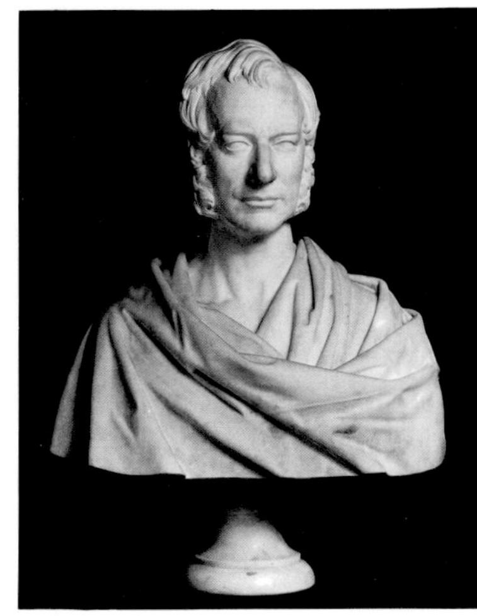

38

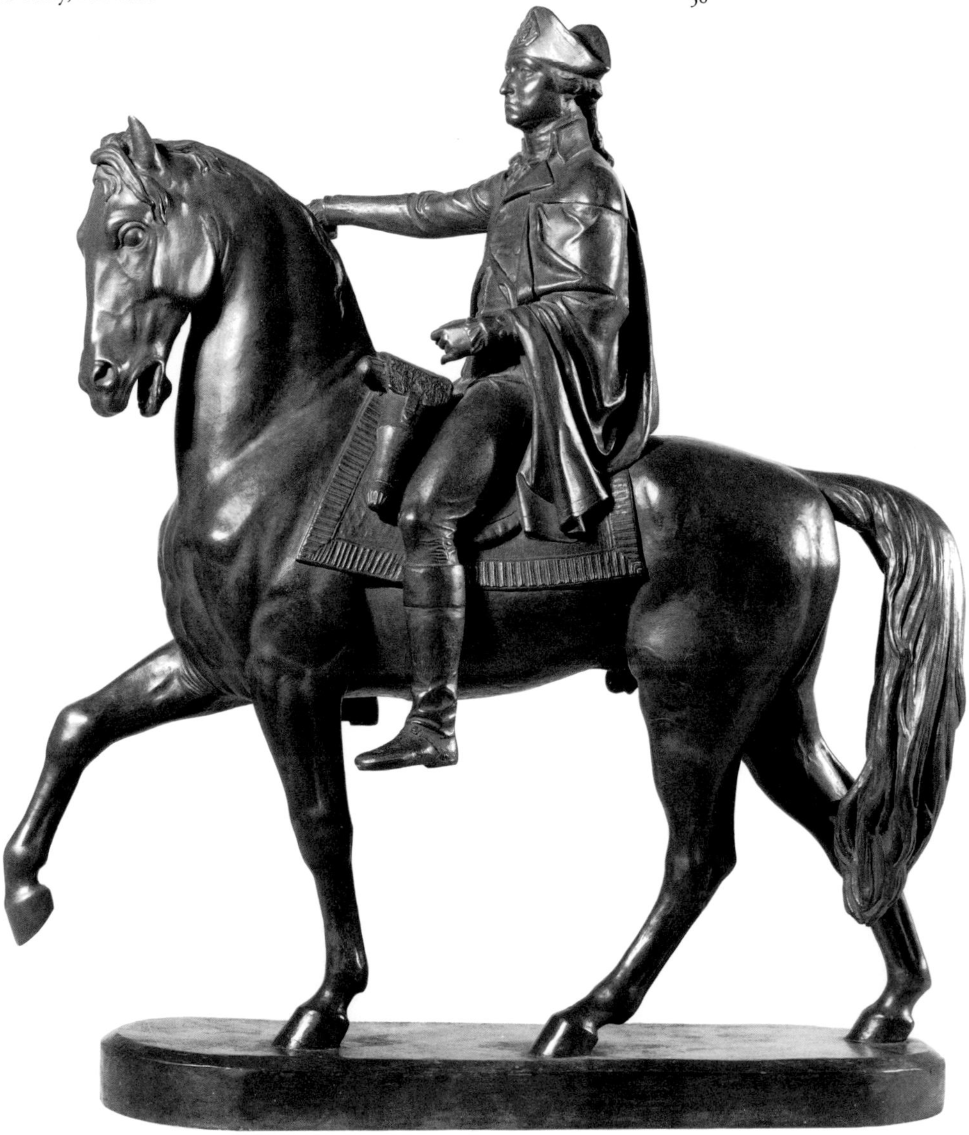

37

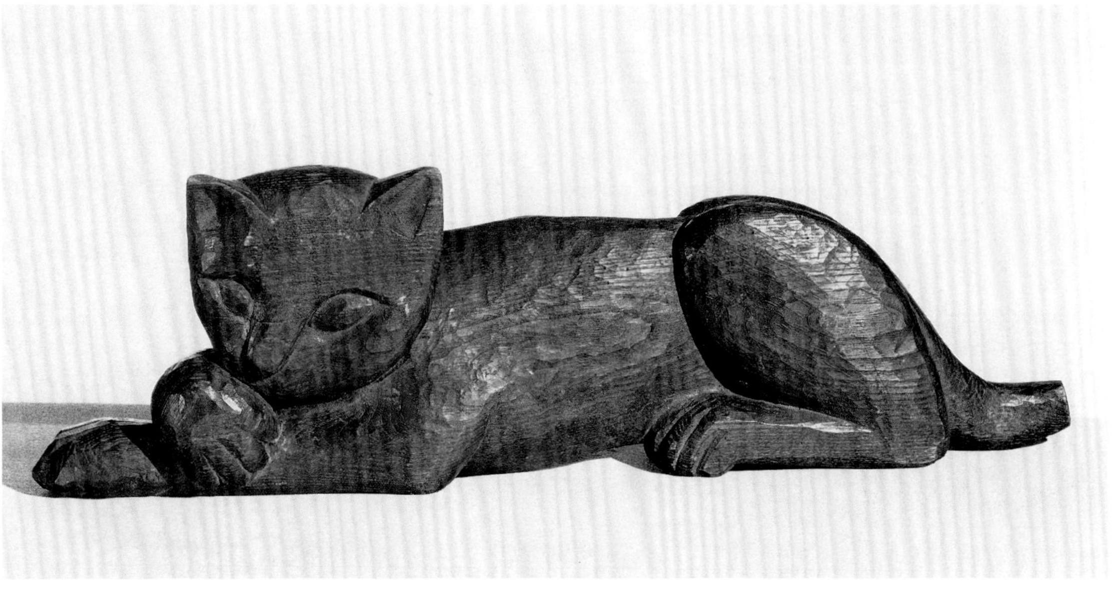

40

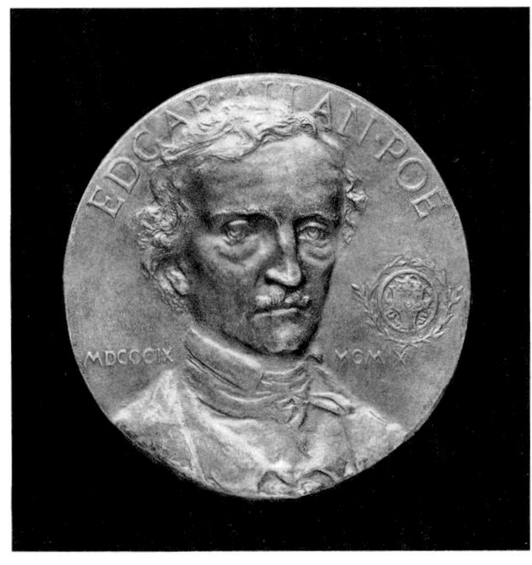

39

EDITH WOODMAN BURROUGHS

1871 Riverdale, New York – 1916 Long Island, New York

39 *Edgar Allan Poe* 1809–1849

1909
Bronze, coppery-brown patina
DIAM. 7 X D. ½ (17.8 X 1.3)

Signed lower left front: Edith Woodman Burroughs

Inscribed in relief upper front: EDGAR · ALLAN · POE; left: MDCCCIX; right: MCMIX; right: Grolier Club seal

Foundry: Roman Bronze Works, New York; mark, bottom edge center: R.B.W. / N.Y.

Gift of Adrian Van Sinderen, B.A. 1910, to the Collection of American Literature, Beinecke Rare Book and Manuscript Library
1980.306

ALEXANDER CALDER

1898 Lawnton (now Philadelphia), Pennsylvania – 1976 New York City

40 *Cat*

c.1930
Wood
7¾ x 26¼ x 3¾ (19.7 x 66.7 x 9.5)

Signed on underside: Calder

Director's Purchase Fund
1967.42

41 *Mobile*

c.1935
Painted wood, painted sheet metal, and thread with a metal hook (damaged)
41½ x 36 x 11 (105.4 x 91.4 x 27.9) approx.

Gift of Henry Russell Hitchcock
1952.49.1

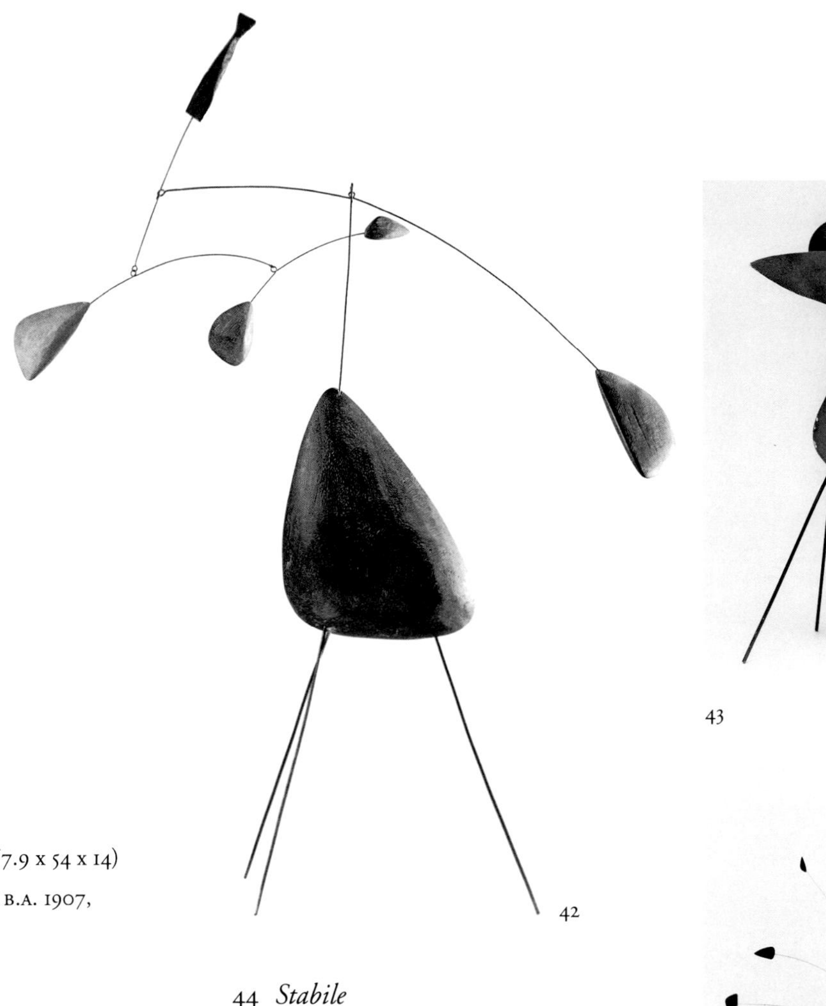

42

43

42 *Standing Mobile*

c.1935
Wood and wire
26¾ x 21¼ x 5½ (67.9 x 54 x 14)

Philip L. Goodwin, B.A. 1907, Collection
1958.16

43 *Bird Form*

c.1936
Painted sheet metal and painted wire
13¼ x 8¼ x 7¼ (33.7 x 21 x 18.4)

Gift of the estate of Katherine S. Dreier
1953.6.2

44 *Stabile*

1943
Painted sheet metal, painted wire and clay
H. 45¾ x maximum extension 46 (116.2 x 116.8)

The Katharine Ordway Collection
1980.12.42

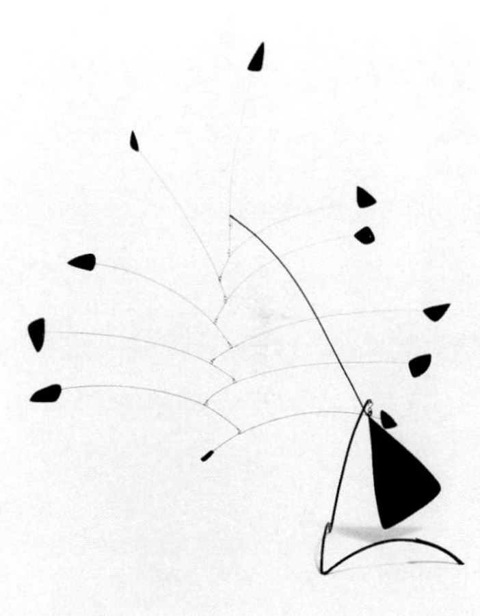

44

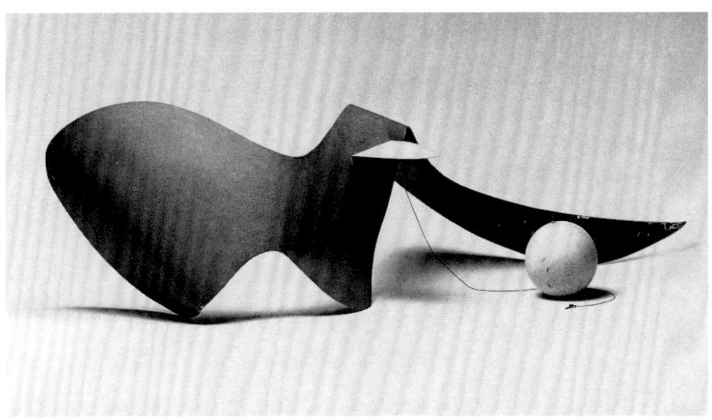

41

45 *Fourth Flurry '48*

1948
Painted sheet metal and wire
H. 80 x maximum extension 76½
(203.2 x 194.3)

Signed and dated on one disc:
Calder / 1948

Edition number on same disc as signature: IV

Gift of Katherine S. Dreier to the Collection Société Anonyme
1948.298

46 *Mobile*

1957
Painted sheet metal and wire
H. 33¾ x maximum extension 97¼
(85.7 x 247)

Signed and dated on vertical plate with hole: CA 57

The Katharine Ordway Collection
1980.12.41

47 *Two Crescents*

1959
Painted sheet metal and wire
H. 106¾ x maximum extension 78¾
(271.1 x 200)

Signed and dated on largest plate:
CA 59

Gift of Mr. and Mrs. Andrew Gagarin, B.A. 1937
1980.115

48 *Gallows and Lollipops*

1960
Painted steel
H. 231 x maximum extension 158
(586.7 x 584.2)

Signed and dated on one leg in relief:
CA / 60

Anonymous gift
1975.123

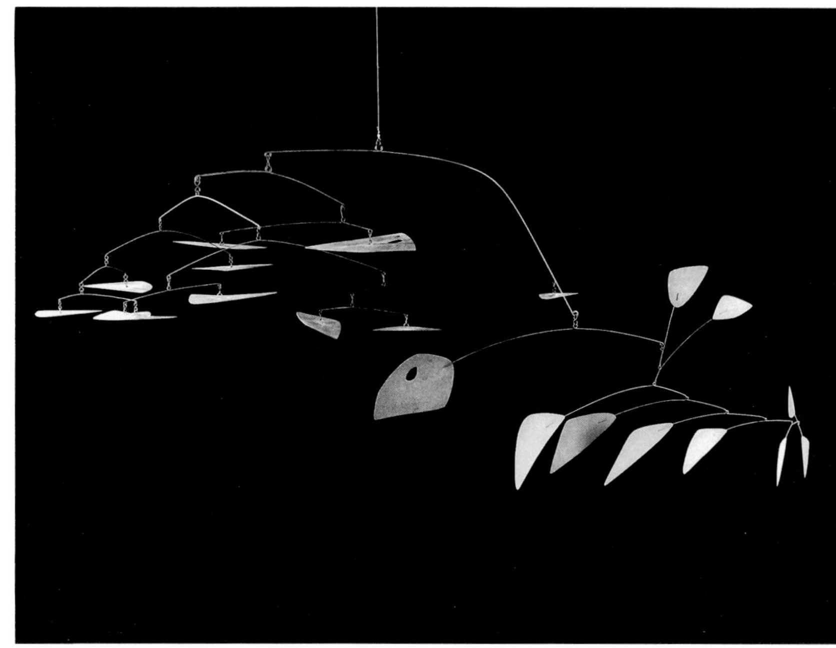

46

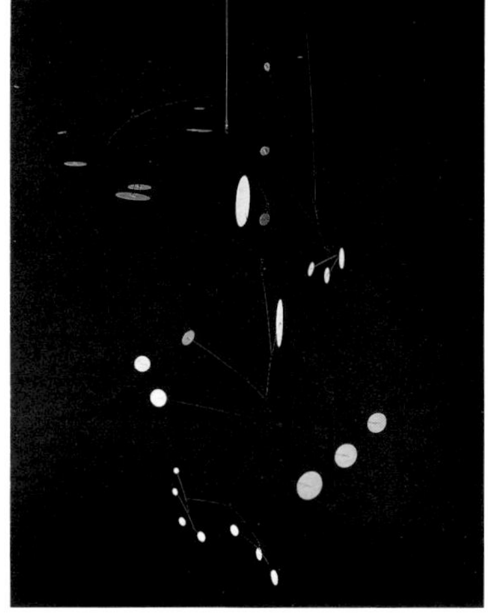

45

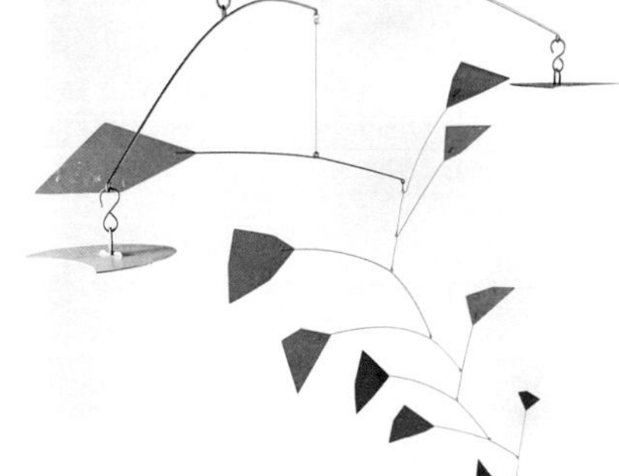

47

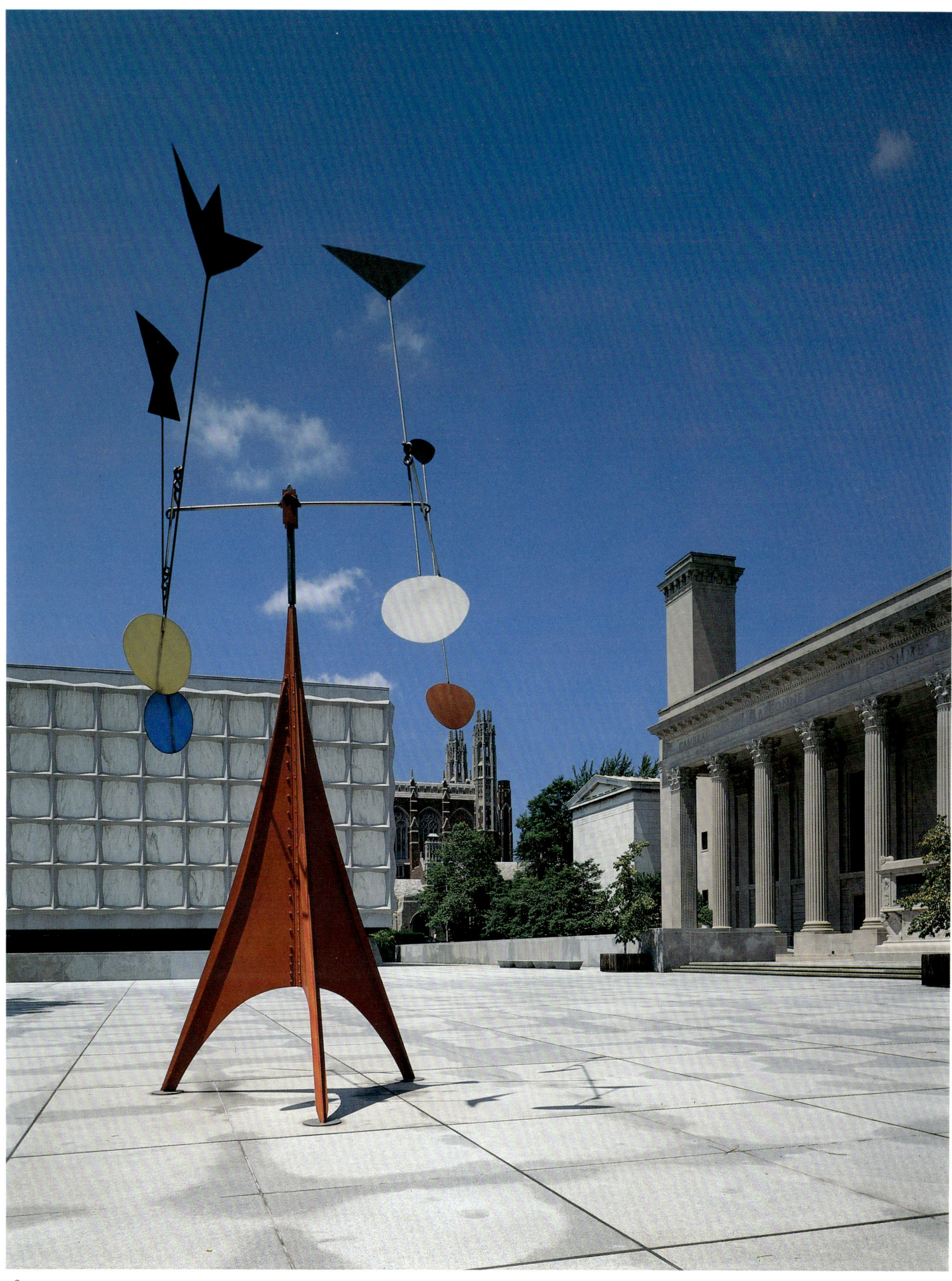

49 *The Tulip*

1967
Painted sheet metal and wire
H. 58½ x maximum extension 87¼ (148 x 221.6)

Signed and dated on largest element: CA / 67

Gift of John Hay Whitney, B.A. 1926, M.A.(hon.) 1956
1977.144

50 *Mobile*

n.d.
Painted sheet metal and wire
H. 23¼ x maximum extension 38 (59.1 x 96.5)

The Katharine Ordway Collection
1980.13.45

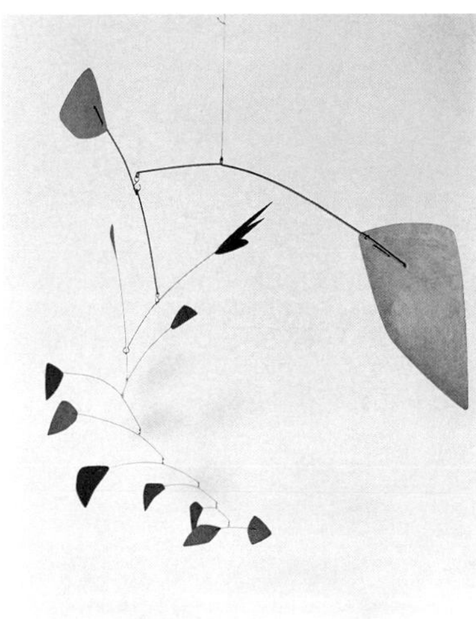

49

CHARLES CALVERLEY

1833 Albany, New York –
1914 Essex Falls, New Jersey

51 *James Russell Lowell* 1819–1891

Cast after 1896, from an original of 1895
Bronze, copper-colored patina
DIAM. 6¾ x D. ½ (17.1 x 1.3)

Signed and dated in relief lower front: CHAS. CALVERLEY. SC MDCCCXCV

Inscribed in relief on front: JAMES RUSSELL LOWELL; lower front: Grolier Club Seal; left: SAPIENS / HAEREDITABIT / HONOREM ET / NOMEN ILLIVS / ERIT VIVENS / IN AETERNVM · / · Ecclus · XXXVII · 26; right: FEB · 22 · 1819 / AUG · 12 · 1891; verso, lower center: COPYRIGHTED 1896

Gift of Adrian Van Sinderen, B.A. 1910, to the Collection of American Literature, Beinecke Rare Book and Manuscript Library
1980.318

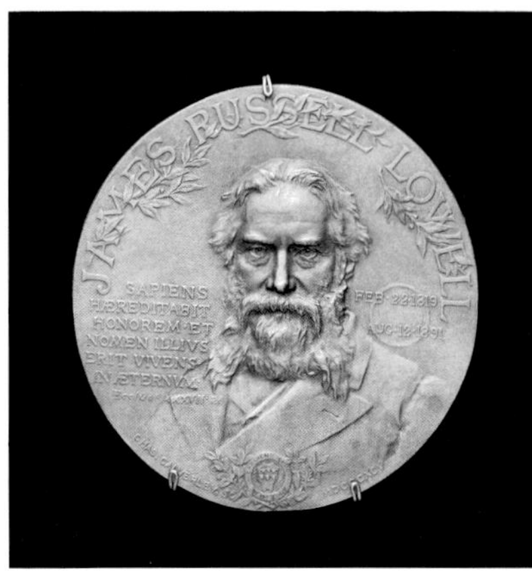

51

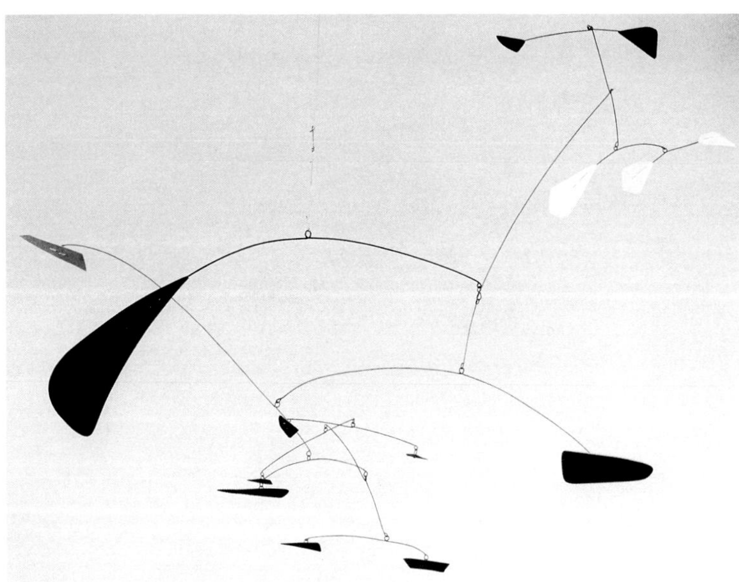

50

52 *Sir Walter Scott* 1771–1832

Cast 1900, after an original of 1896
Bronze, brown patina
16½ x 10¼ x 8¼ (41.9 x 26 x 21)

Signed and dated proper right side of base: COPYRIGHT, 1896, / CHARLES CALVERLEY.

Inscribed in relief front center of base: SCOTT; rear: STUDIED FROM THE / CHANTRY BUST, / SIR THOMAS LAWRENCE S PICTURE / AND THE DEATH MASK. / —— / C. CALVERLEY, Sc. / 1896.

Foundry: The Henry-Bonnard Bronze Company, New York; mark, proper left side: THE HENRY BONNARD BRONZE CO / FOUNDERS. N.Y. 1900

Gift of Dr. James C. Greenway, B.A. 1900, M.A.(hon.) 1916, to the Yale University Library
1931.1297

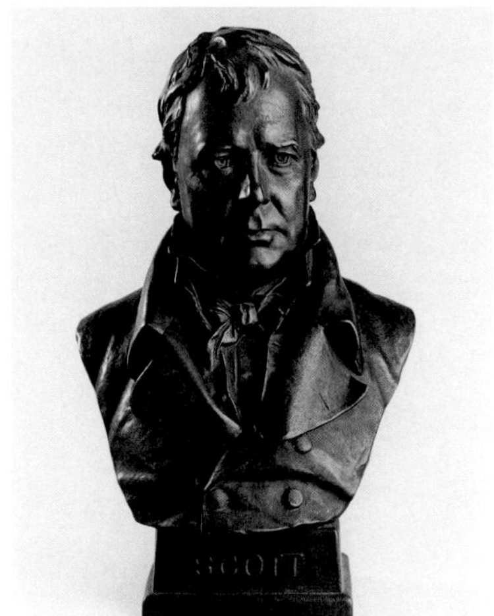

52

RHYS CAPARN

b. 1909 Oneonta Park, New York

53 *Hawk*

1978
Bronze, dark greenish-brown patina
16½ x 14 x 14½ (41.9 x 35.6 x 36.8)

Mica flecked quartz base
8¼ x 14½ x 7¼ (21 x 36.8 x 18.4)

Signed and dated lower rear of proper left wing: Rhys Caparn 78

Foundry: Tallix, Beacon, New York; mark, lower rear of proper left wing:
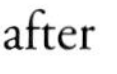

Gift of Bernard Offerman
1981.38

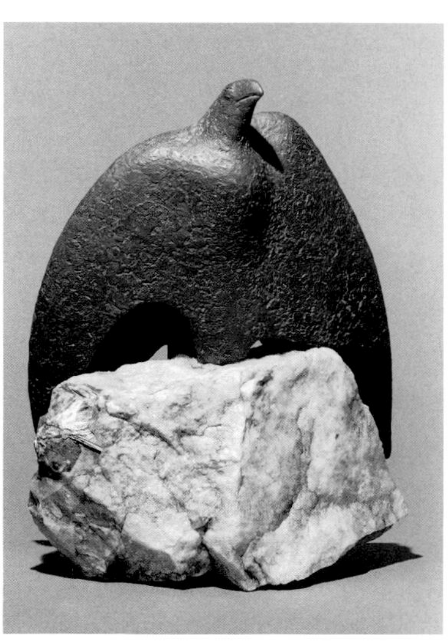

53

after
SHOBAL VAIL CLEVENGER

1812 Middletown, Ohio –
1843 at sea, returning from Italy

54 *Daniel Webster* 1782–1852

19th century
Plaster
29½ x 20½ x 12¼ (74.9 x 52.1 x 31.1)

Provenance unknown
1900.21

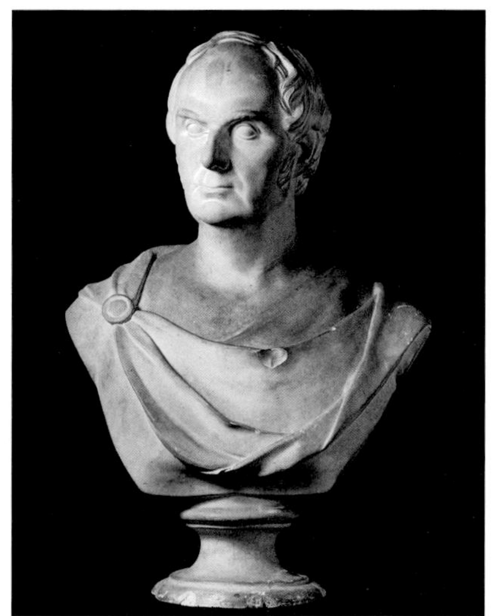

54

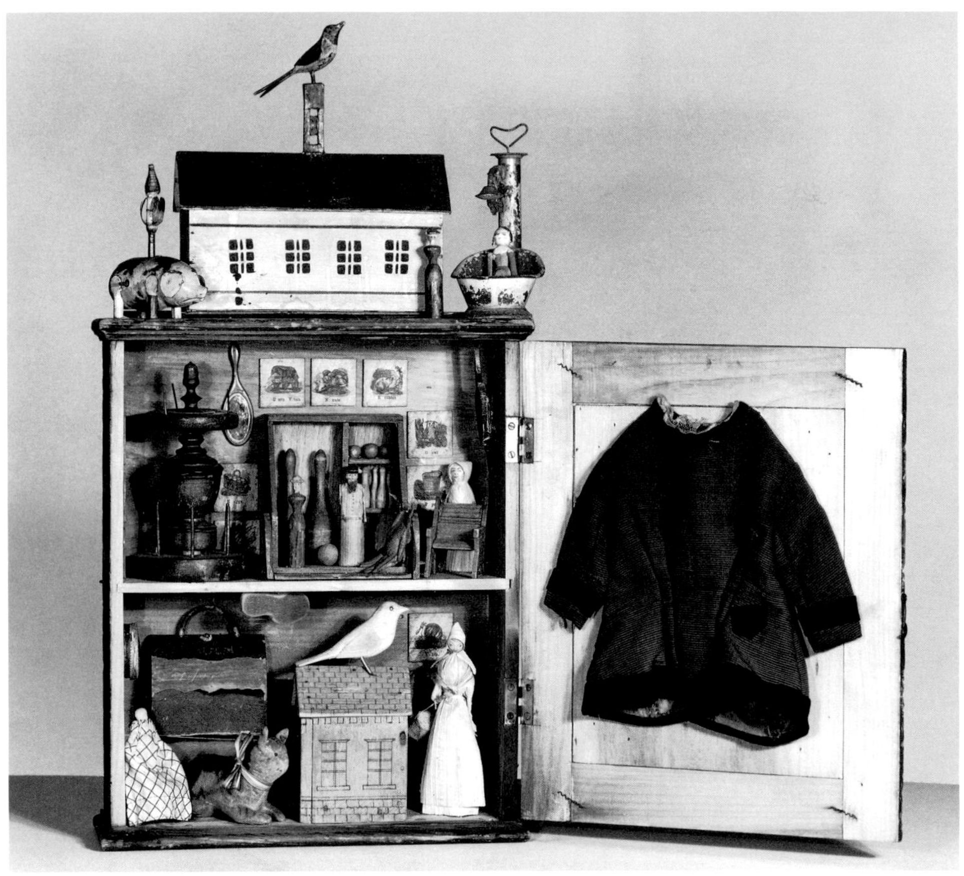

55

BARRY COHEN

1934 – 1990 New York City
M.F.A. 1960

55 *Construction*

c.1970
Wood, metal, textiles, paint, cardboard
27½ x 15 x 6 (69.2 x 38.1 x 15.2) closed

27½ x 28¾ x 6 (69.2 x 73 x 15.2) open

Richard Brown Baker, B.A. 1935, Fund
1973.127

JOSEPH CORNELL

1903 Nyack, New York –
1972 Flushing, New York

56 *Collage*

About 1950–55
Sand, glass, wood, seashells, fabric, paper, and cord
9¾ x 6½ x 1½ (24.8 x 16.5 x 3.8)

Signed in graphite verso:
Joseph Cornell

Gift of Mrs. Carl Schniewind
1958.41

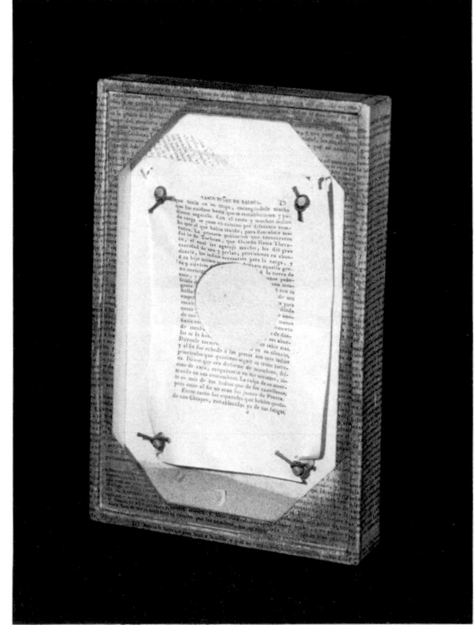

56

NANCY COX-McCORMACK

1885 Nashville, Tennessee – unknown

57 *Life Mask of Ezra Pound*
1885–1972

1921
Bronze, greenish-black patina
9¾ x 7¼ x 5¾ (24.8 x 18.4 x 14.6)

Inscribed upper rear: EZRA POUND – 1921 – PARIS – BY – NANCY COX – McC.

Gift of Mary De Rachewiltz to the Center for the Study of Ezra Pound and His Contemporaries, Collection of American Literature, Beinecke Rare Book and Manuscript Library
1980.152

58 *Charles Upson Clark* 1875–1960
B.A. 1897, PH.D. 1903

1949
Bronze, golden bronze patina
DIAM. 10 x D. ¾ (25.4 x 1.9)

Signed and dated right front in relief: OPVS / COX · McC / 1949

Inscribed on left front in relief: FOR / ANNE · · / JOAN · · / PRISCILLA / GVNTHER; top: · · · CHARLES · VPSON · CLARK . . .; bottom: SEARCHER · AFTER · TRVTH

Yale University Library

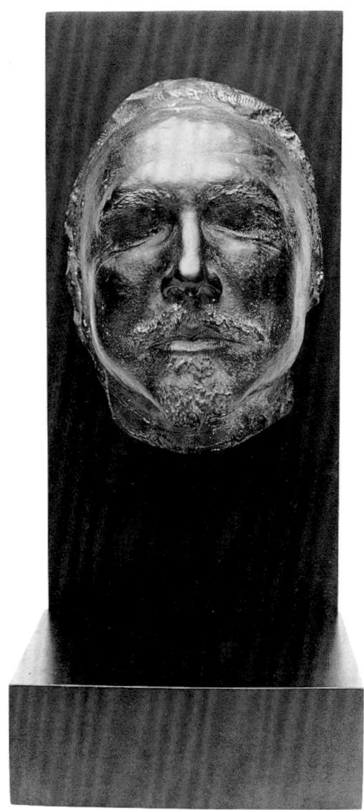

57

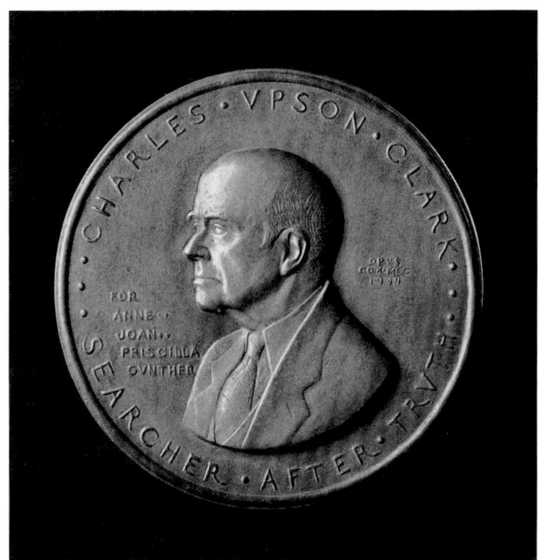

58

THOMAS CRAWFORD

1813? New York City – 1857 London

59 *Cicero*

1837
Marble
22½ x 13½ x 11½ (57.1 x 34.3 x 29.2)

Signed and dated proper left side:
T, C, / Roma / 1837

Presented to Yale College by Professor Edward E. Salisbury, B.A. 1832, M.A. 1835, LL.D. 1869
1900.58

60 *Homer*

1837
Marble
22¼ x 11½ x 11½ (56.5 x 29.2 x 29.2)

Signed and dated proper left side: TC. (monogram) FECT – / ROMA / MDCCXXVII

Presented to Yale College by Professor Edward E. Salisbury, B.A. 1832, M.A. 1835, LL.D. 1869
1900.59

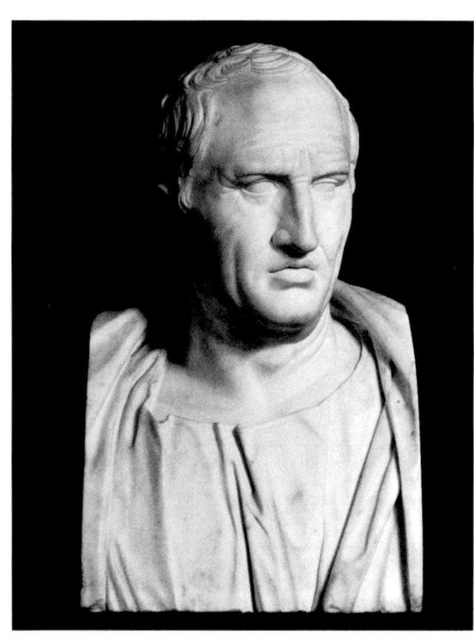

59

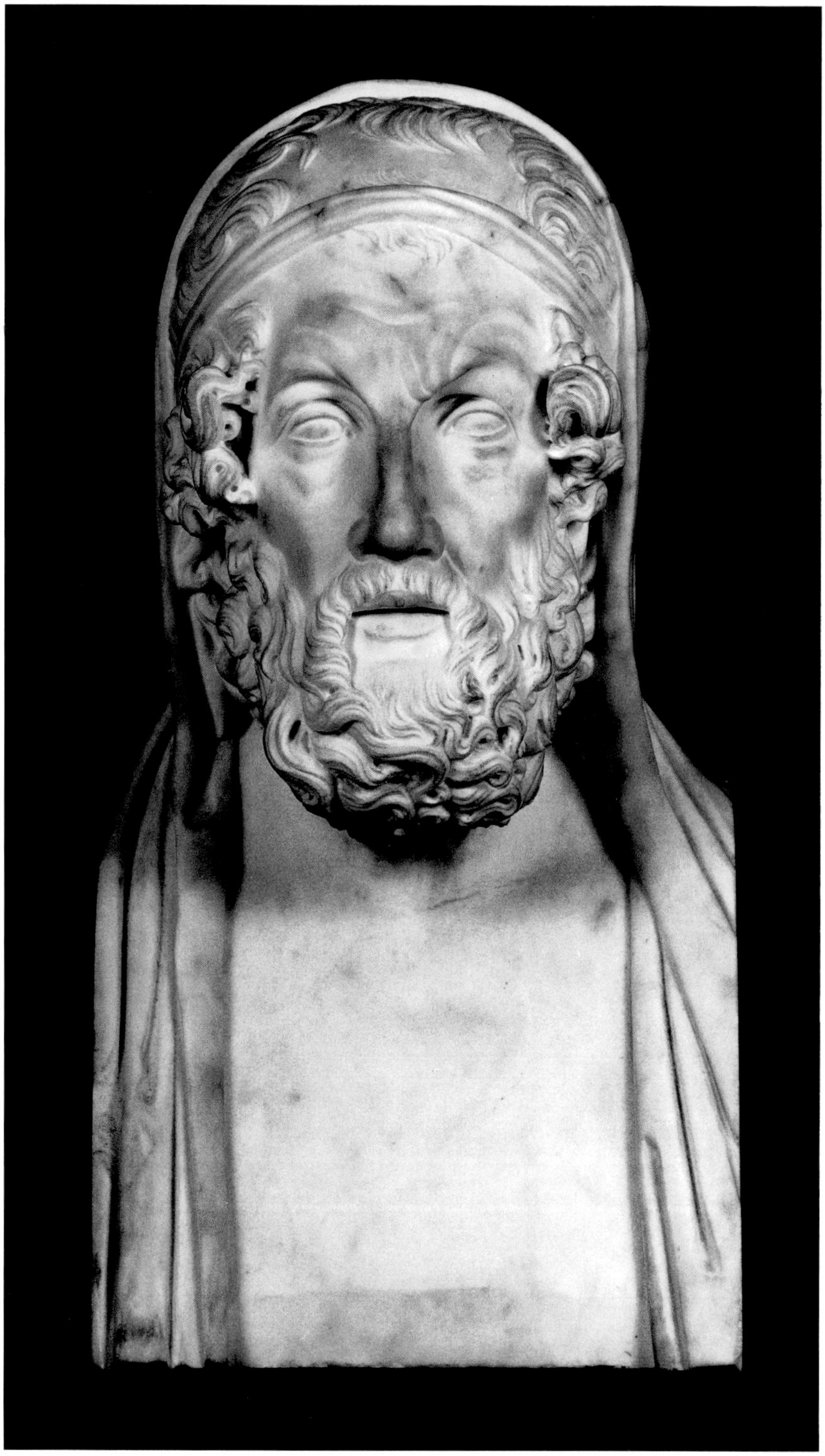

60

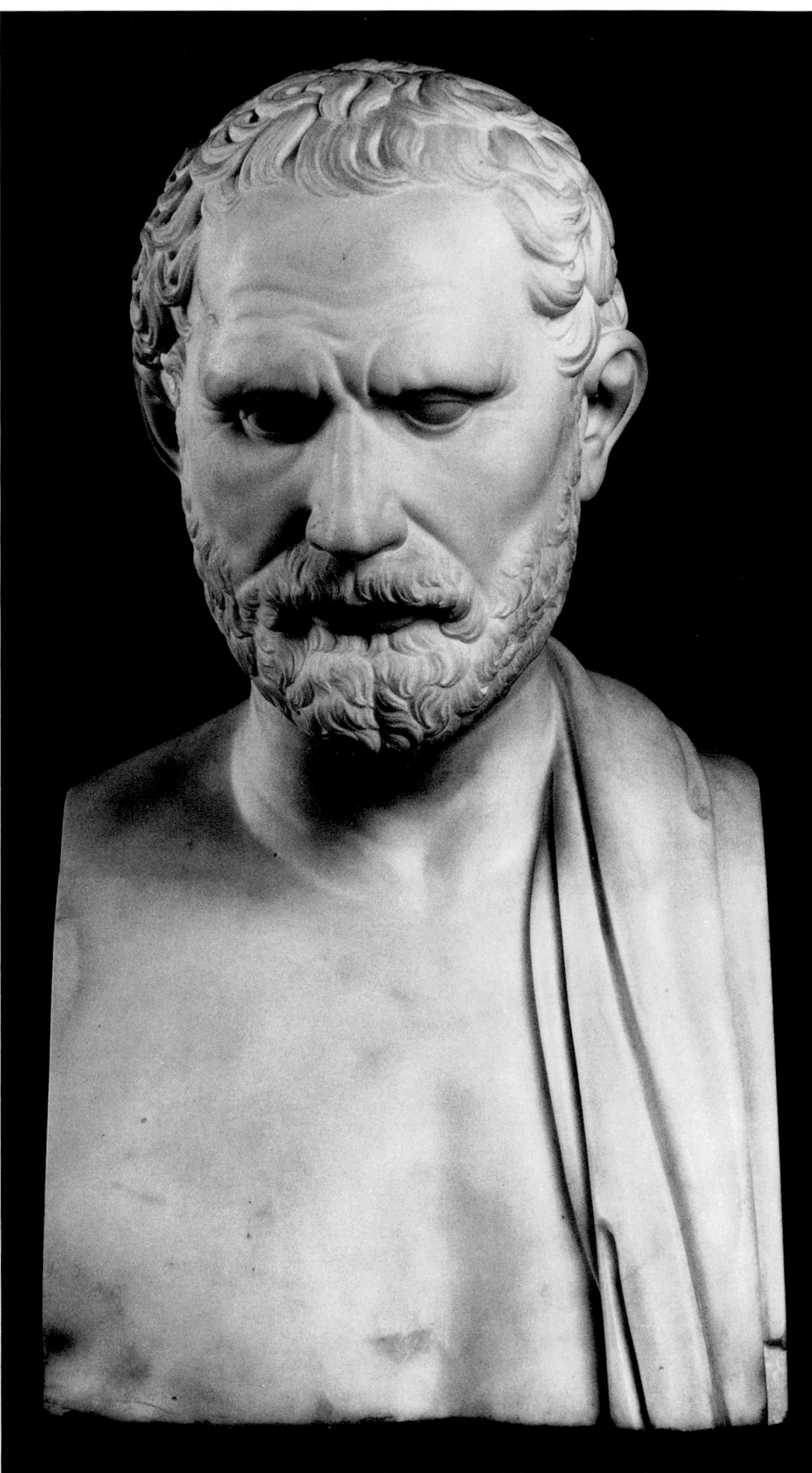

61

61 *Demosthenes*

Probably 1837
Marble
21½ x 12 x 11¼ (54.6 x 30.5 x 28.6)

Signed proper left side:
T, C, / Roma

Presented to Yale College by Professor Edward E. Salisbury, B.A. 1832, M.A. 1835, LL.D. 1869
1900.57

JO DAVIDSON

1883 New York City –
1952 near Tours, France

62 *Gertrude Stein* 1874–1946

Cast 1949, after an original of 1923
Bronze, golden bronze patina
8 x 6¼ x 5¾ (20.3 x 15.9 x 14.6)

Signed proper right lower rear:
J. Davidson / Paris

Gift of Alice B. Toklas, Allan D. Stein, and the artist to the Gertrude Stein Collection in the Yale Collection of American Literature, Beinecke Rare Book and Manuscript Library
1949.291

63 *George Henry Doran* 1869–1956

1929
Bronze, reddish-brown patina
17½ x 18½ x 14 (44.5 x 47 x 35.6)

Signed and dated proper right lower rear: JO DAVIDSON / NY 1929

Foundry: C. Valsuani, Paris; mark, proper left lower rear stamped in relief: CIRE / C VALSUANI / PERDUE

Gift of John Farrar, B.A. 1918, to the Beinecke Rare Book and Manuscript Library
1949.65

64 *Frank Lyon Polk* 1871–1943
B.A. 1894, M.A.(hon.) 1918

c.1930
Bronze, greenish-bronze patina
18 x 8¼ x 10¼ (45.7 x 21 x 26)

Signed proper right rear:
JO DAVIDSON / PARIS

Inscribed lower proper left side:
Frank L. Polk

Foundry: C. Valsuani, Paris; mark, stamped in relief, center rear within a lozenge: CIRE / C. VALSUANI / PERDUE

Gift of Mrs. Frank Lyon Polk to the Yale University Library

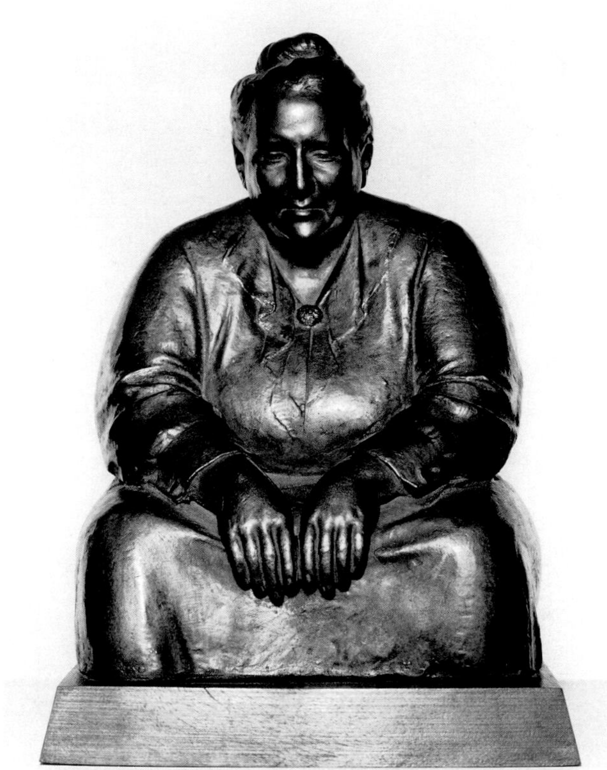

62

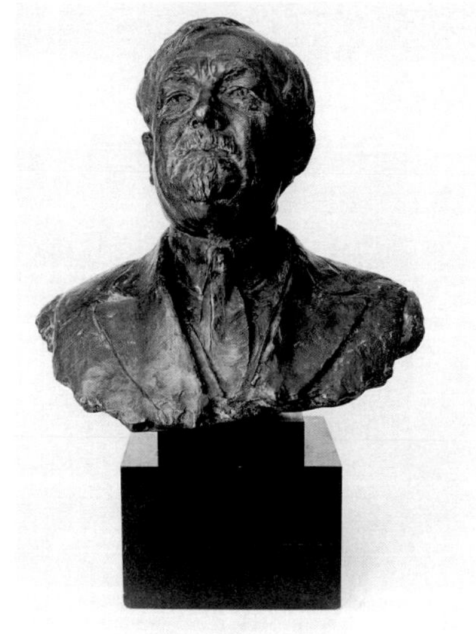

63

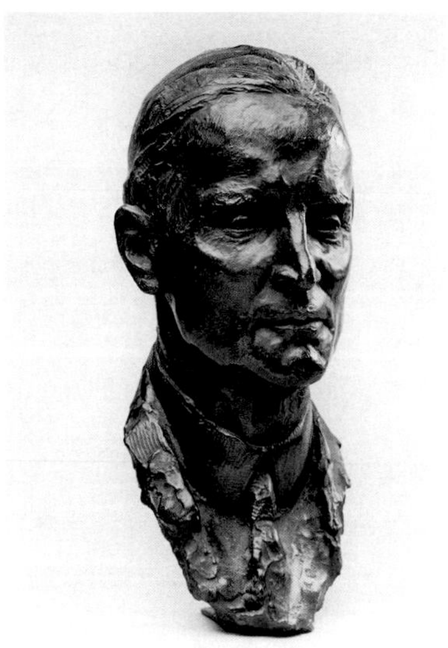

64

65 *William Adams Delano* 1874–1960
B.A. 1895, B.F.A. 1907, M.A.(hon.) 1939

1936
Bronze, black patina
15½ x 8 x 10 (39.4 x 20.3 x 25.4)

Signed and dated on rear edge of collar: JO DAVIDSON PARIS 1936

Foundry: C. Valsuani, Paris; mark, stamped in relief at proper left rear edge of collar: BRONZE / CIRE / VALSUANI / PERDUE

Gift of the sitter
1938.104

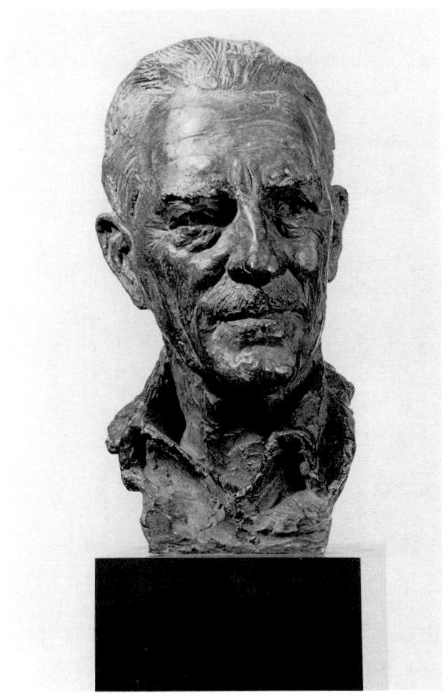

65

EDWARD JAMES DAVIS

1901 Clarksburg, West Virginia – 1974

66 *Plexiglas Mobile*

About 1945–50
Plexiglas
16½ x 11 x 9 (41.9 x 27.9 x 22.9)

Gift of the artist
1950.58

67 *Plexiglas Mobile*

About 1945–50
Plexiglas
15 x 15 x 15 (38.1 x 38.1 x 38.1)

Gift of the artist
1950.59

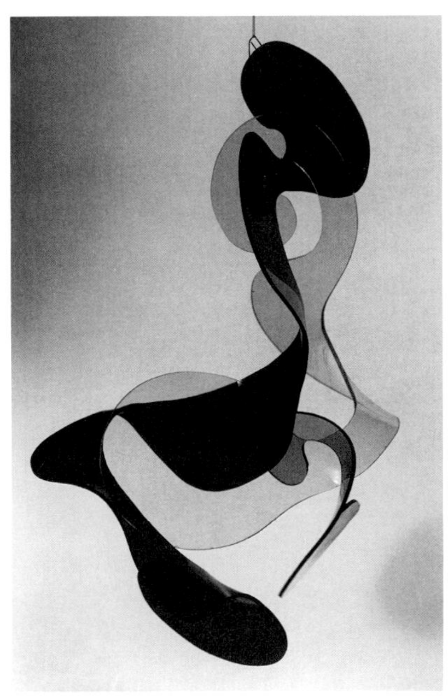

66

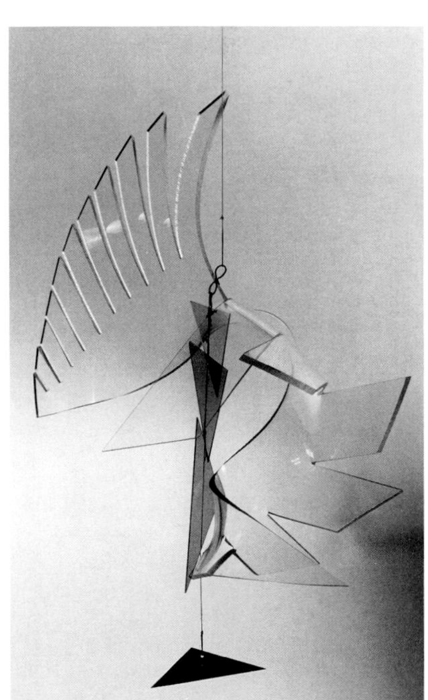

67

RICHARD DEVORE

b. 1933 Toledo, Ohio

68 *Untitled*

1981
Stoneware
16½ x 11¼ x 11 (41.9 x 28.6 x 27.9)

Purchased with the aid of funds from the National Endowment for the Arts and the Eileen Bamberger Matching Fund
1981.63

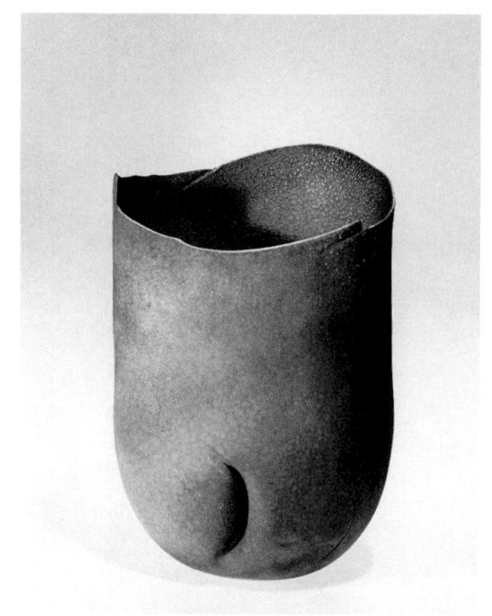

68

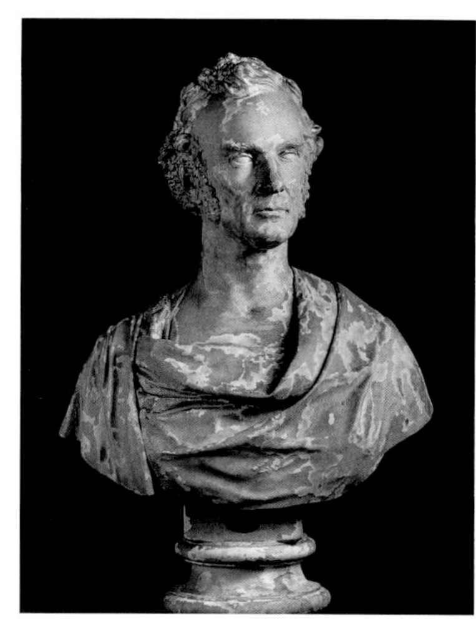

69

HENRY DEXTER

1806 Nelson, New York – 1876

69 *William Alfred Buckingham*
1804–1875
LL.D. 1866

1860
Painted plaster
31 x 21¾ x 14¼ (78.7 x 55.2 x 36.2)

Signed proper left side: SCULPTED BY H. DEXTER

Inscribed and dated center front of base in metal lozenge, in relief: HENRY DEXTER, FECIT. / BOSTON / –1860– COPYRIGHT SECURED

Provenance unknown
1900.25

MARK DI SUVERO

b. 1933 Shanghai, China
To U.S. 1941

70 *Alpha*

1967 or 1968
Steel
144 x 72 x 120 (365.8 x 182.9 x 304.8)

Gift of J. Frederic Byers III, B.A. 1962
1977.182

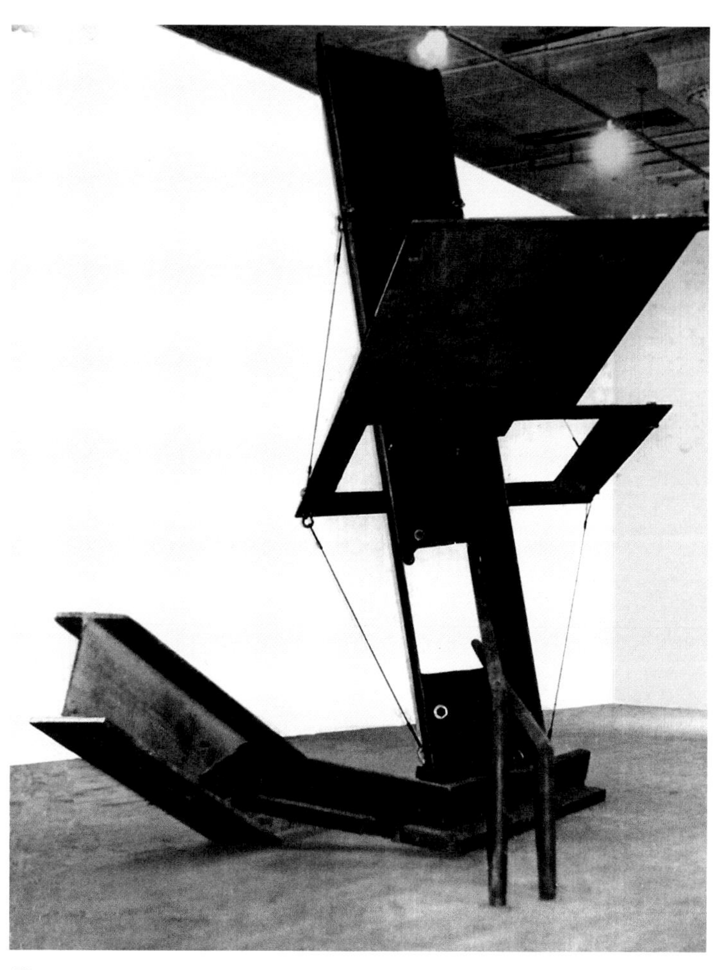

70

MARCEL DUCHAMP

1887 Rouen, France –
1968 Rouen, France
Active U.S. 1915–18; intermittently 1920–27, 1933–36, 1942–68; citizen after 1942

71 *In advance of the broken arm (Snow Shovel)*

1945, replica of lost work of 1915
Wood and galvanized iron snow shovel
48 x 18 x 4 (121.9 x 45.7 x 10.2)

Signed, dated, and inscribed in paint along lower rear of shovel: IN ADVANCE OF THE BROKEN ARM MARCEL DUCHAMP [1915] / replica 1945

Gift of Katherine S. Dreier to the Collection Société Anonyme
1946.99

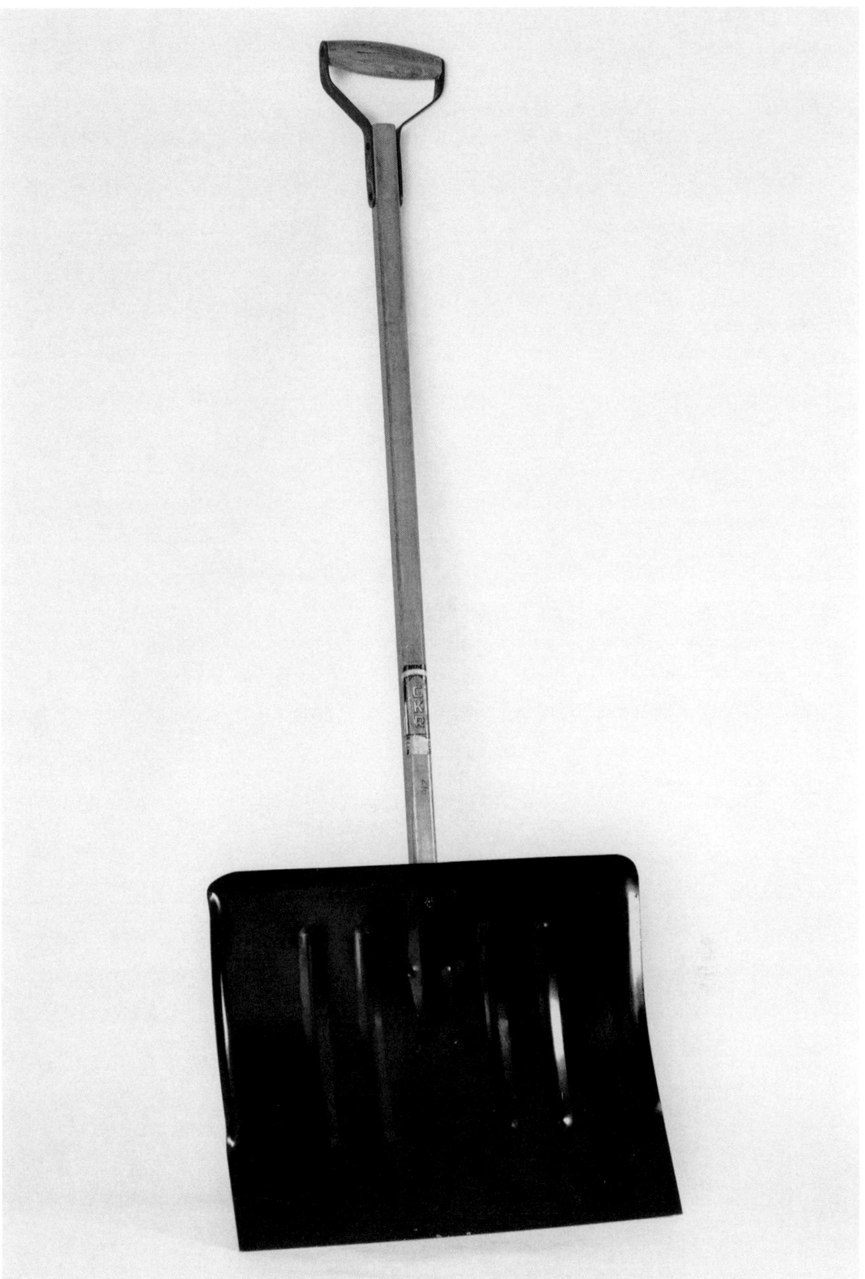

71

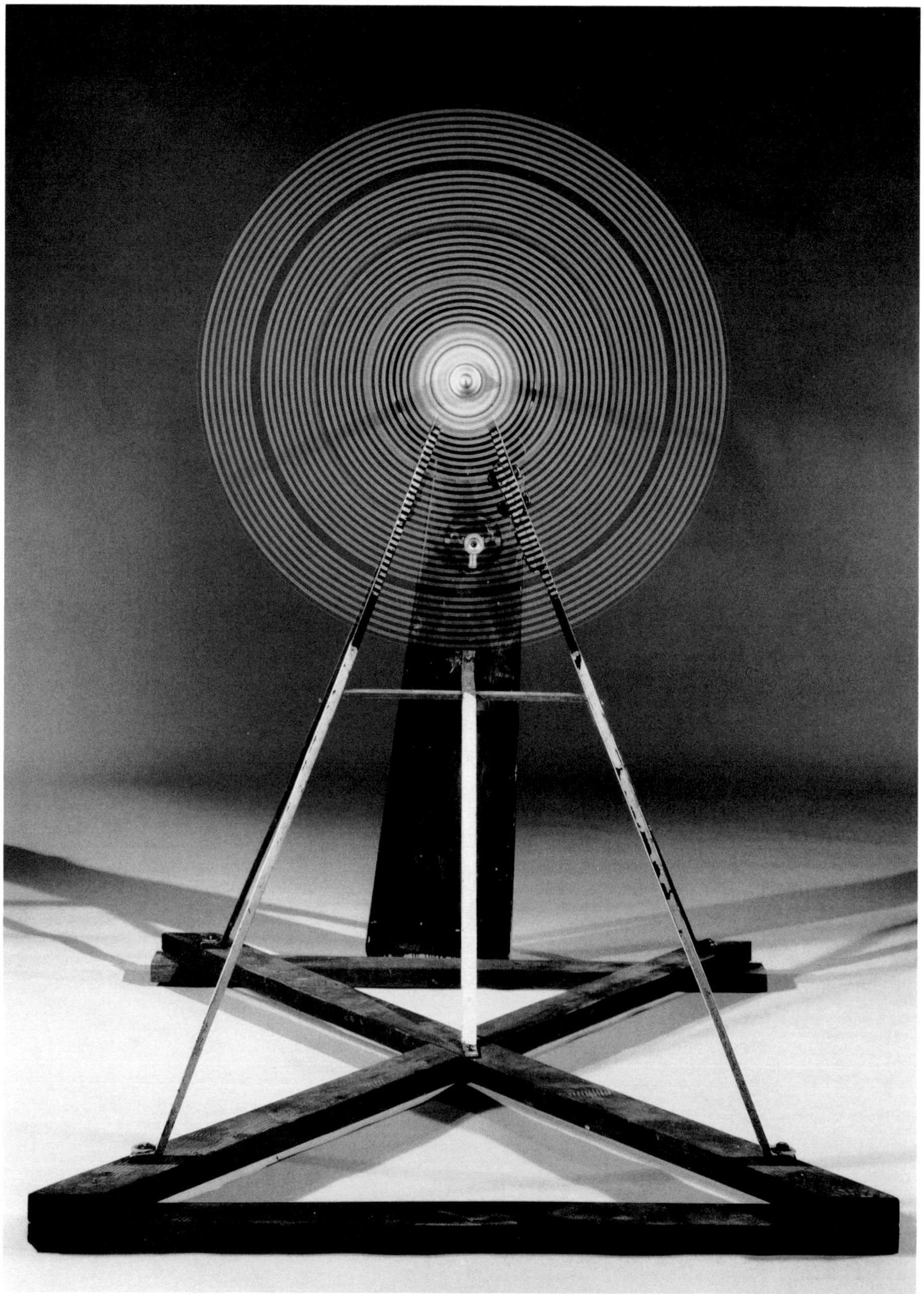

72 B

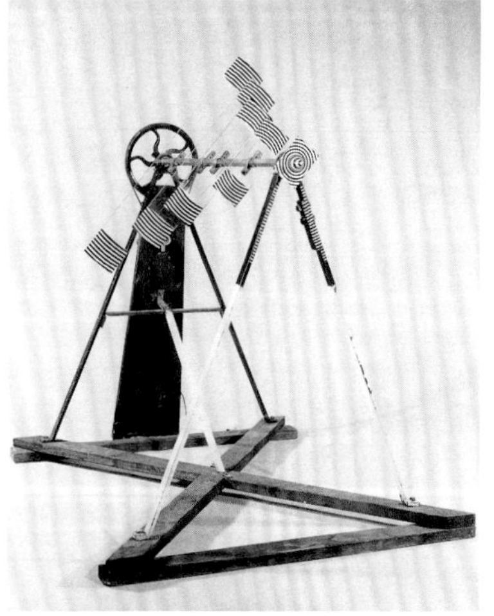

72 A

72 *Rotary Glass Plates (Precision Optics)*
Rotative Plaque Verre (Optique de Précision)
Illustrated at rest (A) and in motion (B)

1920
Five glass plates painted with segments of black and white circles, turning on a metal axis powered by an electric motor, supported by a frame of metal and wood
65¼ x 62 x 38 (165.7 x 157.5 x 96.5)

Inscribed in paint on front of foremost support crossbar, below apex: AV DEV; stenciled on wood above the engine: AR

Gift of the Collection Société Anonyme
1941.446

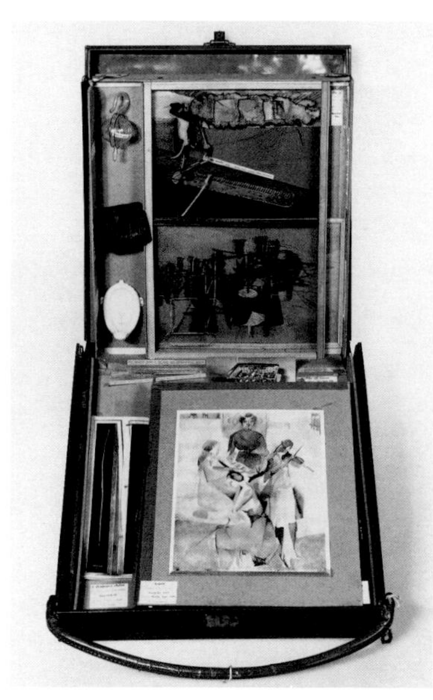

73

73 *Box in a Valise (Boîte-en-valise)*

1942–43
Leather valise containing miniature replicas and color reproductions of works by Duchamp; includes original photographic reproduction of *Tu m'* with additions of graphite and watercolor
4¼ x 15¼ x L. 19 (10.8 x 38.7 x L. 48.3) closed

Signed, dated, and inscribed in ink on interior bottom: Pour Katherine Dreier ce N° 0 / de vingt boîtes-en-valise contenant / chacune 69 items et un original / et par Marcel Duchamp / Marseille 1942 – New York Feb. 1943; on *Tu m'*: coloriage original Marcel Duchamp 1938

Inscription stamped in gold on inside edge: KATHERINE S. DREIER 0/XX

Gift of the estate of Katherine S. Dreier to the Collection Société Anonyme
1953.6.6

74 *Pocket Chess Set*

1943
Leather pocket chessboard, celluloid pieces, pins, in black leather wallet
6½ x 4½ x ½ (16.5 x 11.4 x 1.3) closed
6½ x 8¾ x ¼ (16.5 x 22.2 x 0.6) open

Gift of the estate of Katherine S. Dreier to the Collection Société Anonyme
1953.6.221

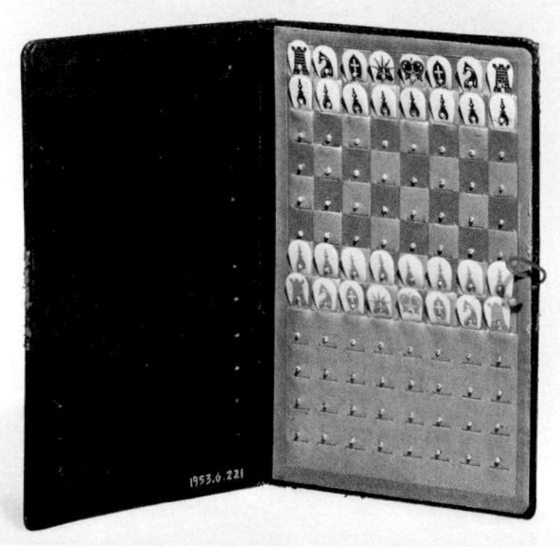

74

75 *Box in a Valise (Boîte-en-valise)*

1948
Leather valise containing miniature replicas and color reproductions of works by Duchamp; includes original ink drawing, *Knight's Head,* on inside cover under leather frame
4¼ x 17 x L. 18 (10.8 x 43.2 x L. 45.7) closed

Signed, dated, and inscribed in ink on bottom of interior: pour Yale University Art Gallery / ce No. XVII de vingt boîtes - en - valise contenant / chacune 69 items et un original et / par Marcel Duchamp New York août 1948; at lower right of *Knight's Head:* M.D. 1920; on mount below drawing: Letterhead of the 'Société Anonyme' / original drawing

Inscription stamped in gold on inside edge: YALE UNIVERSITY ART GALLERY XVII / XX

Gift of Katherine S. Dreier to the Collection Société Anonyme
1948.102

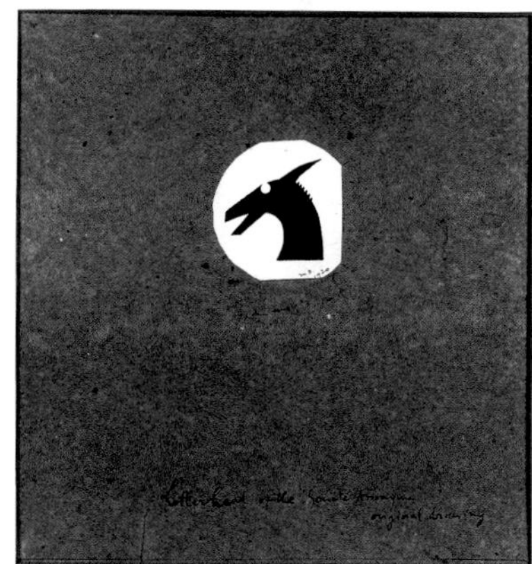

75

RINGEL DULLZACH

Dates unknown

76 *Nathaniel Hawthorne* 1804–1864

1902
Bronze, dark brown patina
DIAM. 7 x D. ½ (17.8 x 1.3)

Signed and dated in relief lower front: · RINGEL · DULLZACH · · MEDr · MDCCCXCII ·

Inscribed in relief upper front: NATHANIEL A HAWTHORNE; left center: · 1804 · / · JULY · 4 ·; right center: · MAY · 18 · / · 1864 ·; lower center within seal, not in relief: GROLIER CLVB / NEW – YORK 1893

Gift of Adrian Van Sinderen, B.A. 1910, to the Collection of American Literature, Beinecke Rare Book and Manuscript Library
1980.317

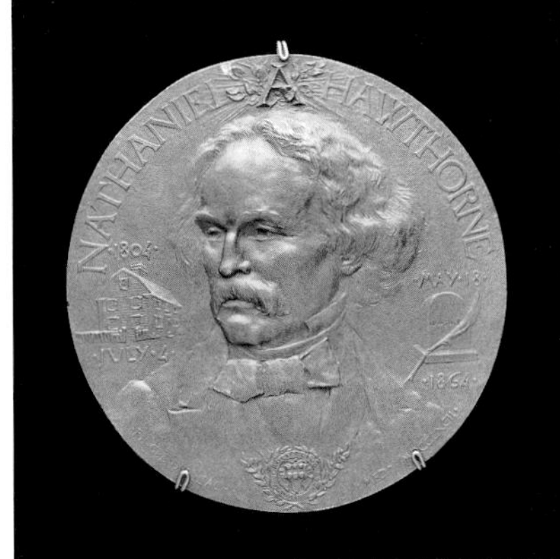

76

ANNA GLENNY DUNBAR

1888 Buffalo, New York – unknown

77 *Francis Hyde Bangs* 1892–1964
B.A. 1915

1930
Bronze, dark reddish-brown patina
13¾ x 6¾ x 9¼ (34.9 x 17.1 x 23.5)

Signed lower proper left side: A. Glenny

Foundry: Roman Bronze Works, New York; mark, lower center rear: ROMAN BRONZE WORKS N.Y.

Bequest of Francis Hyde Bangs, B.A. 1915, to the Collection of American Literature, Beinecke Rare Book and Manuscript Library
1980.371

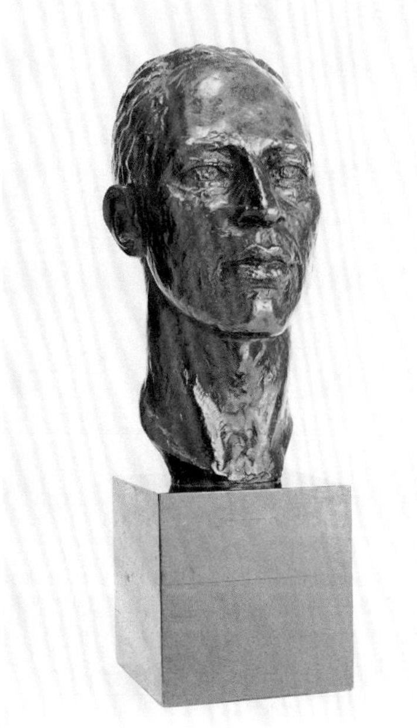

77

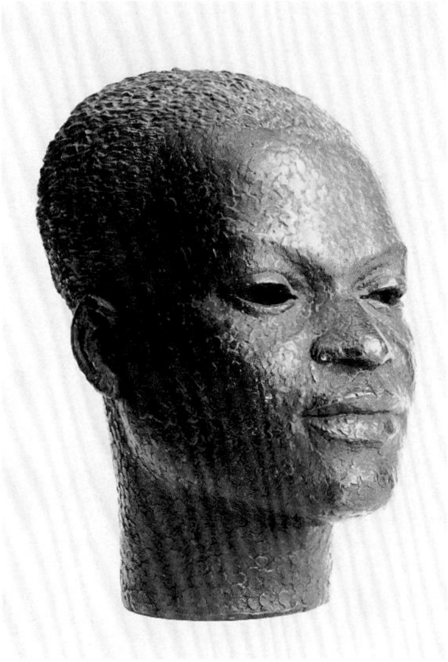

78

NOMMIE DURRELL

Active first half 20th century

78 *Rudolph Dunbar* b. 1917

n.d.
Bronze, dark reddish-brown patina
12¼ x 6½ x 10 (31.1 x 16.5 x 25.4)

Gift of the sculptor, received through Rudolph Dunbar, to the James Weldon Johnson Memorial Collection of Negro Arts and Letters, Beinecke Rare Book and Manuscript Library
1980.169

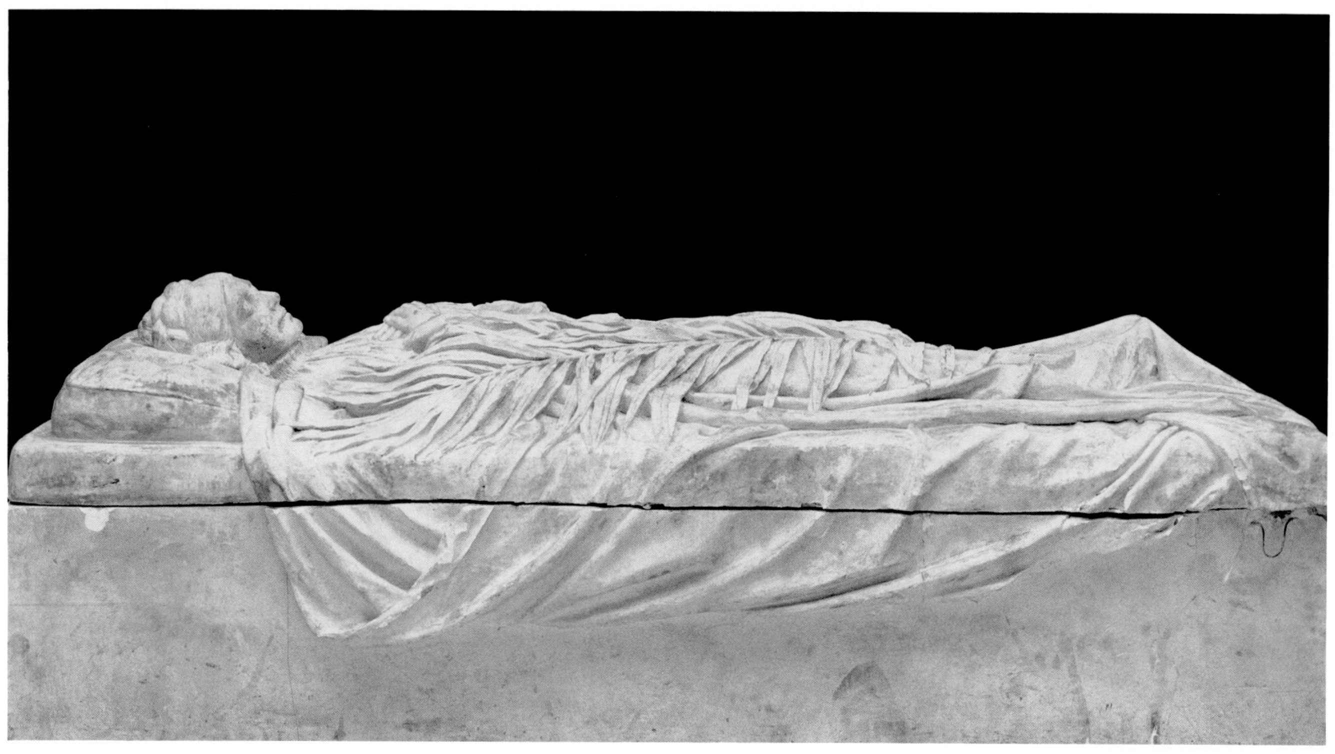

79

FRANK DUVENECK

1848 Covington, Kentucky –
1919 Cincinnati, Ohio

CLEMENT J. BARNHORN

1857 Cincinnati, Ohio –
1935 Cincinnati, Ohio

79 *Tomb Effigy of Elizabeth Boott Duveneck* 1846–1888

About 1900–1915, after original of 1891
Plaster
29 x 40¼ x L. 86
(73.7 x 102.2 x L. 218.4)

Inscribed at upper proper right corner on head of base, partially obscured:
F DUVE

Provenance unknown
1990.17.1

THOMAS EAKINS

1844 Philadelphia – 1916 Philadelphia

80 *Head of William Rush* 1756–1833

Study for *William Rush Carving His Allegorical Figure of the Schuylkill River*

Cast about 1965, after original of 1876–77
Bronze, reddish-brown patina
7¼ x 4 x 4¾ (18.4 x 10.2 x 12.1)

John Hill Morgan, B.A. 1893, Fund
1971.88.1

81 *Water Nymph and Bittern*

Study for *William Rush Carving His Allegorical Figure of the Schuylkill River*

Cast about 1965, after original of 1876–77
Bronze, reddish-brown patina
9¼ x 4¼ x 2¾ (23.5 x 10.8 x 7)

John Hill Morgan, B.A. 1893, Fund
1971.88.2

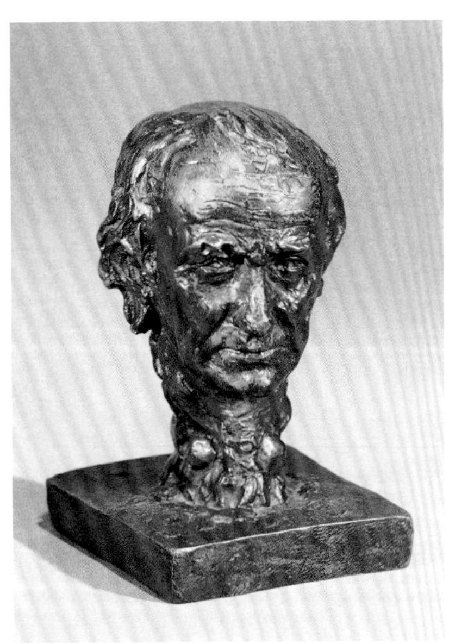

80

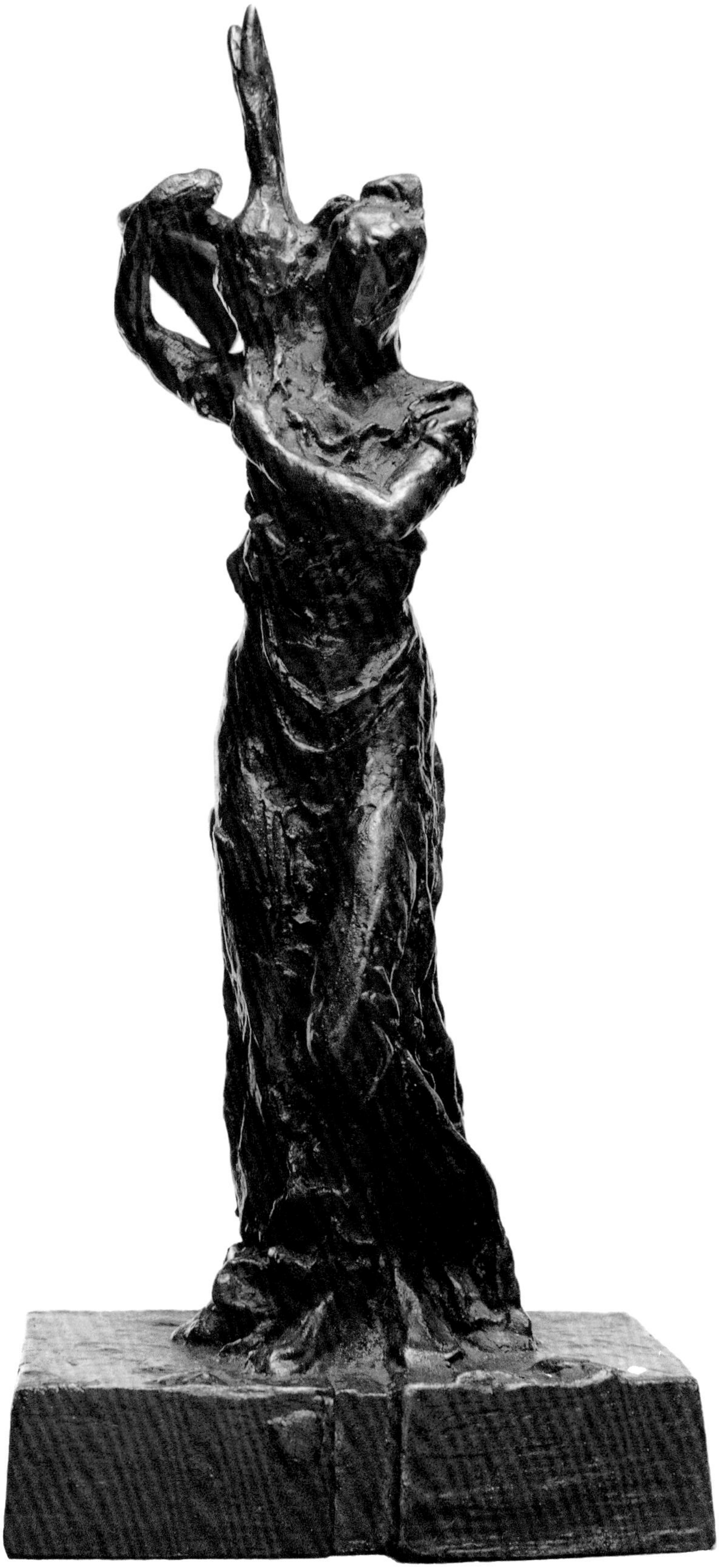

81

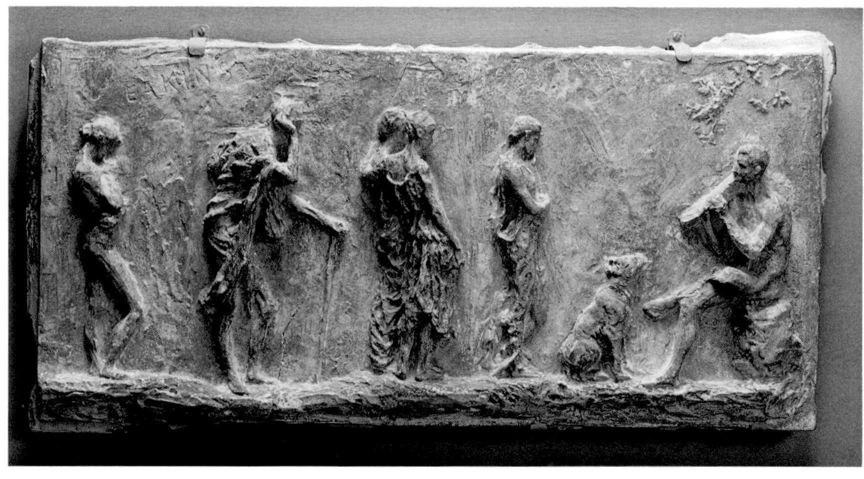

82

82 *Arcadia*

1883
Plaster
12 x 25 x 2½ (30.5 x 63.5 x 6.4)

Signed and dated upper front left: EAKINS; center: 1883

Gift of the H. J. Heinz II Charitable and Family Trust
1975.67

JOSEPH EDIN

Dates unknown

83 *Bust of an Unidentified Man*

Mid–19th century
Painted plaster
22 x 11¼ x 11¼ (55.9 x 28.6 x 28.6)

Signed center rear of base: JOSEPH EDINR I

Yale University Library

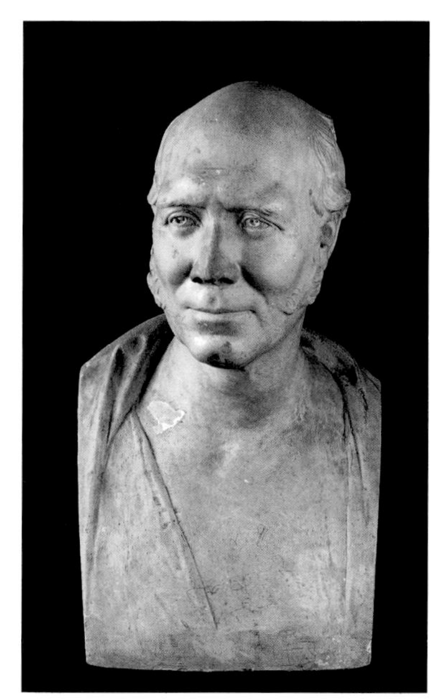

83

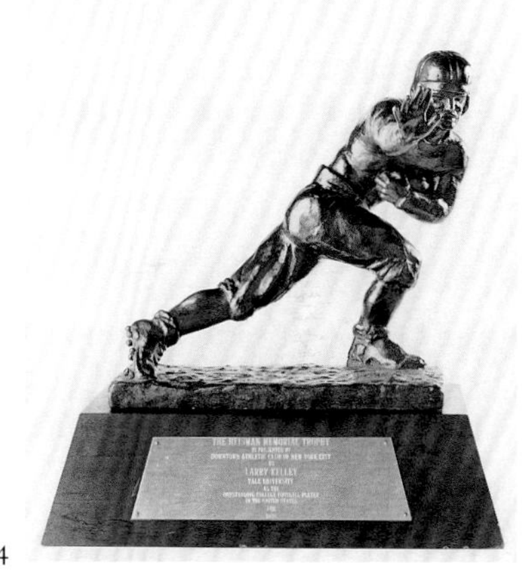

84

FRANK ELISCU

b. 1912 New York City

84 *Heisman Trophy*

1935
Bronze, dark brown patina
13¾ x 14 x 11½ (34.9 x 35.6 x 29.2)

Foundry: Roman Bronze Works, New York; mark, proper right edge of base: ROMAN BRONZE WORKS. N.Y.

Gift of Larry Kelley, B.A. 1937, to the Payne Whitney Gymnasium

FRANCIS EDWIN ELWELL

1858 Concord, Massachusetts – 1922 Darien, Connecticut

85 *Simeon Baldwin Chittenden*
1814–1889
M.A.(hon.) 1871

1890
Marble
36½ x 23 x 14¾ (92.7 x 58.4 x 37.5)

Signed proper left top of base:
F · EDWIN · ELWELL ·

Gift of the Chittenden family to the Yale Divinity School
1890.42

86 *Simeon Baldwin Chittenden*
1814–1889
M.A.(hon.) 1871

1890
Painted plaster with structural iron rods
27¾ x 21 x 12¾ (70.5 x 53.3 x 32.4)

Gift of the Chittenden family to the Yale Divinity School
1890.42

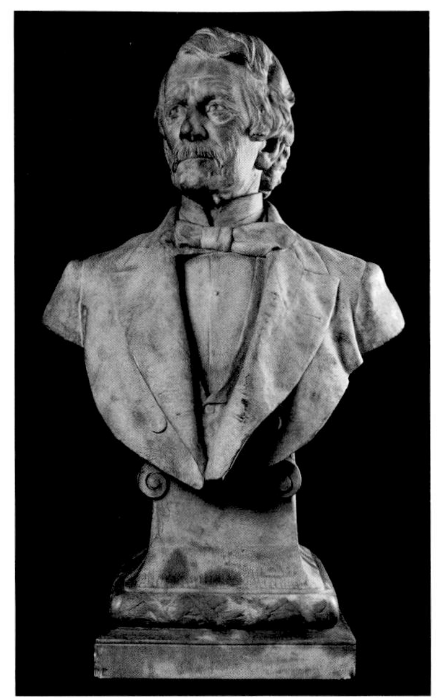

85

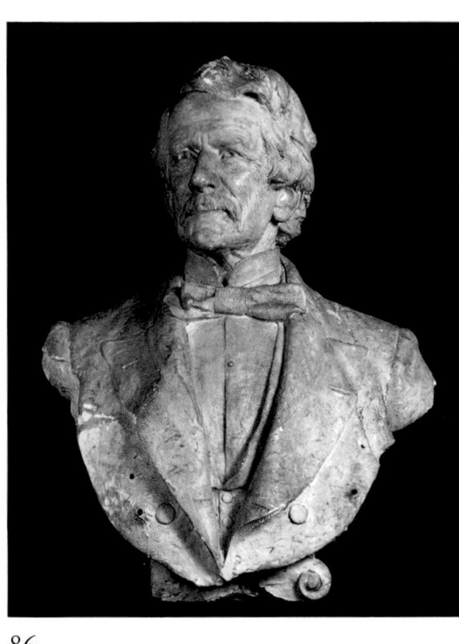

86

ROBERT ENGMAN

b. 1927 Belmont, Massachusetts
M.F.A. 1955

87 *Sculpture*

1959
Muntz metal
45 x 21¾ x 21½ (114.3 x 55.2 x 54.6)

White marble or quartz base
2¼ x 21 x 21 (5.7 x 53.3 x 53.3)

Director's Purchase Fund
1960.31

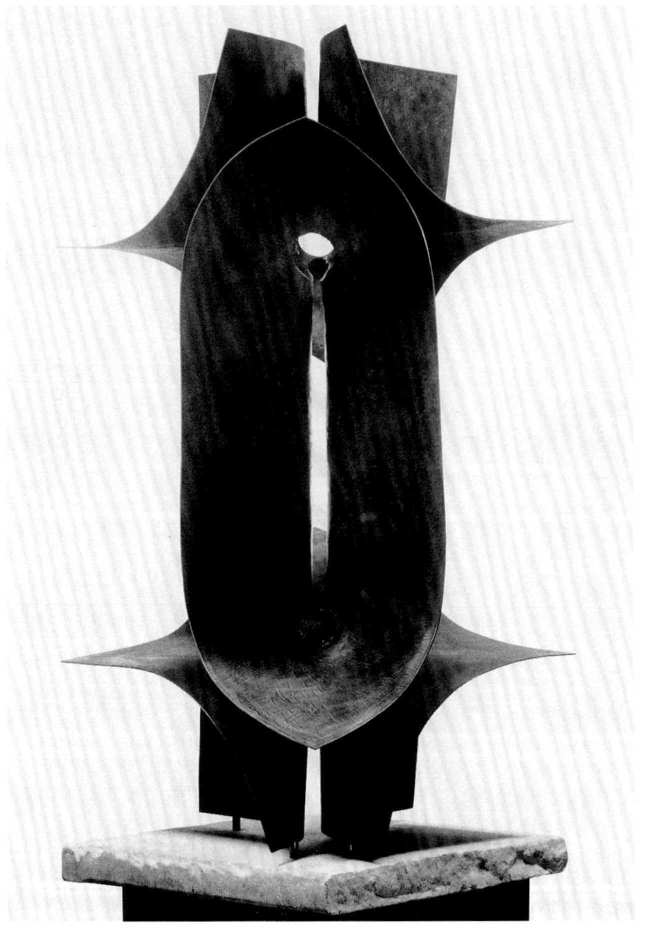

87

88 *Column*

1963
Reinforced concrete and iron bolts
240 x 23½ x 23½ (609.6 x 59.7 x 59.7)

Signed bottom front edge in mirrored letters: ENGMAN

Inscribed along edge from top to bottom proper left side: WU WALTON SCHRAEDER RUDOLPH RITCHIE PFISTERER KLOSZEWSKI KUBLER COUGHLIN [?]ANCY BELOFF ALBERS; proper right side: WILSON WEISS WELLIVER SEWALL SILLMAN ROSATI MILLARD IVES HAMILTON CATLIN BITELMAN ANDREWS

Yale University Schools of Art and Architecture

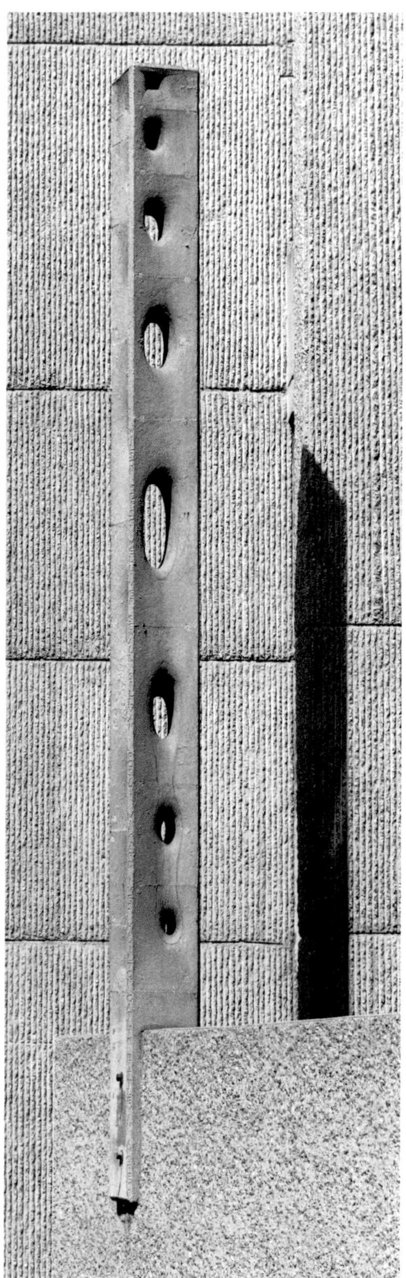

88

ALFEO FAGGI

1885 Sesto Fiorentino, Italy –
1966 Woodstock, New York
Active U.S. 1913–66, citizen about 1919

89 *Cloaked Figure*

1949
Bronze, dark green and light green patina
25½ x 10¼ x 13 (64.8 x 26 x 33)

Signed and dated proper left top of base: A. FAGGI / 1949

Payne Whitney Gymnasium

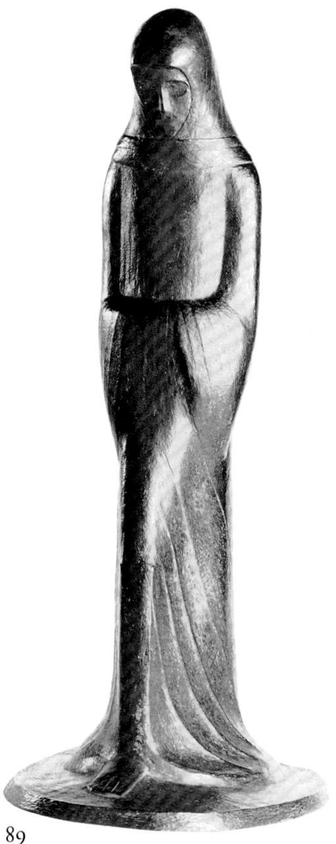

89

HERBERT FERBER

b. 1906 New York City

90 *Pods (Wall Sculpture)*

1953
Copper and brass
37 x 45¾ x 13½ (94 x 116.2 x 34.3)

Signed and dated front center:
Ferber 53

Gift of Mr. and Mrs. Andrew Gagarin, B.A. 1937
1973.3

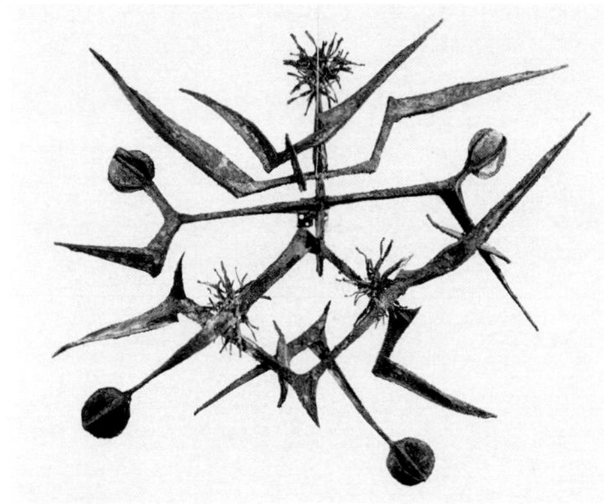

90

91 *Homage to Igor Stravinsky*

1959–60
Brass
43 x 79 x 35 (109.2 x 200.7 x 88.9)

Gift of the artist to Morse College

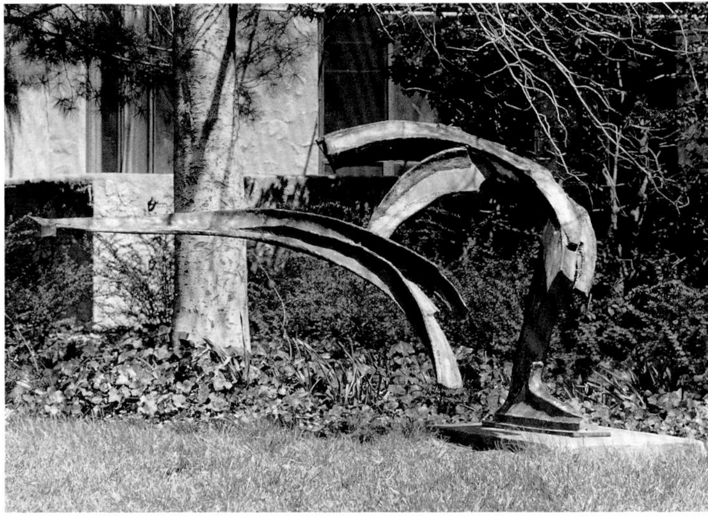

91

92 *Sphere*

1963–64
Bronze, dark brown patina partially obscured by corrosion and rust
27 x 26½ x 31½ (68.6 x 67.3 x 80)

Bronze base, dark brown patina partially obscured by corrosion and rust
2 x 15¾ x 15¾ (5.1 x 40 x 40)

Signed and dated on top of base at corner: *Ferber 63 / 64*

Director's Purchase and Seymour H. Knox, B.A. 1920, Funds
1965.4

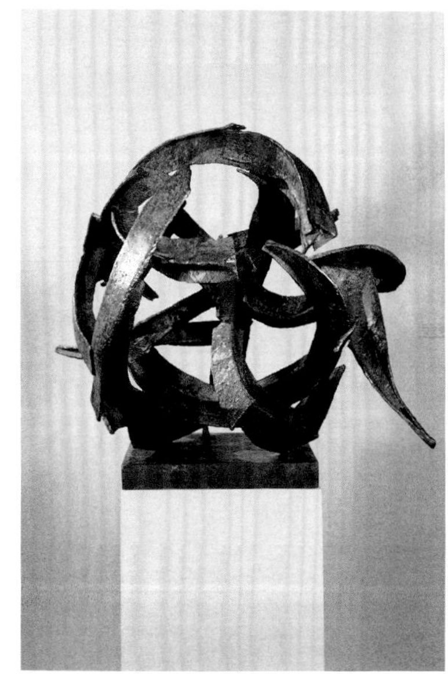

92

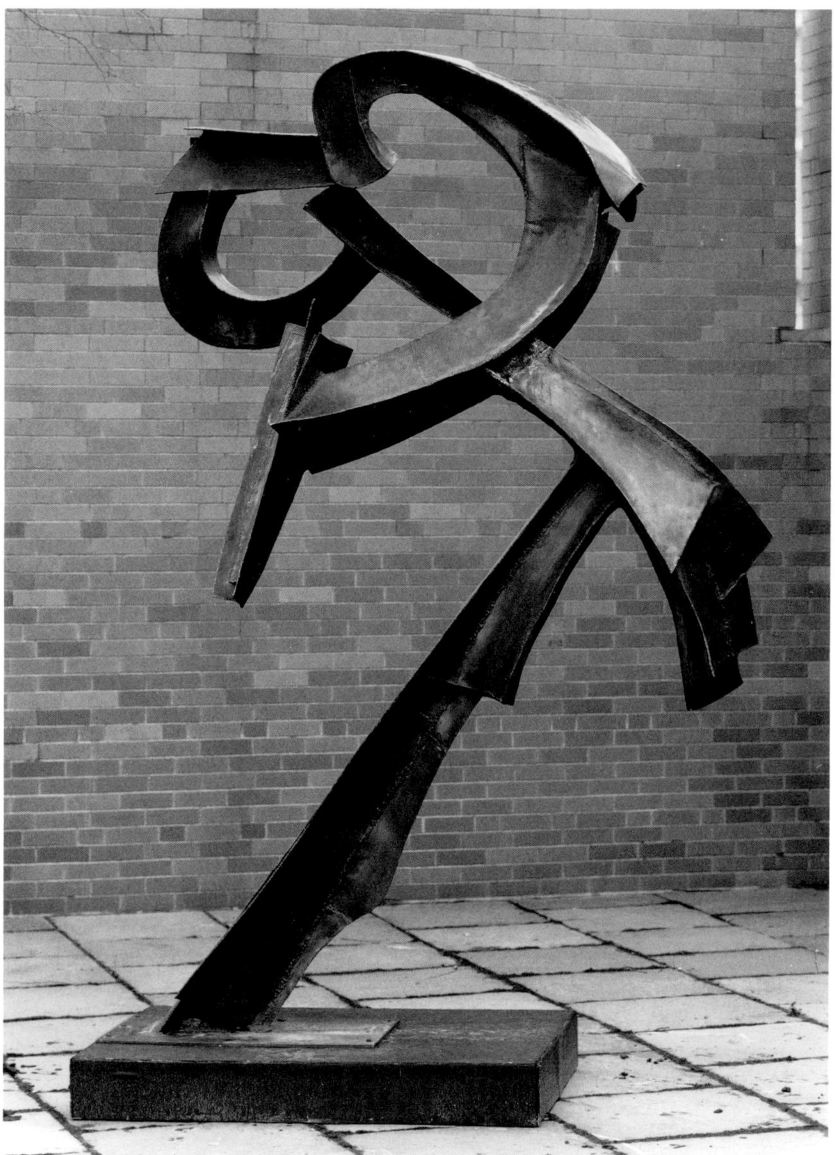

93

93 *Calligraph Gee III*

1964
Copper
105 x 74 x 18 (266.7 x 188 x 45.7)

Signed and dated top of base within applied cast patch, in relief: Ferber 64

Gift of the artist
1969.84

94 *Two Arches*

1964
Copper
34½ x 48 x 36 (87.6 x 121.9 x 91.4)

Signed and dated at foot of one support: Ferber 64

Gift of the artist
1968.28

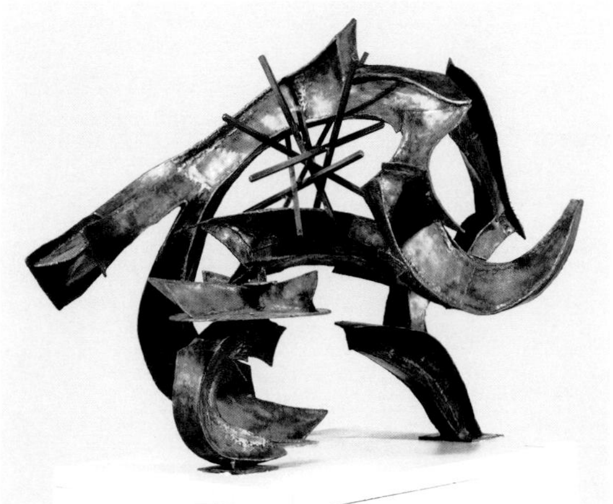

94

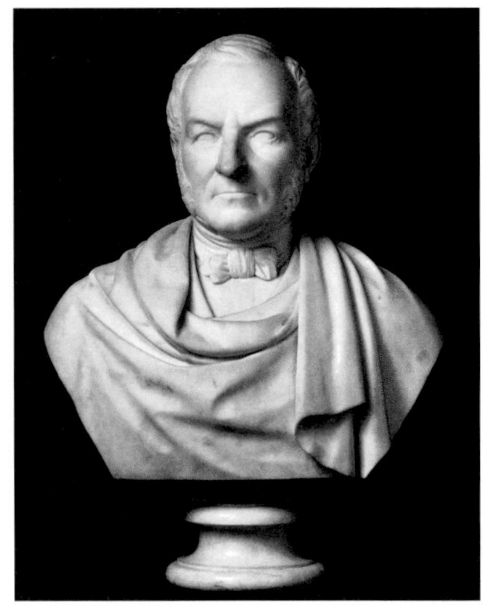

95

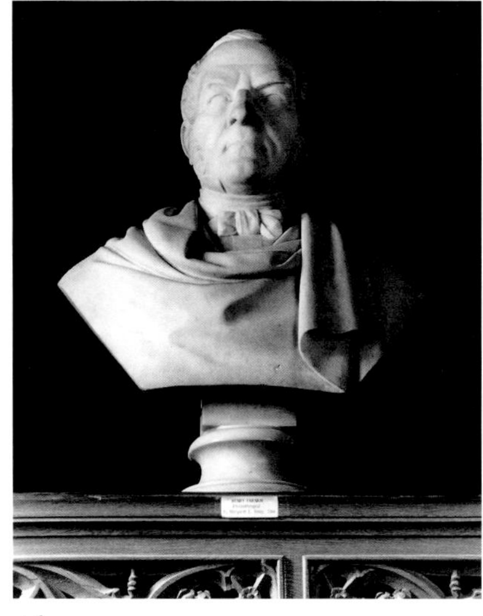

96

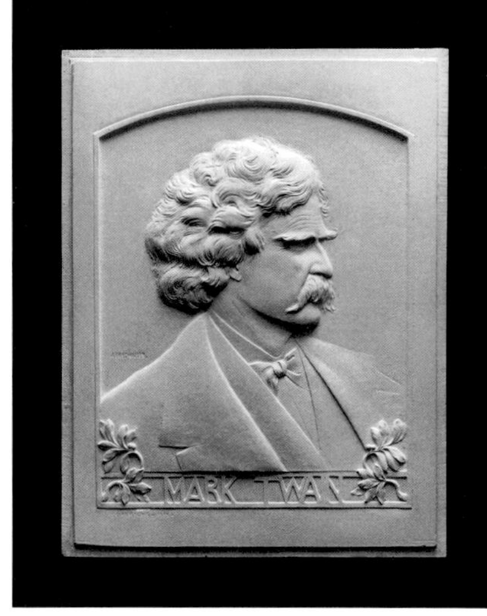

97

MARGARET FOLEY

About 1820 Vermont or New Hampshire – 1877 Austrian Tyrol

95 *Henry Farnam* 1803–1883
M.A.(hon.) 1871

1868
Marble
21½ x 19½ x 11 (54.6 x 49.5 x 27.9)

Signed, dated, and inscribed lower center rear: MARGARET . FOLEY . / SC. IN . ROMA . 1868

Bequest of Henry Farnam, M.A.(hon.) 1871
1883.4

96 *Henry Farnam* 1803–1883
M.A.(hon.) 1871

1875
Marble
21 x 20 x 12 (53.3 x 50.8 x 30.5)

Signed, dated and inscribed lower rear: MARGARET . FOLEY . / SCULPT . IN . ROMA · 1875

Gift of the sitter to the Yale University Library
1875.3

A. FRECHINGER

Dates unknown

97 *Mark Twain*
(Samuel Langhorne Clemens)
1835–1910
M.A.(hon.) 1888, LITT.D. 1901

1914
Plaster
11¼ x 8¾ x 1 (28.6 x 22.2 x 2.5)

Signed and dated on front left center: A · FRECHINGER ·; lower left: COPYRIGHT · 1914

Inscribed lower front in relief: MARK TWAIN

Gift of Willard S. Morse to the Collection of American Literature, Beinecke Rare Book and Manuscript Library
1980.299

HARRIET WHITNEY FRISHMUTH

1880 Philadelphia – 1979 Norwalk or Southbury, Connecticut

98 *The Vine*

1921
Bronze, green patina
12¾ x 7¼ x 5¼ (32.4 x 18.4 x 13.3)

Belgian marble base
¾ x 4¼ x 4¼ (1.9 x 10.8 x 10.8)

Signed and dated proper right rear edge of base: HARRIET W FRISHMUTH / 1921

Foundry: Roman Bronze Works, New York; mark, proper left rear edge of base: ROMAN BRONZE WORKS N–Y–

Bequest of Doris M. Brixey
1984.32.7

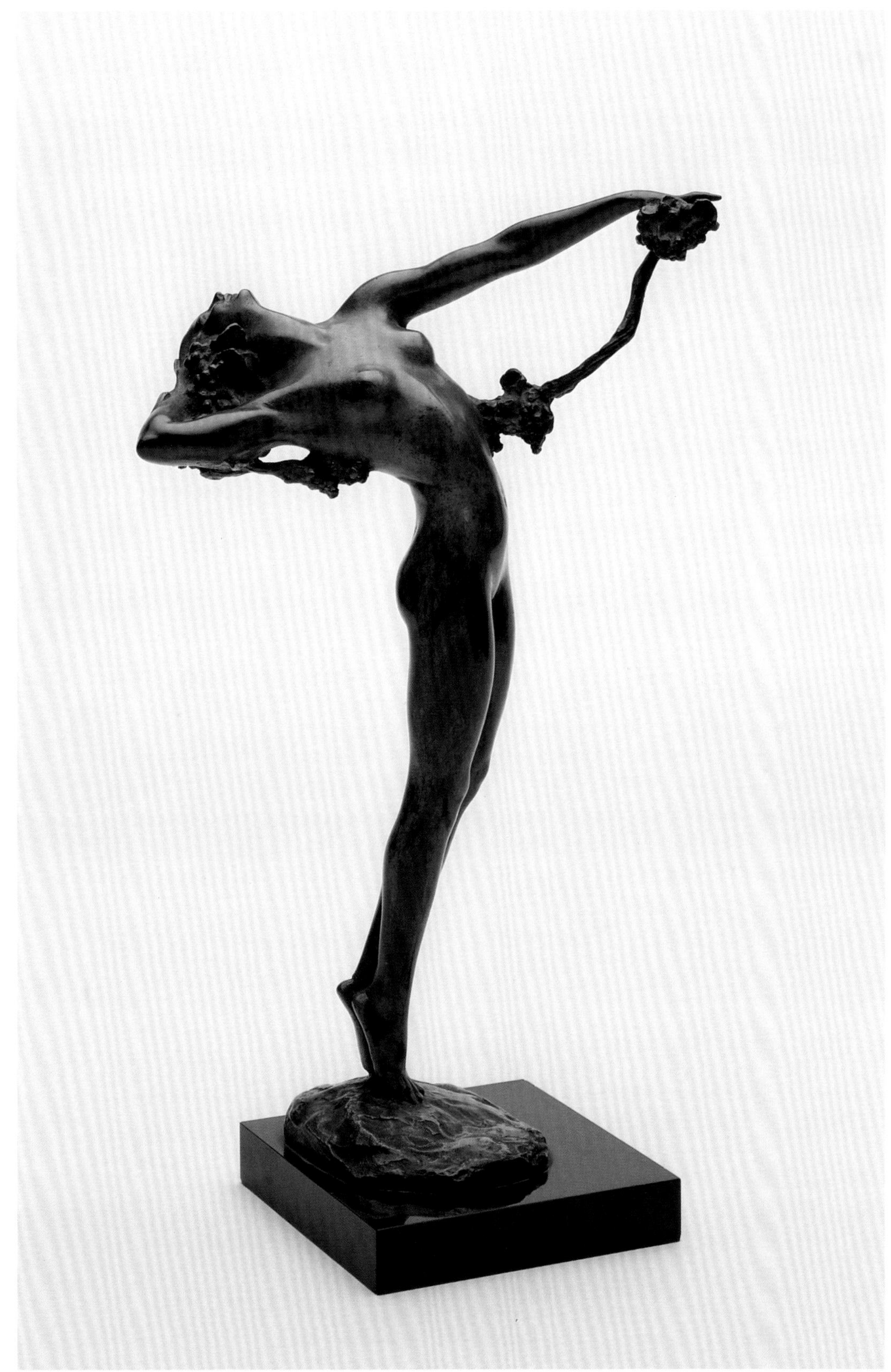

D. WHIPPLE FRY

Dates unknown

99 *Sherman Leland Whipple*
1862–1930
B.A. 1881, LL.B. 1884

c.1930
Bronze, brown patina
21¾ x 14¾ x ¾ (55.2 x 37.5 x 1.9)

Signed lower left front:
D WHIPPLE FRY

Inscribed lower front in relief:
SHERMAN L. WHIPPLE / 1862
1930 / LUX ET VERITAS

Foundry: The Gorham Manufacturing Company, Providence, Rhode Island; mark, lower right front near bottom edge: GORHAMCO FOUNDERS

Gift of the artist to the Yale University Law School
1933.13

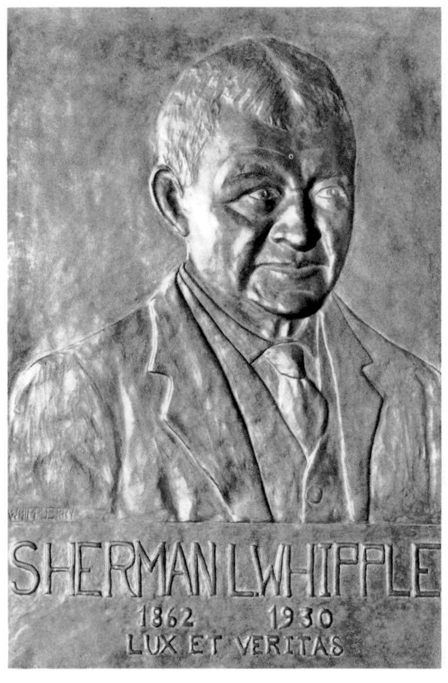

99

META VAUX WARRICK FULLER

1877 Philadelphia – 1968 Framingham, Massachusetts

100 *Phillis Wheatley* c.1753–1784

c.1925, after an engraving published London 1773, after lost oil, possibly by Scipio Moorhead of Boston
Painted plaster
8 x 6¼ x ¾ (20.3 x 15.9 x 1.9) oval

Inscribed along upper front border:
PHILLIS WHEATLEY A NEGRO SERVANT TO MR JOHN WHEATLEY OF BOSTON

Bequest of Grayce Fairfax Nail to the Collection of American Literature, Beinecke Rare Book and Manuscript Library
1980.213

101 *Ethiopia*

c.1930
Bronze, greenish-black patina
13½ x 3½ x 4 (34.3 x 8.9 x 10.2)

Signed lower rear edge of base:
M V W (monogram) FULLER ©

Founder's mark, rear underside edge of base: P.B.u. C° MUNCHEN
MADE IN GERMANY

Bequest of Grayce Fairfax Nail to the Collection of American Literature, Beinecke Rare Book and Manuscript Library
1980.168

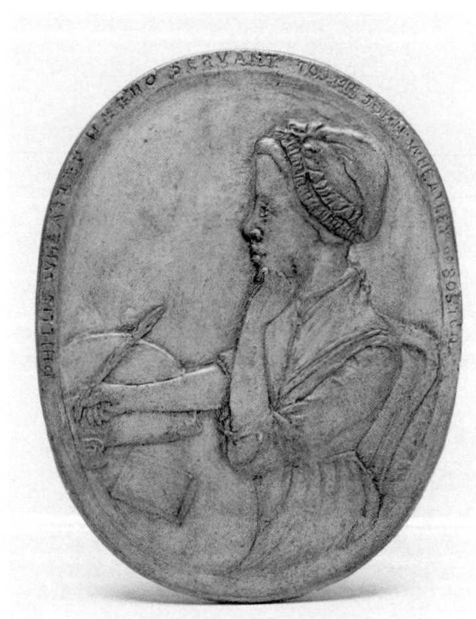

100

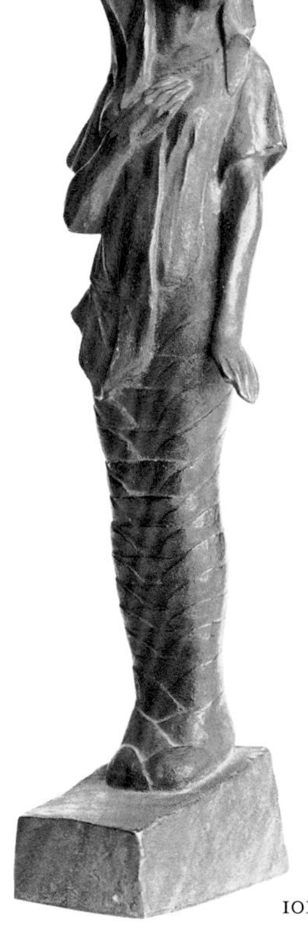

101

JOHANNES SOPHUS GELERT

1852 Denmark – 1923 New York City
Active U.S. 1887–1923

102 *William Frederick Poole* 1821–1894
B.A. 1849

1897
Bronze, dark brown patina
29¾ x 19½ x 12¼ (75.6 x 49.5 x 31.1)

Signed and dated proper left edge: J · GELERT · 1897 ·; rear: *J. GELERT / Sculptor / Aug. 26th 97*

Inscribed center front of base in relief: WILLIAM · FREDERICK · / POOLE · / · QUI · SCIT · VBI · SIT · SCIENTIA · / · HABENTI · EST · PROXIMVS

Gift of the family of William Frederick Poole, B.A. 1849, to the Yale University Library

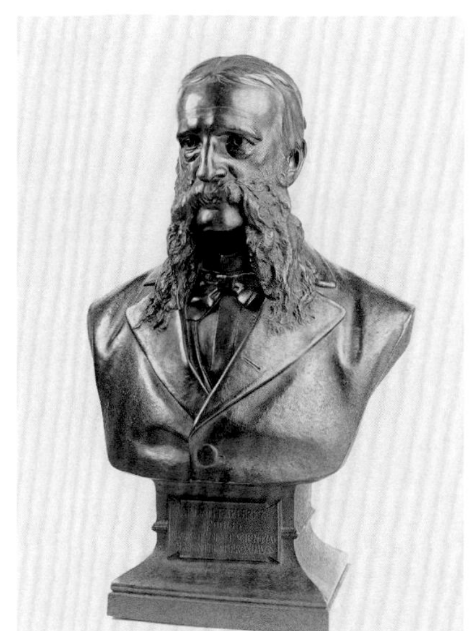

102

I. GELLI

Dates unknown

103 *Mark Twain*
(Samuel Langhorne Clemens)
1835–1910
M.A.(hon.) 1888, LITT.D. 1901

Late 19th – early 20th century
Bronze, copper-brown patina
12¼ x 9¼ x 1 (31.1 x 23.5 x 2.5)

Signed lower left front: *Gelli*

Inscribed on front left center: –COPYRIGHT–; lower center in relief: MARK TWAIN

Founder's mark right center front: M NELLI & C FIRENZI

Collection of American Literature, Beinecke Rare Book and Manuscript Library
1980.315

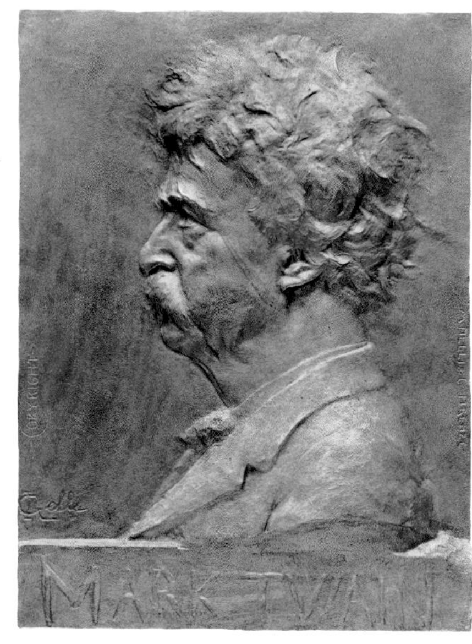

103

KARL GERHARDT

1853 Boston – 1940

104 *Mark Twain and George W. Cable*
(Samuel Langhorne Clemens)
1835–1910
M.A.(hon.) 1888, LITT.D. 1901

George W. Cable, 1844–1925
M.A.(hon.) 1888, LITT.D. 1901

Late 19th – early 20th century
Terra cotta
9¼ x 8½ x 1 (23.5 x 21.6 x 2.5)

Signed lower front:
Karl · Gerhardt · fecit ·

Inscribed in mixed upper and lower case on front left: Mark · Twain; right: Geo · W · Cable ·

Gift of Willard S. Morse to the Collection of American Literature, Beinecke Rare Book and Manuscript Library
1942.357

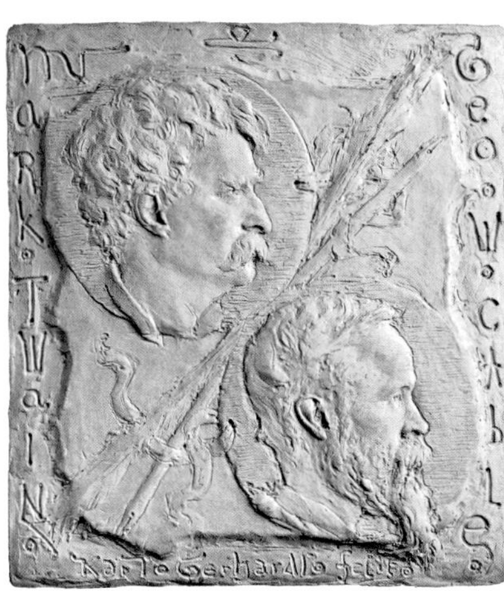

104

LLOYD GLASSON

b. 1931 Chicago

105 *William Clyde DeVane* 1898–1965
B.A. 1920, PH.D. 1926

1968
Bronze, black patina
21 x 11½ x 11 (53.3 x 29.2 x 27.9)

Signed and dated lower proper left side edge: L. Glasson / '68

Gift of Frederic W. Naumberg, B.A. 1920, PH.D. 1926, to Yale University
1968.45

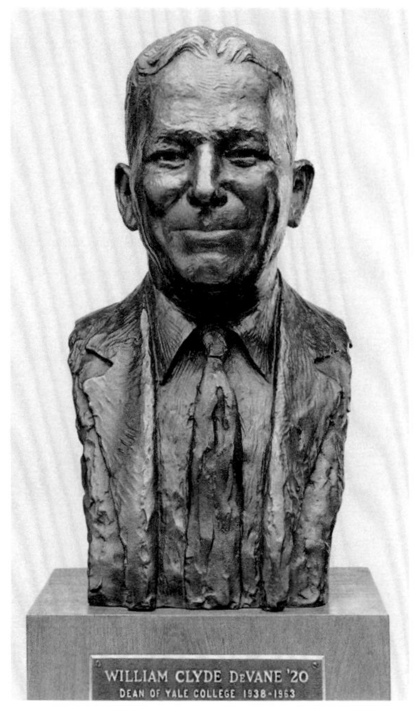

105

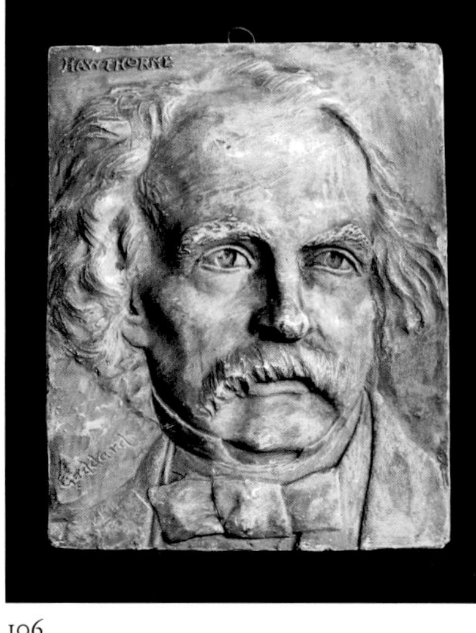

106

RALPH BARTLETT GODDARD

1861 Meadville, Pennsylvania –
1936 Middletown, New York

106 *Nathaniel Hawthorne* 1804–1864

1894
Painted plaster
8¼ x 6¾ x 1½ (21 x 17.1 x 3.8)

Signed lower left front: Goddard

Inscribed upper left front in relief: HAWTHORNE; lower left side edge: copyright 1894 / by R.B. Goddard

Bequest of Norman Holmes Pearson, PH.D. 1941, to the Collection of American Literature, Beinecke Rare Book and Manuscript Library
1980.314

GEORGE GREENE

b. 1908

107 *Blue Horizon II*

1973
Plexiglas
10¾ x 13¼ x 5¼ (27.3 x 33.7 x 13.3)

Signed, dated, and inscribed in ink verso: BLUE HORIZON II
G. Greene '73

The Katharine Ordway Collection
1980.13.25

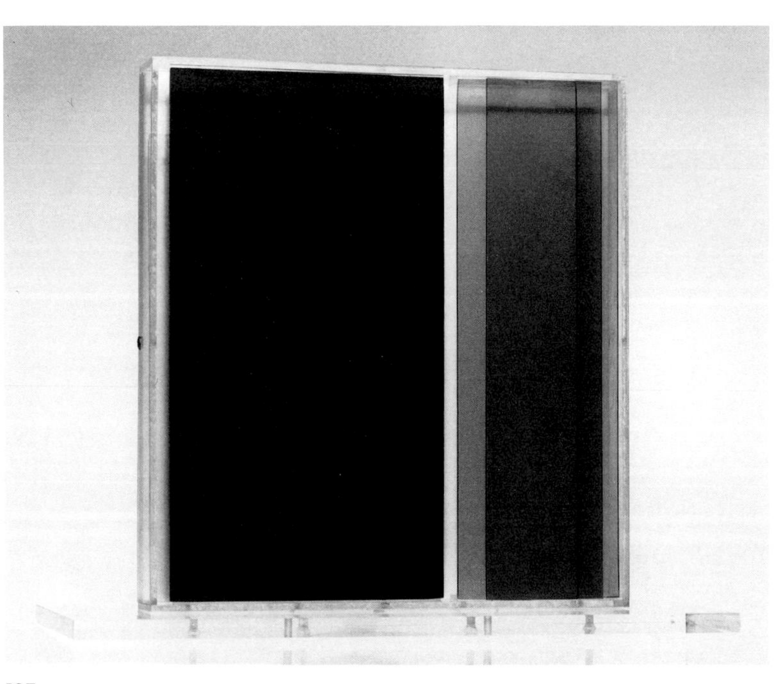

107

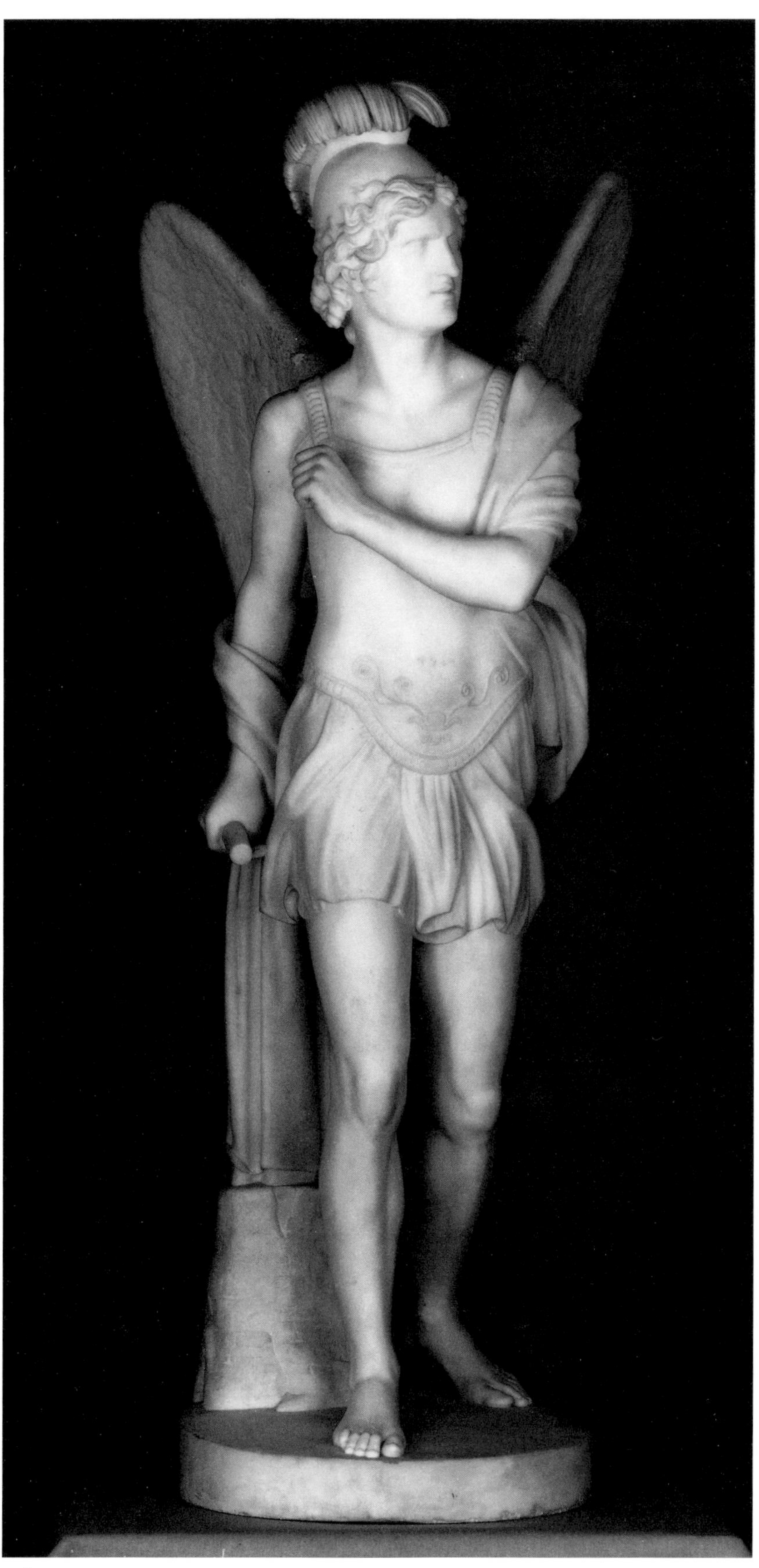

108

HORATIO GREENOUGH

1805 Boston – 1852 Somerville, Massachusetts

108 *The Angel Abdiel*

1839
Marble
41 x 16¾ x 14½ (104.1 x 42.5 x 36.8)

Signed and dated rear edge of base:
HG. 1839

Bequest of Professor Edward E. Salisbury, B.A. 1832, M.A. 1835, LL.D. 1869
1919.13

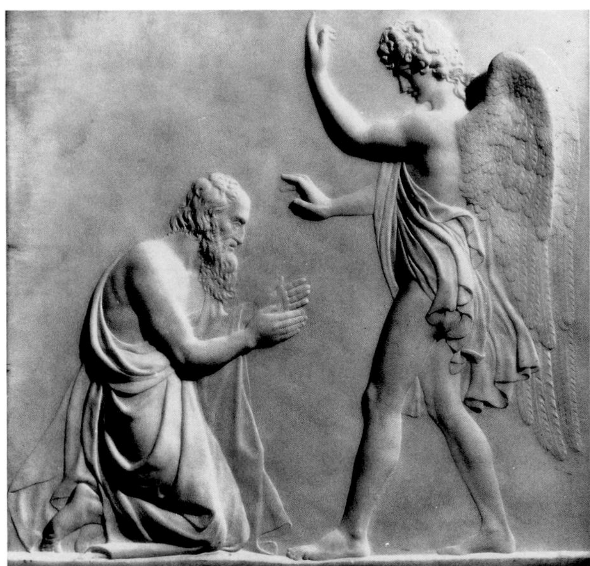

109

109 *The Angel Warning St. John*

c.1839
Marble
21½ x 23¼ x 2¼ (54.6 x 59.1 x 5.7)

Bequest of Professor Edward E. Salisbury, B.A. 1832, M.A. 1835, LL.D. 1869
1919.14

110 *Aeschines*
Formerly known as *Aristides*
After 4th century Roman copy

c.1839
Marble
31¼ x 13½ x 8¼ (79.4 x 34.3 x 21)

Bequest of Professor Edward E. Salisbury, B.A. 1832, M.A. 1835, LL.D. 1869
1919.15

after
HORATIO GREENOUGH
See cat. 423

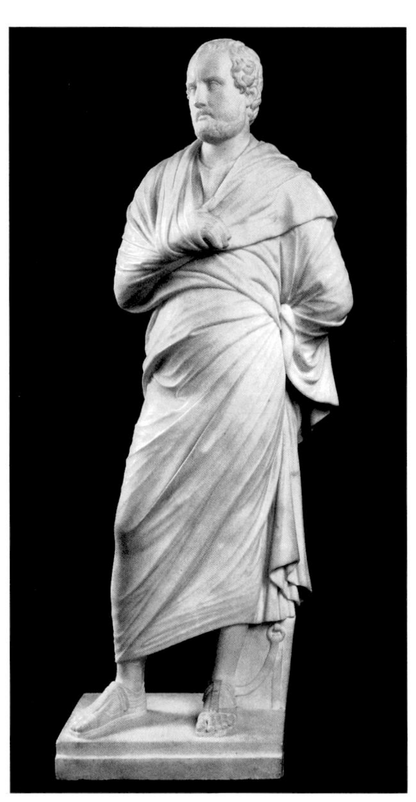

110

JOHN GREGORY

1879 London – 1958 New York City
Active U.S. 1891–1958

111 *Philomela*

1922
Bronze, reddish-brown and green patina
12¼ x 9¼ x 4¼ (31.1 x 23.5 x 10.8)

Marble base
2 x 8 x 4 (5.1 x 20.3 x 10.2)

Signed and dated proper right top rear on bronze base: *John Gregory / 1922* ©

Inscribed proper left top front on bronze base: PHILOMELA

Foundry: Roman Bronze Works, New York; mark, proper left side on bronze base: ROMAN BRONZE WORKS N–Y–

Cast number proper left top rear of bronze base: No3

Gift of Miss Elisabeth Achelis
1956.15.2

HENRY GUDGELL

1826 Livingston County, Kentucky –
1895 Livingston County, Kentucky

112 *Afro-Missourian Cane with Figural Relief*

c.1863
Wood
H. 37 X DIAM. 1½ (94 x 3.8)
Director's Purchase Fund
1968.23

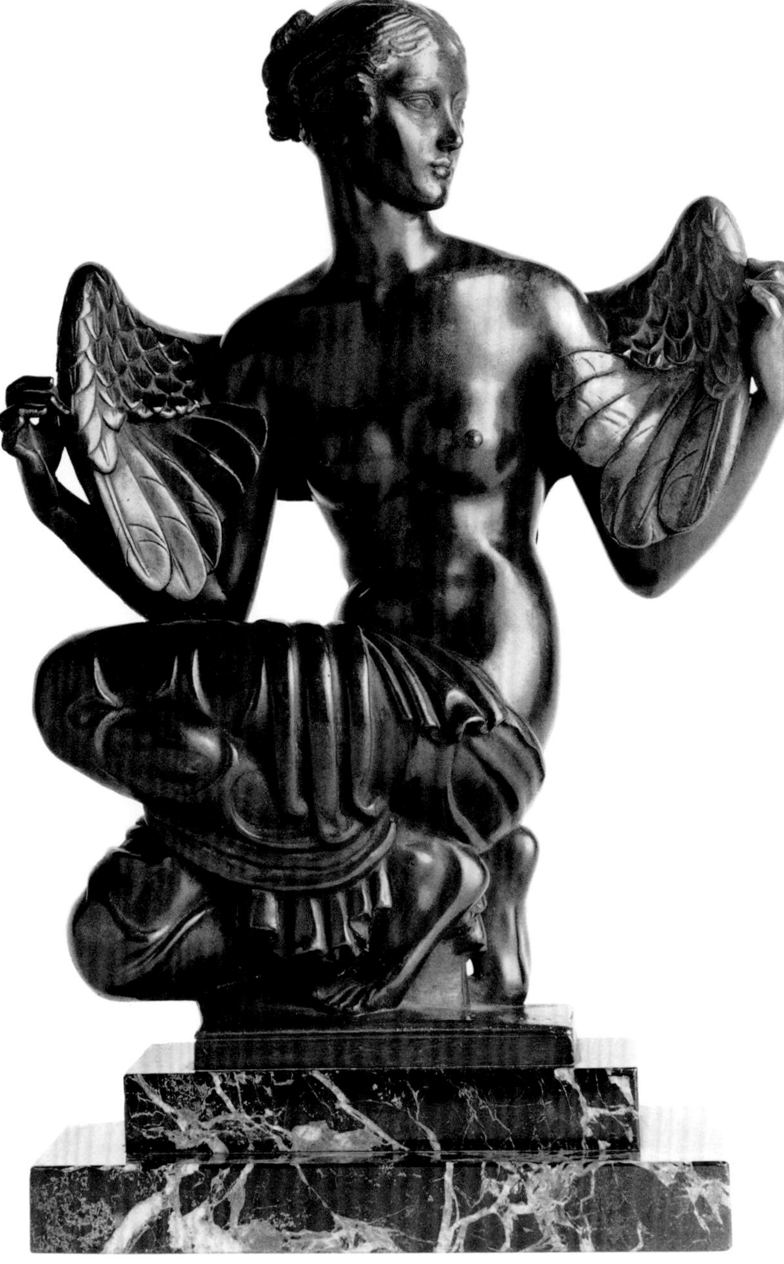

111

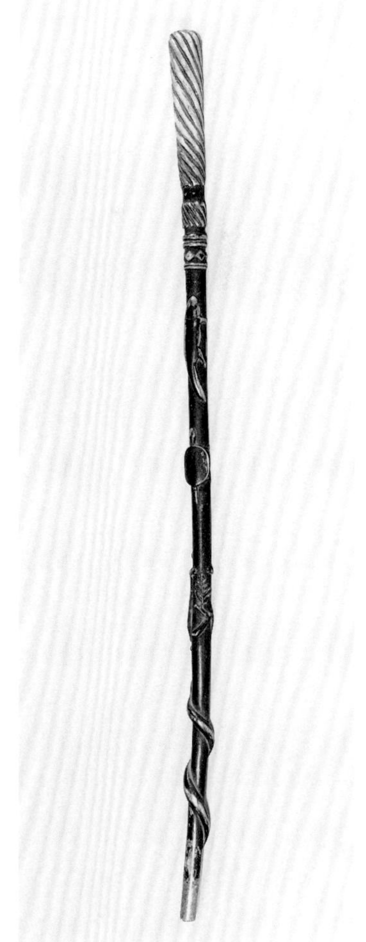

112

DIMITRI HADZI

b. 1921 New York City

113 *Floating Helmets*

1965
Bronze, black patina
136 x 54¼ x 52½ (345.4 x 137.8 x 133.4)

Travertine base
19½ x 36 x 36 (49.5 x 91.4 x 91.4)

Signed outside edge of one concave element near side bottom of sculpture: D. HADZI I/IV

Inscribed in relief on bottom of another concave element near side bottom of sculpture: TOM

Leonard C. Hanna, Jr., B.A. 1913, Fund
1965.53

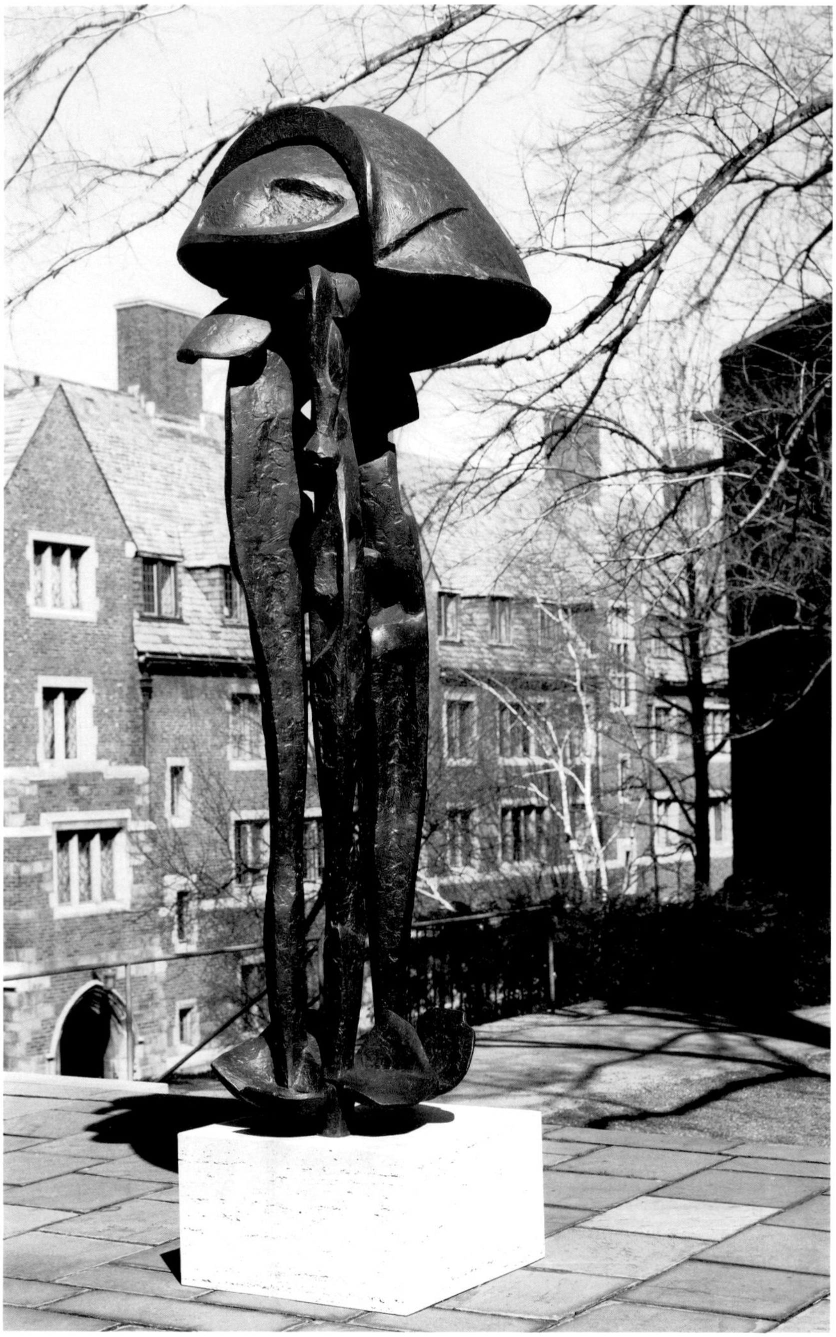

113

DAVID HARE

b. 1917 New York City

114 *Red Knight*

c.1940
Painted plaster and wood
58 x 21½ x 20¾ (147.3 x 54.6 x 52.7)

Painted wood base
2¾ x 17½ x 16¼ (7 x 44.5 x 41.3)

Gift of Miss Peggy Guggenheim
1947.216

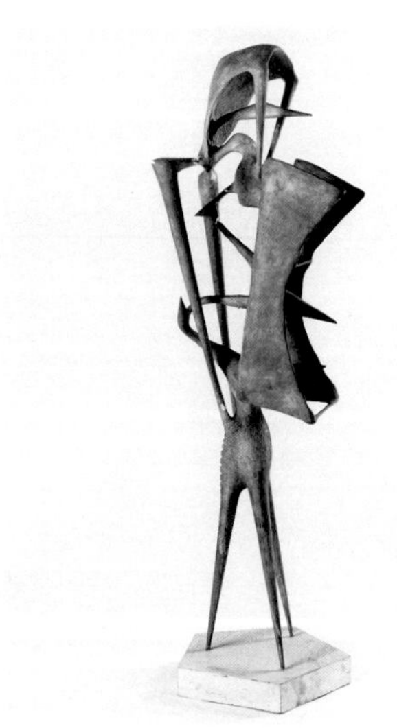

114

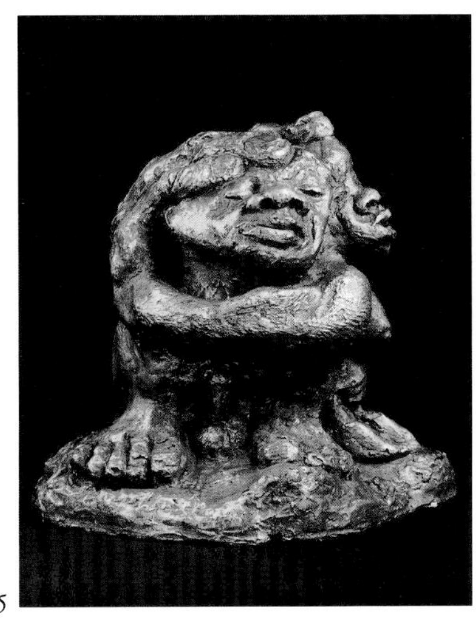
115

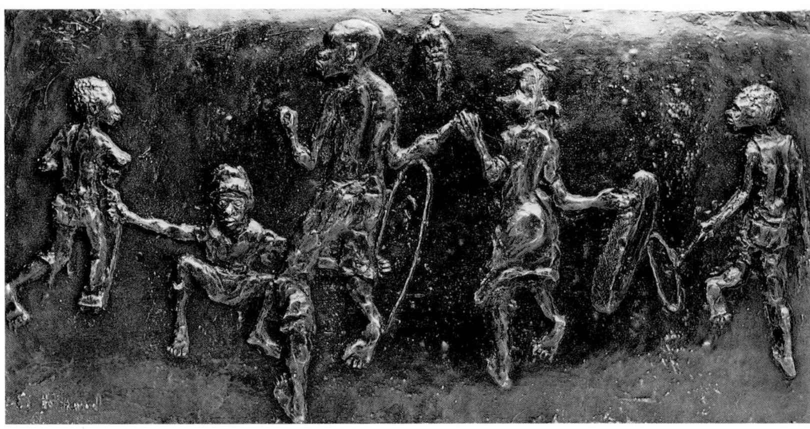
116

HUGH HARRELL

b. 1926 Hampton, Virginia

115 *Untitled*

1981
Painted plaster
14¾ x 16 x 14½ (37.5 x 40.6 x 36.8)

Dated proper right side: ©1981

Gift of the Mildred Andrews Fund
to the Afro-American Cultural Center
at Yale

116 *Untitled*

1981
Bronze, dark brown and exposed
bronze patina
13¼ x 26½ x 1¾ (33.7 x 67.3 x 4.4)

Signed and dated proper right lower
front corner in relief: © H. Harrell / 81

Gift of the Mildred Andrews Fund
to the Afro-American Cultural Center
at Yale

117 *Untitled*

1981
Bronze, dark brown and exposed
bronze patina
47½ x 31½ x 2¾ (120.7 x 80 x 7)

Signed and dated proper right lower
front corner: © Harrell / 1981

Gift of the Mildred Andrews Fund
to the Afro-American Cultural Center
at Yale

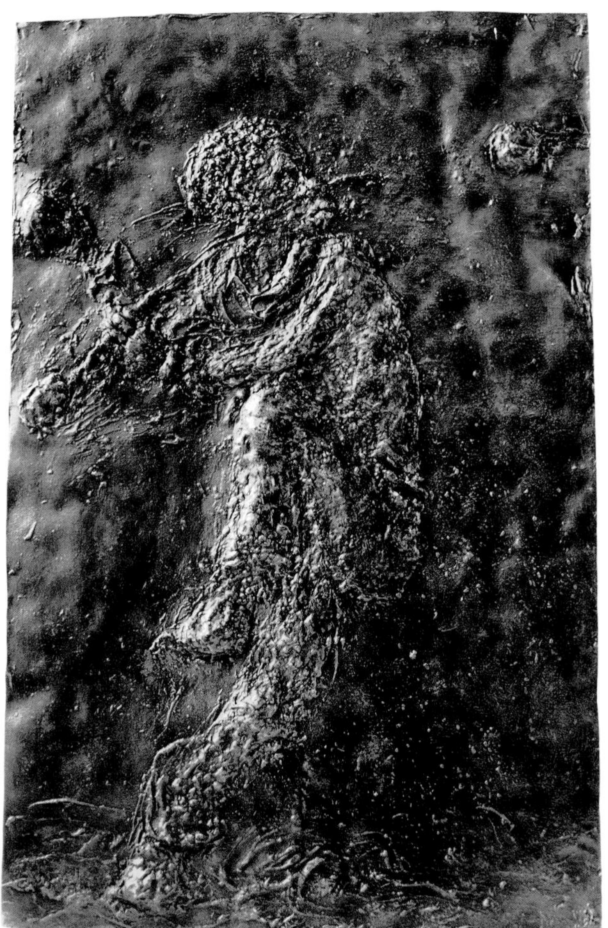
117

HERBERT HASELTINE

1877 Rome, Italy – 1962 Paris

118 *Suffolk Punch*

1931
Bronze, brown patina with gilt
11 x 11 x 7 (27.9 x 27.9 x 17.8)

Marble base
6½ x 11¼ x 8 (16.5 x 28.6 x 20.3)

Signed and dated proper right side lower center of marble base:
HASELTINE · MCMXXXI

Gift of William Adams Delano, B.A. 1895, B.F.A. 1907, M.A.(hon.) 1939
1950.57

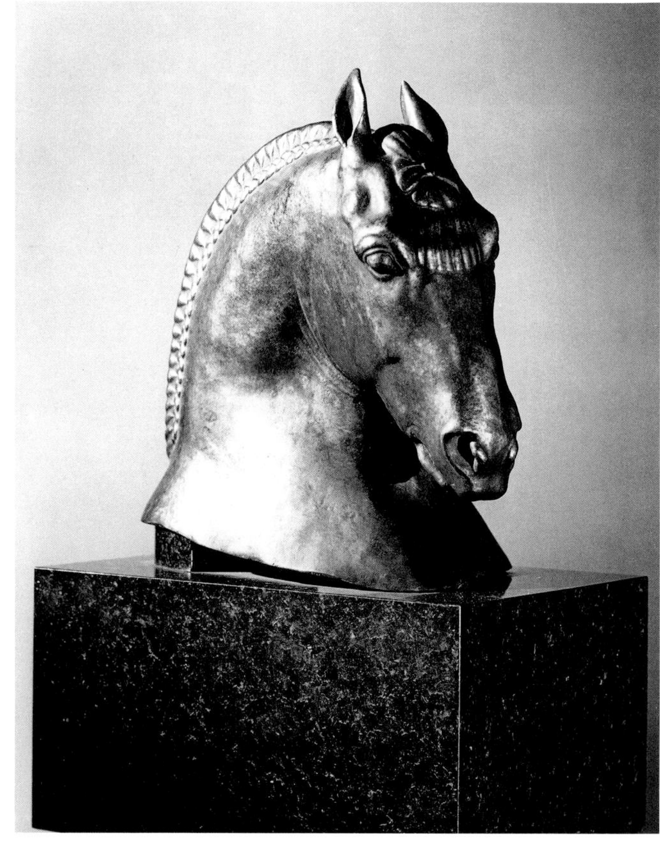

118

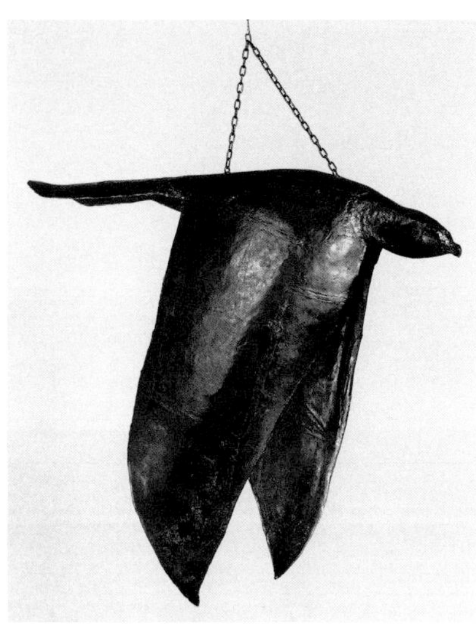

119

DAVID VINCENT HAYES

b. 1931 Hartford, Connecticut

119 *Flying Hawk*

c.1960
Forged steel, black patina
26¾ x 12 x 30 (67.9 x 30.5 x 76.2)

Gift of Mrs. John D. Rockefeller III
1969.38.1

120 *Gladiator*

1963
Forged steel, black patina
24 x 17¾ x 12¼ (61 x 45.1 x 31.1)

Gift of Mrs. John D. Rockefeller III
1969.38.2

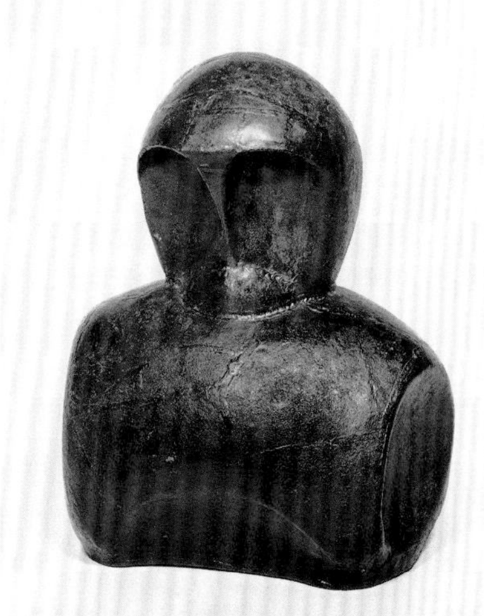

120

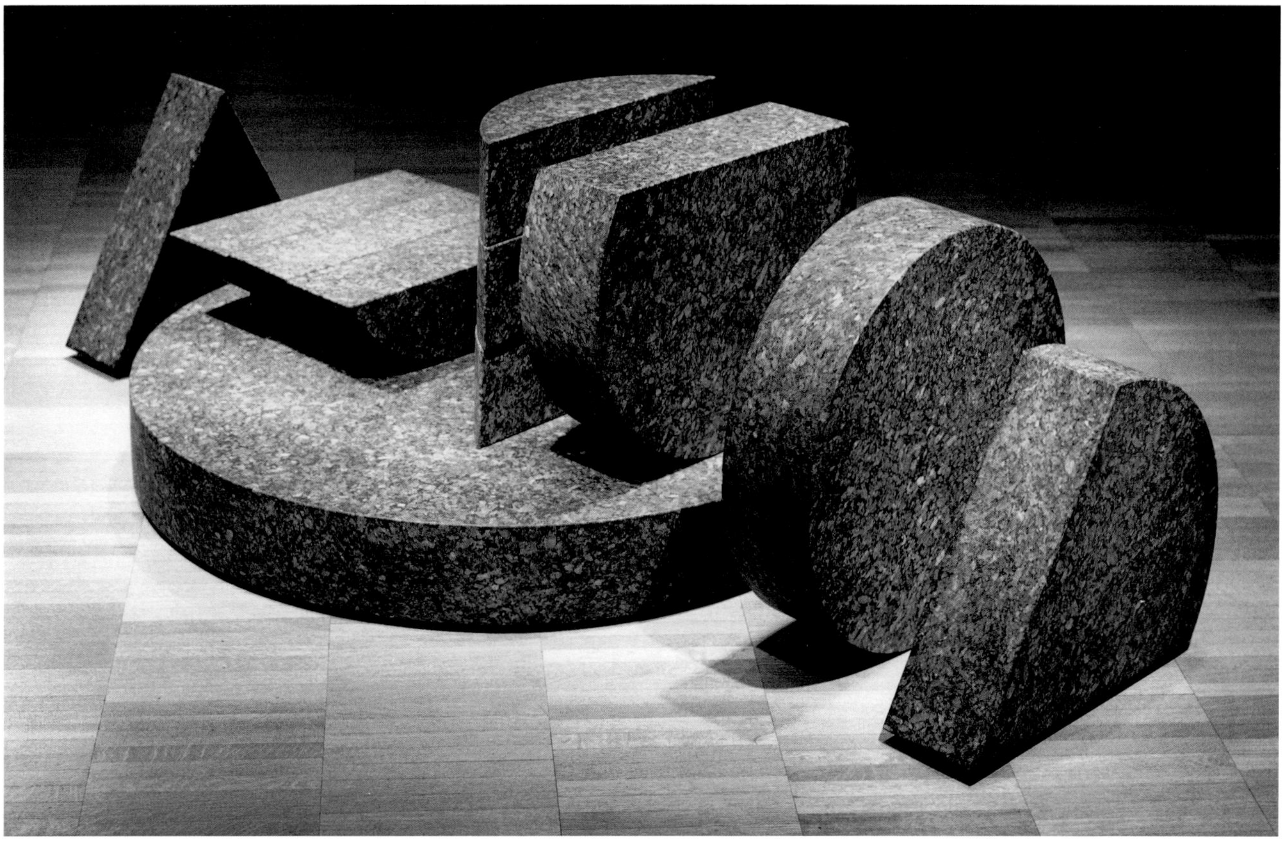

122

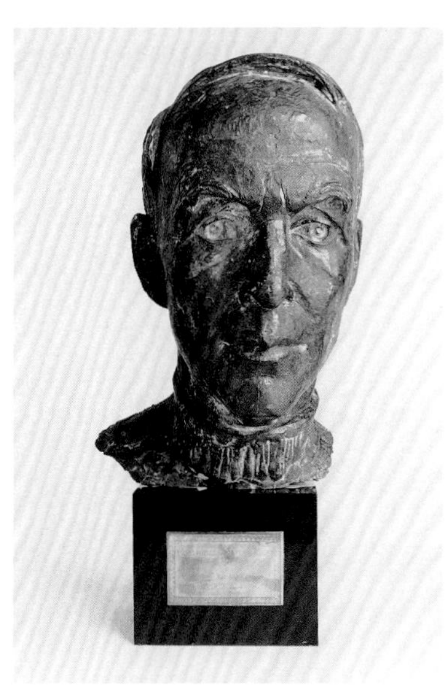

121

MILTON ELTING HEBALD

b. 1917 New York City

121 *Archibald MacLeish* 1892–1982
B.A. 1915

n.d.
Bronze, dark brown and exposed bronze patina
14 x 10¼ x 10 (35.6 x 26 x 25.4)

Signed and inscribed lower proper left side: HEBALD ROMA

Gift of Mr. and Mrs. Holstead B. Vander Poel, PH.B. 1933, to the Collection of American Literature, Beinecke Rare Book and Manuscript Library
1980.140

MICHAEL HEIZER

b. 1944 Berkeley, California

122 *Sweden*

c.1970
Blue pearl granite
24¼ x 75½ x 47¾ (61.6 x 191.8 x 121.3)

Dimensions variable, according to installation

Gift of Susan Morse Hilles
1984.75.1

PEACE CROWNS THEIR
ACT OF SACRIFICE

123

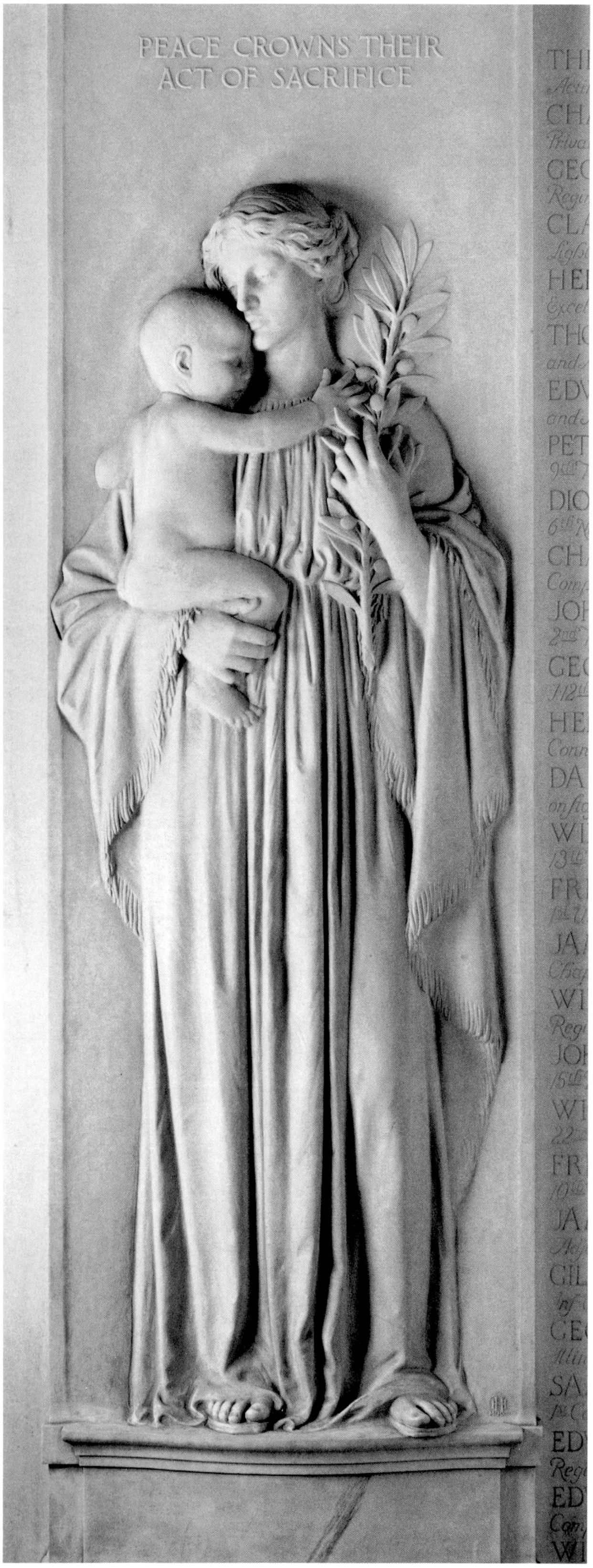

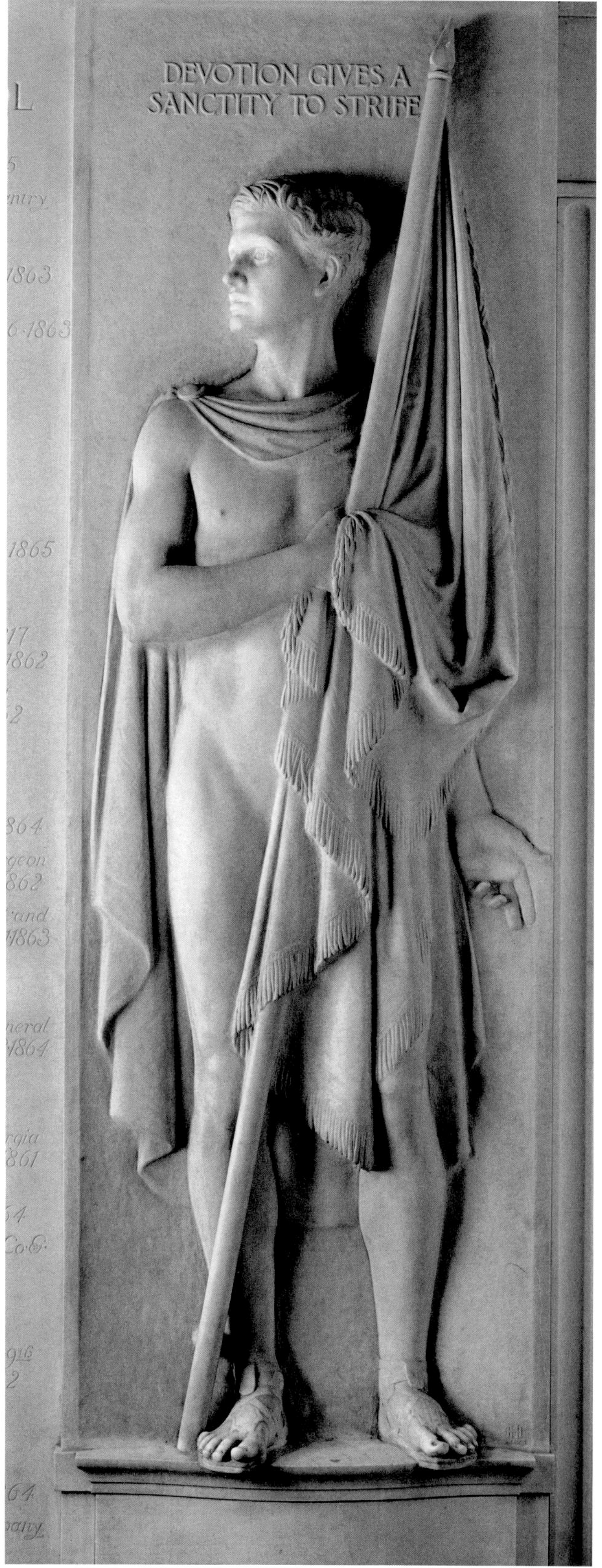
DEVOTION GIVES A
SANCTITY TO STRIFE

124

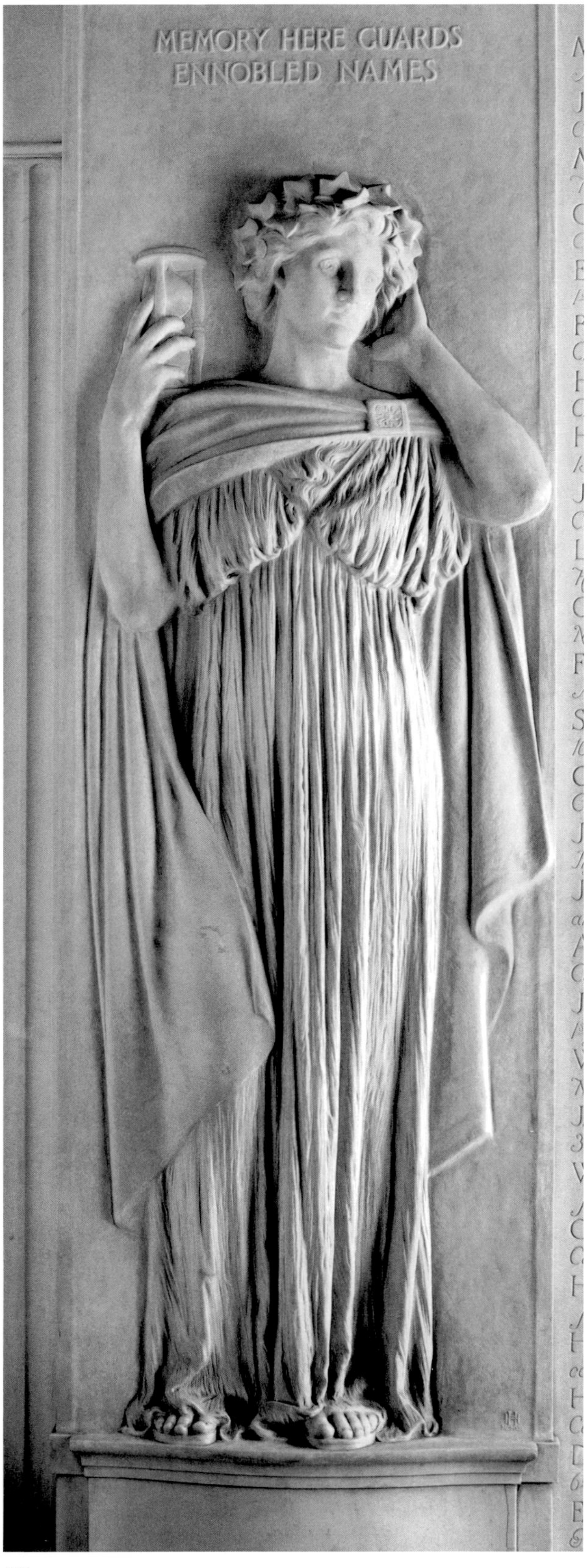

MEMORY HERE GUARDS
ENNOBLED NAMES

125

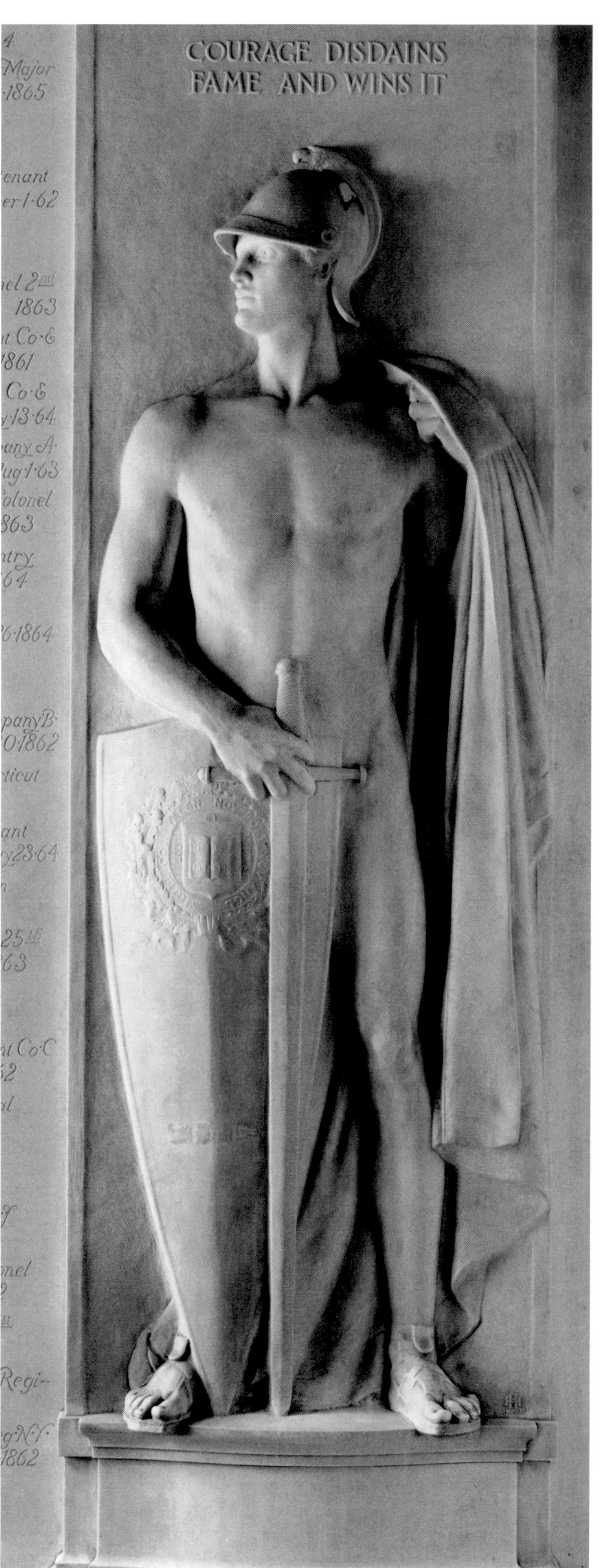

126

HENRY HERING

1874 New York City –
1949 New York City

123 *Peace*

1913
Marble
117 x 35½ x 5¾ (297.2 x 90.2 x 14.6)

Signed and dated lower right front in relief: HHH (monogram) / MCMXIII

Inscribed upper center front in relief: PEACE CROWNS THEIR / ACT OF SACRIFICE

Dedicated by the University to the men of Yale who gave their lives in the Civil War

124 *Devotion*

1913
Marble
117 x 35½ x 9½ (297.2 x 90.2 x 24.1)

Signed and dated lower right front in relief: HHH (monogram) / MCMXIII

Inscribed upper center front in relief: DEVOTION GIVES A / SANCTITY TO STRIFE

Dedicated by the University to the men of Yale who gave their lives in the Civil War

125 *Memory*

1913
Marble
117 x 35¼ x 5¾ (297.2 x 89.5 x 14.6)

Signed and dated lower right front in relief: HHH (monogram) / MCMXIII

Inscribed upper center front in relief: MEMORY HERE GUARDS / ENNOBLED NAMES

Dedicated by the University to the men of Yale who gave their lives in the Civil War

126 *Courage*

1913
Marble
117 x 35½ x 7 (297.2 x 90.2 x 17.8)

Signed and dated lower right front in relief: HHH (monogram) / MCMXIII

Inscribed upper center front in relief: COURAGE DISDAINS FAME AND WINS IT; on shield: Yale University seal

Dedicated by the University to the men of Yale who gave their lives in the Civil War

R.Y.M. HITCHCOCK

Dates unknown

127 *James Donnelly*

1912
Plaster
9 x 5¼ x 4¼ (22.9 x 13.3 x 10.8)

Signed and dated proper right side of base: R.Y.M. Hitchcock. / ©1912 / 1Ŷ4

Inscribed on front edge of base: JIM DONNELLY; rear edge: –YALE UNIV– and Yale University seal

Manuscripts and Archives, Yale University Library

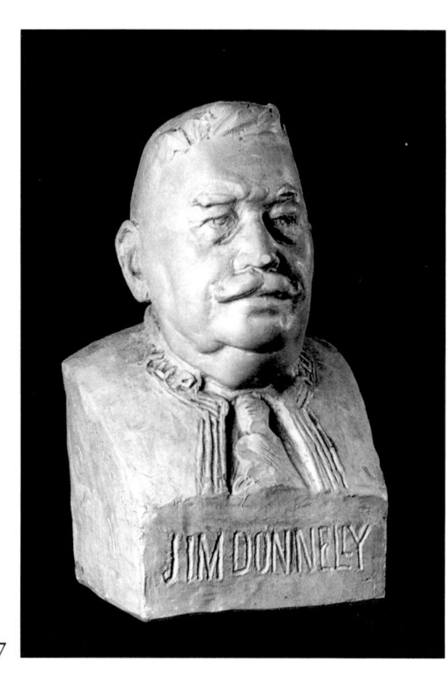

127

DAVID HOCKNEY

b. 1937 Bradford, England
Active U.S. intermittently 1963 on

128 *Blue Plastercine Mountain Where the Queen of the Night Lives*

c.1977
Plastiline
11½ x 11¼ x 9¾ (29.2 x 28.6 x 24.8)

Foamcore base
¼ x 14¾ x 13 (0.64 x 37.5 x 33)

Signed, dated, and inscribed in ink at lower left top of foamcore base: *a blue plastercine / mountain where / the Queen of the Night lives. / DH. 197[7?]*

Gift of Mr. and Mrs. Robert Peter Miller
1981.95

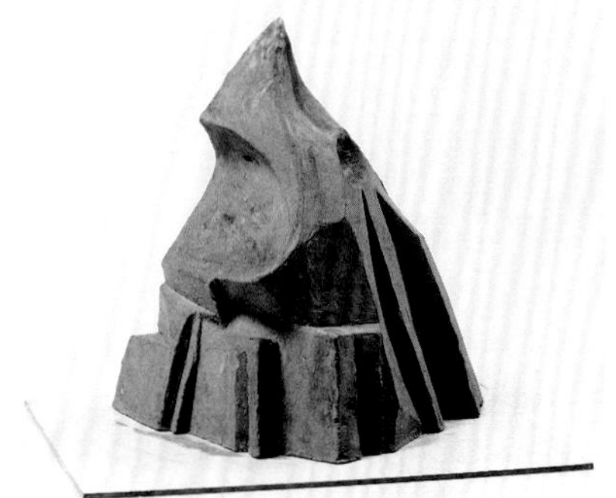

128

MALVINA CORNELL HOFFMAN

1885 or 1887 New York City – 1966 New York City

129 *Pavlova and Novikoff in "La Péri"*
Anna Pavlova, 1882–1931
Laurent Novikoff, 1888–1956

1921
Bronze, mottled reddish-brown, black and green patina
11½ x 9½ x 6¼ (29.2 x 24.1 x 15.9)

Marble base
1 x 7⅞ x 7⅛ (2.5 x 20 x 18.1)

Signed in mixed upper and lower case, and dated proper left top center of bronze base: Malvina Hoffman / © 1921 I

Foundry: Alexis Rudier, Paris; mark, proper left top rear corner of bronze base: Alexis Rudier / Fondeur Paris

Gift of Miss Elisabeth Achelis
1956.15.3

130 *Dr. Harvey W. Cushing* 1869–1939
B.A. 1891, M.A.(hon.) 1913, SC.D.(hon.) 1919

1948
Bronze, dark reddish-brown patina
22¾ x 10¼ x 10¼ (57.8 x 26 x 26)

Signed and dated proper left edge: MALVIN – HOFFMAN / 1948

Inscribed center front of base in relief: HARVEY CUSHING / 1869–1939

Foundry: Roman Bronze Works, New York; mark, lower center rear of base: ROMAN BRONZE WORKS N–Y–

Gift of the artist to the Yale School of Medicine
1948.299

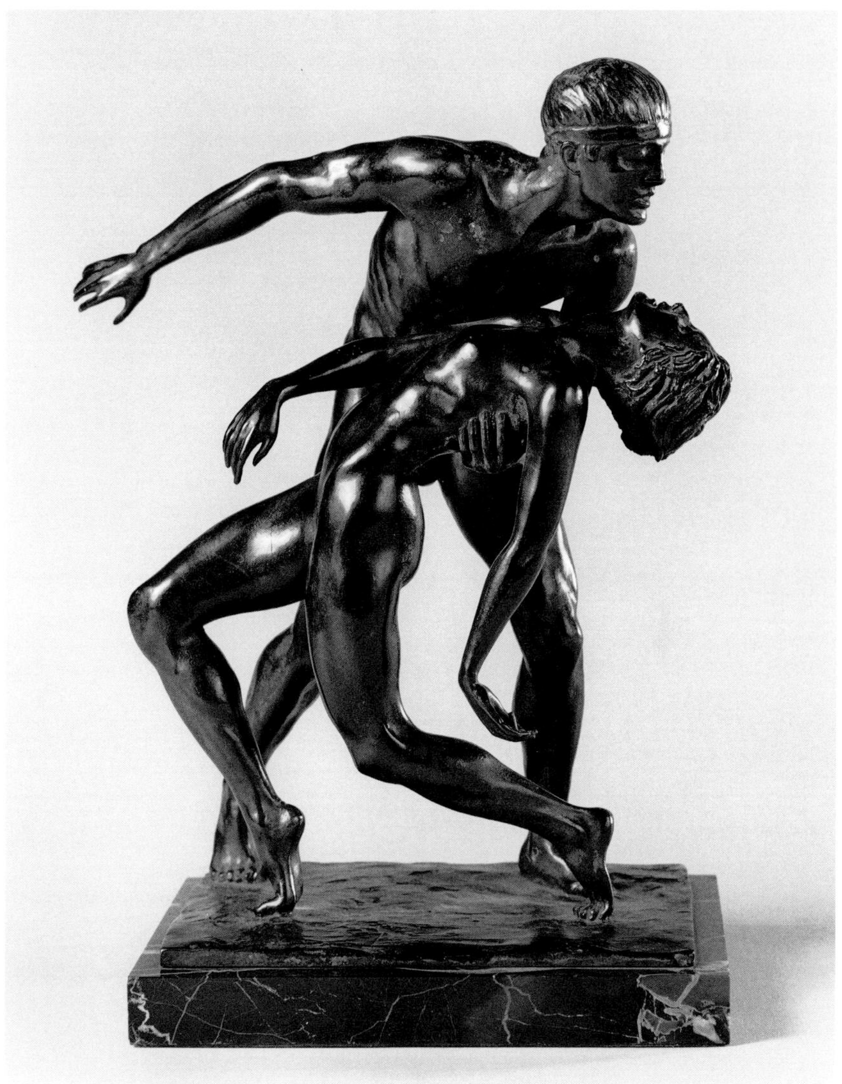

129

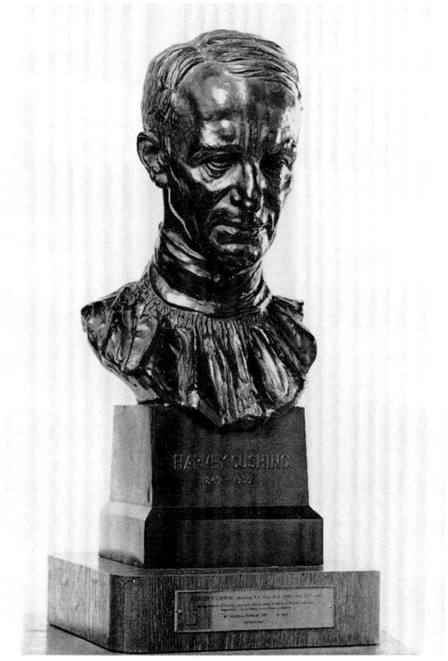

130

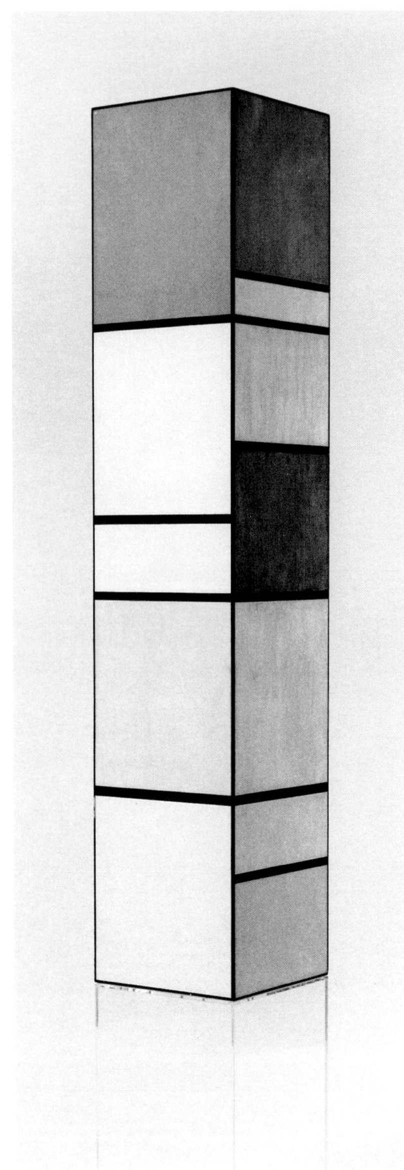

131

HARRY HOLTZMAN

1912 New York City –
1987 Lyme, Connecticut

131 *Sculpture*

1941–42
Oil and tempera on cheesecloth or muslin laid down on masonite
60 x 12 x 12 (152.4 x 30.5 x 30.5)

Plexiglas base, 1976 (original wood base replaced with present plexiglas base by the artist)
18 x 12 x 12 (45.7 x 30.5 x 30.5)

Signed, dated, and inscribed on top edge, painted twice, in black and in white: SCULPTURE / 1941–42 HARRY HOLTZMAN

Gift of the artist to the Collection Société Anonyme
1950.112

WILL HORWITT

1934 New York City – 1985

132 *Corinth*

1963–66
Bronze, black patina
43 x 72 x 42 (109.2 x 182.8 x 106.7)

Signed and dated near bottom edge of base adjacent to center seam: HORWITT 63–66

Cast number above signature: 1/4

Gift of Mr. and Mrs. Richard Shields, B.A. 1929
1967.21

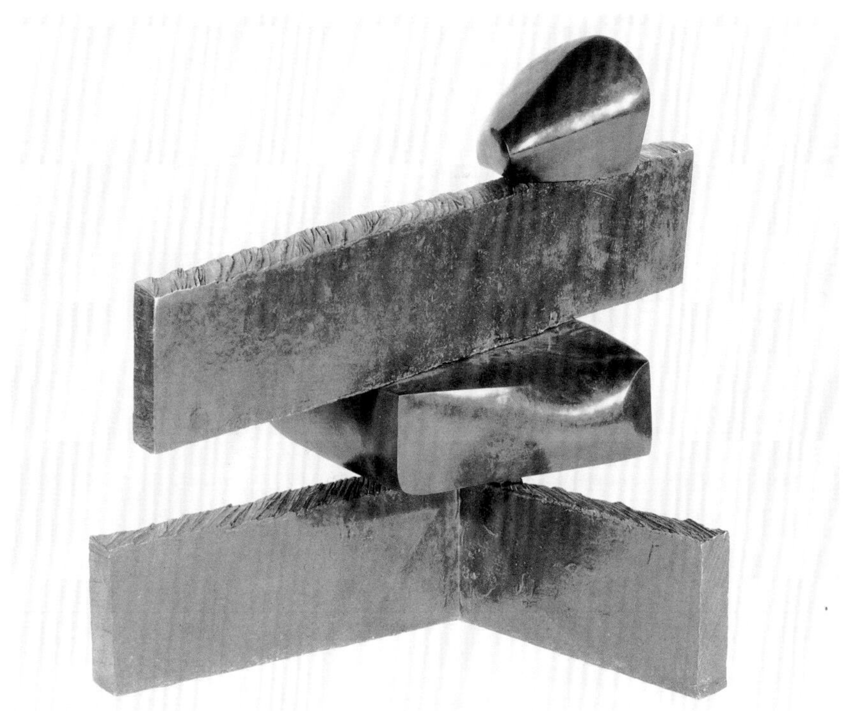

132

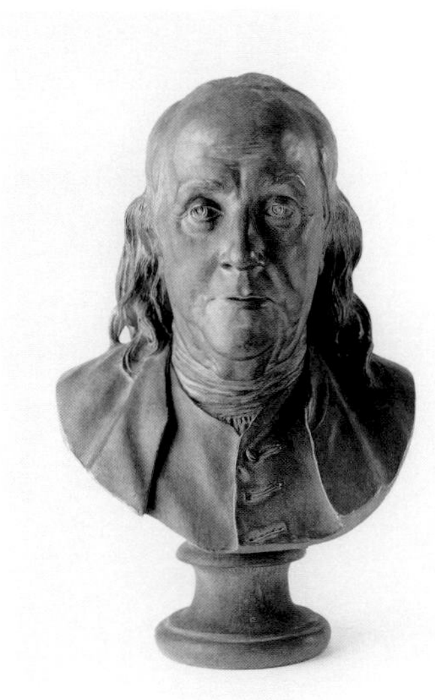
133

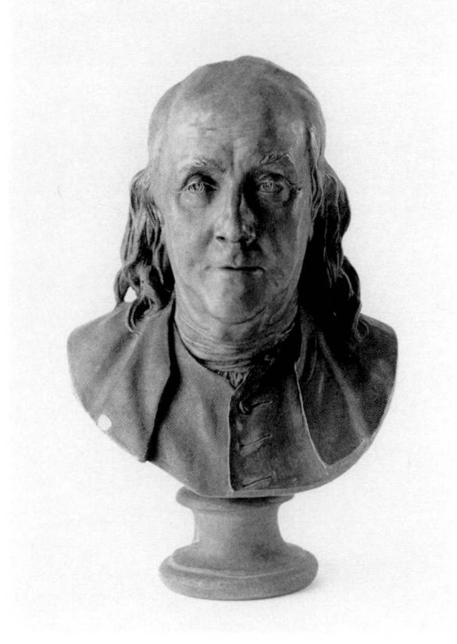
134

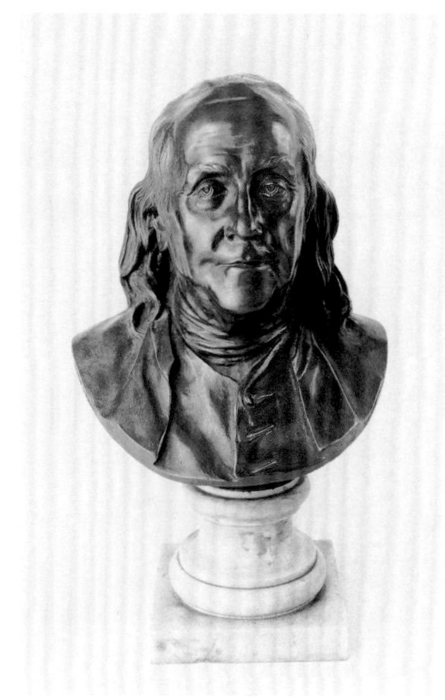

135

after
JEAN ANTOINE HOUDON

1741 Versailles, France – 1828 Paris
Active U.S. 1785

See also Hiram Powers, cat. 244

133 *Benjamin Franklin* 1706–1790
M.A.(hon.) 1753

After an original of 1777
Painted plaster
16¾ x 12¼ x 9¾ (42.5 x 31.1 x 24.8)

Signed and dated proper right edge:
Houdon ft. 1777

Benjamin Franklin Collection,
Yale University Library

134 *Benjamin Franklin* 1706–1790
M.A.(hon.) 1753

After an original of 1778
Painted plaster
18½ x 13 x 10 (47 x 33 x 25.4)

Signed and dated proper right edge:
Houdon Ft. 1778

Benjamin Franklin Collection,
Yale University Library

135 *Benjamin Franklin* 1706–1790
M.A.(hon.) 1753

After an original of 1778
Bronze, greenish-black patina
13¼ x 11 x 8½ (33.7 x 27.9 x 21.6)

Signed and dated proper right side
edge: *houdon f · 1778*

Benjamin Franklin Collection,
Yale University Library

136 *Benjamin Franklin* 1706–1790
M.A.(hon.) 1753

Probably 19th century, after an original
of 1778
Marble
21 x 13¾ x 10½ (53.3 x 34.9 x 26.7)

Signed and dated proper right side
edge: *Houdon f. 1778*

Benjamin Franklin Collection,
Yale University Library

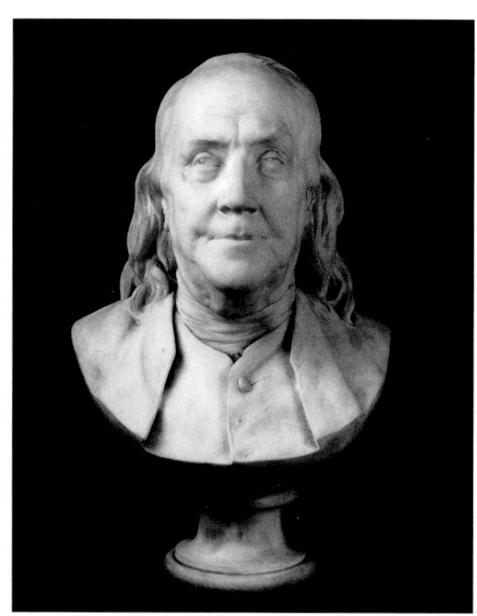
136

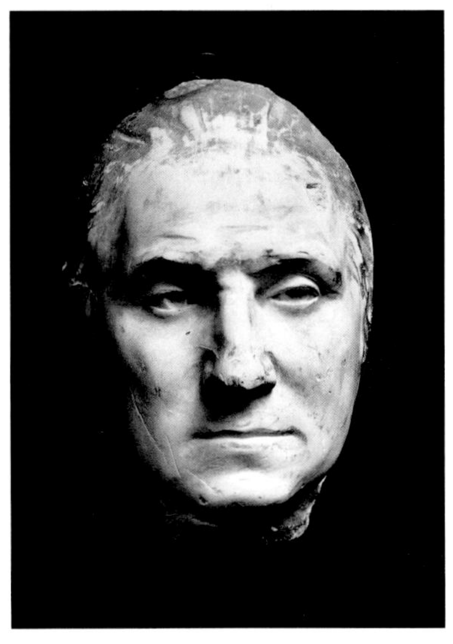

137

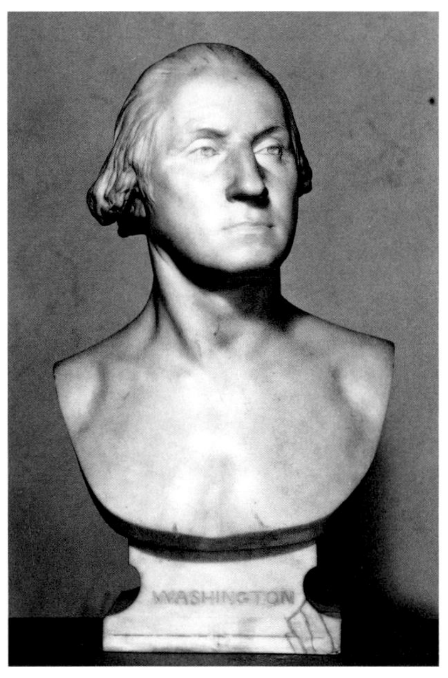

138

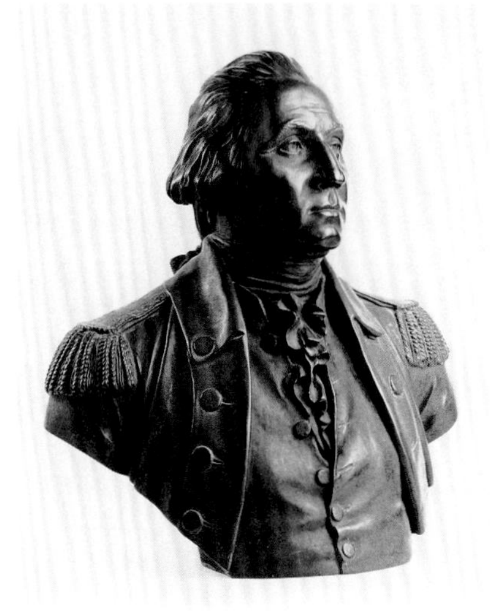

139

137 *Life Mask of George Washington*
1732–1799
LL.D. 1781

After an original of 1785
Painted plaster
11 x 7½ x 5 (27.9 x 19.1 x 12.7)

John Hill Morgan, B.A. 1893, LL.B. 1896, Collection
1943.96

138 *George Washington* 1732–1799
LL.D. 1781

Probably 19th century, after an original of 1785
Marble
24 x 14¾ x 12¼ (61 x 37.5 x 31.1)

Inscribed center front of base: WASHINGTON

Gift of deLancey Kountze, B.A. 1899
1939.50

139 *General George Washington*
1732–1799
LL.D. 1781

Cast after 1909, after an original of 1785
Bronze, black patina
23 x 21½ x 12¾ (58.4 x 54.6 x 32.4)

Foundry: The Gorham Manufacturing Company, Providence, Rhode Island; mark, proper right lower rear: THE GORHAM CO 0488

Gift of Mc A. Donald Ryan, B.A. 1934, and William H. Ryan, B.A. 1921
1957.47.2

140 *Joel Barlow* 1754–1812
B.A. 1778, M.A. 1781

Possibly 1912, after an original of 1803
Painted plaster
24½ x 20 x 12¾ (62.2 x 50.8 x 32.4)

Gift of Peter T. Barlow to the Yale University Library
1914.19

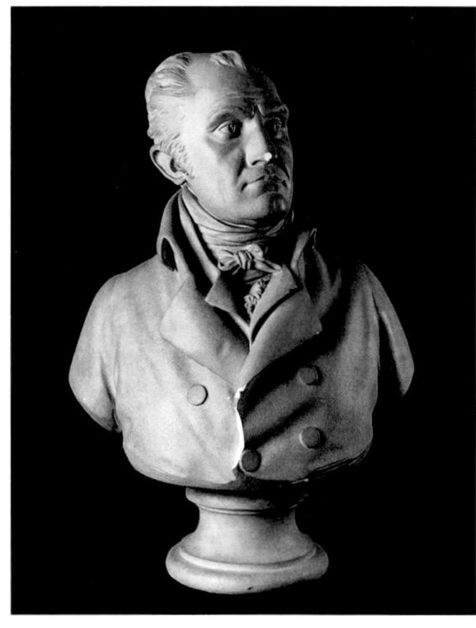

140

ROBERT BALL HUGHES

1806 London – 1868 Dorchester, Massachusetts
Active U.S. 1829–68

141 *John Trumbull* 1756–1843

c.1834
Marble
24 x 20¼ x 9¼ (61 x 51.4 x 23.5)

University Purchase
1851.2

ANNA VAUGHN HYATT HUNTINGTON

1876 Cambridge, Massachusetts – 1973 New York City or Redding Ridge, Connecticut

142 *Jaguar Eating*

1907
Bronze, black patina over red
18¼ x 40 x 15¾ (46.4 x 101.6 x 40)

Signed center, proper left top of base: ANNA·V·HYATT.

Foundry: Kunst Foundry, New York; mark, center rear proper left side of base: KUNST–FOUNDRY–N–Y–

Gift of the artist
1939.273

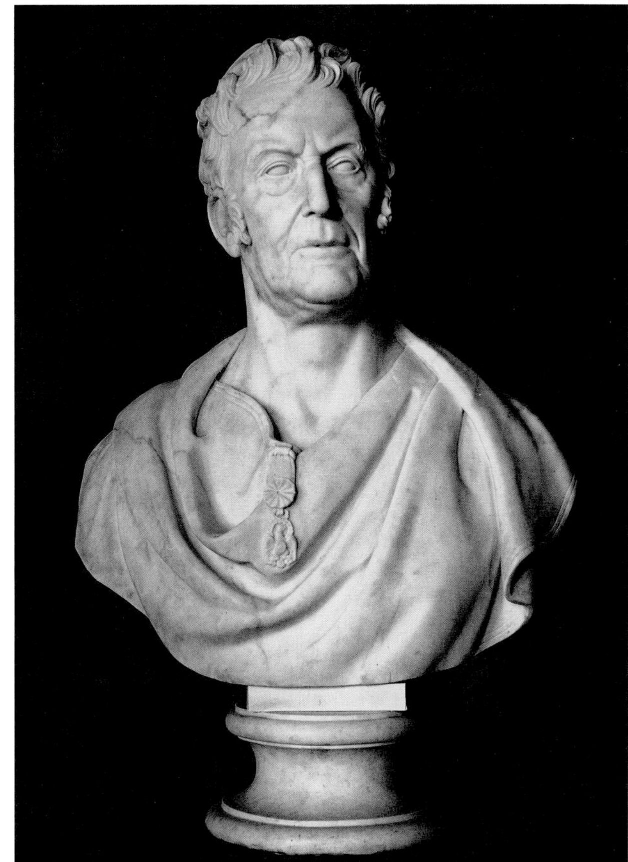

141

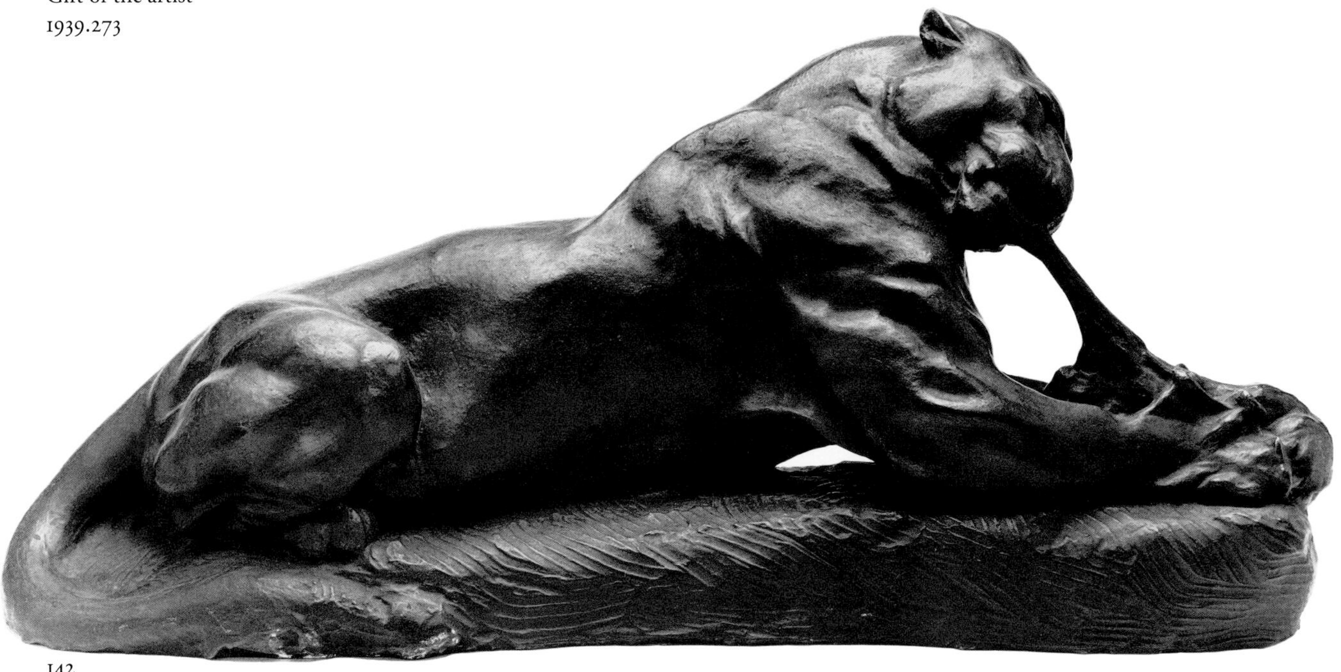

142

after
MAUDE PHELPS McVEIGH HUTCHINS

b. 1899 Long Island, New York
B.F.A. 1926

143 *A Yale Oarsman*
(Thomas Gerard Curtain Early)
b. 1907
B.A. 1931

c.1926
Painted plaster
19 x 18 x 11 (48.3 x 45.7 x 27.9)

Gift of Hollon A. Farr, B.A. 1896, M.A. 1902, PH.D. 1904, to the Yale University Library
1948.309

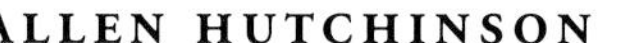

ALLEN HUTCHINSON

1855 Handford, Stotre on Trent, England – 1929

144 *Robert Louis Stevenson* 1850–1894

1893
Bronze, black patina
13 x 8½ x 8 (33 x 21.6 x 20.3)

Signed, dated, and inscribed lower rear proper right: © / Allen Hutchinson / Honolulu 1893; proper left: Tusitala

Founder's mark proper left side edge of base: P.B.U. CO MUNCHEN MADE IN GERMANY

Cast number stamped proper left inside of neck: (104)

Bequest of Edwin J. Beinecke, B.A. 1907, to the Robert Louis Stevenson Collection, Beinecke Rare Book and Manuscript Library
1952.36.5

LEWIS ISELIN

1913 New Rochelle, New York – 1990 Camden, Maine

145 *Dr. Frederick C. Redlich* b. 1910
M.A.(hon.) 1950

1968
Bronze, dark brown and bronze patina
12 x 8½ x 9¼ (30.5 x 21.6 x 23.5)

Pink granite base
54½ x 10½ x 10½ (138.4 x 26.7 x 26.7)

Signed and dated lower rear edge on collar: *1968 L. Iselin*

Inscribed front edge of granite base: F.C. REDLICH

Gift of the friends of Dr. Frederick C. Redlich, M.A.(hon.) 1950, to the Connecticut Mental Health Center
1968.44

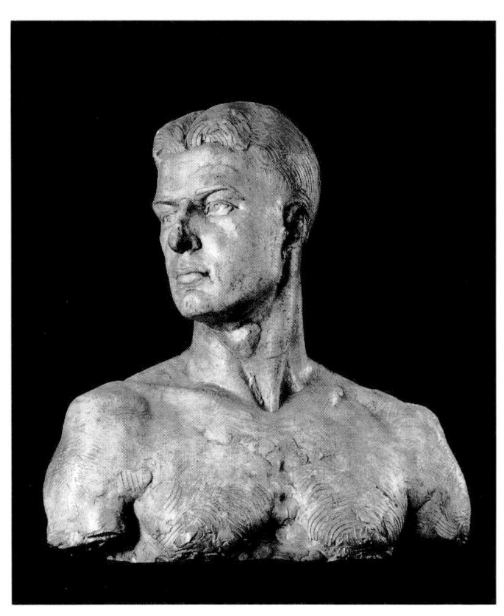

143

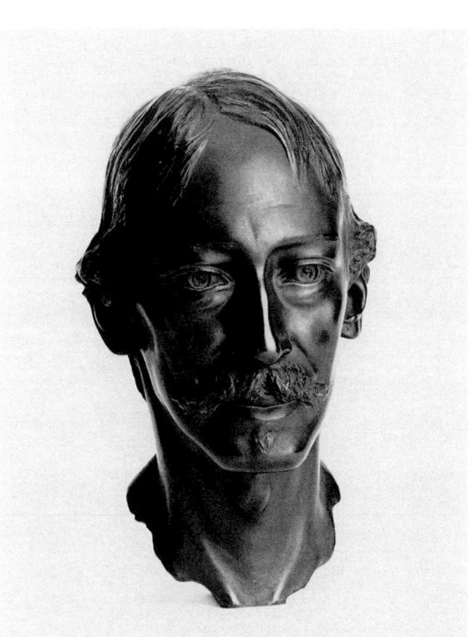

144

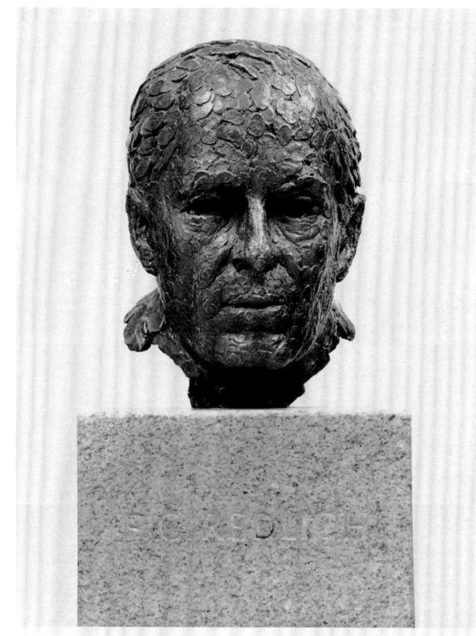

145

CHAUNCEY BRADLEY IVES

1810 Hamden, Connecticut – 1894 Rome, Italy

146 *David Daggett* 1764–1851
B.A. 1783, M.A. 1786, LL.D. 1826

After an original of 1839
Plaster
30 x 21¾ x 12¼ (76.2 x 55.2 x 31.1)

Signed and dated upper proper left rear: *Ives / Sculp 1839*

Provenance unknown
1968.34.1

147 *David Daggett*
30½ x 22 x 14¾ (77.5 x 55.9 x 37.5)

1968.34.2

Same as cat. 146 except for measurements as shown above

148 *William Wolcott Ellsworth*
1791–1868
B.A. 1810

After an original of 1840
Painted plaster
30½ x 19½ x 11¼ (77.5 x 49.5 x 28.6)

Signed and dated center rear: *C.B.I. 1840.*

Provenance unknown
1900.26

149 *Noah Webster* 1758–1843
B.A. 1778, LL.D. 1823

c.1841
Bronze, dark brown patina
28¼ x 9¼ x 8½ (71.8 x 23.5 x 21.6)

Signed and inscribed on rear edge of base: *A Study by C. B. Ives / Roma*

Gift of Mr. and Mrs. Theodore L. Bailey
1964.72

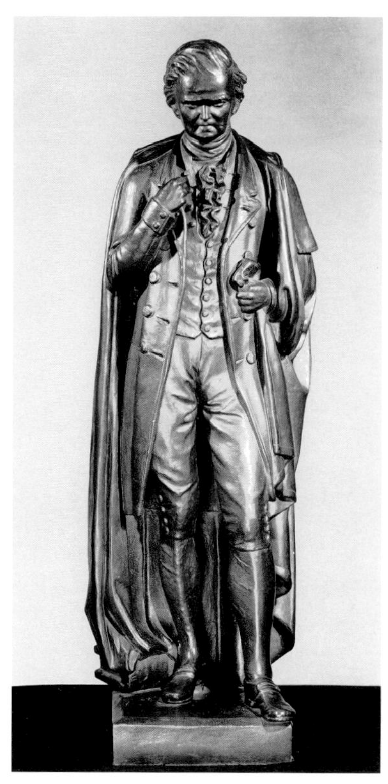
149

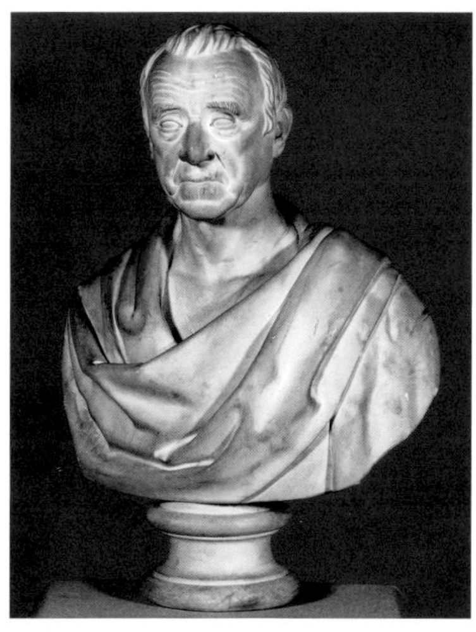
146

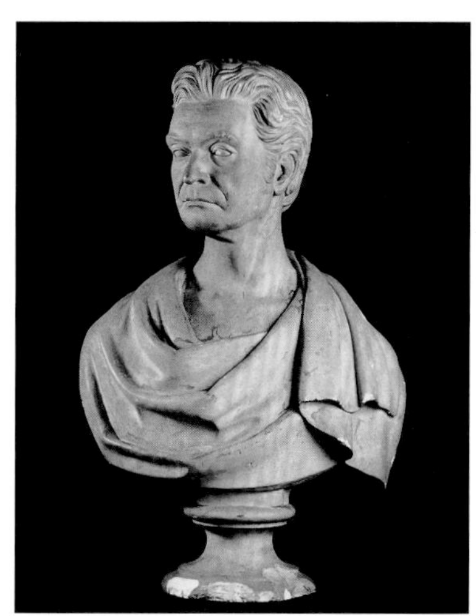
148

150 *Jeremiah Day* 1773–1867
B.A. 1795, M.A. 1798

After an original of 1842
Plaster
22 x 15 x 10¾ (55.9 x 38.1 x 27.3)

Signed and dated proper left side: *C B Ives / Sculp.*; rear center: *C.B.I. / Sculpt. / 1842*

Gift of Charles Seymour, B.A. 1908, PH.D. 1911, LL.D. 1950
1950.684

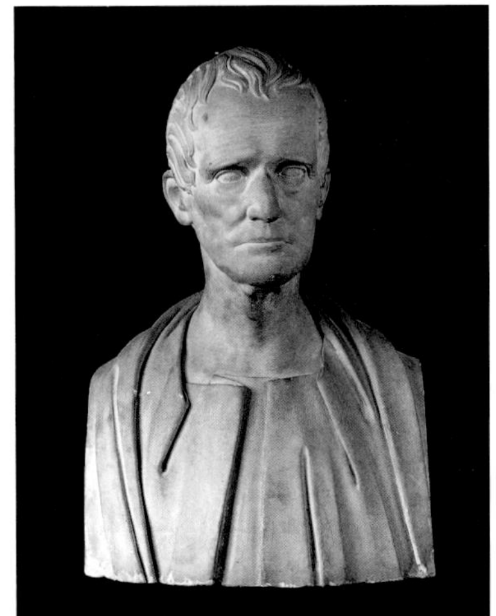

150

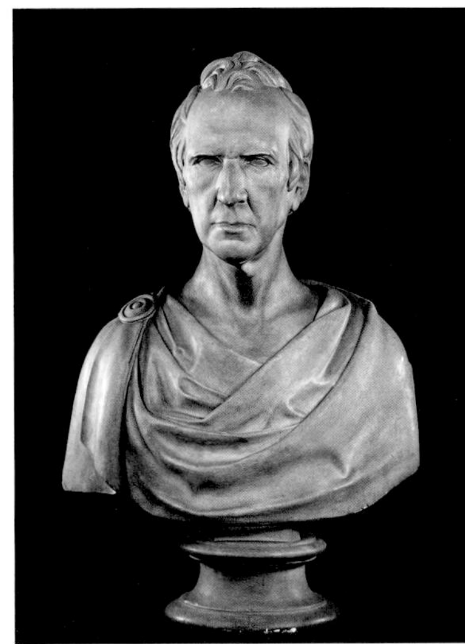

151

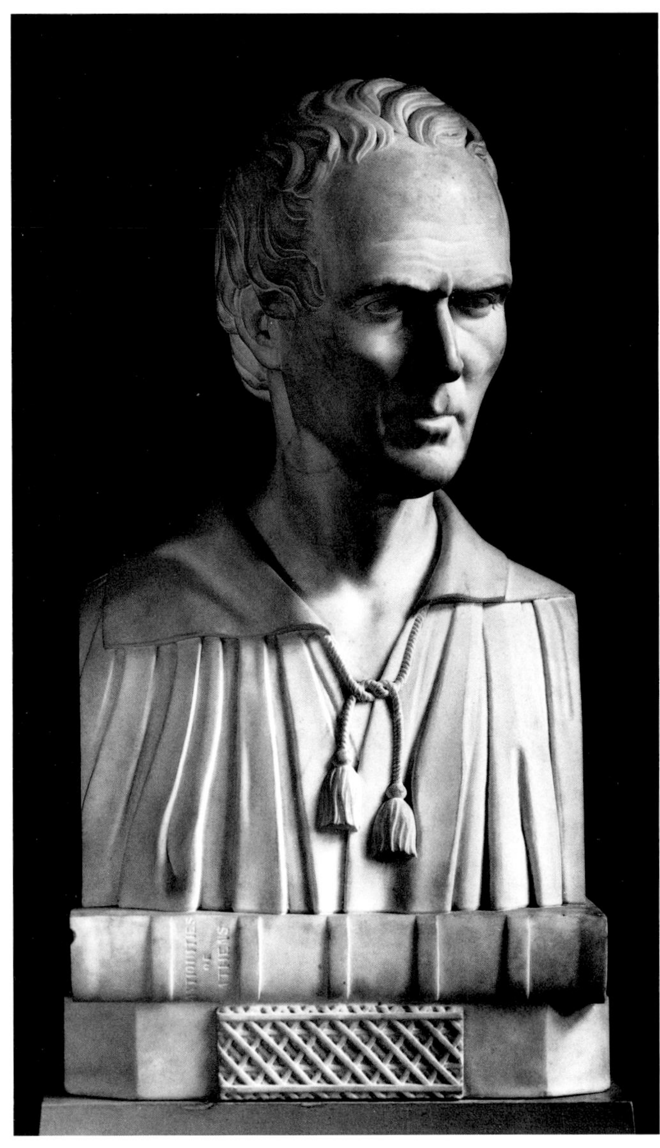

152

151 *Thomas Day* 1777–1865
B.A. 1797, M.A. 1800, LL.D. 1847

After an original of 1842
Painted plaster
29½ x 18¼ x 12 (74.9 x 46.4 x 30.5)

Signed and dated upper proper right rear: *C B Ives Sculpt. 1842*

Gift of Charles Seymour, B.A. 1908, PH.D. 1911, LL.D. 1950
1950.683

152 *Ithiel Town* 1784–1844
M.A.(hon.) 1825

1842
Marble
26 x 14½ x 11¼ (66 x 36.8 x 28.6)

Signed and dated center rear: *C.B. IVES Sculpt. / 1842*

Inscribed on spine of book: ANTIQUITIES OF ATHENS

Gift of Dr. William Thompson Peters, B.A. 1825, M.D. 1830
1844.3

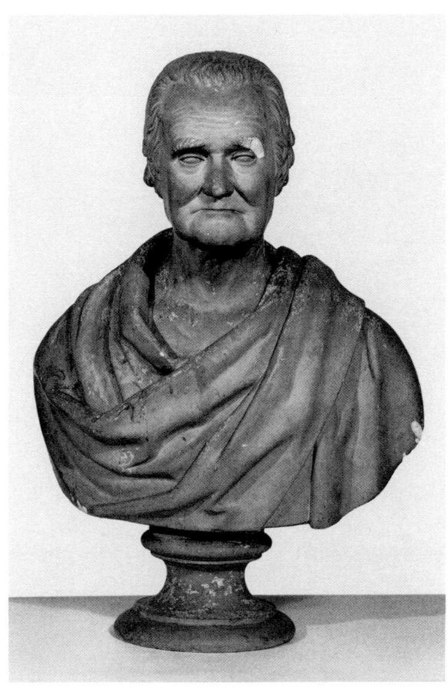
153

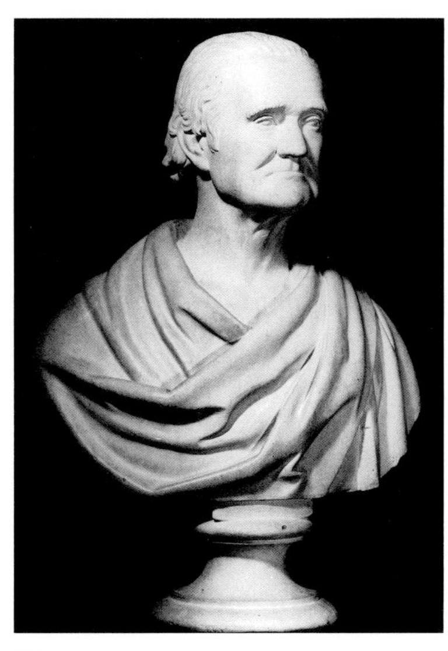
154

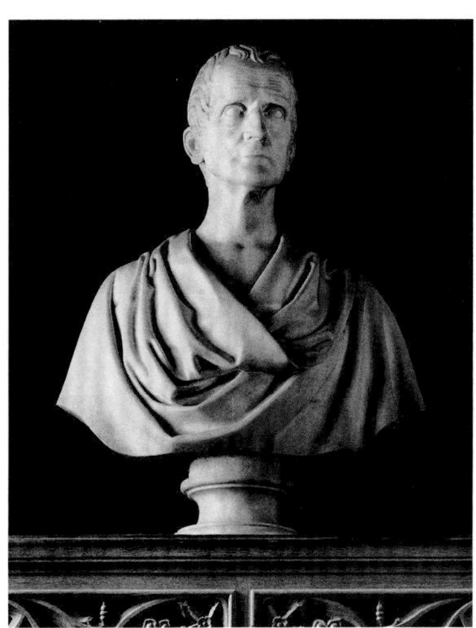
155

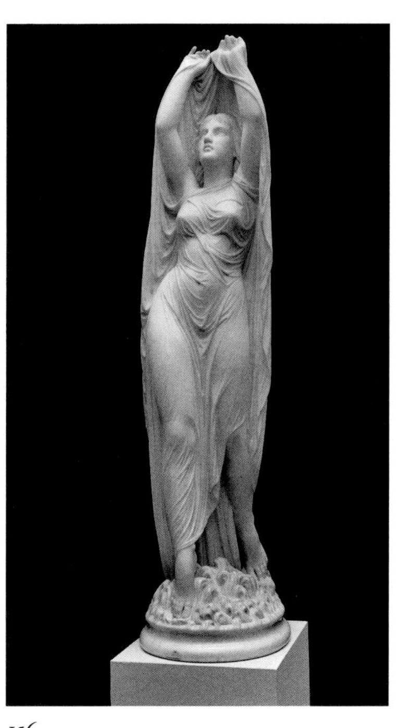
156

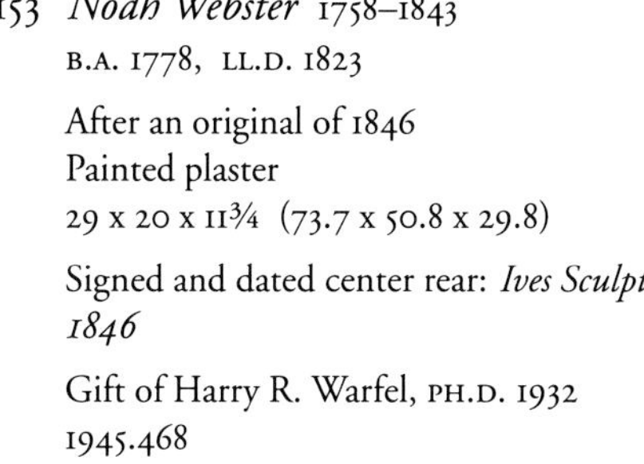
153 *Noah Webster* 1758–1843
B.A. 1778, LL.D. 1823

After an original of 1846
Painted plaster
29 x 20 x 11¾ (73.7 x 50.8 x 29.8)

Signed and dated center rear: *Ives Sculpt 1846*

Gift of Harry R. Warfel, PH.D. 1932
1945.468

154 *Noah Webster* 1758–1843
B.A. 1778, LL.D. 1823

After an original of about 1846
Plaster
29 x 20¾ x 11 (73.7 x 52.7 x 27.9)

Gift of Mrs. Brinton Dulles to the Yale University Library
1944.82

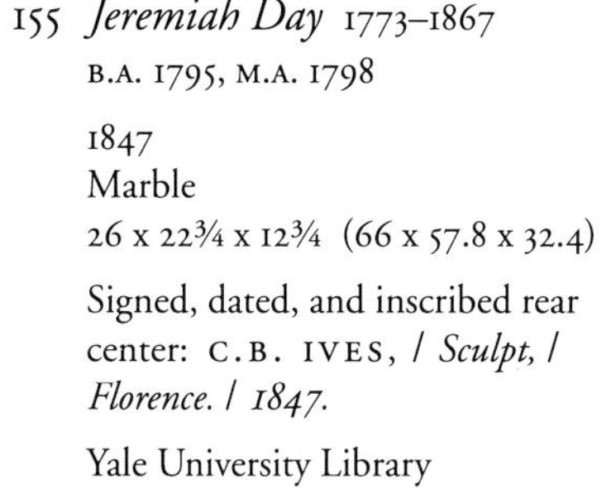
155 *Jeremiah Day* 1773–1867
B.A. 1795, M.A. 1798

1847
Marble
26 x 22¾ x 12¾ (66 x 57.8 x 32.4)

Signed, dated, and inscribed rear center: C.B. IVES, / *Sculpt, / Florence. / 1847.*

Yale University Library
1847.2

156 *Undine*

Between 1880–92
Marble
60½ x 19 x 15½ (153.7 x 48.3 x 39.4)

Signed, and inscribed proper left side of base: C.B. IVES. FECIT. /
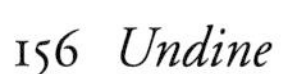
ROMÆ.

Given by Mrs. Alice A. Allen in memory of Simon Sterne
1926.116

Also illustrated on cover

157 *Benjamin Silliman, Sr.* 1779–1864
B.A. 1796, M.A. 1799

1860
Marble
27½ x 19½ x 11¾ (69.9 x 49.5 x 29.8)

Signed, dated, and inscribed lower rear center: C.B. IVES / FECIT. / ROMA. / 1860

Gift of the friends and pupils of the sitter to the Yale University Library
1862.1

158 *Rev. Dr. Nathaniel William Taylor*
1786–1858
B.A. 1807, M.A. 1810

1860
Marble
26¼ x 21 x 11 (66.7 x 53.3 x 27.9)

Inscribed lower center rear: C.B. IVES / ROME / 1860

Gift of the students of the sitter to Yale University
1860.3

159 *Rev. Dr. Nathaniel William Taylor*
1786–1858
B.A. 1807, M.A. 1810

After an original of 1860
Plaster
21 x 13½ x 11¼ (53.3 x 34.3 x 28.6)

Signed proper left side: *C.B. Ives / Sculpt.*

Gift of Mrs. Brinton Dulles
1944.83

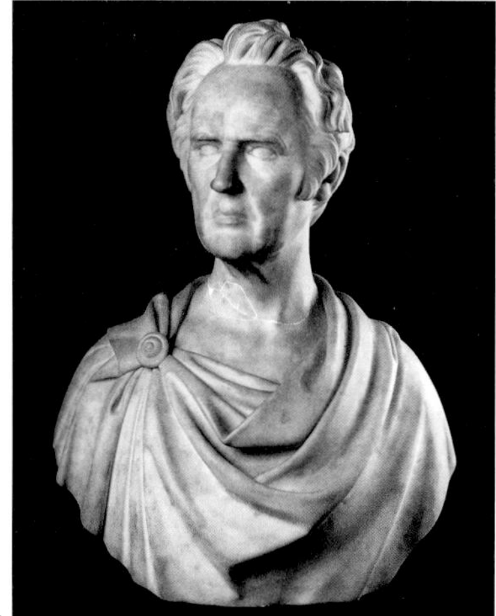

157

160 *Bust of an Unidentified Man*

1870
Marble
26½ x 21 x 12¼ (67.3 x 53.3 x 31.1)

Signed, dated, and inscribed lower center rear: C.B. IVES / FECIT / ROMÆ 1870

Provenance unknown
1900.60

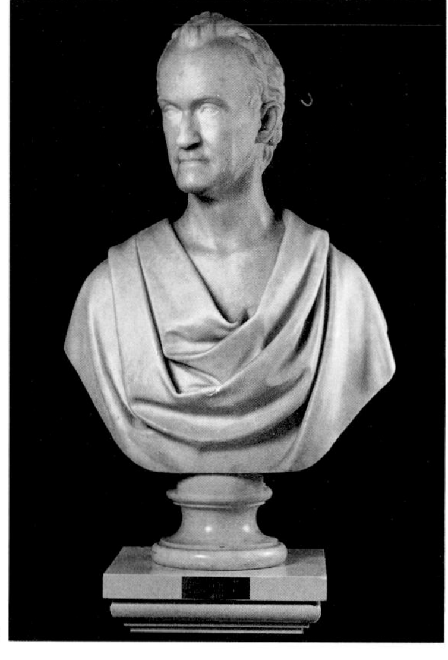

158

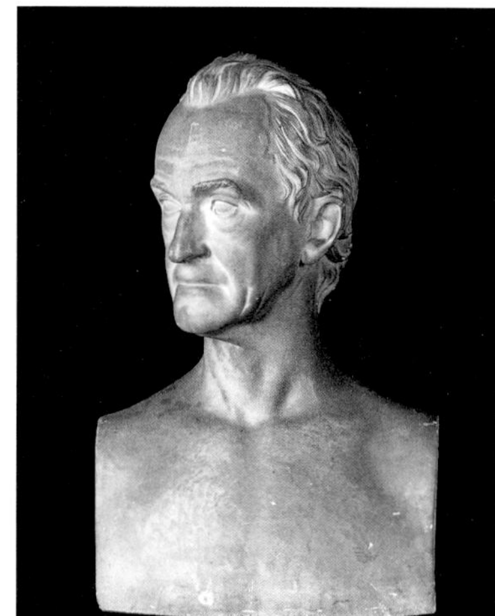

159

161 *Chauncey Allen Goodrich*
1790–1860
B.A. 1810, M.A. 1813

1873
Marble
22¼ x 15¾ x 12 (56.5 x 40 x 30.5)

Signed, dated, and inscribed rear center: C.B. IVES / FECIT / ROMÆ. 1873.

Gift of Dr. William Henry Goodrich, B.A. 1843, M.A. 1846, to Yale University
1873.4

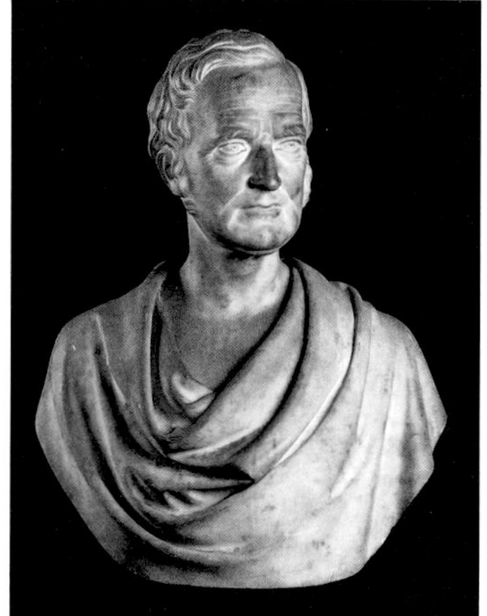

160

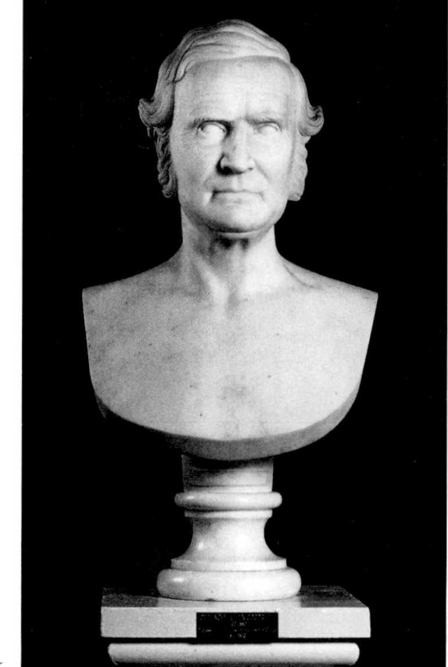

161

after
THOMAS DOW JONES

1811 Oneida County, New York –
1881 Columbus, Ohio

162 *Abraham Lincoln* 1809–1865

c.1862
Painted plaster
32 x 20½ x 17½ (81.3 x 52 x 44.5)

Signed and dated center rear:
T.D. Jones, Sculptor 1861.

Inscribed proper right side: *Patented June, 1862*

Provenance unknown
1900.23

JENO JUSKO (JUSZKO)

1880 Ungvar, Hungary –
1954 New York City
Active U.S. 1906–54

163 *Walt Whitman* 1819–1892

1913
Bronze, copper and bronze colored patina
DIAM. 7 X D. 1 (17.8 x 2.5)

Wood mount
12 x 9½ x ½ (30.5 x 24.1 x 1.3)

Signed lower left front: J. Jusko

Inscribed lower right front:
Walt / Whitman

Foundry: Metal Products Manufacturing Company, Inc., New York; mark, on front in relief, lower center: METAL PRODUCTS MFG. CO. INC. NY; lower left: 19©13 M.P.M.CO.

Gift of Adrian Van Sinderen, B.A. 1910, to the Collection of American Literature, Beinecke Rare Book and Manuscript Library
1980.313

CHARLES KECK

1875 New York City –
1951 Carmel, New York

164 *William Whiting Borden*
1887–1913
B.A. 1909

c.1913
Bronze, dark green and bronze patina
41¾ x 16½ x 11¾ (106 x 41.9 x 29.8)

Signed lower proper left rear edge:
CHARLES KECK

Inscribed around trough in relief: LET HIM THAT IS ATHIRST COME; top of plaque: WILLIAM WHITING BORDEN / YALE COLLEGE 1909 / BORN IN CHICAGO / NOVEMBER 1ST 1887 / DIED IN CAIRO EGYPT / APRIL 9TH 1913 / ERECTED BY HIS CLASSMATES / A TRIBUTE TO HIS CHARACTER

Foundry: Roman Bronze Works, New York; mark, proper right, lower edge: ROMAN BRONZE WORKS INC. N–Y–

Gift of his classmates to Yale University

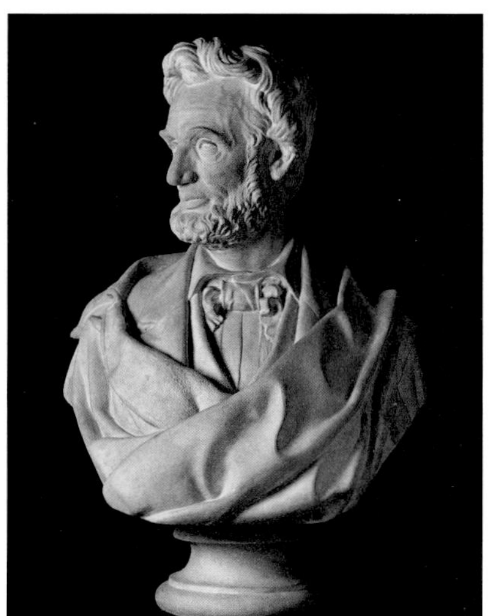

162

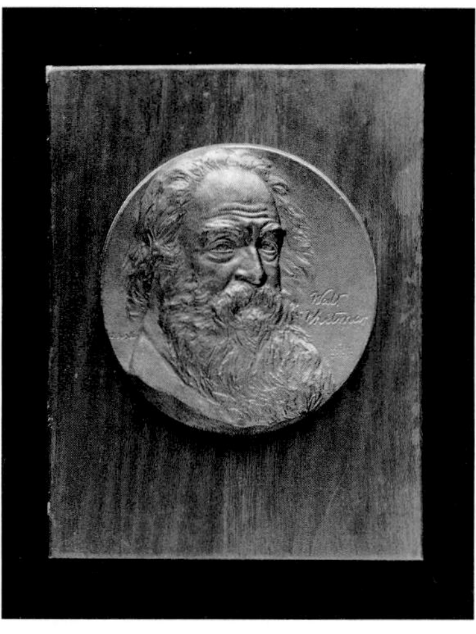

163

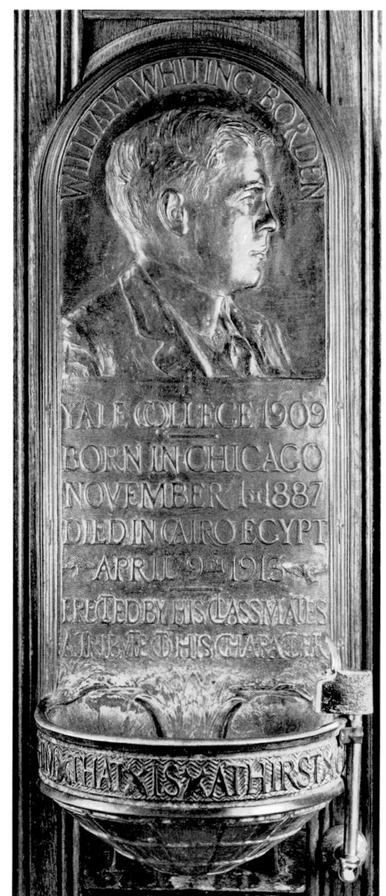

164

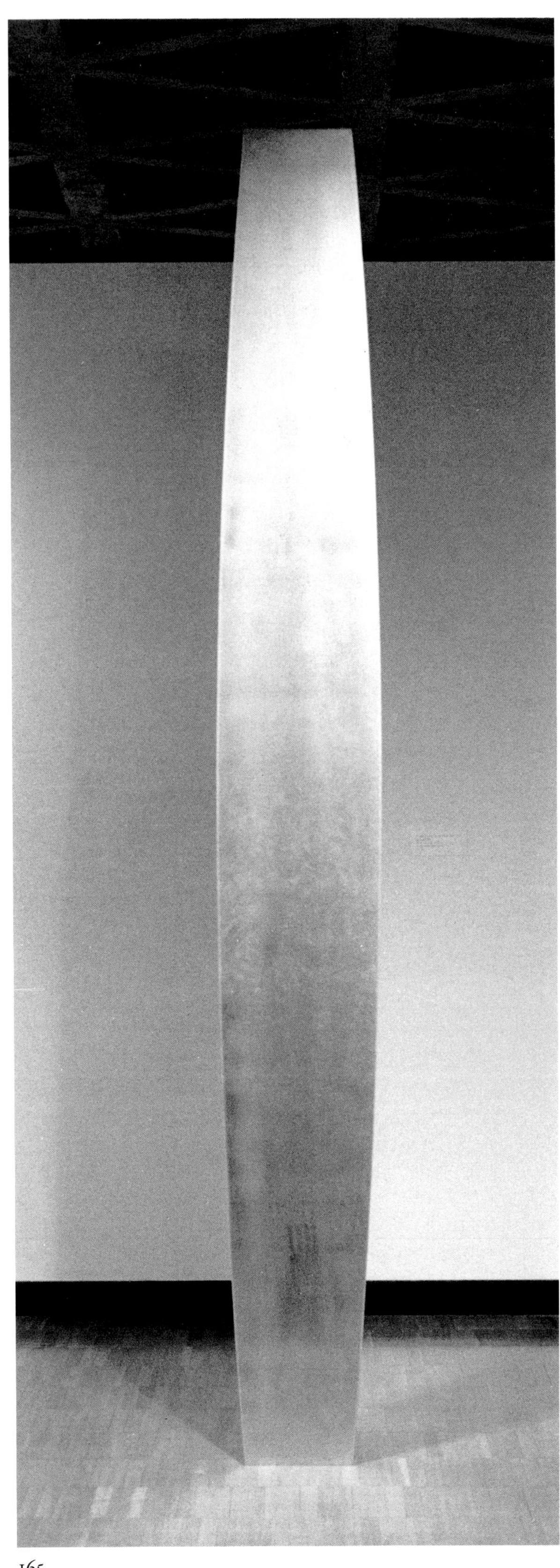

165

ELLSWORTH KELLY

b. 1923 Newburgh, New York

165 *Untitled (Curve XXIII)*

1981
Buffed stainless steel
120 x 15 x 10 (304.8 x 38.1 x 25.4)

Signature, date, and inscription on rear edge of base: EK 617 KELLY 81

Gift of Susan Morse Hilles
1981.58

JULIO KILENYI

1885 Arad, Hungary –
1959 New York City
Active U.S. 1916–59, citizen 1924

166 *John Campbell Greenway*
1872–1926
PH.B. 1895

1927
Bronze, greenish-brown patina
47½ x 24¾ x ¾ (120.7 x 62.9 x 1.9)

Signed lower right front: KILENYI

Inscribed center front in relief:
· JOHN · CAMPBELL · GREENWAY · / · 1895'S · / · BORN · 1872 · · DIED · 1926 · / · STUDENT · ENGINEER · / · ATHLETE · SOLDIER · / · IN · ALL · THINGS · FAITHFUL · / · ERECTED · BY · HIS · CLASS · / · 1927 ·

Gift of the Class of 1927 to the Payne Whitney Gymnasium
1927.133

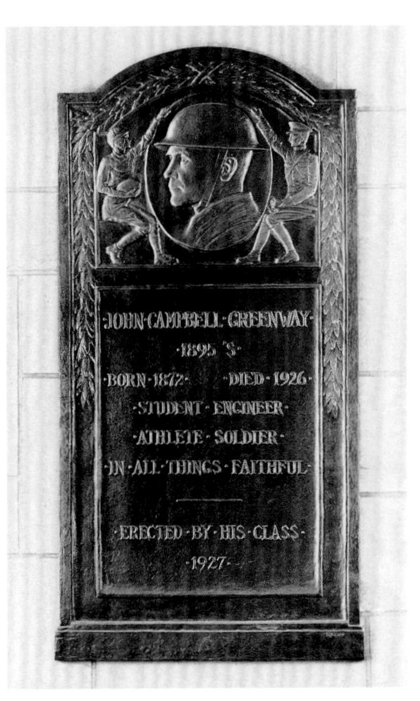

166

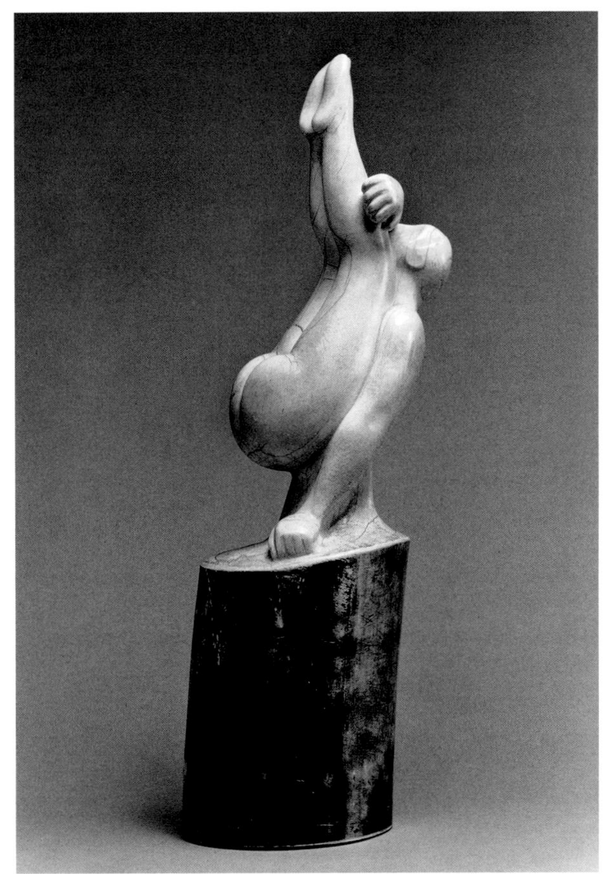

168

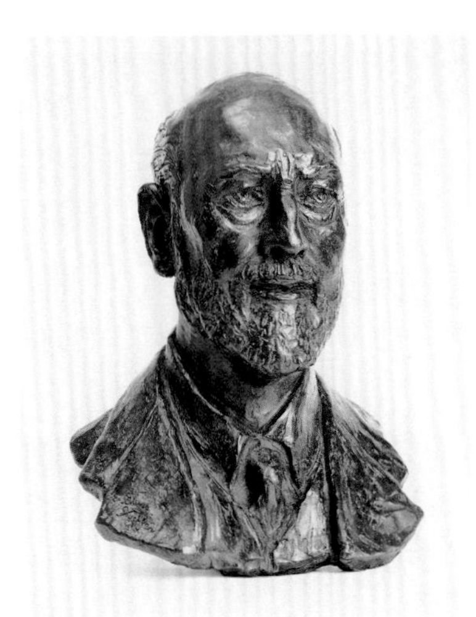

167

BRUCE KUEFFER

Dates unknown

167 *Charles E. Ives* 1874–1954
B.A. 1898

c.1950
Bronze, dark brown and bronze patina
17 x 12 x 10 (43.2 x 30.5 x 25.4)

Signed proper right side: *Bruce Kueffer*

Yale University School of Music Library

GASTON LACHAISE

1882 Paris – 1935 New York City
Active U.S. after 1906, citizen 1916

168 *Acrobat*

1930
Ivory
23 x 9 x 5¼ (58.4 x 22.9 x 13.3)

Signed and dated lower center proper right side: G. LACHAISE / 1930

Philip L. Goodwin, B.A. 1907, Collection
1951.29.1

HENRY LEE LAVENTHOL

b. 1927 Philadelphia
B.A. 1947

169 *Head of a Mexican*

c.1948
Stone
19¾ x 9½ x 9 (50.2 x 24.1 x 22.9)

Gift of the artist to Jonathan Edwards College
1948.300

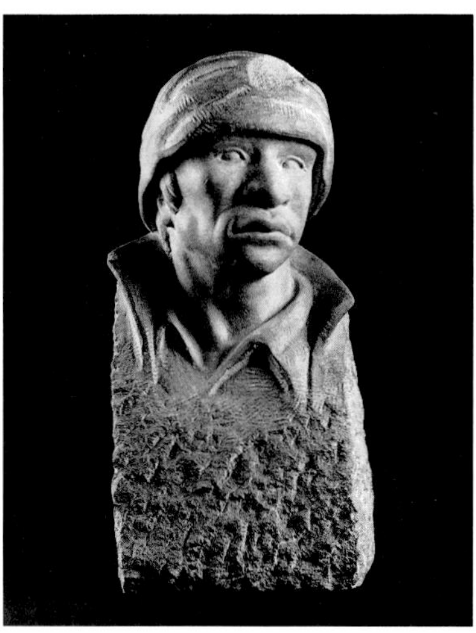

169

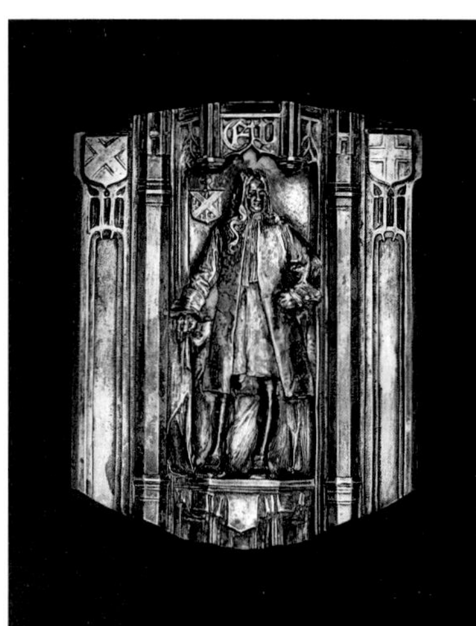

170

LEE OSCAR LAWRIE

1877 Rixford, Germany –
1963 Easton, Massachusetts
To U.S. as an infant
B.F.A. 1910, M.A.(hon.) 1932

170 *Elihu Yale* 1649–1721

Probably 1909
Bronze, silver gilt
8¾ x 6½ x 1 (22.2 x 16.5 x 2.5)

Signed bottom right edge: LEE LAWRIE / FECIT

Inscribed verso center: HENRICO PARKS WRIGHT / COLLEGII YALENSIS / DECANATV ANNOS XXV / SVMMA CVM LAVDE / PERFVNCTO GRATI ET / AMANTES COLLEGAE / MCMIX; upper center: Yale University seal / LUX ET VERITAS; lower center flanking raised design of a sailing ship: MARE LIBERVM

Foundry: Roman Bronze Works, New York; mark, bottom left edge: ROMAN BRONZE WORKS, N.Y.

Gift of Henry P. Wright to the Yale University Library

171 *Josiah Willard Gibbs* 1839–1903
B.A. 1858, M.A. 1861, PH.D. 1863

1912
Bronze, dark reddish-brown patina
44½ x 35 x 5 (113 x 88.9 x 12.7)

Signed and dated lower proper left front corner: LEE LAWRIE / MCMXII

Inscribed lower center front in relief: JOSIAH WILLARD GIBBS LLD / PROFESSOR OF MATHEMATICAL PHYSICS / IN YALE COLLEGE MDCCCLXXI TO / MCMIII DISCOVERER AND / INTERPRETER OF THE LAWS OF CHEMICAL EQUILIBRIUM

Foundry: The Gorham Manufacturing Company, Providence, Rhode Island; mark, lower proper left front corner: GORHAM CO. FOUNDERS

Gift of Walter Nernst, Professor and Director of the Institute of Physical Chemistry, University of Berlin, to the J.W. Gibbs Physics Laboratory

172 *James Gamble Rogers* 1867–1947
B.A. 1889, M.A.(hon.) 1921

1921
Cast stone
41 x 27½ x 1¾ (104.1 x 69.9 x 4.4)

Signed and dated on front corner lower proper right: LEE LAWRIE; upper proper left: MCM / XXI / AD

Inscribed lower front center in relief: JAMES GAMBLE ROGERS / CLASS OF MDCCCLXXXIX / ARCHITECT OF THESE BUILDINGS / HIS ASSOCIATES IN THE WORK / HAVE PLACED HERE A TRIBUTE / TO THE ARTIST MASTER AND FRIEND

Placed at Saybrook College in tribute to James Gamble Rogers, B.A. 1889, M.A.(hon.) 1921, by his work associates

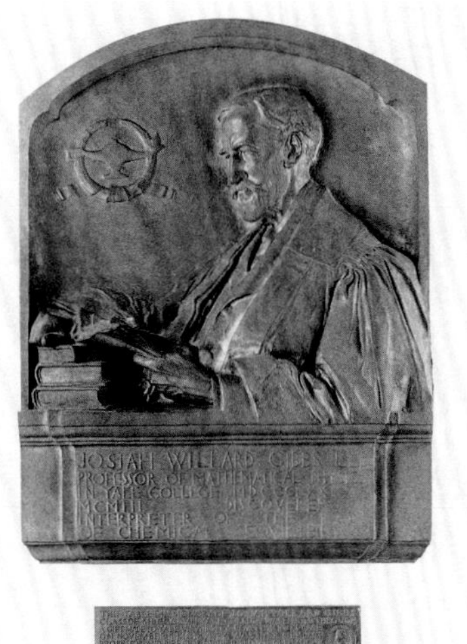

171

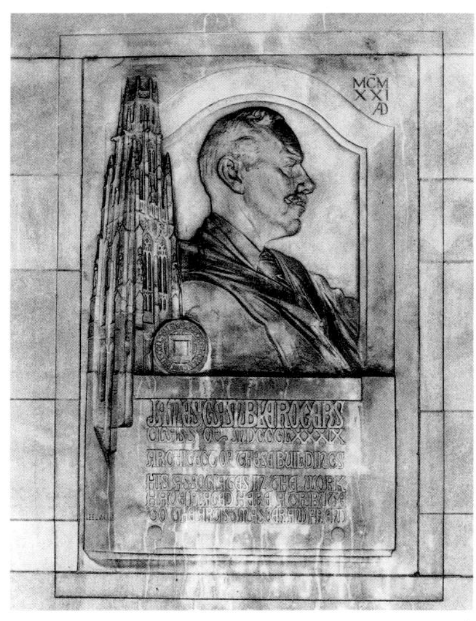

172

MARYLA LEDNICKA-SZCZYTT

1895 Moscow – 1947
To U.S. before World War II

173 *Edward Mandell House* 1858–1938

1934
Bronze, dark brown patina
22¼ x 17¾ x 1½ (56.5 x 45.1 x 3.8)

Signed in mixed upper and lower case, and dated lower right front:
Lednicka / 1934

Foundry: Roman Bronze Works, New York; mark, lower right front:
ROMAN BRONZE WORKS, N.Y.

Gift of the Polish-American Committee to the Yale University Library in honor of Colonel Edward M. House

ARTHUR LEE

1881 Trondjem, Norway –
1961 Newtown, Connecticut
To U.S. 1888 or 1889

174 *Volupté*

c.1915
Rosa Milano marble
33¾ x 11 x 9½ (85.7 x 27.9 x 24.1)

Signed center rear edge of base:
ARTHVR LEE

Inscribed center front edge of base:
VOLVPTÉ

Bequest of Dorothea Nolan
1955.37.1

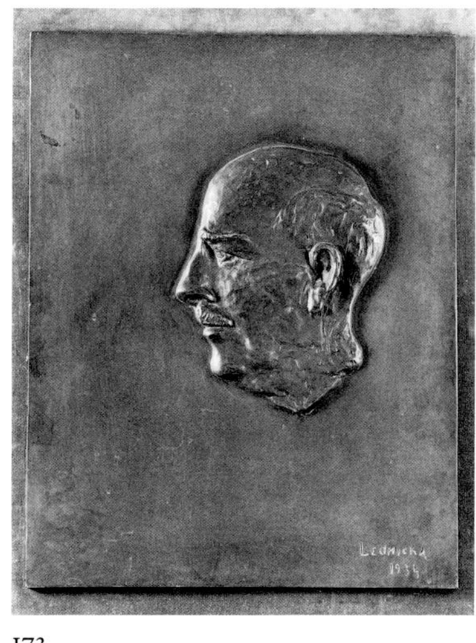

173

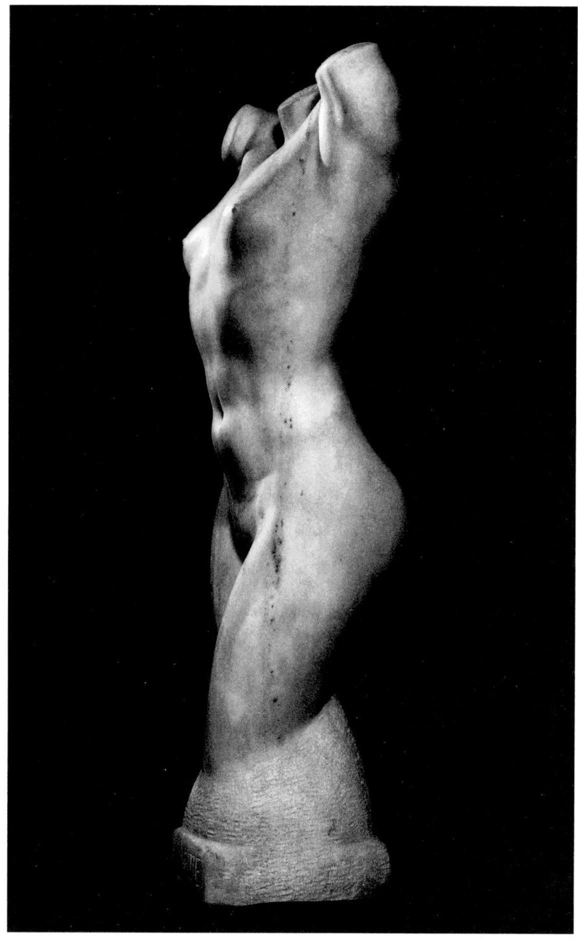

174

ALEXANDER LIBERMAN

b. 1912 Kiev, Russia
Active U.S. since 1941, citizen 1946

175 *Turning*

1965
Welded steel, painted black
112 x 213 x 130 (284.5 x 541 x 330.2)

Inscribed in relief on a welded steel plate located on inside wall of cylindrical base segment: AL 65 (inscription visible only when sculpture is disassembled)

Fabricator: William J. Layman & Sons, Warren, Connecticut

Gift of Enid A. Haupt
1969.40

176 *Untitled*

c.1965
Welded steel, painted black
90¾ x 94¼ x 72¼
(230.5 x 239.4 x 183.5)

Gift of Mr. and Mrs. Burton G. Tremaine, Jr., B.A. 1944, to the Yale Schools of Art and Architecture

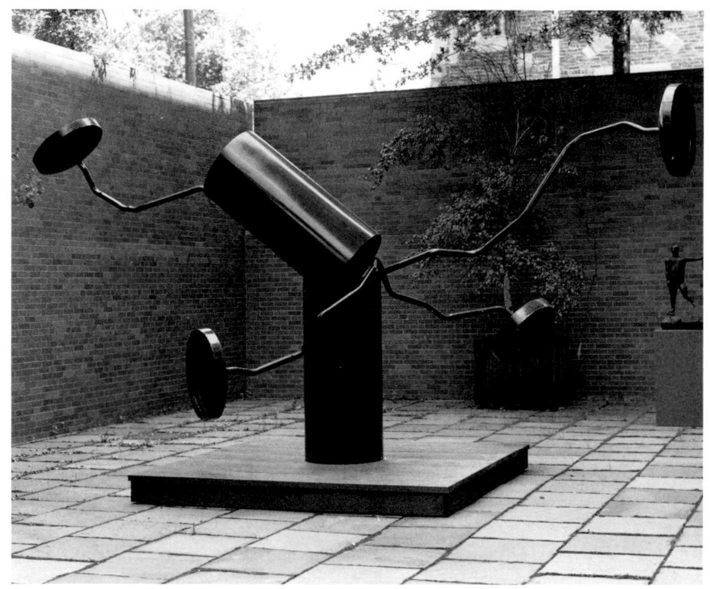

175

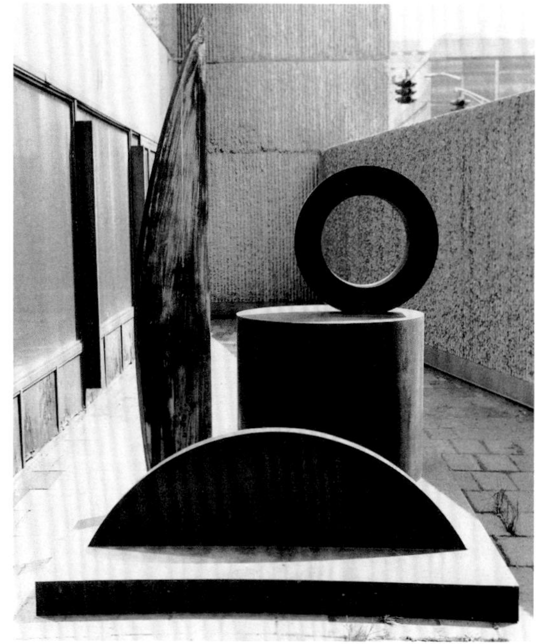

176

177 *On High*

1978
Welded steel maquette, painted red
23¾ x 16 x 16 (60.3 x 40.6 x 40.6)

Signature and date stamped on a top corner of base: AL 78

Gift of William F. Pedersen
1981.111

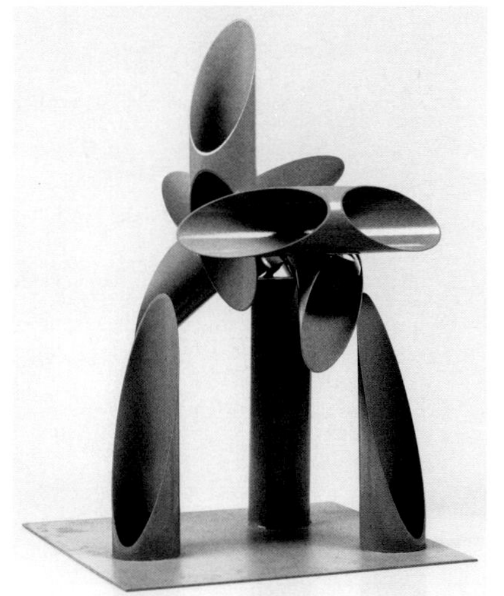

177

PETER LIPMAN-WULF

b. 1905 Berlin, Germany

178 *Hermann Broch* 1886–1951

c.1951
Bronze, greenish-copper colored patina
9½ x 6½ x 4¾ (24.1 x 16.5 x 12.1)

Wood mount
17 x 10½ x 2¾ (43.2 x 26.7 x 7)

Signed proper left bottom front of mount: PETER LIPMAN WULF

Inscription carved in relief lower center front of mount: HERMANN BROCH / POET AND PHILOSOPHER / BORN VIENNA · NOVEMBER 1 1886 / DIED NEW HAVEN · MAY 30 1951

Collection of German Literature, Beinecke Rare Book and Manuscript Library

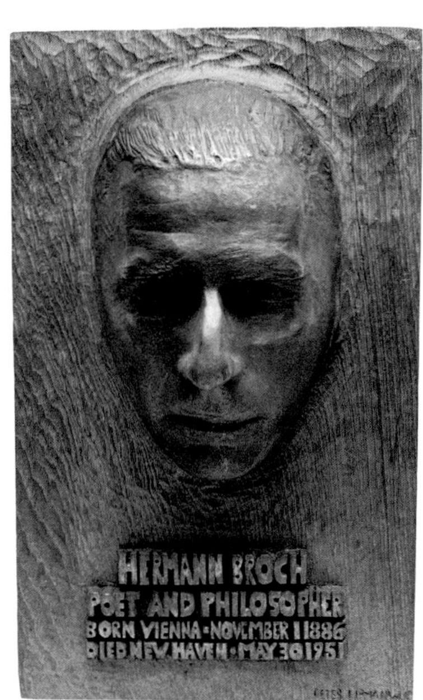

178

RICHARD LIPPOLD

b. 1915 Milwaukee, Wisconsin

179 *Ganymede*

c.1955
Brass and wire
88 x 60 x 60 (223.5 x 152.4 x 152.4)

Bequest of Susan Vanderpoel Clark
1967.82.5

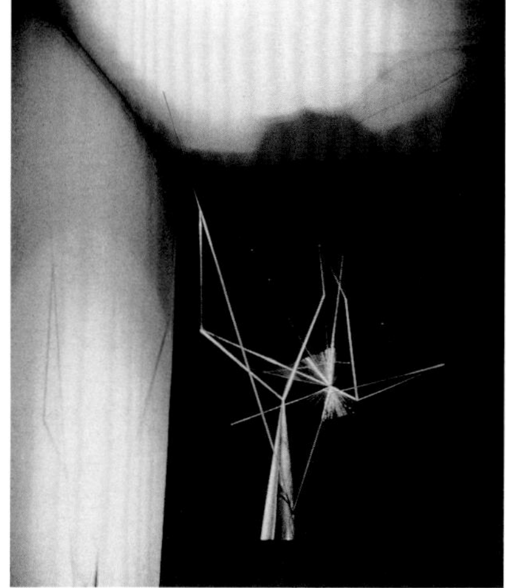

179

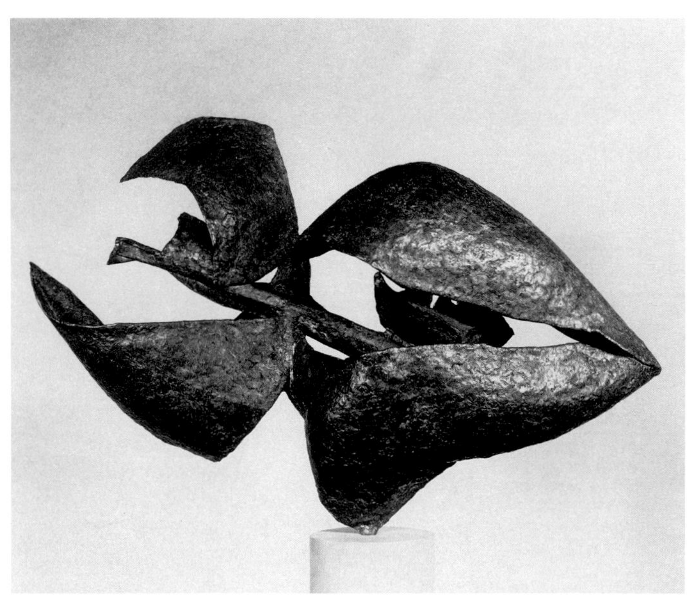

180

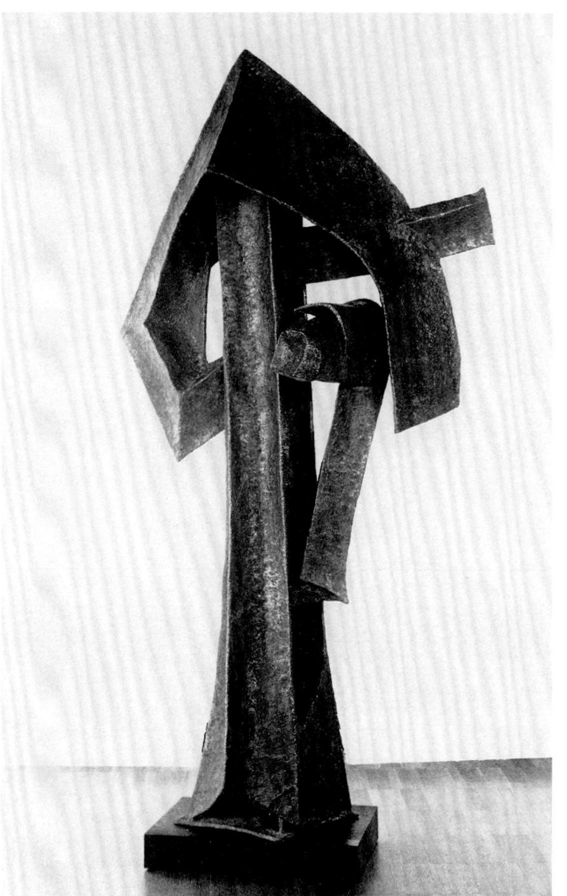

181

SEYMOUR LIPTON

1903 New York City –
1986 Locust Valley, New York

180 *Jungle Bloom*

1954
Gilded bronze
21 x 32½ x 14½ (53.3 x 82.6 x 36.8)

Gift of Susan Morse Hilles
1955.35.1

181 *Sentinel*

1959
Nickel silver on monel metal
90 x 47 x 29 (228.6 x 119.4 x 73.7)

Signed and dated top of base:
Lipton '59

University Purchase, Leonard C. Hanna, Jr., B.A. 1913, Fund
1959.49

RICHARD EDGAR LØVSTRØM

See Thomas Wilfred, cats. 405–07

GWEN LUX

b. 1908 Chicago

182 *Sergei Rachmaninoff* 1873–1943

1946
Cast stone
16 x 11 x 11¼ (40.6 x 27.9 x 28.6)

Signed and dated center rear:
Gwen Lux / 46

Gift of Irving S. Gilmore, B.A. 1923, to the Yale University School of Music Library
1953.53

ROBERT TAIT McKENZIE

1867 Almonte, Ontario, Canada – 1938 Philadelphia
Active U.S. 1904–38

183 *The Athlete*

1903
Bronze, dark reddish-brown patina
17 x 5¼ x 5¾ (43.2 x 13.3 x 14.6)

Signed and dated top rear of base:
R. Tait McKenzie / 1903 / ©

Foundry: The Gorham Manufacturing Company, Providence, Rhode Island; mark, rear edge of base:
Q H J G GORHAM CO.

Whitney Collections of Sporting Art, given in memory of Harry Payne Whitney, B.A. 1894, and Payne Whitney, B.A. 1898, by Francis P. Garvan, B.A. 1897, M.A.(hon.) 1922
1932.217

184 *The Competitor*

1906
Bronze, reddish-brown patina
20¼ x 10½ x 16 (51.4 x 26.7 x 40.6)

Signed and dated front of base:
06 / R. Tait McKenzie

Foundry: Roman Bronze Works, New York; mark, rear of base: ROMAN BRONZE WORKS N–Y–

Whitney Collections of Sporting Art, given in memory of Harry Payne Whitney, B.A. 1894, and Payne Whitney, B.A. 1898, by Francis P. Garvan, B.A. 1897, M.A.(hon.) 1922
1932.213

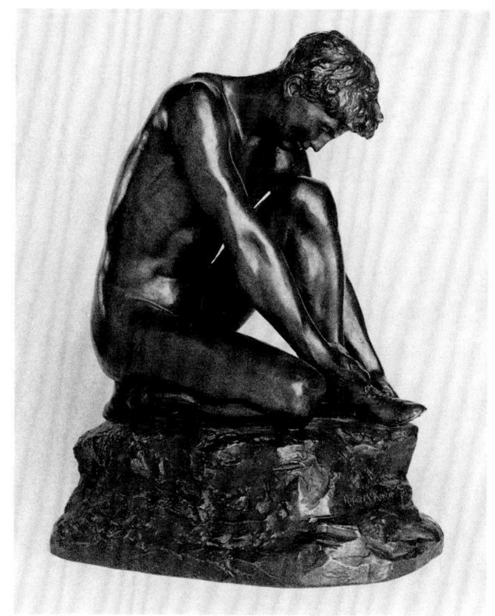

184

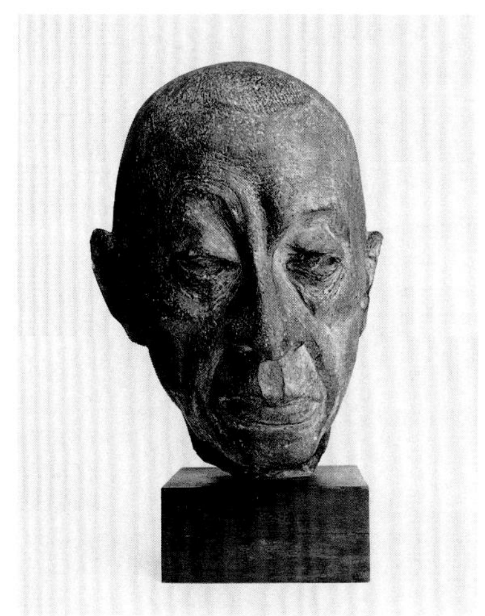

182

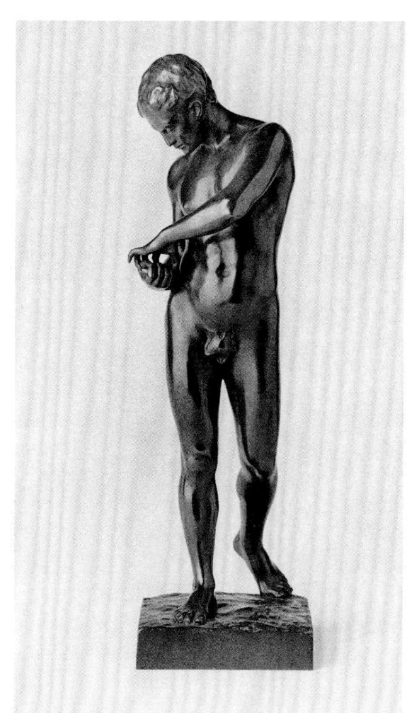

183

185 *The Relay*

1910
Bronze, dark reddish-brown patina
21½ x 14½ x 14¼ (54.6 x 36.8 x 36.2)

Signed and dated center front of base:
R. Tait McKenzie / 1910

Foundry: The Gorham Manufacturing Company, Providence, Rhode Island; mark, rear of base: Q H W N
GORHAM CO. FOUNDERS

Whitney Collections of Sporting Art, given in memory of Harry Payne Whitney, B.A. 1894, and Payne Whitney, B.A. 1898, by Francis P. Garvan, B.A. 1897, M.A.(hon.) 1922
1932.215

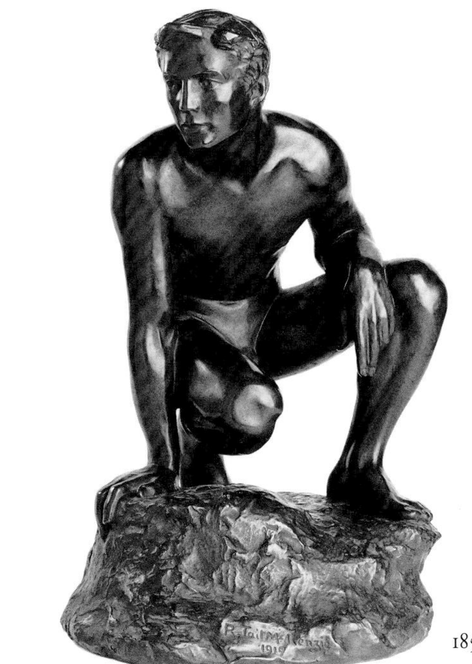

185

186 *The Joy of Effort*

1914
Bronze, dark reddish-brown patina
DIAM. 44½ x D. 2 (112.4 x 5.1)

Signed and dated lower front center in relief: © / R. Tait McKenzie / 1914

Inscribed in relief above signature:
The Joy of Effort

Foundry: The Gorham Manufacturing Company, Providence, Rhode Island; mark, center of bottom edge:
THE GORHAM CO FOUNDERS

Whitney Collections of Sporting Art, given in memory of Harry Payne Whitney, B.A. 1894, and Payne Whitney, B.A. 1898, by Francis P. Garvan, B.A. 1897, M.A.(hon.) 1922
1932.205

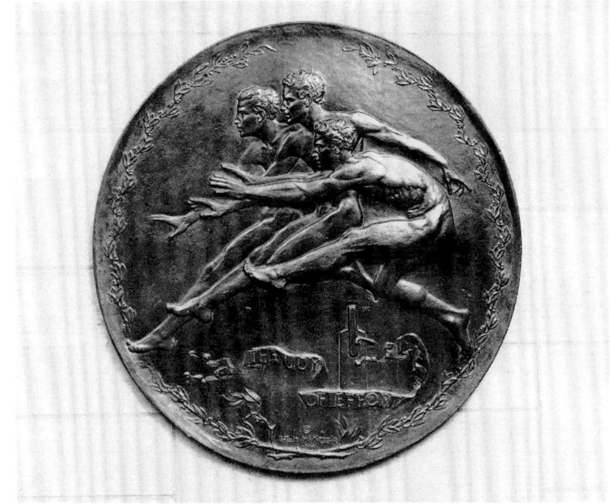

186

187 *The Sprinter*

c.1915
Bronze, dark brown patina
9 x 12 x 6 (22.9 x 30.5 x 15.2)

Signed proper left top of base:
R. Tait McKenzie

Foundry: Roman Bronze Works, New York; mark, rear edge of base: ROMAN BRONZE WORKS N.Y.

Whitney Collections of Sporting Art, given in memory of Harry Payne Whitney, B.A. 1894, and Payne Whitney, B.A. 1898, by Francis P. Garvan, B.A. 1897, M.A.(hon.) 1922
1932.216

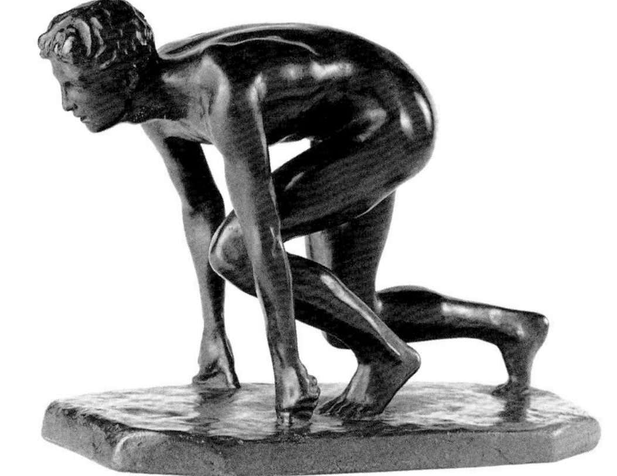

187

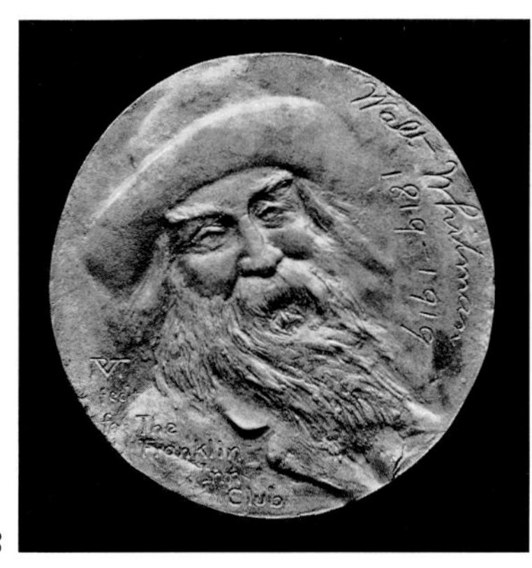

188

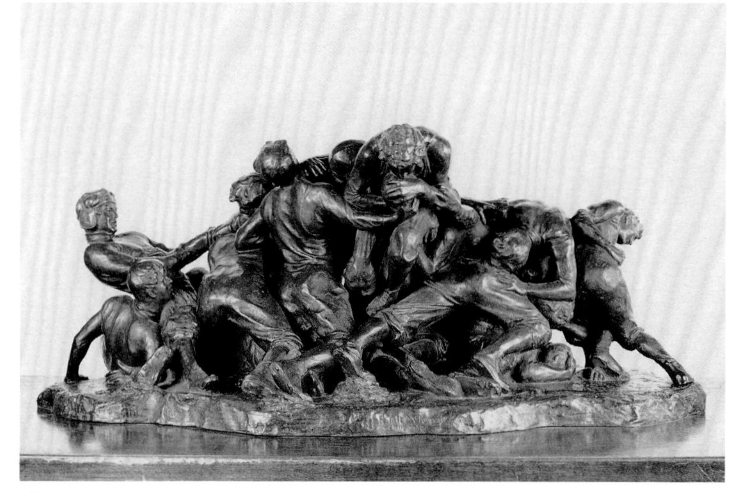

189

188 *Walt Whitman* 1819–1892

Probably 1919
Bronze, coppery-bronze patina
DIAM. 5 x D. 1/4 (12.7 x 0.64)

Signed and inscribed on front lower left: R T M (monogram) / Fecit / for The / Franklin / Inn / Club; upper right: *Walt Whitman / 1819–1919*

Gift of Adrian Van Sinderen, B.A. 1910, to the Collection of American Literature, Beinecke Rare Book and Manuscript Library
1980.312

189 *The Onslaught (Study of a Football Scrum)*

c.1920
Bronze, grey-brown patina
15 x 38 x 23 1/2 (38.1 x 96.5 x 59.7)

Signed center front edge of base: R. Tait McKenzie / copyright

Foundry: Roman Bronze Works, New York; mark, proper left front edge of base: ROMAN BRONZE WORKS N.Y.

Cast number on top rear of base: © EXAMPLE No1 OF AN EDITION OF SIX

Whitney Collections of Sporting Art, given in memory of Harry Payne Whitney, B.A. 1894, and Payne Whitney, B.A. 1898, by Francis P. Garvan, B.A. 1897, M.A.(hon.) 1922
1932.204

190 *The Plunger*

c.1920
Bronze, dark reddish-brown patina
24 x 22 x 18 (61 x 55.9 x 45.7)

Signed proper left top of base: R. Tait McKenzie

Cast number on center rear of base: NO13

Whitney Collections of Sporting Art, given in memory of Harry Payne Whitney, B.A. 1894, and Payne Whitney, B.A. 1898, by Francis P. Garvan, B.A. 1897, M.A.(hon.) 1922
1932.214

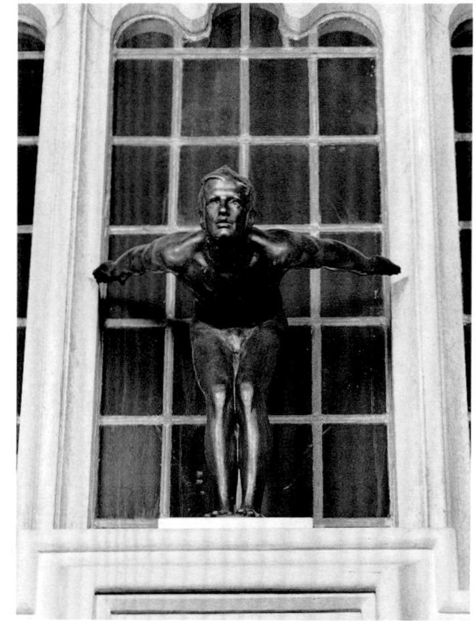

190

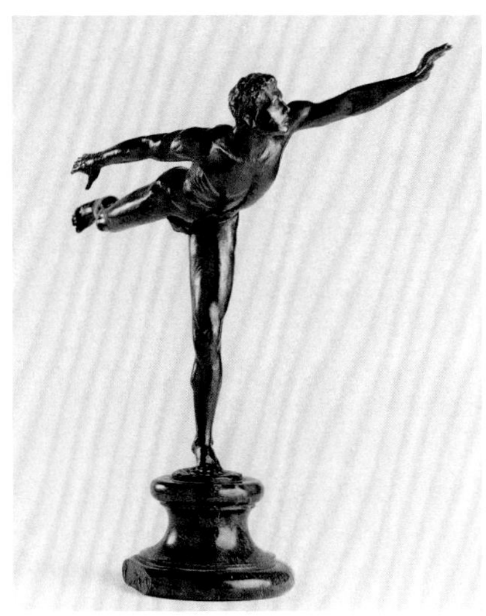

191

191 *The Flying Sphere*

1923
Bronze, dark brown patina
17 x 20½ x 9½ (43.2 x 52.1 x 24.1)

Signed and dated proper right top of base: R. Tait McKenzie / 1923

Foundry: The Gorham Manufacturing Company, Providence, Rhode Island; mark, rear of base: Q F V T GORHAM CO

Whitney Collections of Sporting Art, given in memory of Harry Payne Whitney, B.A. 1894, and Payne Whitney, B.A. 1898, by Francis P. Garvan, B.A. 1897, M.A.(hon.) 1922
1932.212

192 *The Ice Bird*

1923
Bronze, dark brown patina
20 x 28 x 13¼ (50.8 x 71.1 x 33.7)

Signed and dated proper left top of base: R. Tait McKenzie / 1923; proper right top of base: ©

Inscribed proper left top of base: ICE BIRD

Foundry: The Gorham Manufacturing Company, Providence, Rhode Island; mark, proper left rear of base: Q G W X GORHAM CO.

Whitney Collections of Sporting Art, given in memory of Harry Payne Whitney, B.A. 1894, and Payne Whitney, B.A. 1898, by Francis P. Garvan, B.A. 1897, M.A.(hon.) 1922
1932.207

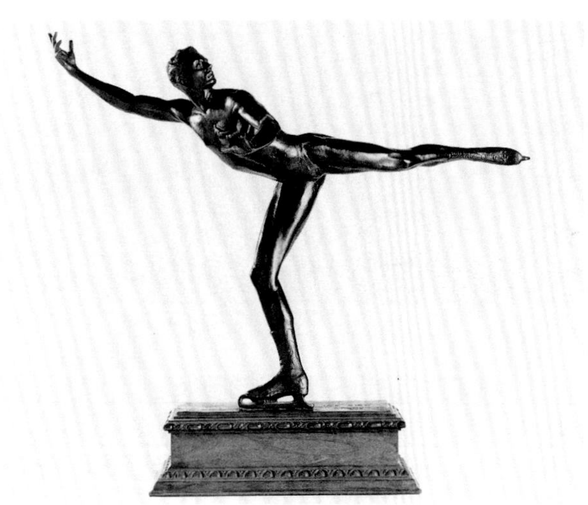

192

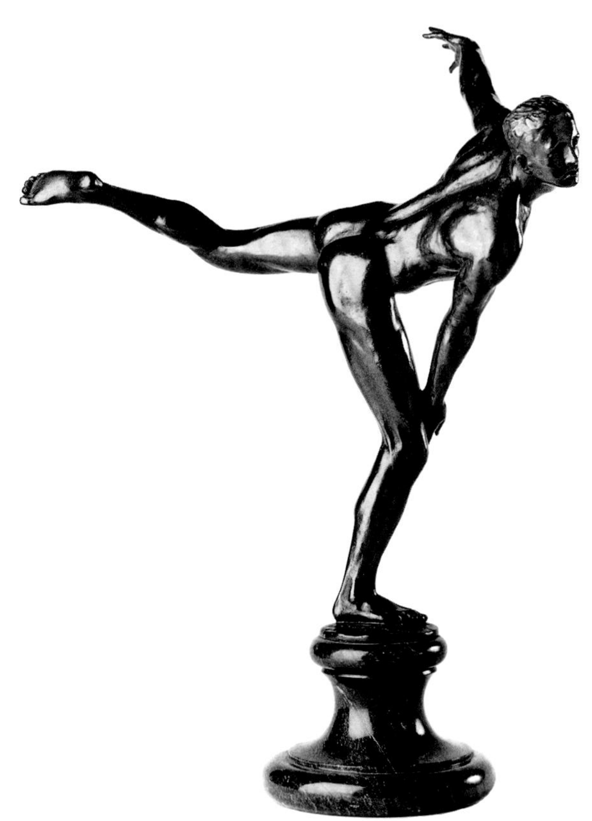

193

193 *The Javelin Cast*

1923
Bronze, dark brown patina
17½ x 9 x 17¼ (44.5 x 22.9 x 43.8)

Signed and dated front top of base: R. Tait McKenzie / 1923

Foundry: The Gorham Manufacturing Company, Providence, Rhode Island; mark, rear edge of base: R.G.W. Gorham Co.

Whitney Collections of Sporting Art, given in memory of Harry Payne Whitney, B.A. 1894, and Payne Whitney, B.A. 1898, by Francis P. Garvan, B.A. 1897, M.A.(hon.) 1922
1932.208

194 *The Pole Vaulter*

1923
Bronze, dark brown patina
18¼ x 3½ x 5 (46.4 x 8.9 x 12.7)

Signed and dated lower front: R / TAIT / MCKENZIE / FECIT / 1923 / ·

Inscribed lower rear: NELSON I SHERRILL / OF THE UNIVERSITY / OF PENNSYLVANIA / VAULTED OVER A BAR / THIRTEEN FEET IN / HEIGHT MAY 1923 / THE WORLD / MAY YET PRODUCE / AN ATHLETE WHO / WILL SOAR HIGHER / BY ANOTHER FOOT

Whitney Collections of Sporting Art, given in memory of Harry Payne Whitney, B.A. 1894, and Payne Whitney, B.A. 1898, by Francis P. Garvan, B.A. 1897, M.A.(hon.) 1922
1932.206

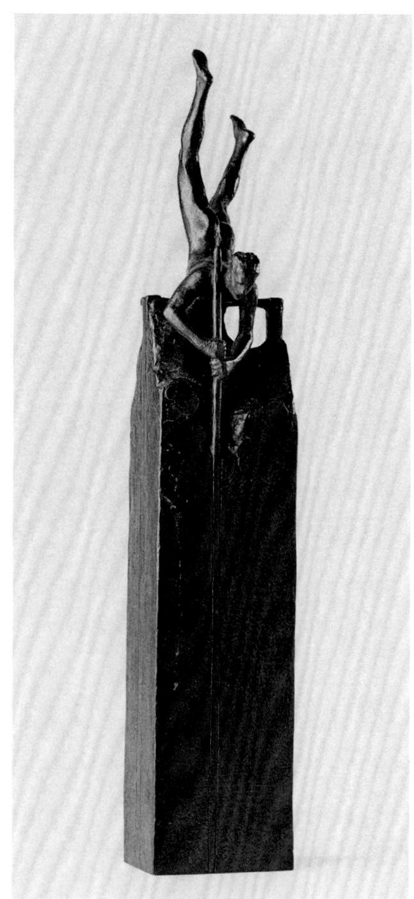

194

195 *The Shot Putter*

1923
Bronze, green and brown patina
12¼ x 7 x 6¼ (31.1 x 17.8 x 15.9)

Signed and dated proper left top front of base: R. Tait McKenzie / 1923

Foundry: The Gorham Manufacturing Company, Providence, Rhode Island; mark, rear of base: Q H L F / GORHAM CO.

Whitney Collections of Sporting Art, given in memory of Harry Payne Whitney, B.A. 1894, and Payne Whitney, B.A. 1898, by Francis P. Garvan, B.A. 1897, M.A.(hon.) 1922
1932.211

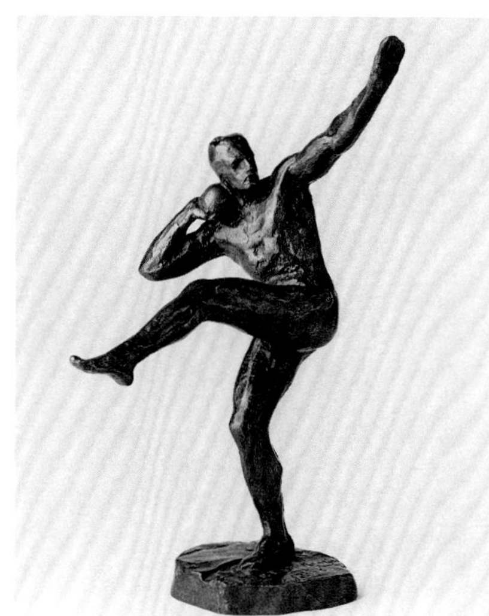

195

196 *The Modern Discus Thrower*

1926
Bronze, dark reddish-brown patina
28½ x 21¼ x 11¼ (72.4 x 54 x 28.6)

Signed and dated proper right top of base: R. Tait McKenzie / 1926

Foundry: Roman Bronze Works, New York; mark, proper left side of base: ROMAN BRONZE WORKS N–Y–

Whitney Collections of Sporting Art, given in memory of Harry Payne Whitney, B.A. 1894, and Payne Whitney, B.A. 1898, by Francis P. Garvan, B.A. 1897, M.A.(hon.) 1922
1932.210

197 *The Upright Discus Thrower*

1928
Bronze, green and brown patina
11 x 10 x 3 (27.9 x 25.4 x 7.6)

Signed and dated on front of base: R. Tait McKenzie / '28

Inscribed proper right side of base: The Upright Discus Thrower

Foundry: The Gorham Manufacturing Company, Providence, Rhode Island; mark, proper right side edge of base: Q H L G GORHAM CO. FOUNDERS

Whitney Collections of Sporting Art, given in memory of Harry Payne Whitney, B.A. 1894, and Payne Whitney, B.A. 1898, by Francis P. Garvan, B.A. 1897, M.A.(hon.) 1922
1932.209

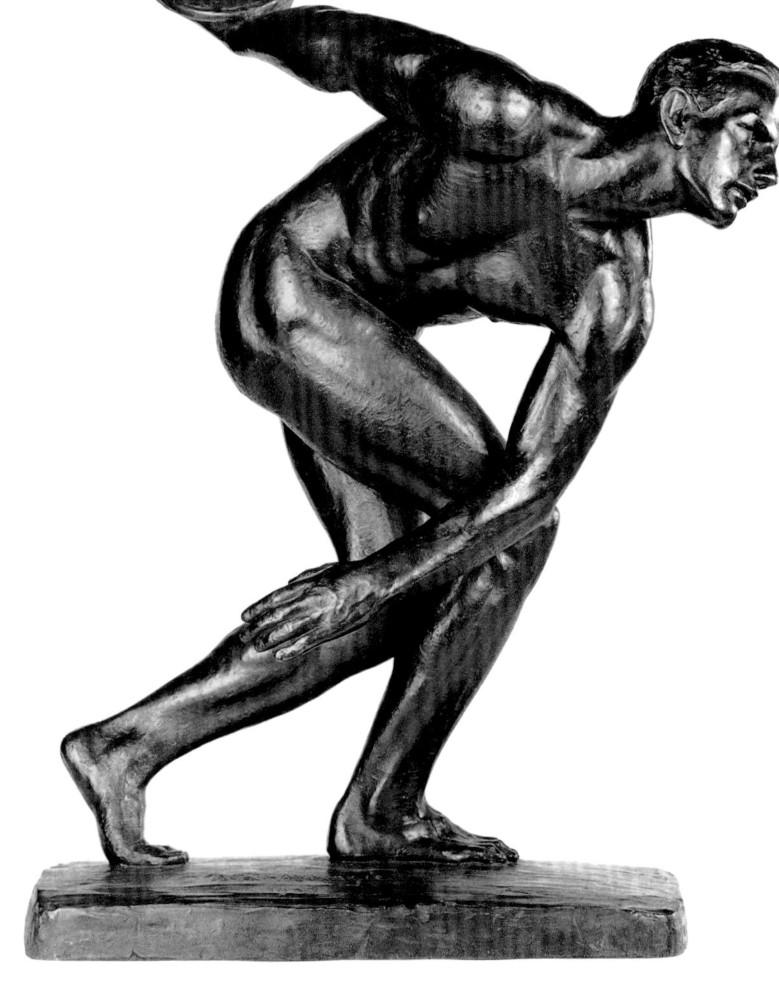

196

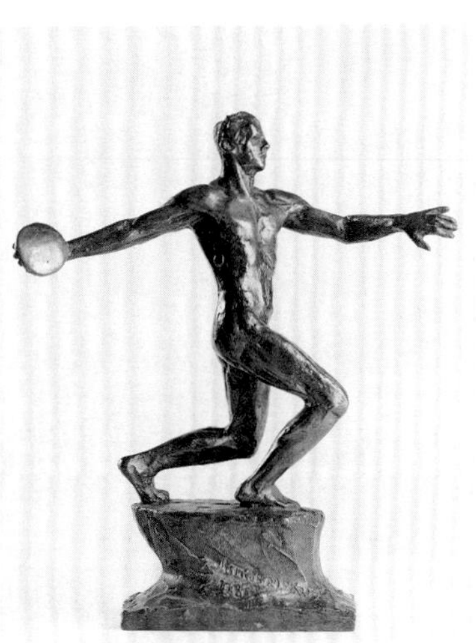

197

FREDERICK WILLIAM MacMONNIES

1863 Brooklyn, New York –
1937 New York City

198 *Nathan Hale* 1755–1776
B.A. 1773, M.A. 1776

1890
Bronze, dark brown patina
28½ x 9¼ x 6¼ (72.4 x 23.5 x 15.9)

Signed and dated proper left side of base: *F. MacMonnies 1890*

Foundry: Jaboeuf & Rouard, Paris; mark, in circular stamp, proper right rear corner: J A BOEUF & ROUARD / 10 & 12 R. DE L'ASILE POPINCOURT / FONDEURS / A / PARIS

Bequest of George Dudley Seymour, M.A.(hon.) 1913
1945.55

after
FREDERICK WILLIAM MacMONNIES

199 *Nathan Hale* 1755–1776
B.A. 1773, M.A. 1776

1893
Bronzed white metal
7 x 2¼ x 2 (17.8 x 5.7 x 5.1)

Inscribed front edge of base in relief: NATHAN HALE; proper right side: NEW YORK; back edge: NOVEMBER 25 – 1893; proper left side: SONG OF THE REVOLUTION

Yale University Library

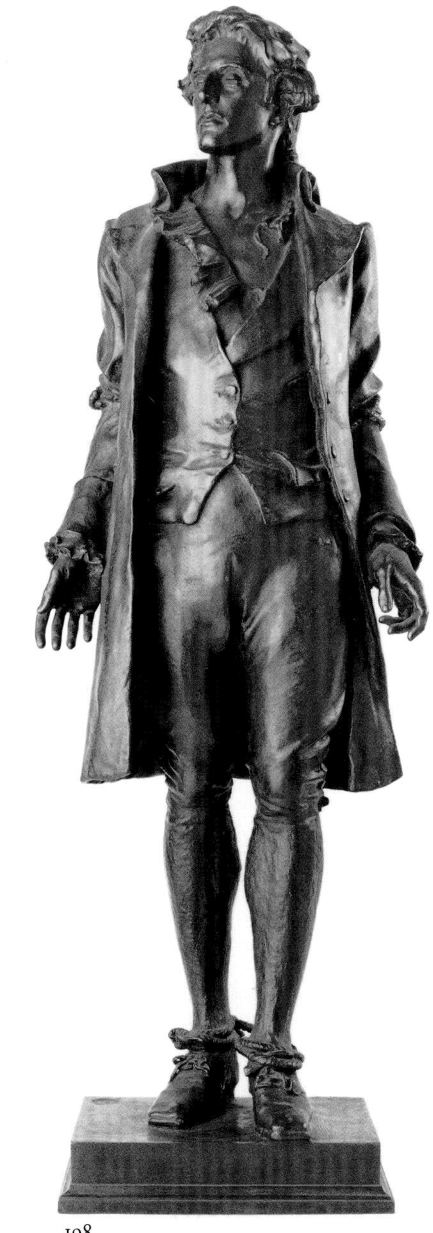

198

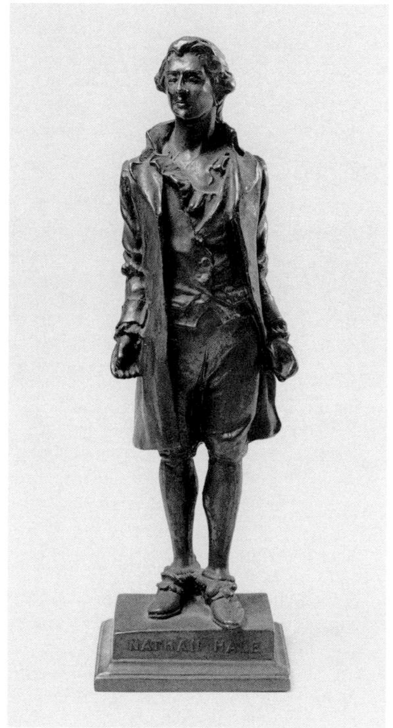

199

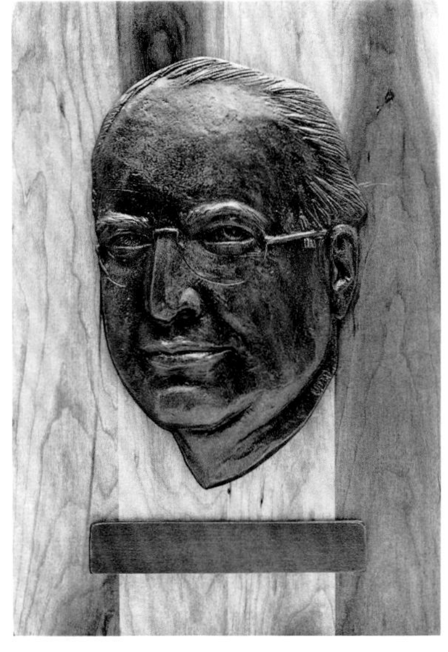

200

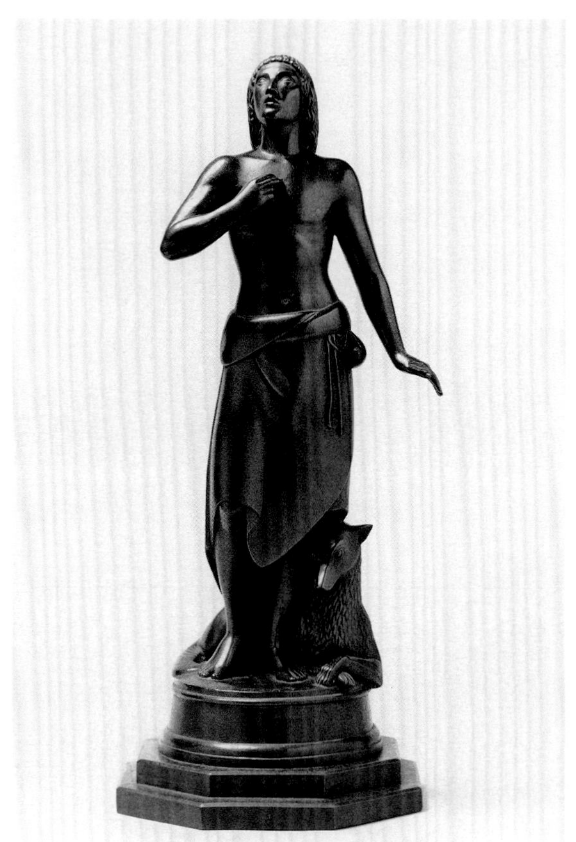

201

WILLIAM M. McVEY

b. 1905 Boston

200 *James Marshall Osborn* 1906–1976

1977
Bronze, dark reddish-brown and black patina
13 x 7¼ x 1 (33 x 18.4 x 2.5)

Wood mount
16 x 11 x 1 (40.6 x 27.9 x 2.5)

Signed lower right on neck: W M

Given by the artist in memory of James Marshall Osborn to the James M. and Marie-Louise Osborn Collection, Beinecke Rare Book and Manuscript Library

PAUL MANSHIP

1885 St.Paul, Minnesota – 1966 New York City

201 *David*

1921
Bronze, brown patina
19¾ x 8 x 6½ (50.2 x 20.3 x 16.5)

Signed and dated between feet at top front of base, in relief: PAUL MANSHIP / © 1921

Foundry: Roman Bronze Works, New York; mark, center rear of base: ROMAN BRONZE WORKS N–Y–

Gift of Miss Elisabeth Achelis
1960.55.1

202 *Spear Thrower*

1921
Bronze, dark green patina
20 x 28½ x 7½ (50.8 x 72.4 x 19.1)

Signed and dated top center of base: PAUL MANSHIP / © 1921

Foundry: Roman Bronze Works, New York; mark, proper right lower rear edge of base: ROMAN BRONZE WORKS N–Y–

Cast number proper left top of base: N$^{\underline{o}}$4

Whitney Collections of Sporting Art, given in memory of Harry Payne Whitney, B.A. 1894, and Payne Whitney, B.A. 1898, by Francis P. Garvan, B.A. 1897, M.A.(hon.) 1922
1932.203

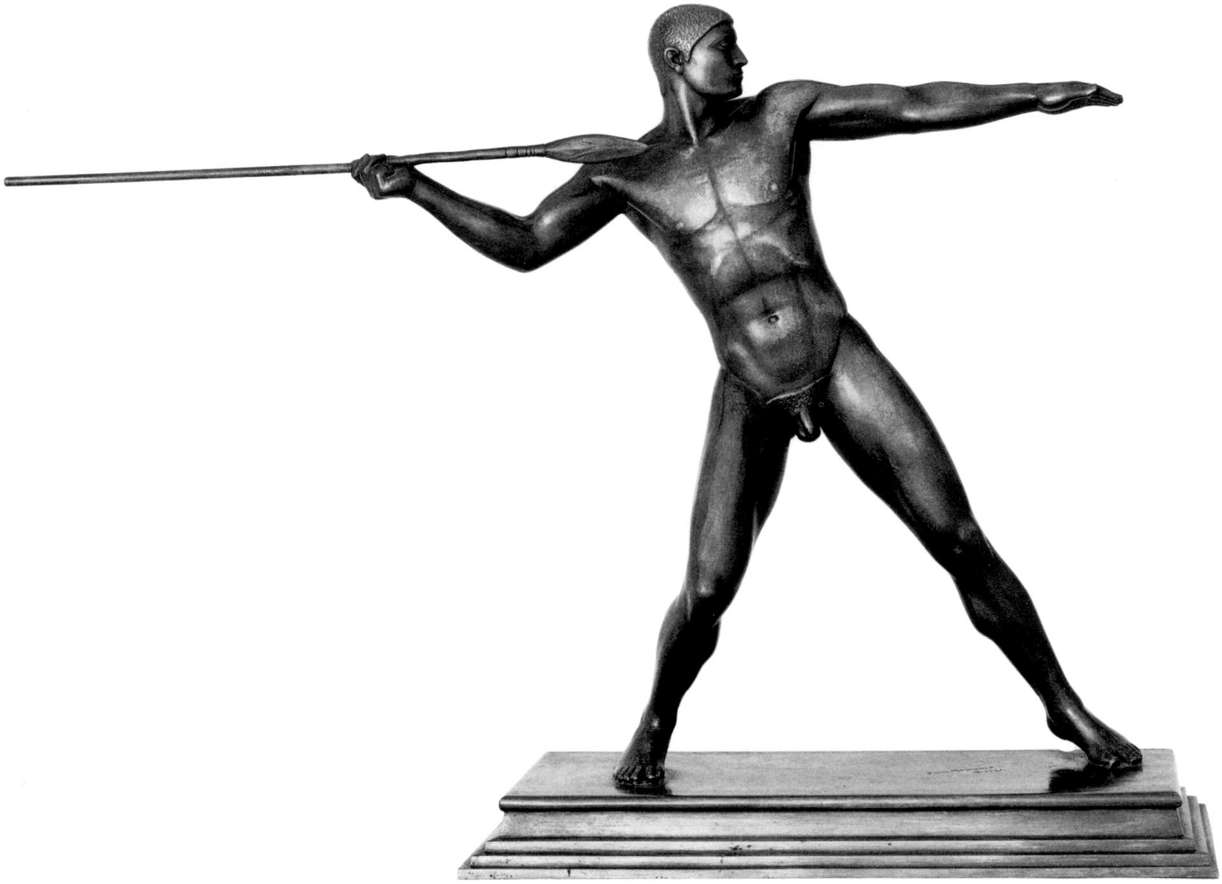

202

203 *Europa and the Bull*

1924
Bronze, brown patina and gilt
9½ x 11¼ x 6¾ (24.1 x 28.6 x 17.1)

Brescian marble base
1½ x 13¾ x 8½ (3.8 x 34.9 x 21.6)

Signed and dated proper left lower rear on hoof: P. MANSHIP / © 1924

Gift of Shepherd Stevens, B.F.A. 1922
1963.28.1

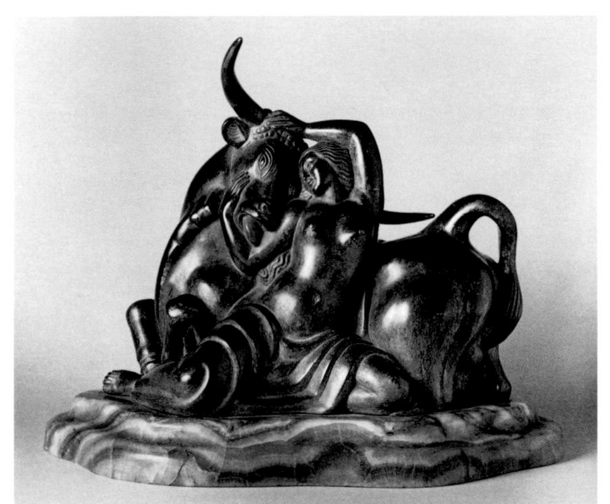

203

MARISOL (ESCOBAR)

b. 1930 Paris
Active U.S. since 1950

204 *Dinner Date*

1963
Painted wood, plaster, textiles, oil on canvas, metal fork, leather boots, paint, graphite
55 x 53½ x 44 (139.7 x 135.9 x 111.8)

Inscribed in ink, bottom of table and of each chair: (—·)

Gift of Susan Morse Hilles
1973.86

PHILIP MARTINY

1858 Strasbourg, Alsace, France – 1927 New York City
Active U.S. after c.1876

205 *Charles James Osborn* 1840–1885

1888
Bronze, black patina
47½ x 31½ x 1¾ (120.7 x 80 x 4.4)

Signed bottom edge of figure in relief: P H · MARTINY – SC · NY

Inscribed lower front in relief: IN MEMORIAM / CAROLI IACOBI OSBORN / NEO–EBORACENSIS / MARITI VXOR / MIRIAM ADALINA OSBORN / HOC AEDIFICIVM / EXSTRVENDVM CVRAVIT / MDCCCLXXXVIII / MVLTS ILLE BONIS FLEBILIS OCCIDIT; upper left top: A–D–XV–KAL– / IAN MDCCCXXXX.; upper right top: A–D–III IDVS / NOV – MDCCCLXXXV.

Gift of Mrs. Charles James Osborn to the Osborn Memorial Laboratories

LARKIN GOLDSMITH MEAD

1835 Chesterfield, New Hampshire, or Brattleboro, Vermont – 1910 Florence, Italy

206 *Bust of a Young Boy*

c.1860
Marble
17¼ x 11¼ x 6¼ (43.8 x 28.6 x 15.9)

Signed on front of base: *Mead · Sculpt*

Gift of James Jackson Jarves
1868.2

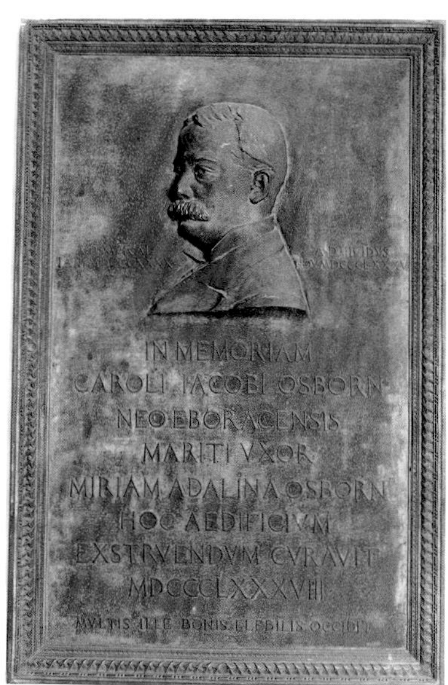

205

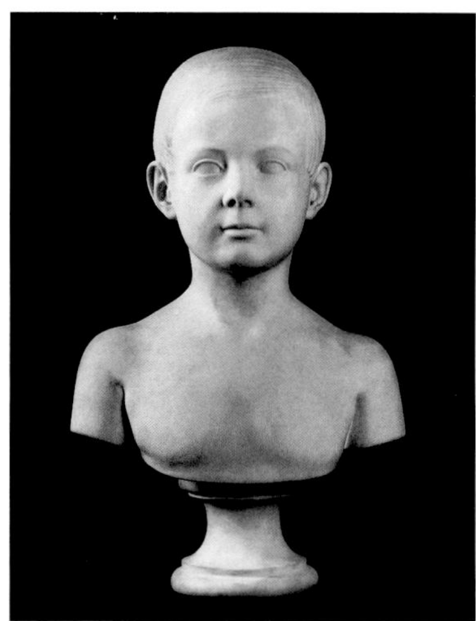

206

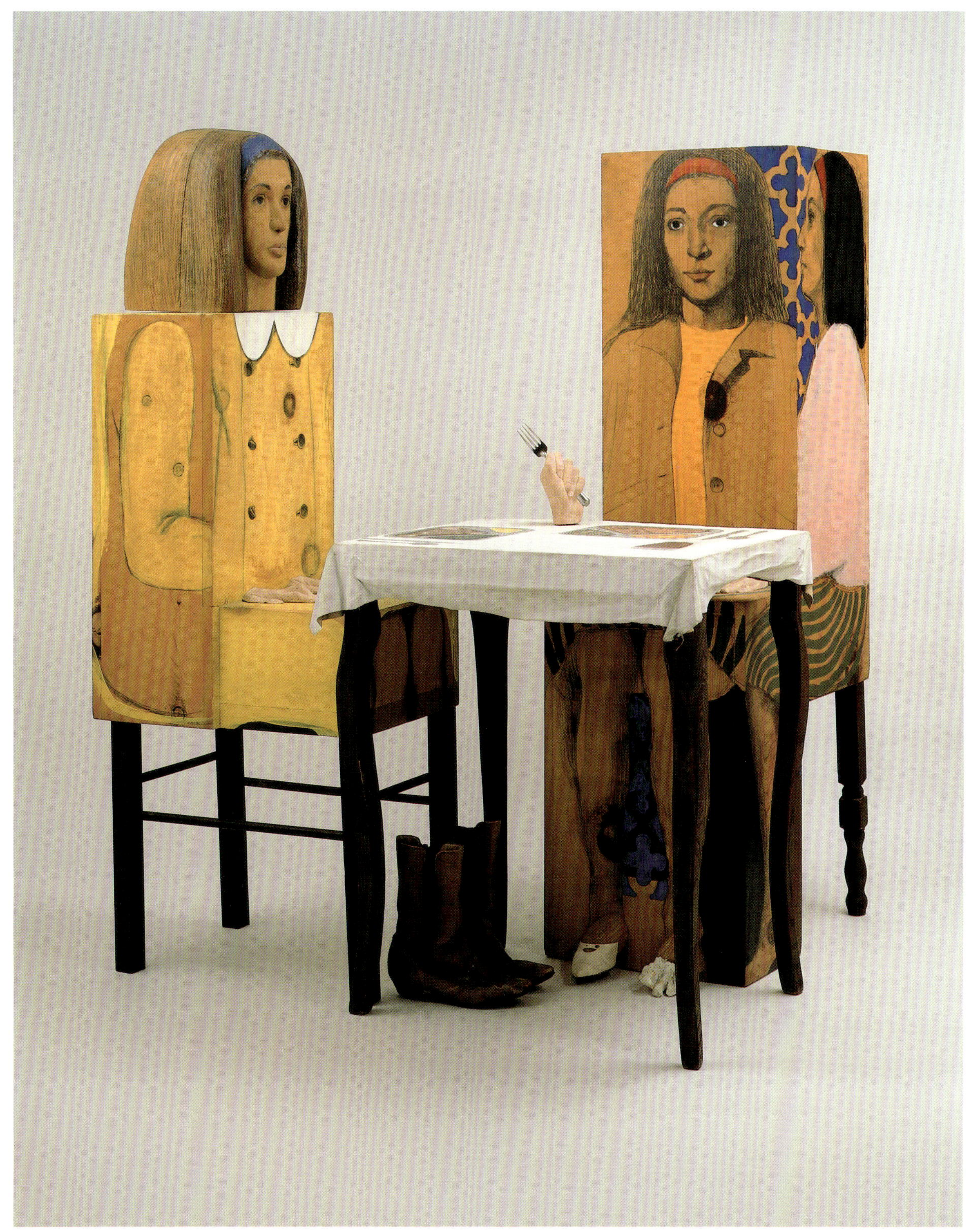

207 *James Jackson Jarves* 1818–1888

1883
Bronze, dark brown and bronze patina
16½ x 13 x 2 (41.9 x 33 x 5.1)

Signed and dated lower left front:
L G Mead 1883

Inscribed in mixed upper and lower case, upper left front: J. Jackson Jarves

Founder's mark lower center, under edge of bust: *Carradori e Cie* (?) / *Pistoia*

Given in memory of James Jackson Jarves by his daughter, Mrs. Walter Raleigh Kerr
1930.331

DOROTHEA P. MICHALSON

b. 1906 Chicago

208 *Thurman W. Arnold* 1891–1969
M.A.(hon.) 1931

1961
Bronze, reddish-brown and green patina
13 x 8¼ x 9¼ (33 x 21 x 23.5)

Signed and dated lower proper right rear: 1961 D P Michalson

Gift of Joseph Borkin, Ernest Meyers, LL.B. 1934, Laporte and Mayers, Manuel Gorman, LL.B. 1936, and Monroe Karasik to the Yale University Law School

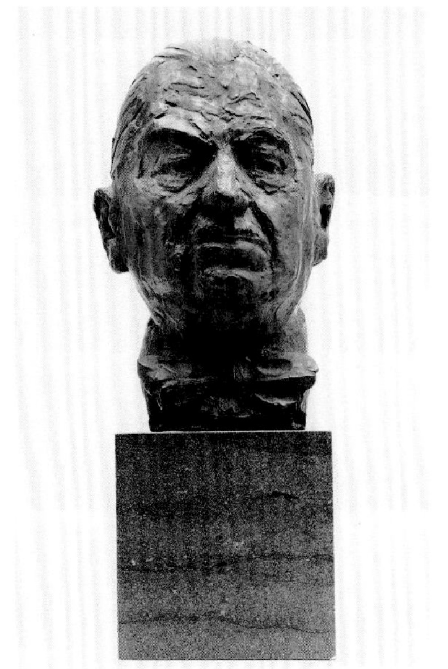

208

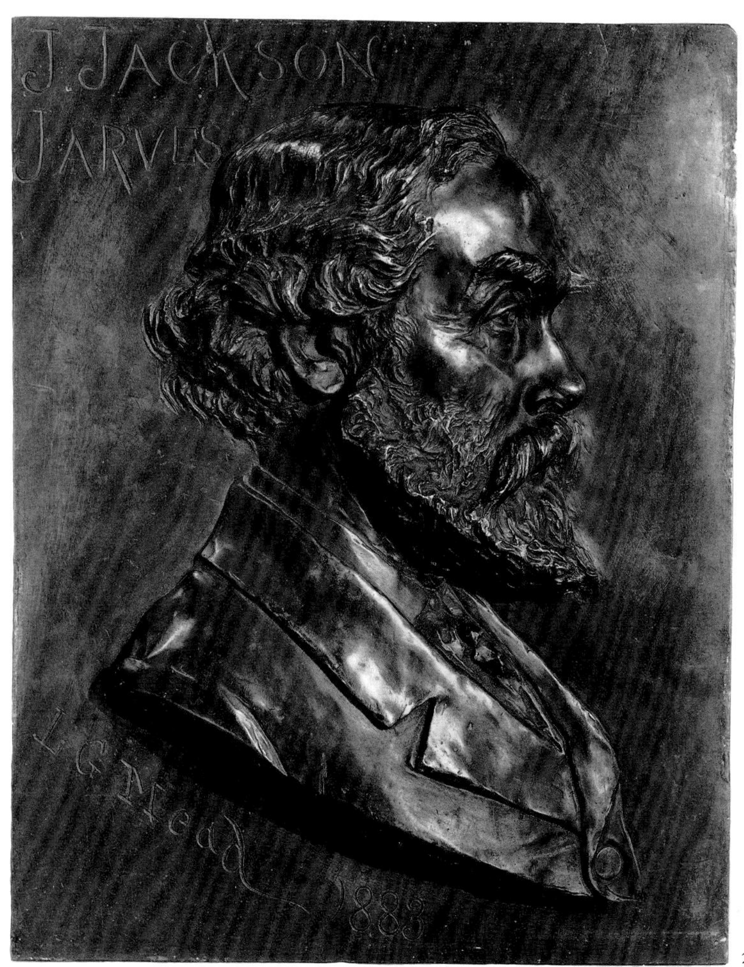

207

WILLIAM MILLER

1850 possibly New York City –
1923 possibly Providence, Rhode Island

209 *Noah Porter* 1811–1892
B.A. 1831, M.A. 1834

1890
Bronze, yellow-green patina
DIAM. 22¾ x D. 2 (57.8 x 5.1)

Wood frame
DIAM. 32 x D. 2 (81.3 x 5.1)

Yale University Library

210 *Theodore Dwight Woolsey*
1801–1889
B.A. 1820, M.A. 1823

c.1890
Bronze, yellow-green patina
DIAM. 22½ x D. 2 (57.2 x 5.1)

Wood frame (hexagon)
31 x 31 x 2 (78.7 x 78.7 x 5.1)

Yale University Library

CARL MILLES

1875 Lagga, Sweden –
1955 Lidingö, Sweden
L.H.D.(hon.) 1936
Active U.S. intermittently after 1929, citizen 1945

211 *Diana*

c.1940
Gilded bronze
59 x 21¼ x 24 (149.9 x 54 x 61)

Signed lower proper left rear of base: C. Milles

Philip L. Goodwin, B.A. 1907, Collection
1958.47

FISK MILLS

Dates unknown

212 *Walter Hilliard Bidwell* 1798–1881
B.A. 1827, Divinity School 1833

c.1850
Plaster
25 x 13¾ x 11 (63.5 x 34.9 x 27.9)

Signed lower center front: Fisk Mills / Sculpt.

Gift of Mrs. Frank A. DeWitt to the Yale University Library
1964.50

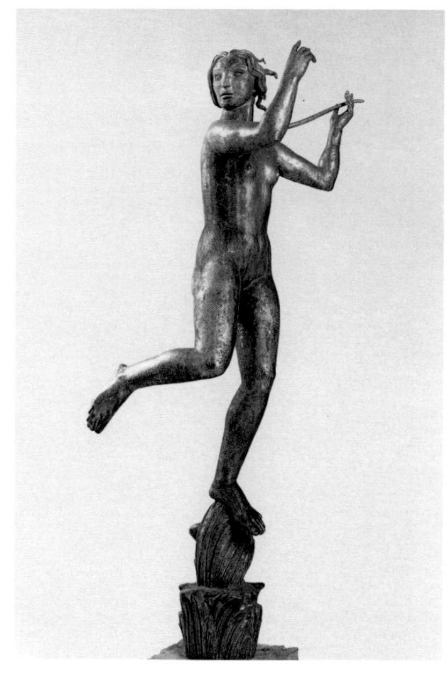

211

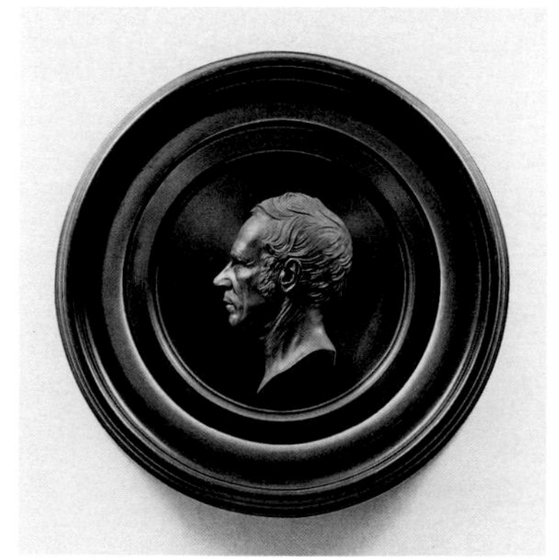

209

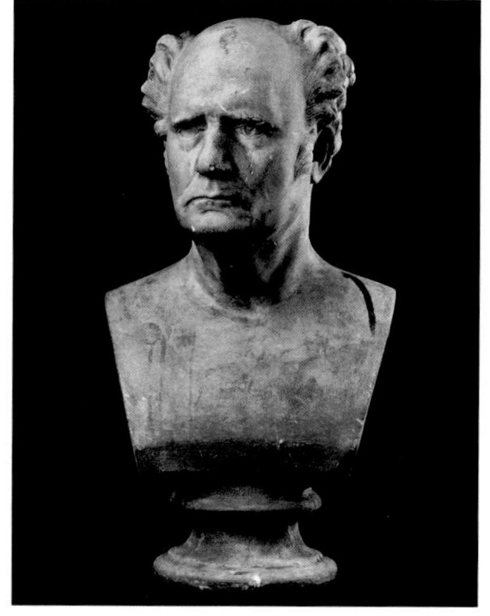

212

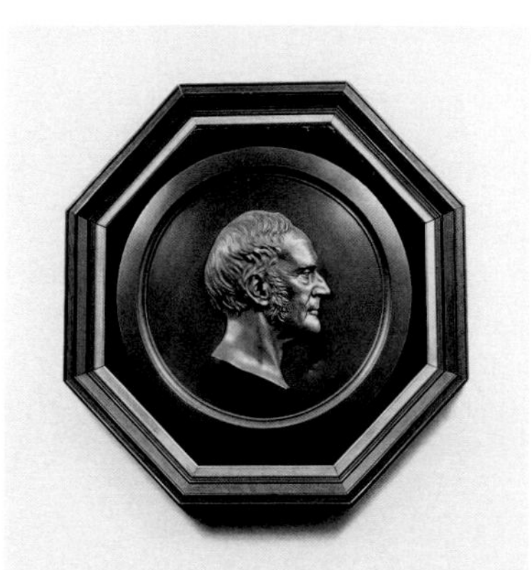

210

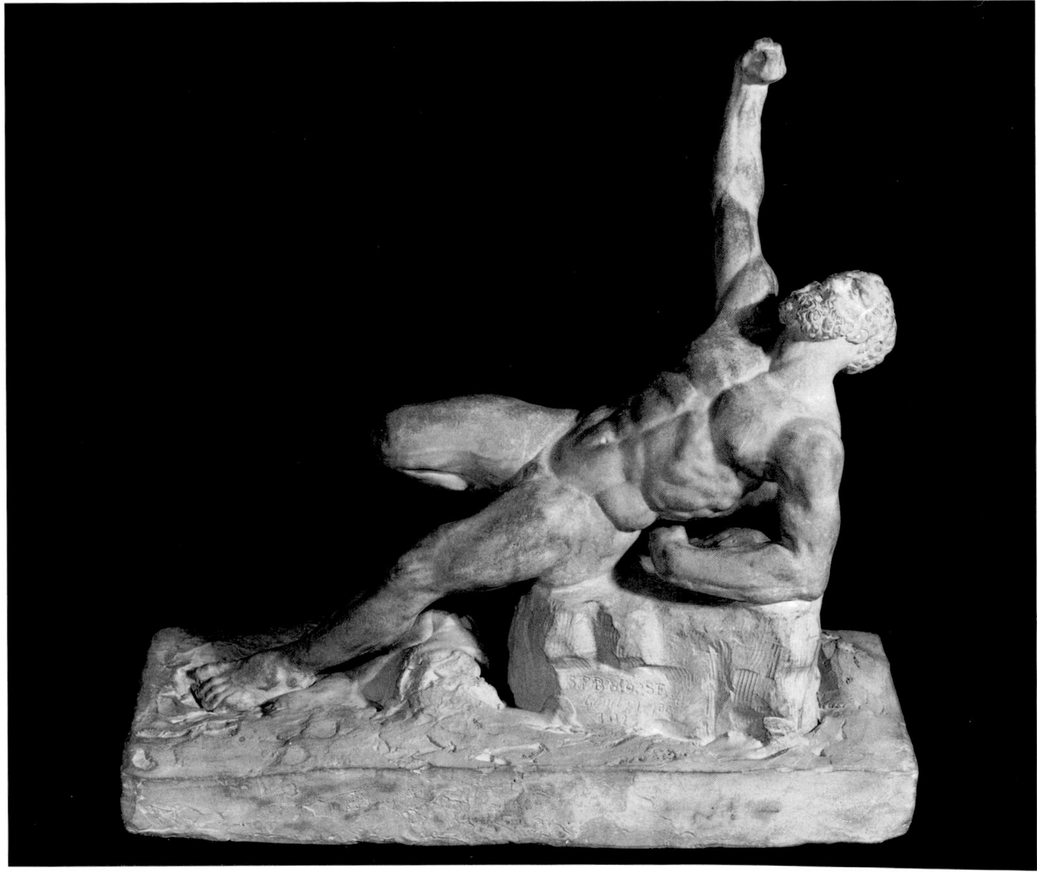

214

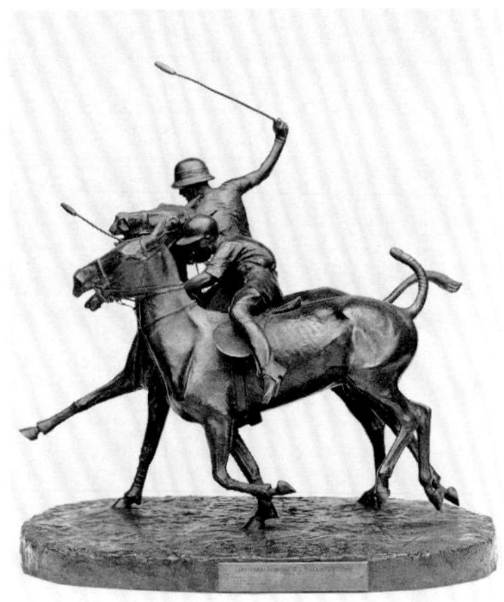

213

N. MOELLER

Dates unknown

213 *Polo (Lieutenant General R.L. Bullard Trophy)*

1916
Bronze, dark green-brown patina
19 x 19½ x 14¼ (48.3 x 49.5 x 36.2)

Signed and dated proper left front top of base beneath an incised image of two crossed polo mallets: N. MOELLER / 1916 / ©

Inscribed on metal plaque attached to base: LIEUTENANT GENERAL R.L. BULLARD TROPHY / WON BY / 1922 – YALE / 1924 – PRINCETON / 1926 – HARVARD / 1928 – YALE

Foundry: Roman Bronze Works, New York; mark, rear edge of base: ROMAN BRONZE WORKS N.Y.

Payne Whitney Gymnasium

SAMUEL FINLEY BREESE MORSE

1791 Charlestown, Massachusetts – 1872 New York City
B.A. 1810, M.A. 1816, LL.D. 1846

214 *Dying Hercules*

1812
Plaster
19¾ x 23 x 11 (50.2 x 58.4 x 27.9)

Signed, dated, and inscribed center front on largest rock: S.F.B. Morse. / London. fec^t / 1812

Gift of the Rev. E. Goodrich Smith, B.A. 1822, M.A. 1825
1866.4

SIDNEY A. MORSE

1832–1903

215 *Walt Whitman* 1819–1892

1887
Plaster
24 x 17½ x 13½ (61 x 44.5 x 33.7)

Signed and dated proper right side:
Sidney Morse / Sculpt. / 1887

Provenance unknown
1900.22

JOSEPH MOZIER

1812 Burlington, Vermont –
1870 Faido, Switzerland

216 *The Wept of Wish-ton-Wish*

1859
Marble
66 x 28¾ x 23¼ (167.6 x 73 x 59.1)

Signed and dated proper right edge of base: J. MOZIER. SC: / ROME. 1859

Inscribed front edge of base: THE WEPT OF WISH–TON–WISH

Gift of the heirs of Mrs. Joseph E. Sheffield
1889.5

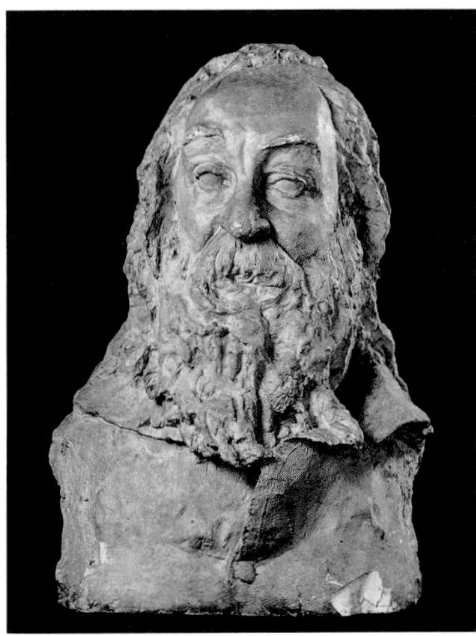

215

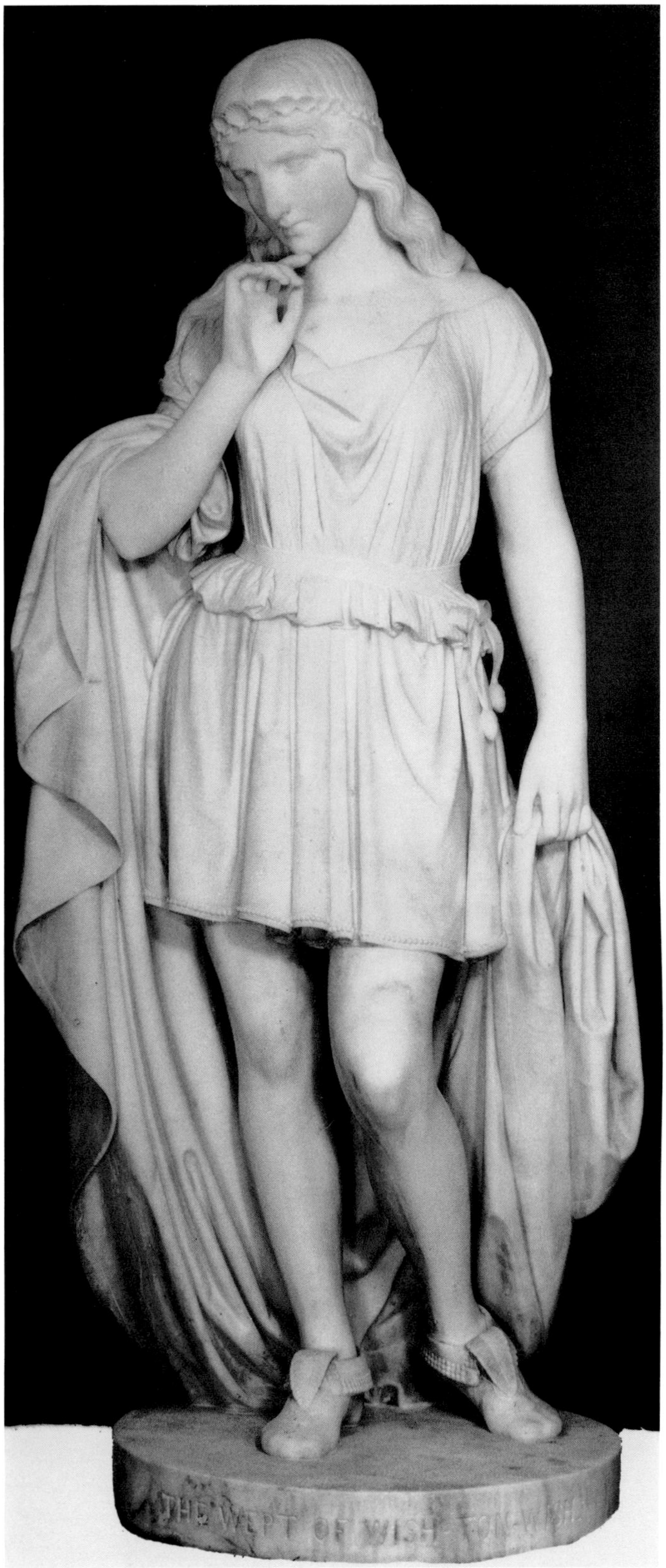

216

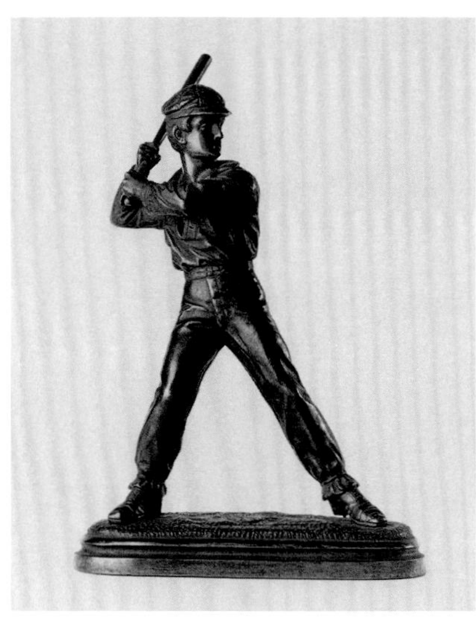

217

K. MULLER and J. DEACON

Dates unknown

217 *The Batsman*

Patented 1868
Bronze, green and black patina
11 x 7½ x 5 (27.9 x 19.1 x 12.7)

Signed and dated top front of base: K. MULLER & J. DEACON PAT. 1868

Whitney Collections of Sporting Art, given in memory of Harry Payne Whitney, B.A. 1894, and Payne Whitney, B.A. 1898, by Francis P. Garvan, B.A. 1897, M.A.(hon.) 1922
1932.200

218 *The Pitcher*

Patented 1868
Bronze, green and black patina
10 x 8¼ x 3½ (25.4 x 21 x 8.9)

Signed and dated top front of base: K. MULLER & J. DEACON PAT. 1868

Whitney Collections of Sporting Art, given in memory of Harry Payne Whitney, B.A. 1894, and Payne Whitney, B.A. 1898, by Francis P. Garvan, B.A. 1897, M.A.(hon.) 1922
1932.201

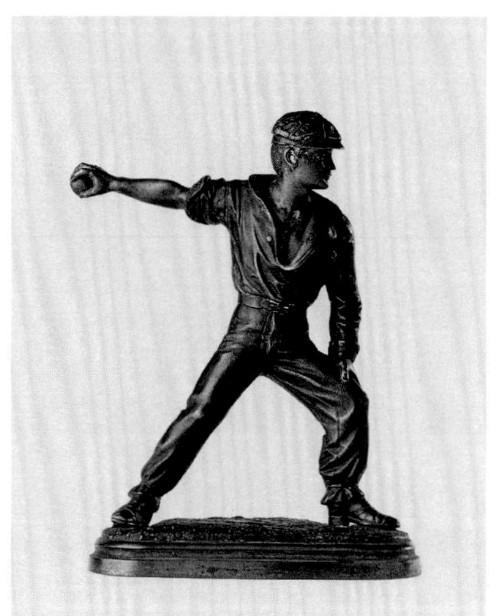

218

SAMUEL ALOYSIUS MURRAY

1869 Philadelphia – 1941 Philadelphia

219 *Walt Whitman* 1819–1892

1892
Painted plaster
13¾ x 7 x 5¼ (34.9 x 17.8 x 13.3)

Signed and dated lower center rear of base: COPY'RIGHT / MURRAY 1892

Inscribed center rear of base: To Mr Talcott Williams / from his friend; front in relief: Walt / Whitman

Gift of Adrian Van Sinderen, B.A. 1910, to the Collection of American Literature, Beinecke Rare Book and Manuscript Library
1980.311

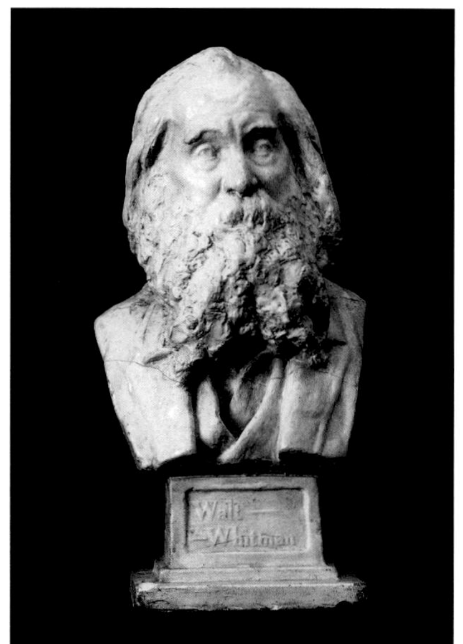

219

220 *William Hance MacDowell*
1816–1906

1897
Painted plaster
13½ x 7½ x 5 (34.3 x 19.1 x 12.7)

Signed, dated, and inscribed lower center rear: To My / Friend / MRS. EAKINS / SAML. MURRAY / 1897; lower proper left side: APRIL 97; in graphite on underside of base: (?) / McDowell / fr Sam Murray

Collection of Mary C. and James W. Fosburgh, B.A. 1933, M.A. 1935
1979.14.60

221 *The Boxer*

1899
Bronze, dark brown patina
30½ x 22¼ x 9½ (77.5 x 56.5 x 24.1)

Signed and dated proper right front top of base: MURRAY / COPYRIGHT 1899

Foundry: Bureau Brothers, Philadelphia; mark, proper left rear top of base: BUREAU BROS. / PHILA.

Whitney Collections of Sporting Art, given in memory of Harry Payne Whitney, B.A. 1894, and Payne Whitney, B.A. 1898, by Francis P. Garvan, B.A. 1897, M.A.(hon.) 1922
1932.202

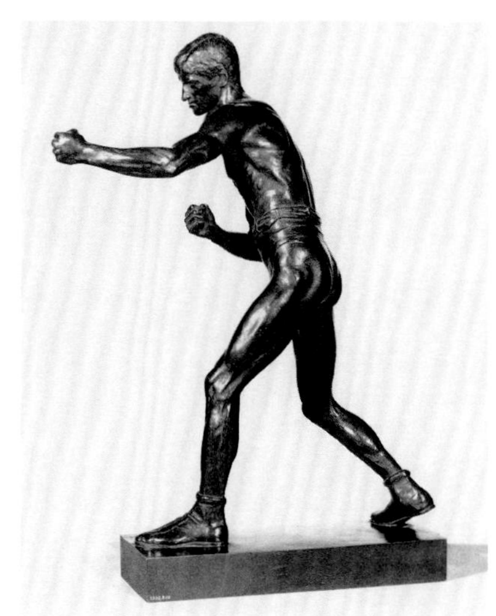

221

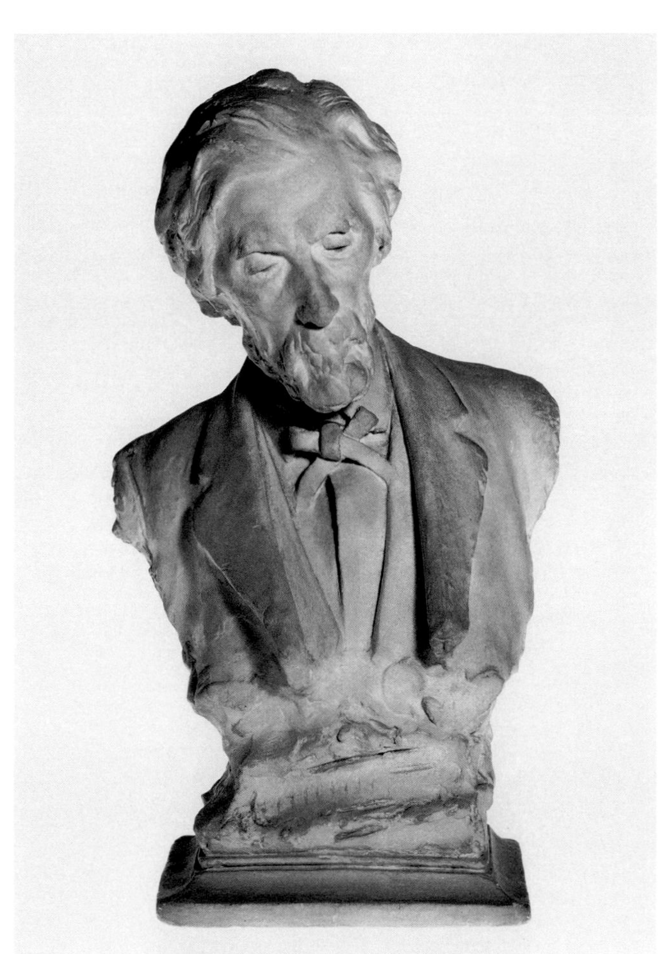

220

ELIE NADELMAN

1882 Warsaw, Poland –
1946 Riverdale, New York
Active U.S. after 1914, citizen 1927

222 *Classical Head*

c.1910
Marble
14½ x 9½ x 10¾ (36.8 x 24.1 x 27.3)

Marble base
5½ x 6½ x 6½ (14 x 16.5 x 16.5)

Signed lower rear at base of neck: ELIE NADELMAN

Gift of Mrs. Francis P. Garvan
1950.724

223 *Patricia Garvan* 1911–1918

After 1918
Marble
20 x 14½ x 8¼ (50.8 x 36.8 x 21)

Marble base
2¼ x 16 x 9 (5.7 x 40.6 x 22.9)

Signed lower proper left rear near edge: ELIE NADELMAN

Gift of Mabel Brady Garvan
1977.176.1

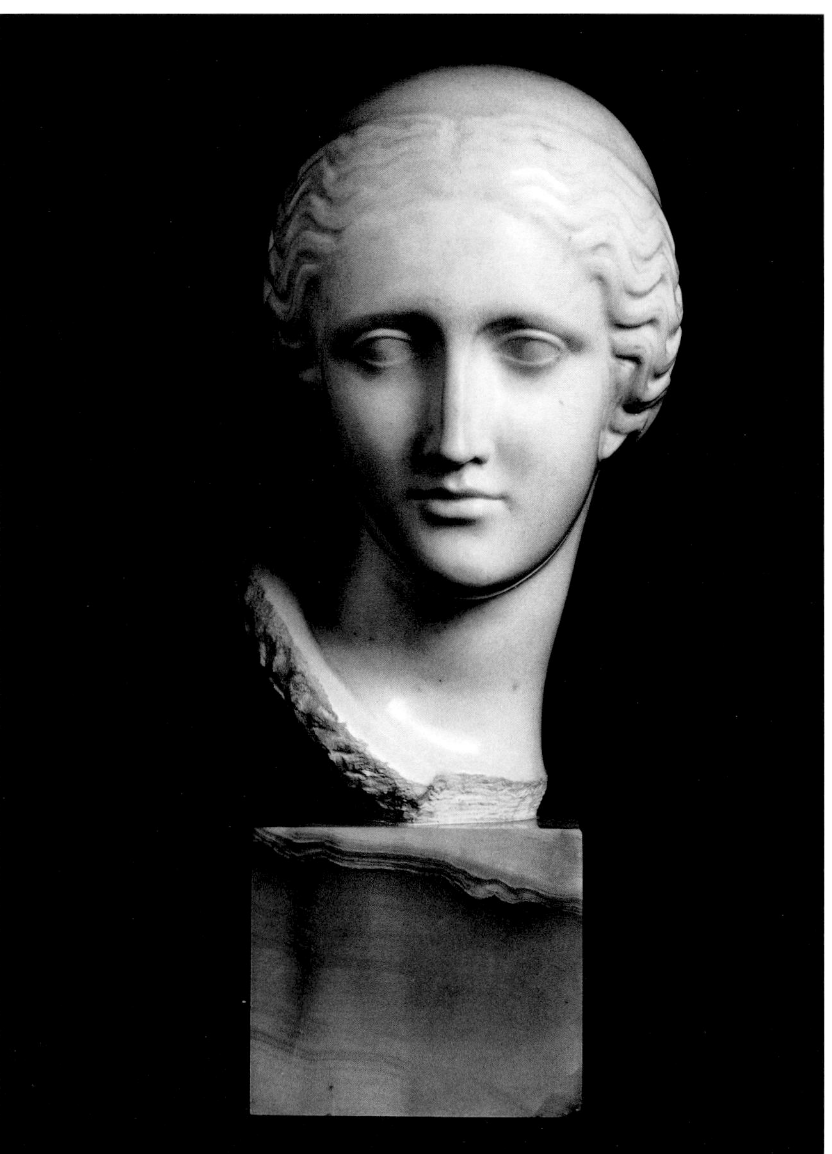

222

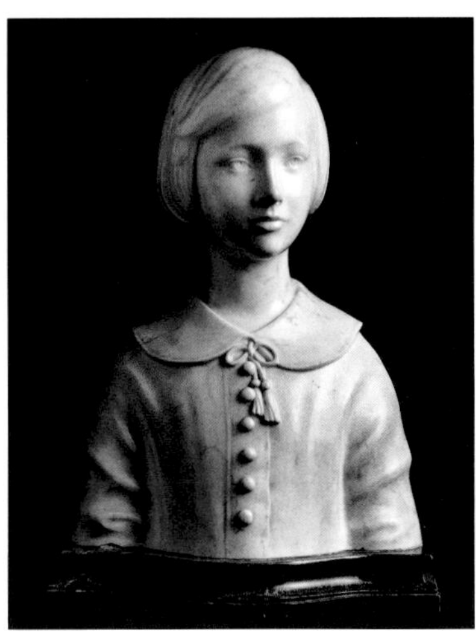

223

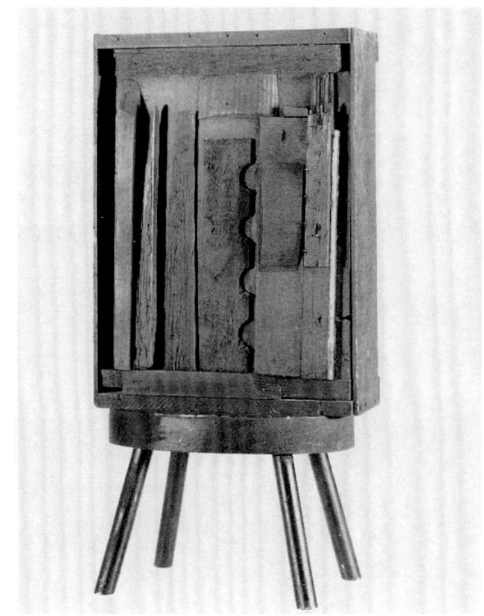

224

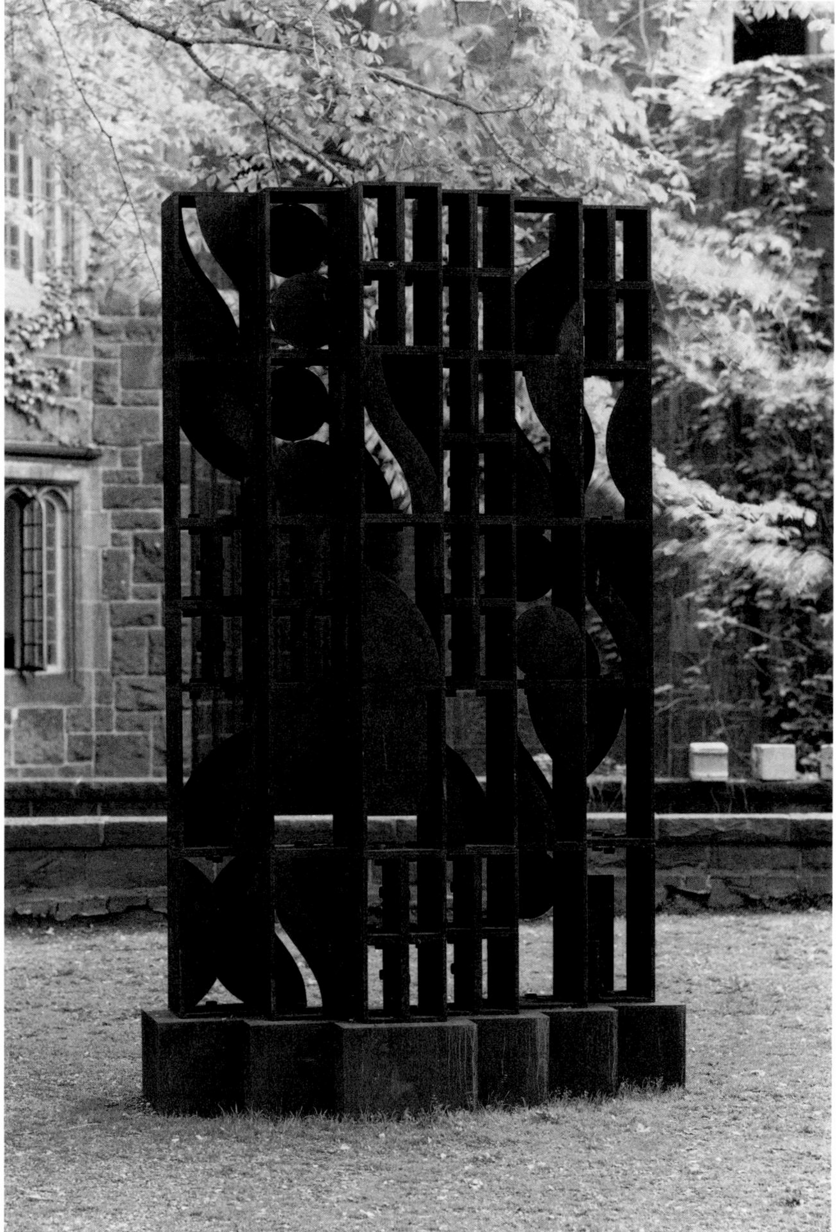

225

LOUISE NEVELSON

1900 Kiev, Russia –
1988 New York City
To U.S. 1905

224 *Dark Treasure*

1958
Wood, painted black
26 x 13¼ x 8¾ (66 x 33.7 x 22.2)

Signed and dated proper right rear of top: NEVELSON – 1958

Inscribed proper right rear of top: B (or 73); on underside of stool, may be original mark on readymade stool: *GG 398.c. / 4*[?]

Gift of Mr. Rufus Stillman, Class of 1943, and Mrs. Rufus Stillman
1980.9.2

225 *Atmosphere and Environment XI*

Fabricated 1971, designed 1969
Cor-ten steel
98 x 60 x 31¼ (248.9 x 152.4 x 79.4)

Cor-ten steel base
12 x 66 x 37¼ (30.5 x 167.6 x 94.6)

Fabricator's mark stamped on proper left top of base: WORK EXECUTED BY / Lippincott / NORTH HAVEN CONN

Metal fabricator: Lippincott, Inc., North Haven, Connecticut

Seymour H. Knox, B.A. 1920, Fund
1971.96

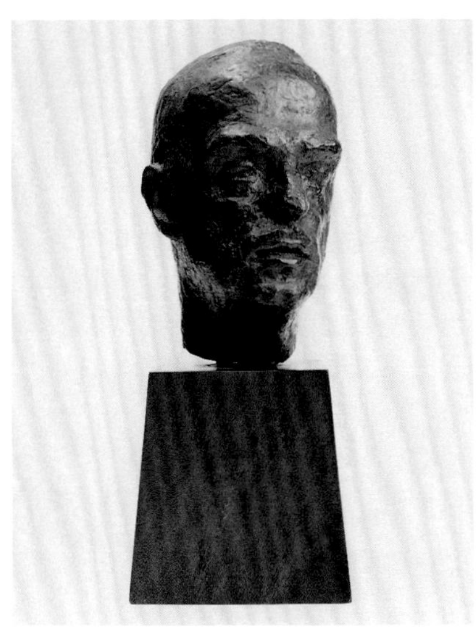

226

ISAMU NOGUCHI

1904 Los Angeles –
1988 New York City

226 *Thornton Niven Wilder* 1897–1975
B.A. 1920, LITT.D. 1947

After an original of 1932
Bronze, black patina
13 x 11 x 8¼ (33 x 27.9 x 21)

Signed proper right underside: ISAMU

Gift of Thornton Wilder, B.A. 1920, LITT.D. 1947, to the Collection of American Literature, Beinecke Rare Book and Manuscript Library
1980.165

227 *Metamorphosis*

1946
Marble
69 x 17 x 15 (175.3 x 43.2 x 38.1)

Henry J. Heinz II, B.A. 1931, Fund
1968.48

228 *The Garden*

1963
Marble
114 x 833½ x 520½
(289.6 x 2117.1 x 1322.1)

Gift of Edwin J. Beinecke, B.A. 1907, Frederick W. Beinecke, PH.B. 1909, and Walter Beinecke, B.A. 1910, to the Yale University Library

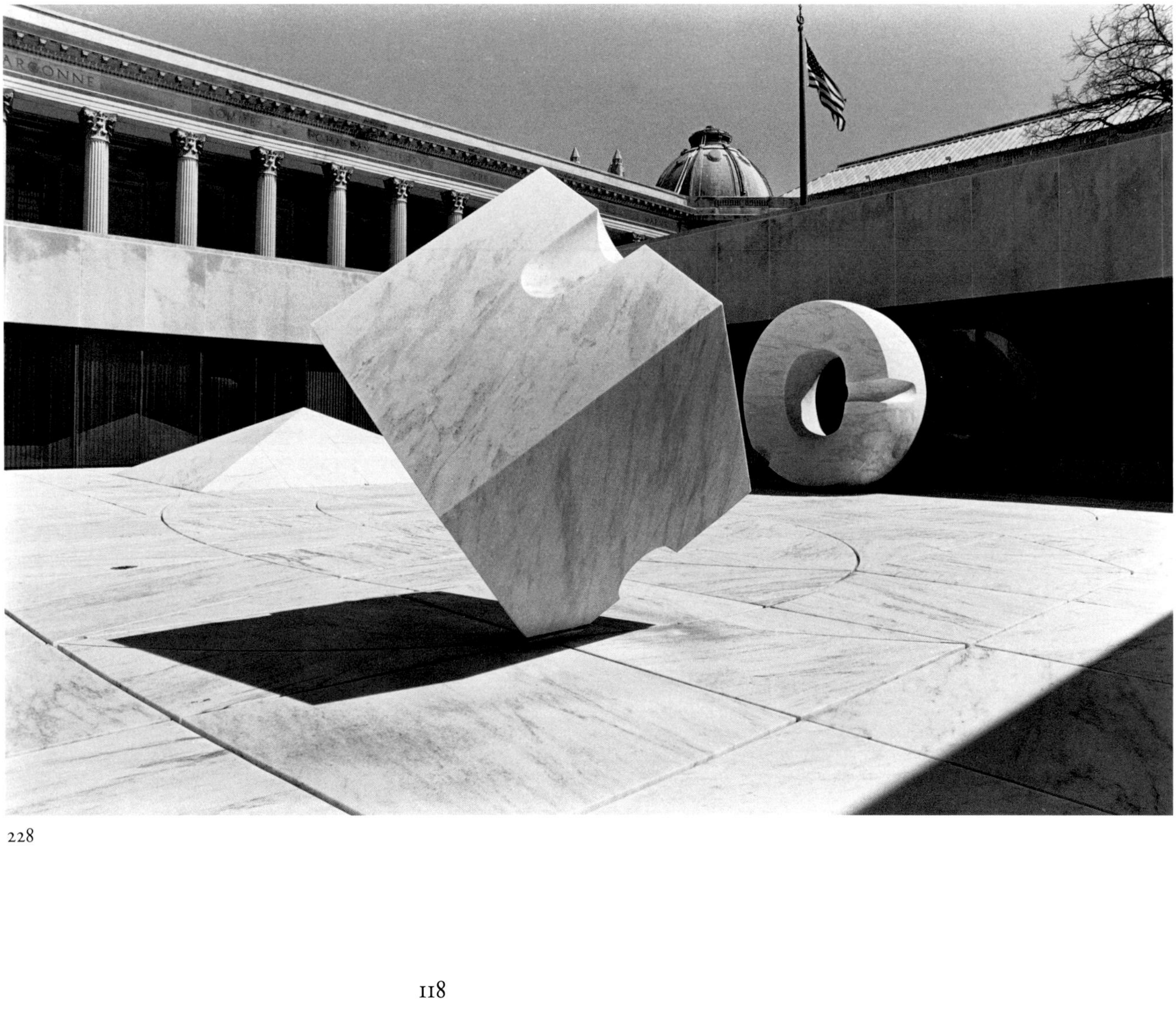

228

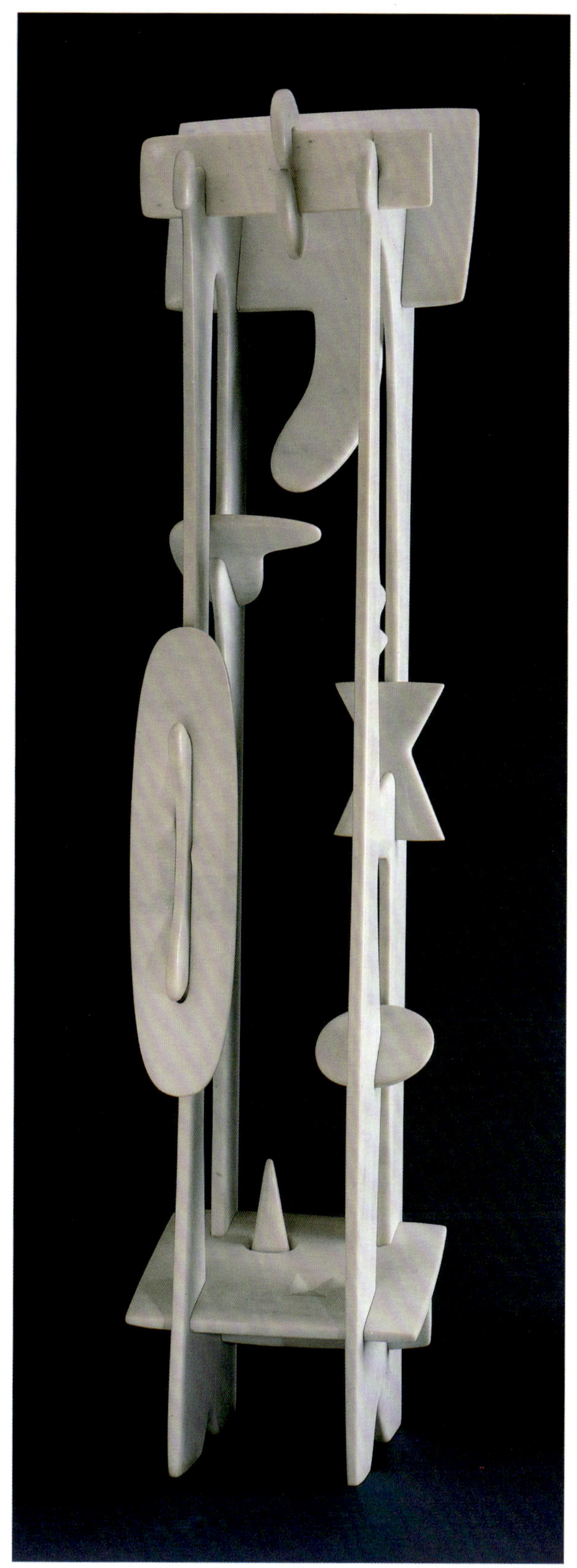

227

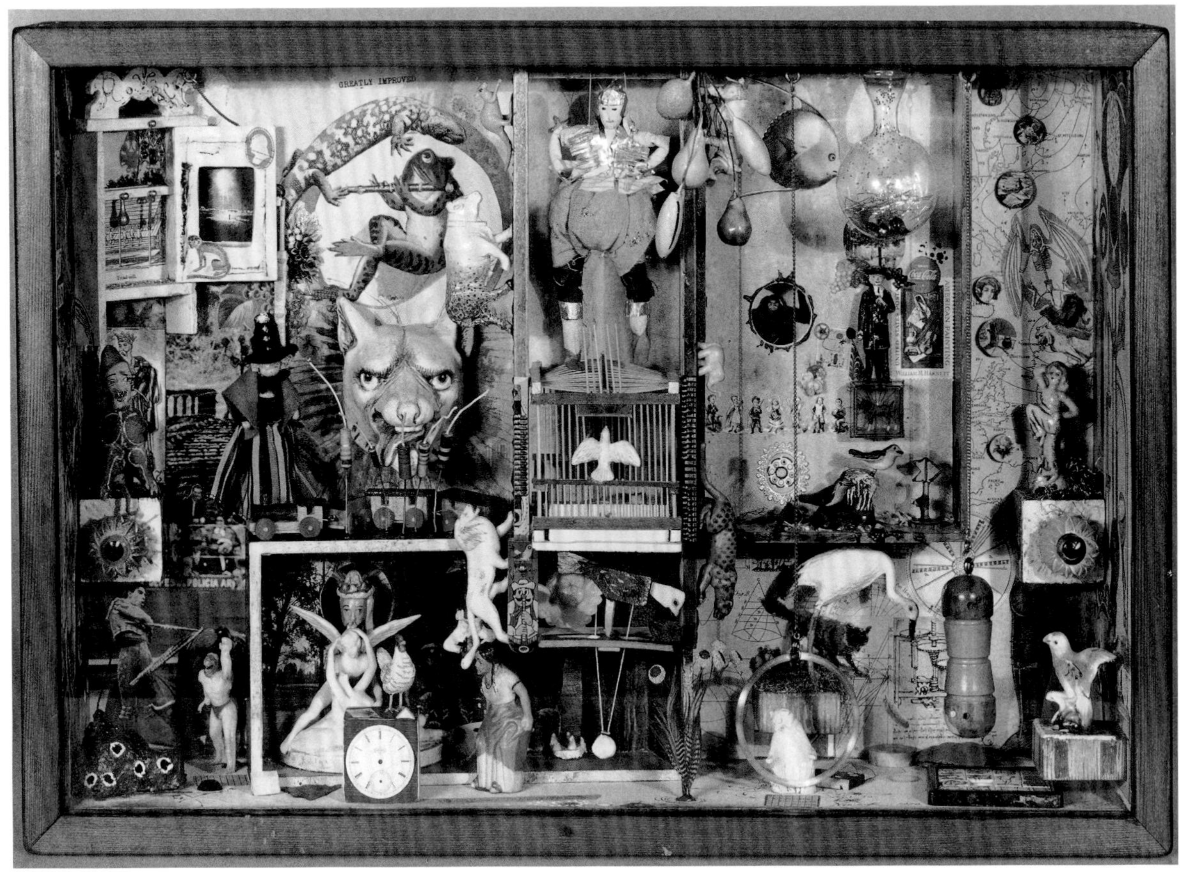

229

WAYNE KENYON NOWACK

b. 1923 Des Moines, Iowa

229 *Revolt in the Menagerie*

1970
Mixed media
15 x 22 x 5¾ (38.1 x 55.9 x 14.6)

Signed and dated in ink at bottom right front: Nowack 1970

Inscribed in paint upper rear left: REVOLT IN THE MENAGERIE / Wayne Nowack / April 29th 1970 / Des Moines, Iowa; upper rear: DO NOT USE PICTURE WIRE FOR HANGING. THIS CAUSES / CHAINS TO HANG OFF PLUMB HANG THE BOX DIRECTLY / FROM SCREW EYES TO WALL HOOKS. CHECK FOR LEVEL.; left and right: ← SCREW EYE / SCREW EYE → ; left center: NOTICE: BLUE RING / SHOULD HANG IN FRONT / OF THE WHITE BEAR.; lower rear: ↓ LEAVE THESE SCREW EYES IN PLACE / THEY WILL KEEP BOX VERTICAL / WITH WALL . . . ↓

Purchased with the aid of funds from the National Endowment for the Arts and the J. Frederic Byers III, B.S. 1962, and the Thomas B. Hess, B.A. 1942, Matching Funds
1975.51

WILLIAM RUDOLPH O'DONOVAN

1844 Preston County, Virginia – 1920 New York City

230 *Bayard Taylor* 1825–1878

c.1870
Bronze, golden bronze patina
18½ x 18½ x 1½ (47 x 47 x 3.8)

Signed lower right front:
V / O'DONOVAN

Inscribed upper left front in relief: three-leaf clover followed by OD (monogram); right: BAYARD TAYLOR

Collection of German Literature, Beinecke Rare Book and Manuscript Library
1980.241

231 *Edwin Austin Abbey* 1852–1911
M.A.(hon.) 1897

About 1877
Plaster
15 x 14¾ x 2¼ (38.1 x 37.5 x 5.7)

Inscribed lower right front:
OD (monogram); upper left:
Ÿ / Ty / le · M / anne.

Edwin Austin Abbey Memorial Collection

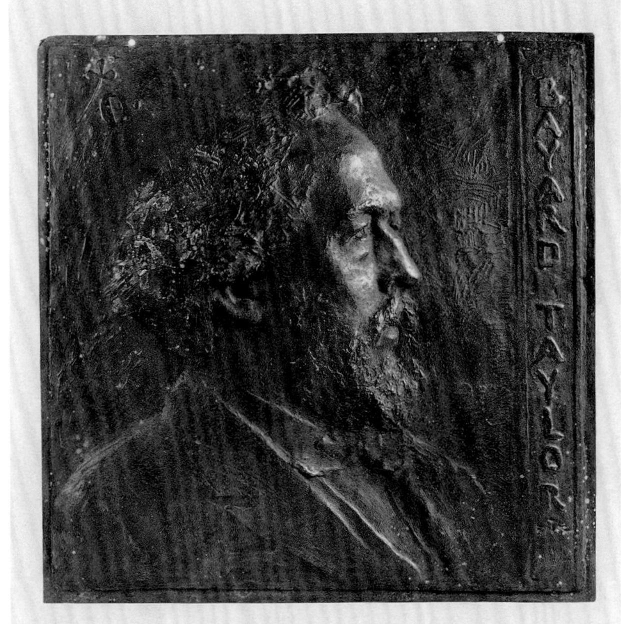

230

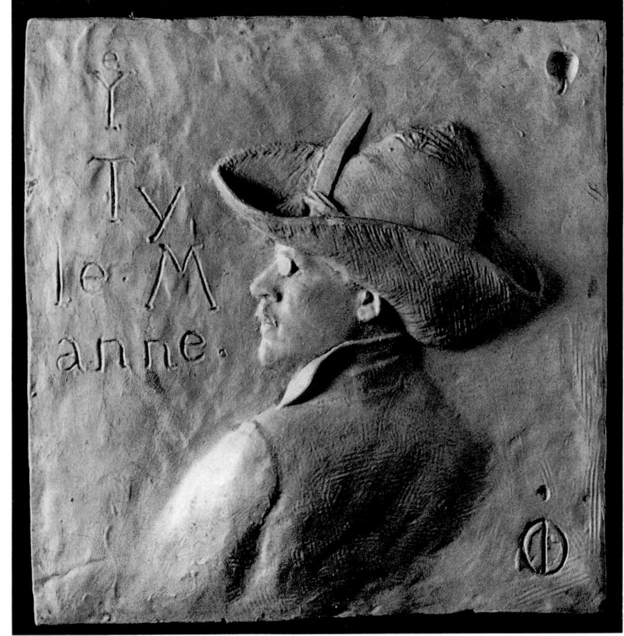

231

RICHARD EMMETT O'HANLON

b. 1906 Long Beach, California

232 *Young Hawk*

Before 1958
Quartzite
7 x 3½ x 5½ (17.8 x 8.9 x 14)

Signed on underside: O H (monogram)

Gift of Miss Caroline Hunter
1958.30

CLAES THURE OLDENBURG

b. 1929 Stockholm, Sweden
To U.S. 1936, citizen 1952
B.A. 1950

233 *Lipstick (Ascending) on Caterpillar Tracks*

1969, reworked 1974
Painted steel body, aluminum tube and fiber glass tip
264 x 234 x 131 (670.6 x 594.4 x 332.7)

Metal fabricator: Lippincott, Inc., North Haven, Connecticut

Gift of the Colossal Keepsake Corporation
1974.86

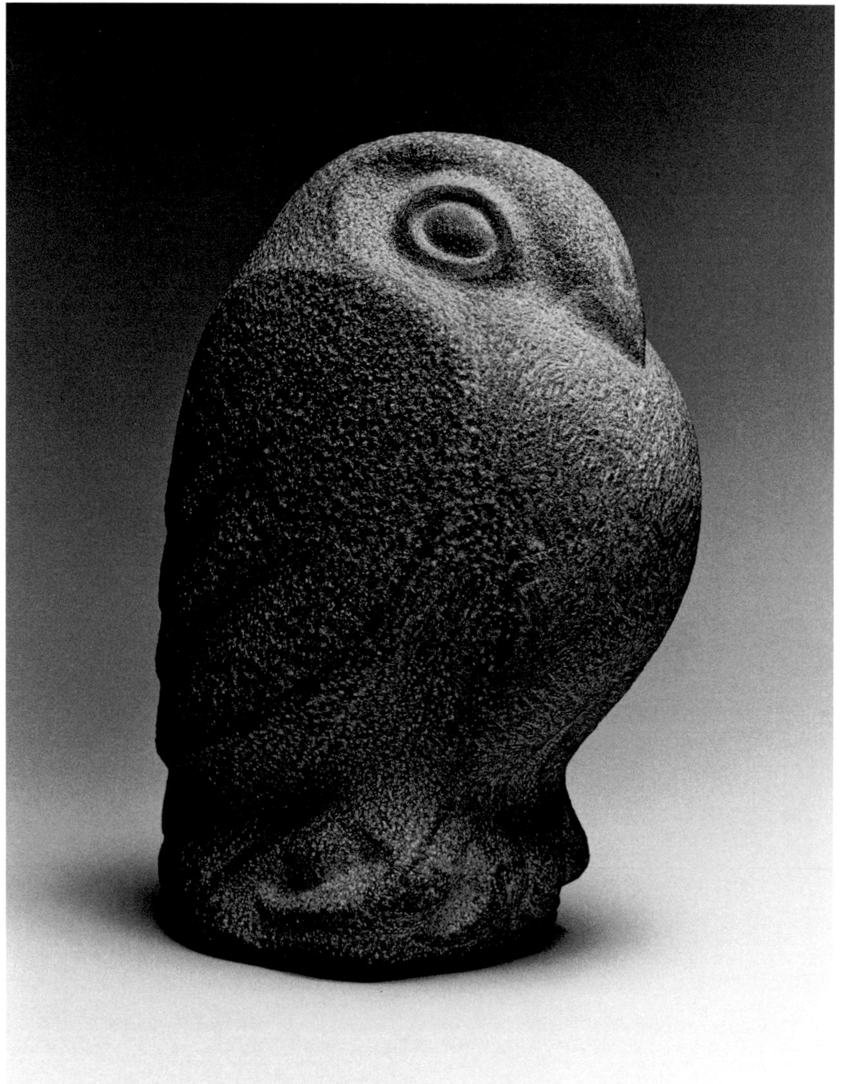

232

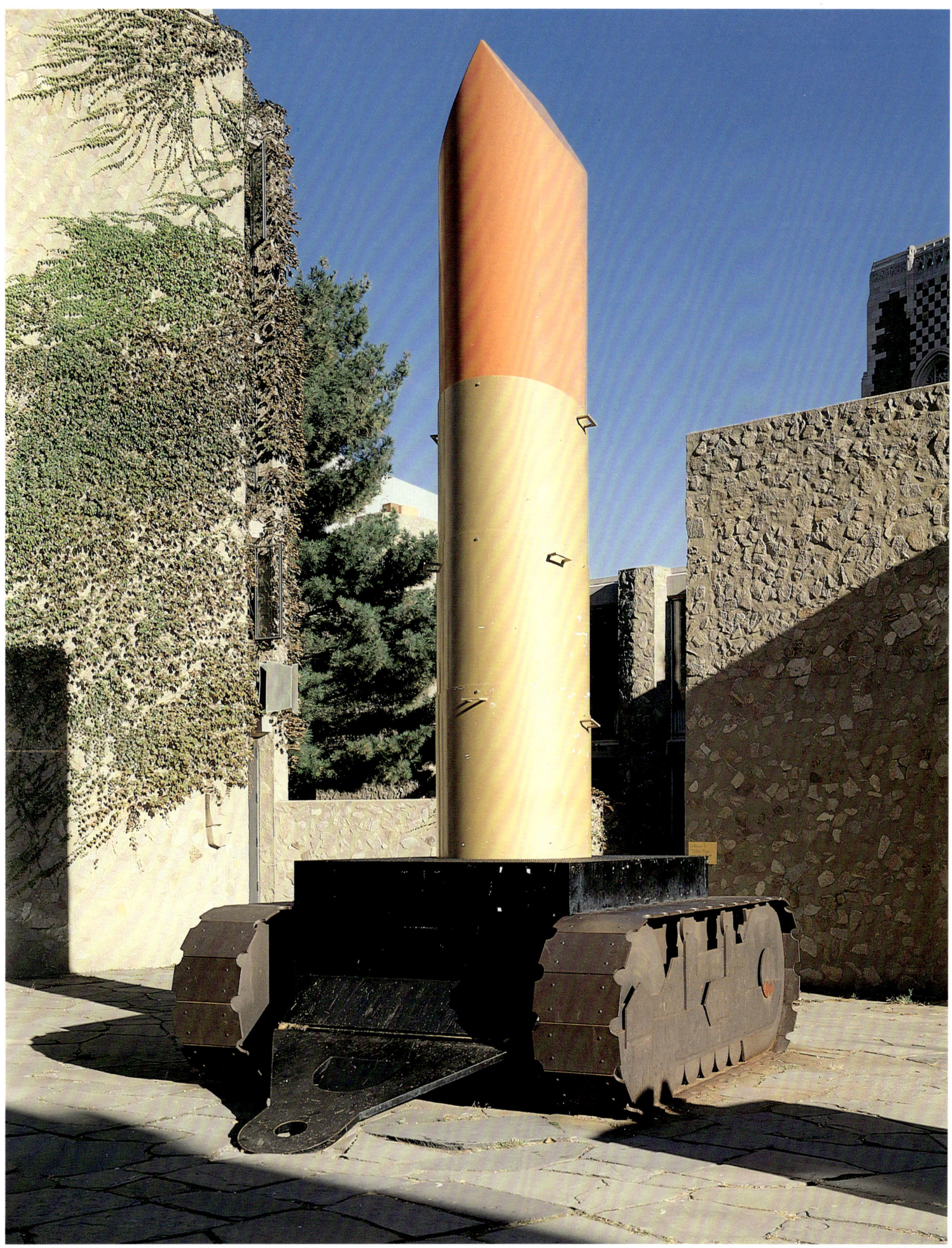

JOSÉ BENITO ORTEGA

See cat. 424

WILLARD DRYDEN PADDOCK

1873 Brooklyn, New York –
1956 Brooklyn, New York

234 *Roger Sherman* 1721–1793
M.A.(hon.) 1768

1937
Painted plaster
20 x 16¼ x 10½ (50.8 x 41.3 x 26.7)

Signed and dated proper left side:
Willard Paddock / 1937

Inscribed proper left side beneath signature: Study / John T mbull / for R SHERMAN.

Yale University Library, gift of Mr. Carl F. Tiedemann, B.S. 1929, and Mrs. Tiedemann
1959.1

ERASTUS DOW PALMER

1817 Pompey, New York –
1904 Albany, New York

235 *Edward Claudius Herrick*
1811–1862
M.A.(hon.) 1838

1865
Marble
21¼ x 16¾ x 3½ (54 x 42.5 x 8.9)

Wood frame with velvet matting
29½ x 26 x 3 (74.9 x 66 x 7.6)

Signed lower left front:
E.D. PALMER

Dated verso, center: 1865

Gift of friends of the sitter to the Yale University Library
1867.8

WILLIAM ORDWAY PARTRIDGE

1861 Paris – 1930 New York City

236 *Robert Burns* 1759–1796

1899
Bronze, golden brown patina
21 x 14 x 8¾ (53.3 x 35.6 x 22.2)

Signed and dated proper left side:
Partridge / 1899

Inscribed center front of base in relief:
BURNS

Foundry: The Gorham Manufacturing Company, Providence, Rhode Island; mark, top of proper right shoulder:
GORHAM MFG · CO · FOUNDERS

Gift of Dr. James C. Greenway, B.A. 1900, M.A.(hon.) 1916, to the Yale University Library, 1931

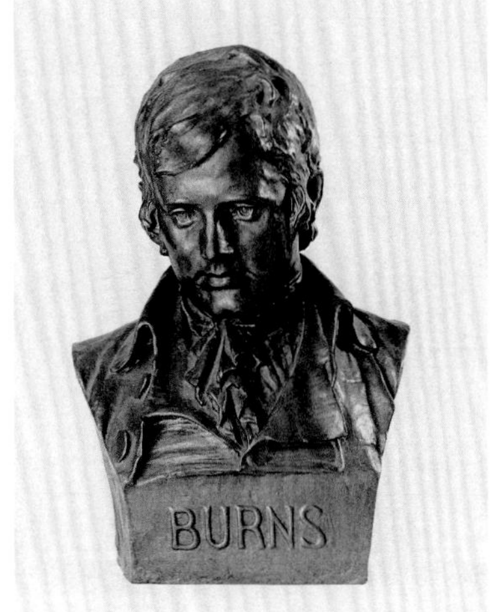

236

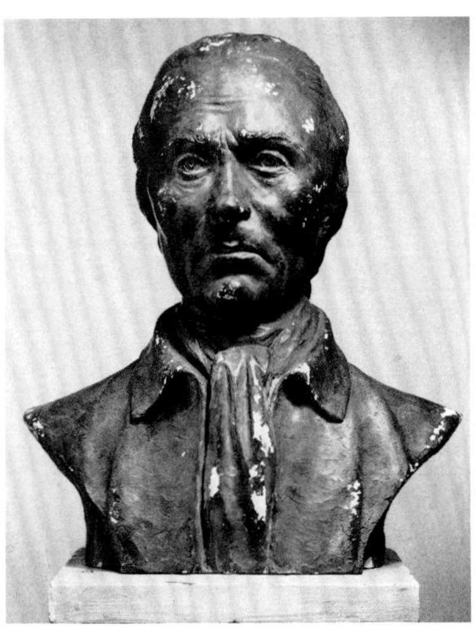

234

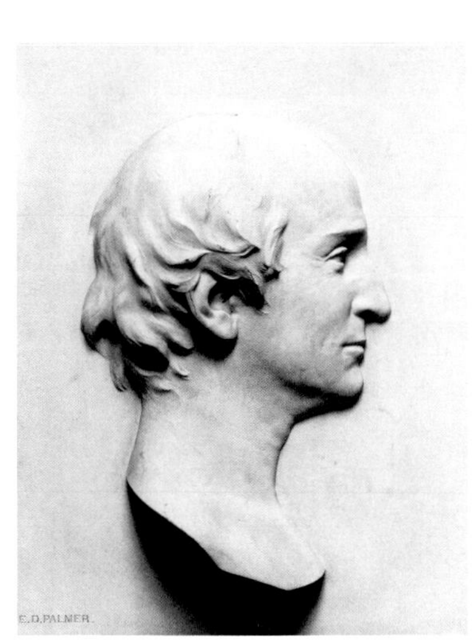

235

237 *Alfred, Lord Tennyson* 1809–1892

Cast about 1901, after original of 1899
Bronze, dark brown patina
21 x 12½ x 11 (53.3 x 31.8 x 27.9)

Signed and dated rear of base: Wm Ordway Partridge / Copyright 1899; affixed plaque at lower proper left center: WM. ORDWAY PARTRIDGE. SC. / COPYRIGHTED 1901.

Inscribed center front of base in relief: TENNYSON

Foundry: Roman Bronze Works, New York; mark, within a circle at proper left rear of base: ROMAN BRONZE WORKS / N.Y.

Yale University Library

238 *Dr. Silas Weir Mitchell* 1829–1914

1914
Bronze, dark brown patina
24 x 22¼ x 16 (61 x 56.5 x 40.6)

Signed and dated proper left side of base: *Ordway Partridge / 1914*

Foundry: Roman Bronze Works, New York; mark, lower center rear: ROMAN BRONZE WORKS N–Y–

Gift of Mrs. Mitchell Macdonough to the Mitchell Collection, Yale University School of Medicine
1967.87

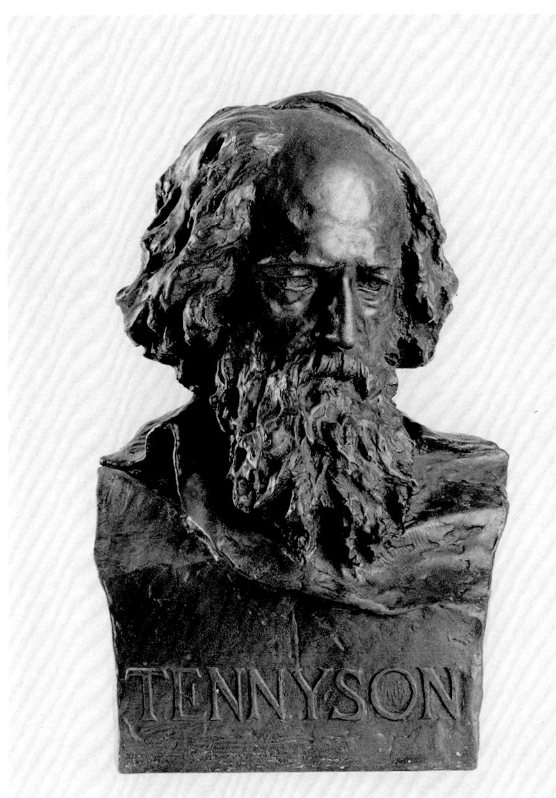

237

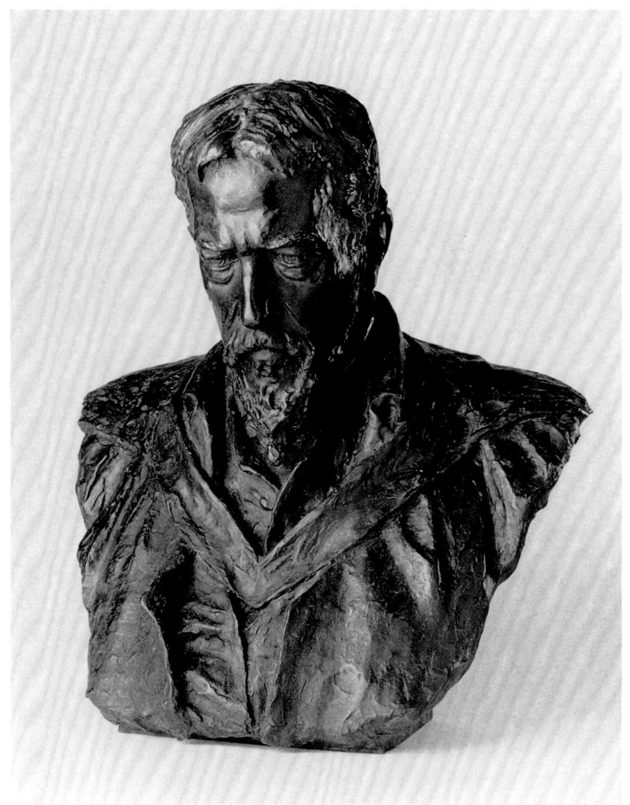

238

JOHN PAULDING

1883 Dark County, Ohio –
1935 Chicago

239 *Benjamin Franklin* 1706–1790
M.A.(hon.) 1753

Probably early 20th century
Bronze, greenish-brown patina
Bookends, each: 5¾ x 5½ x 3¾
(14.6 x 14 x 9.5)

Signed proper left side at bottom:
John Paulding / Sculptor

Inscribed center front at bottom:
Benj. Franklin / 1706–1790

Benjamin Franklin Collection, Yale University Library

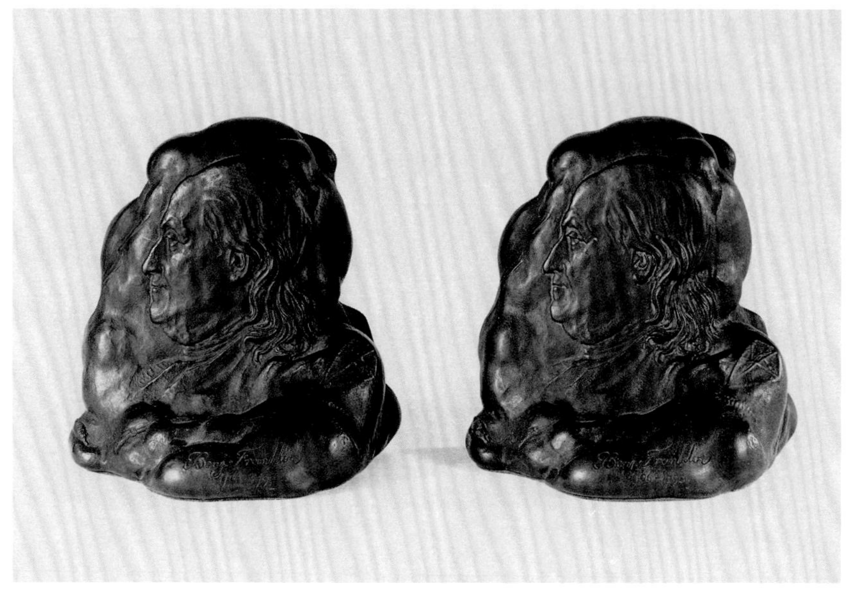

239

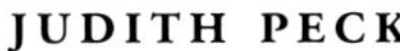

JUDITH PECK

b. 1930 New York City

240 *Race*

1964
Walnut
31 x 21½ x 21½ (78.7 x 54.6 x 54.6)

Signed and dated upper proper left front on shoulder: JSP '64

Gift of Harvey M. Peck, M.D. 1953, to the Yale University School of Medicine
1969.90

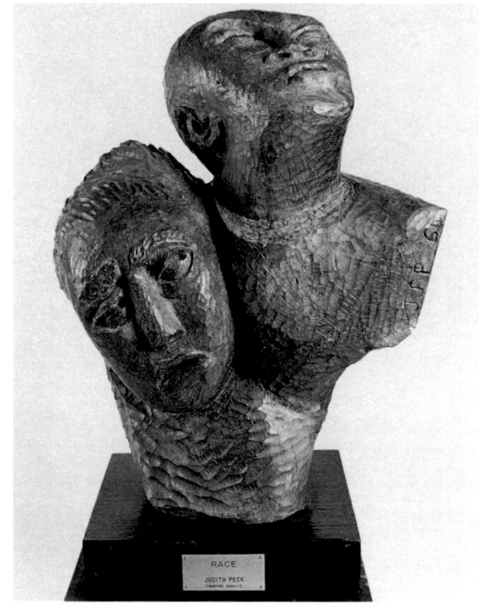

240

VALERIE THORPE PEED

b. 1950
M.A.DIV. 1978

241 *Roland Herbert Bainton* 1894–1984
B.D. 1917, PH.D. 1921

1978
Bronze, greenish-brown patina
15½ x 11¾ x 10¼ (39.4 x 29.8 x 26)

Signed and dated lower center rear:
V. PEED 1978

Foundry: Tallix, Beacon, New York; mark, beneath proper right shoulder:
木

Gift of the artist to the Yale Divinity School

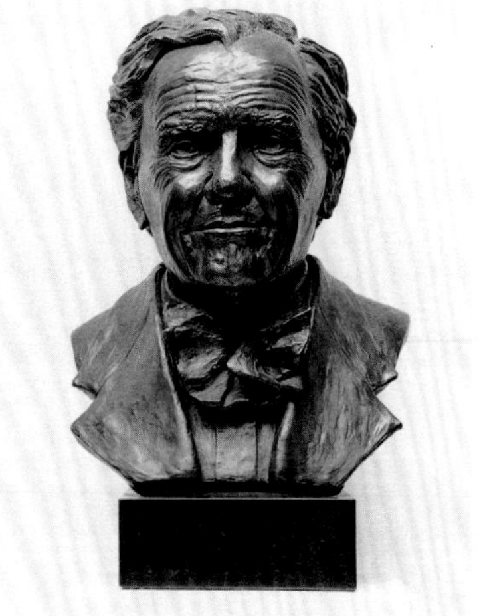

241

JAMES TANK PORTER

1883 Tientsin, China – 1962

242 *Chester Smith Lyman* 1814–1890
B.A. 1837, Yale Divinity School, 1842

1922
Marble
18½ x 19½ x 11½ (47 x 49.5 x 29.2)

Signed and dated lower proper left rear: *James Tank Porter / 1922*

Gift of Chester W. Lyman, B.A. 1882, M.A. 1895
1925.149

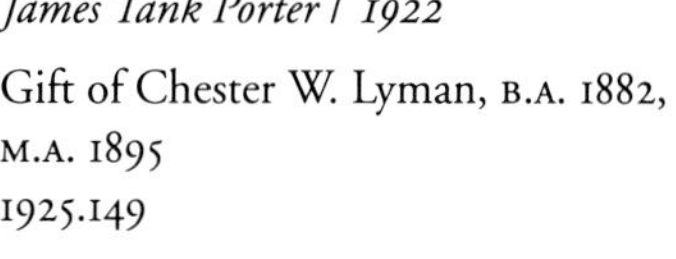

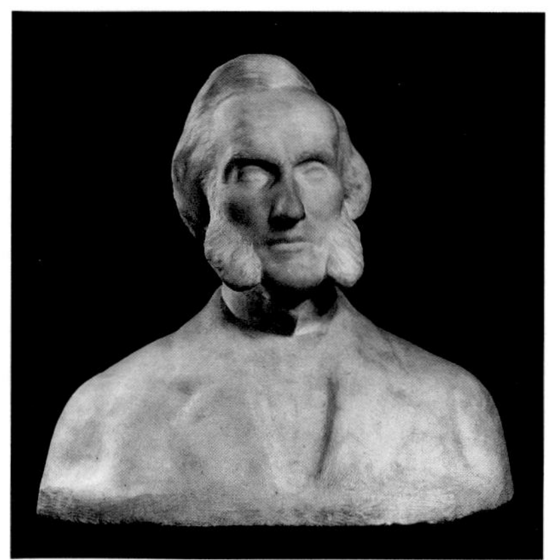

242

ALEXANDER PORTNOFF

1887 Russia – 1949 Philadelphia
Active U.S. after 1908

243 *William Smith Mason* 1866–1961
PH.B. 1888, M.A.(hon.) 1924

c.1925
Bronze, yellow-brown patina
19¼ x 8½ x 9½ (48.9 x 21.6 x 24.1)

Signed lower rear: *A. Portnoff*

Foundry: Roman Bronze Works, New York; mark, rear edge of base: ROMAN BRONZE WORKS N–Y–

Gift of the sitter to the Benjamin Franklin Collection, Yale University Library

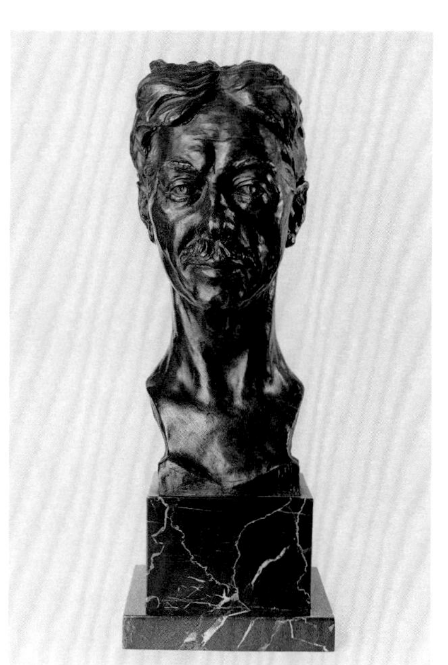

243

HIRAM POWERS

1805 Woodstock, Vermont – 1873 Florence, Italy

244 *Benjamin Franklin,* after Jean Antoine Houdon, see cats. 133–36
1706–1790
M.A.(hon.) 1753

1848–49
Marble
20¾ x 17 x 13¾ (52.7 x 43.2 x 34.9)

Signed center rear: H. POWERS. *Sculp.*

Gift of Mrs. Alfred P. Rockwell and Lawrence Godkin to the Yale University Library
1900.18

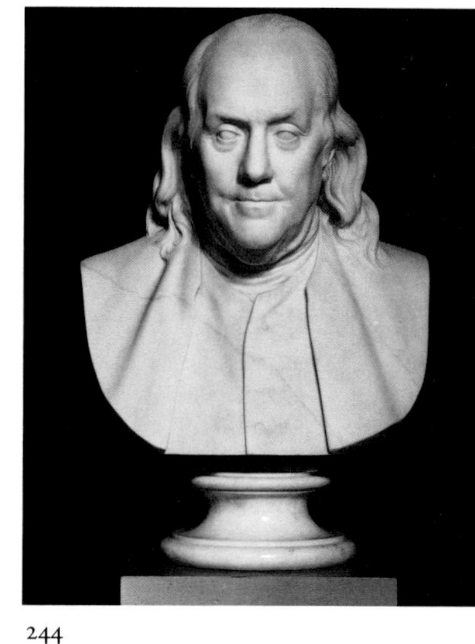

244

245 *John Caldwell Calhoun* 1782–1850
B.A. 1804, LL.D. 1822

1835
Plaster
24 x 18¾ x 13¼ (61 x 47.6 x 33.7)

Inscribed in ink on proper right front on shoulder: *John C. Calhoun*

Given by the fellows and associate fellows in memory of Stanley Thomas Williams, B.A. 1911, M.A. 1914, PH.D. 1915, to Calhoun College
1956.51

246 *William Cranch* 1769–1855

After an original of 1837
Plaster
22¼ x 12½ x 9¾ (56.5 x 31.8 x 24.8)

Signed and dated upper center rear: *Hiram Powers, / Sculp. / 1837*

Gift of J. Henry Korson, M.A. 1942, PH.D. 1947
1981.45

247 *The Greek Slave*

1851, after an original of 1844
Marble
65¼ x 21 x 18¼ (165.7 x 53.7 x 46.4)

Marble base
H. 25 x DIAM. 34 (63.5 x 86.4)

Signed lower proper right rear edge: HIRAM POWERS. / *Sculp.*

Olive Louise Dann Fund
1962.43

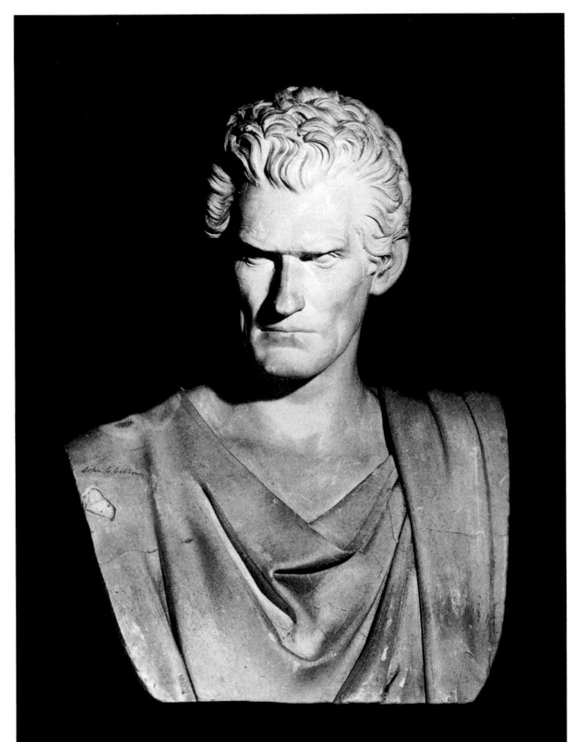

245

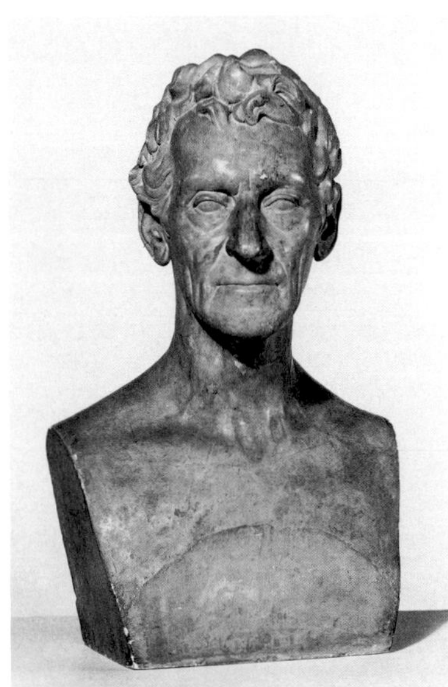

246

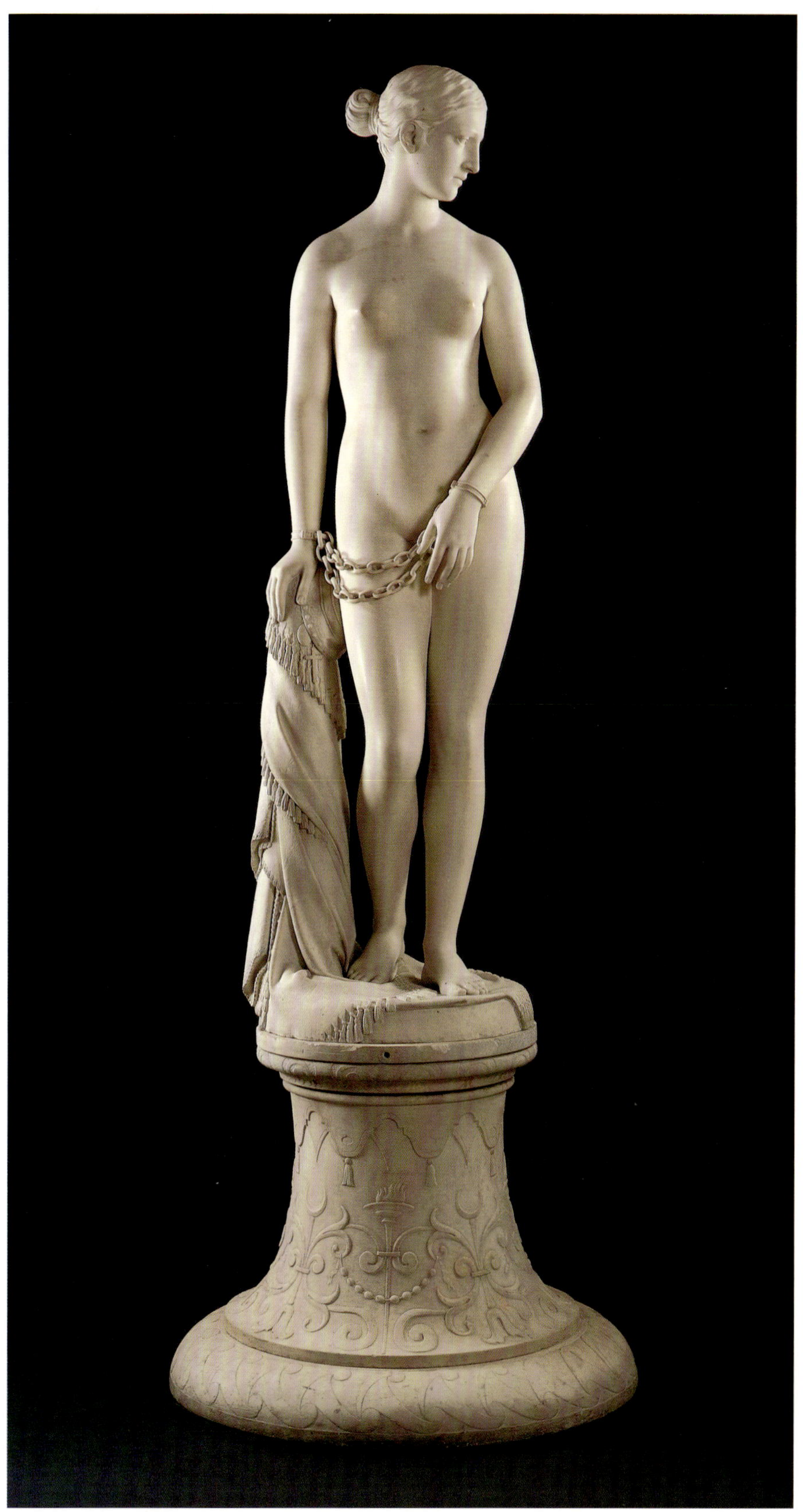

BELA LYON PRATT

1867 Norwich, Connecticut –
1917 Boston
B.F.A. 1899

248 *Nathan Hale* 1755–1776
B.A. 1773, M.A. 1776

Probably 1912
Bronzed plaster
36 x 9¼ x 9¼ (91.4 x 23.5 x 23.5)

Inscribed in paint on front of base: NATHAN HALE / by BELA L. PRATT

Bequest of George Dudley Seymour, M.A.(hon.) 1913
1945.53

249 *Nathan Hale* 1755–1776
B.A. 1773, M.A. 1776

1913
Bronze, dark brown patina
78¼ x 23½ x 23 (198.8 x 59.7 x 58.4)

Granite pedestal
36 x 27½ x 27½ (91.4 x 69.9 x 69.9)

Signed and dated proper left top of bronze base: B L Pratt / 1913

Inscribed around edge of bronze base: I ONLY REGRET THAT I HAVE BUT ONE LIFE TO LOSE FOR MY COUNTRY ✠; front of granite pedestal: NATHAN HALE / 1755–1776 / CLASS OF 1773; rear: A GIFT TO YALE COLLEGE / BY GRADUATES AND FRIENDS / ANNO DOMINI MCMXIV

Foundry: Roman Bronze Works, New York; mark, rear edge of bronze base: ROMAN BRONZE WORKS N–Y–

A gift to Yale College by graduates and friends
1914.21

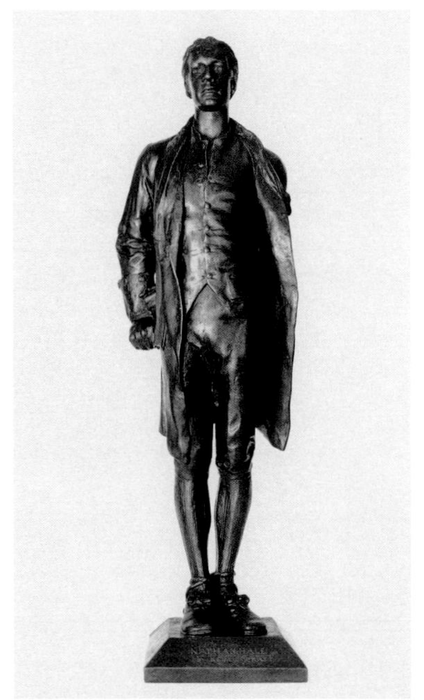
248

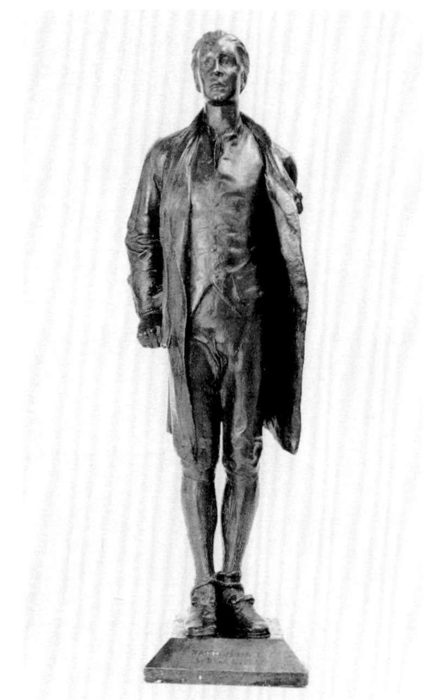
250

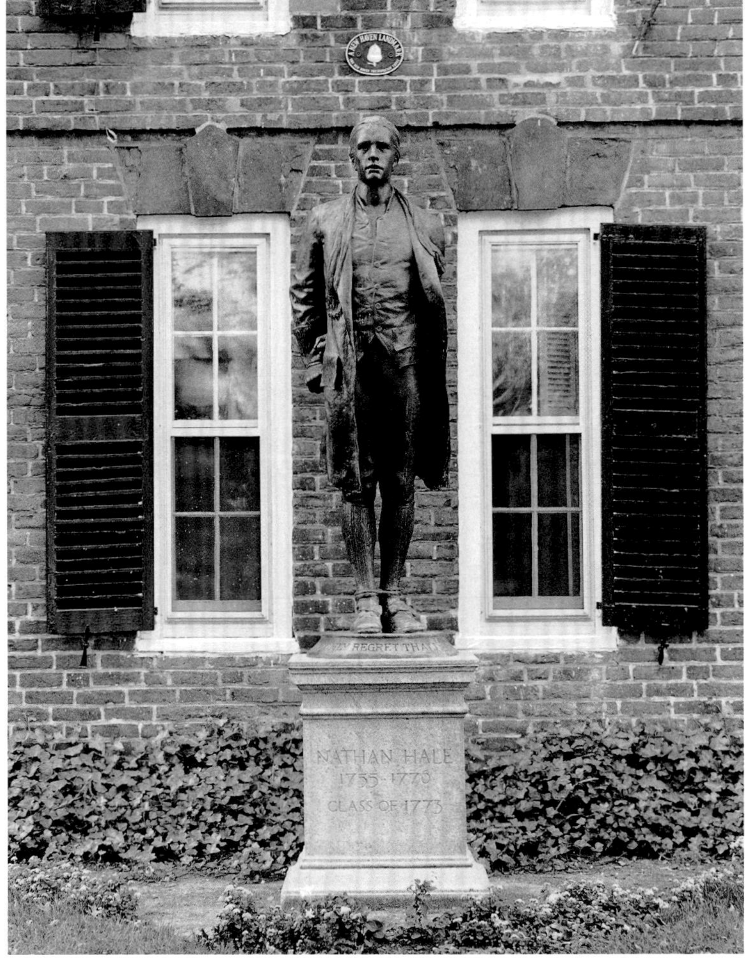

249

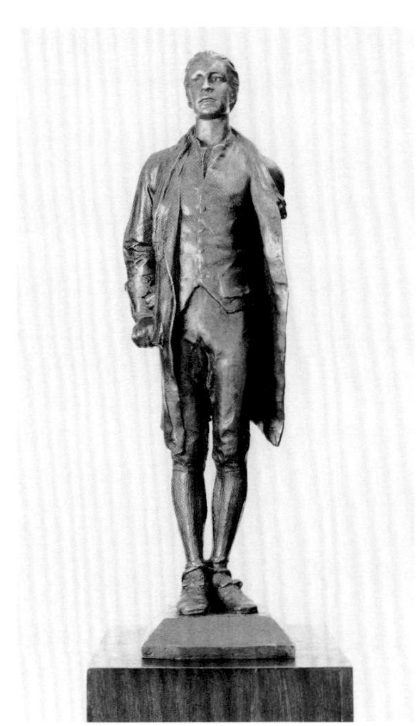
251

250 *Nathan Hale* 1755–1776
B.A. 1773, M.A. 1776

c.1913
Bronze, reddish-brown patina
35¼ x 10¾ x 9¼ (89.5 x 27.3 x 23.5)

Signed and inscribed front edge of base in relief: NATHAN HALE / by BELA L. PRATT

Foundry: Roman Bronze Works, New York; mark, rear edge of base: ROMAN BRONZE WORKS N.Y.

Bequest of George Dudley Seymour, M.A.(hon.) 1913, in memory of Theodore Thornton Munger, B.A. 1851, M.DIV. 1855, D.D. 1908
1945.54

251 *Nathan Hale* 1755–1776
B.A. 1773, M.A. 1776

c.1913
Bronze, dark reddish-brown, green and exposed bronze patina
34 x 9¾ x 8¾ (87.6 x 24.8 x 22.2)

Signed and inscribed front edge of base in relief: NATHAN HALE / by BELA L PRATT; rear edge of base: BL[?]

Yale Club of New York

EDMOND THOMAS QUINN

1868 Philadelphia – 1929

252 *Two Figures,* after *Brother and Sister* by Auguste Rodin
French, 1840–1917

About 1900–1920
Plaster, painted in simulation of terra cotta
15½ x 7 x 9 (39.4 x 17.8 x 22.9)

Gift of Mrs. Edmond Quinn
1932.52

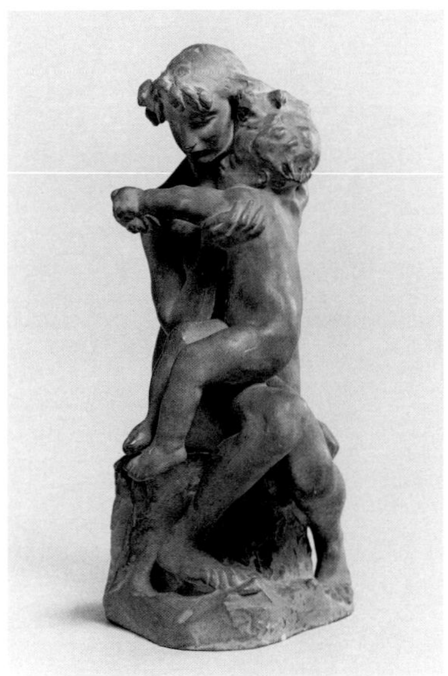
252

253

253 *Eugene Gladstone O'Neill*
1888–1953
LITT.D. 1926

c.1920
Painted plaster
13½ x 9½ x 8 (34.3 x 24.1 x 20.3)

Signed lower rear beneath neck: QVINN. Sc

Gift of Emily Quinn Stevens to the Collection of American Literature, Beinecke Rare Book and Manuscript Library
1980.486

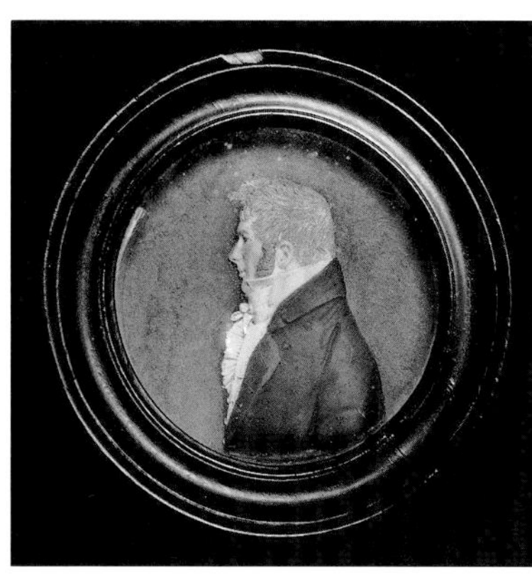

254

JOHANN CHRISTIAN RAUSCHNER

1760 Frankfurt, Germany –
after 1812, possibly Boston
Active U.S. about 1799–1812

254 *Thomas W. Brewer of Roxbury, Massachusetts* possibly 1766–1812

Probably 1809–10
Colored wax and cloth mounted on wood
DIAM. 4 (10.2) sight

Wood frame
DIAM. 5¼ x D. 1¼ (13.3 x 3.2)

John Hill Morgan, B.A. 1893, LL.B. 1896, Collection
1943.95

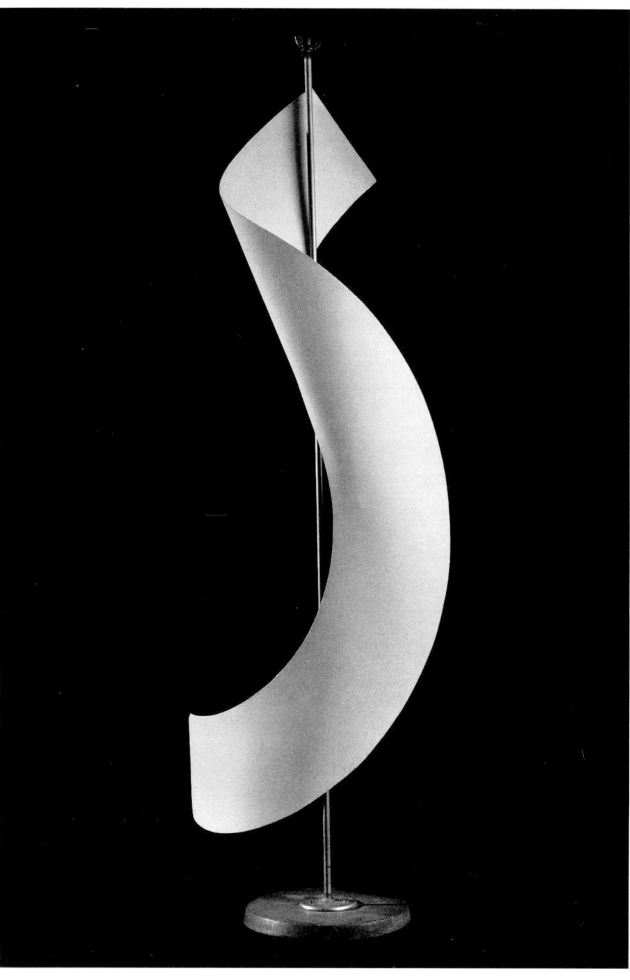

255

MAN RAY

1890 Philadelphia – 1976 Paris

255 *Lampshade*

1921
Painted tin, metal rod, wing bolt, square bolt, round metal flange, wood base
46½ x 18 x 9 (118.1 x 45.7 x 22.9)

Signed, dated, and inscribed in ink on top of base: LAMPSHADE / MAN RAY · N·Y· 1921

Gift of the estate of Katherine S. Dreier
1953.6.1

FREDERIC SACKRIDER REMINGTON

1861 Canton, New York –
1909 Ridgefield, Connecticut
B.F.A.(hon.) 1900

256 *The Wounded Bunkie*

1896
Bronze, dark reddish-brown and black patina
20¼ x 33¼ x 12¾ (51.4 x 84.5 x 32.4)

Signed, dated, and inscribed proper left top of base, front: Frederic Remington; rear: Copyrighted by / Frederic Remington 1896 / E

Foundry: The Henry-Bonnard Bronze Company, New York; mark, on proper right top of base, rear: CAST BY THE HENRY BONNARD BRONZE CO N.Y. 1896.

Gift of the artist
1900.3

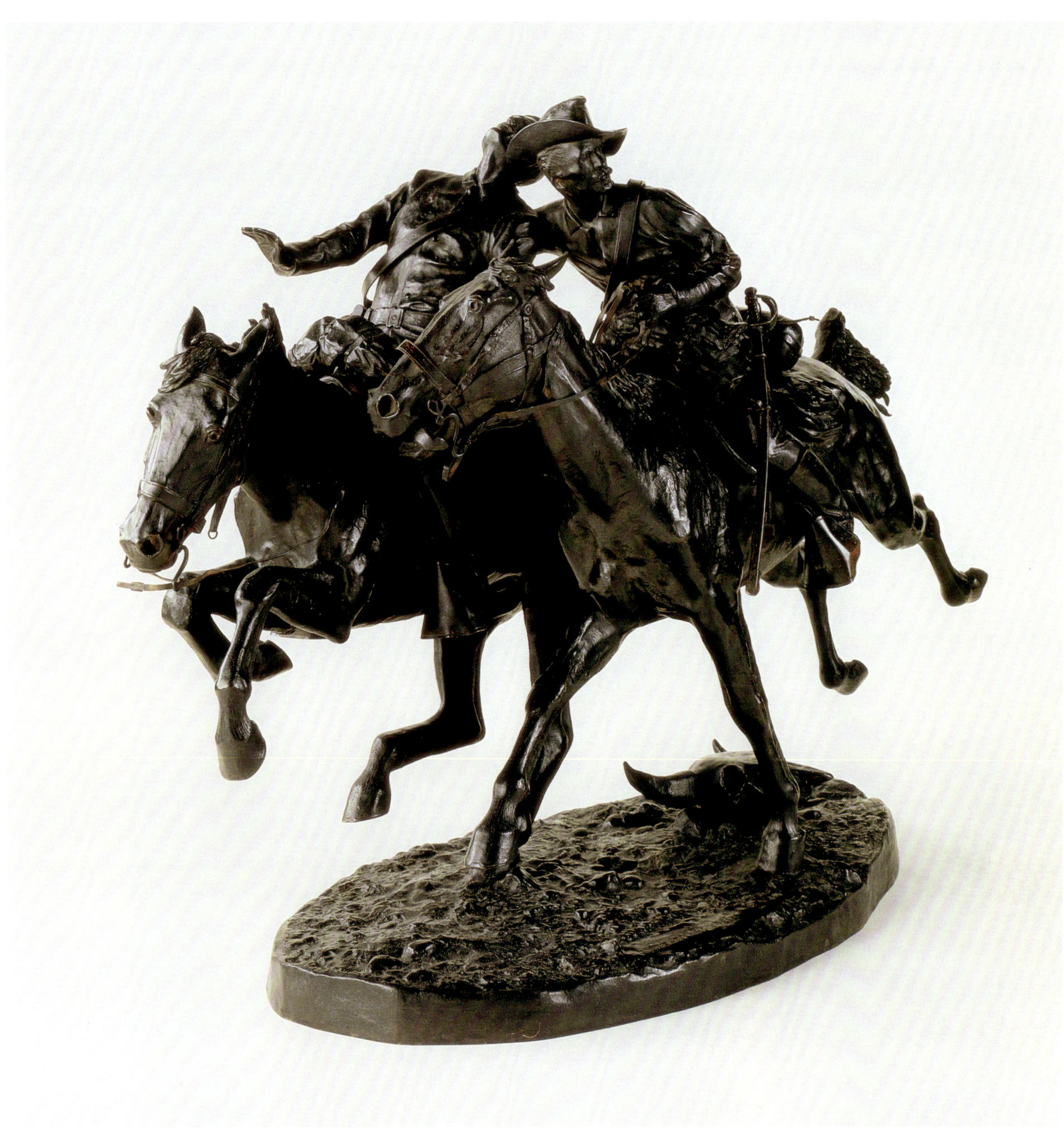

FRANCES L. RICH

b. 1910 Spokane, Washington

257 *Virgil Thompson* 1896–1989

1961
Bronze, green and black patina
11¼ x 7¾ x 9¼ (28.6 x 19.7 x 23.5)

Inscribed near edge at lower center rear: RICH

Foundry: Georges Rudier, Paris; mark, proper right side edge of base: . G . Rudier · Fondeur · Paris ·

Yale University School of Music Library

GEORGE WARREN RICKEY

b. 1907 South Bend, Indiana

258 *Two Planes Vertical – Horizontal II*

1969–70
Burnished stainless steel
152 x 124¼ x 5 vertical position (59 horizontal) (386.1 x 315.6 x 12.7 [149.9])

Gift of Mr. and Mrs. Richard Shields, B.A. 1929
1970.45

WILLIAM RIMMER

1816 Liverpool, England – 1879 South Milford, Massachusetts
To U.S. 1818 or 1826

259 *Dying Centaur*

Probably 1905, after original plaster of 1869
Painted plaster
22¼ x 27 x 24½ (56.5 x 68.6 x 62.2)

Signed proper right top of base: W Rimmer

John Hill Morgan, B.A. 1893, LL.B. 1896, Leonard C. Hanna, Jr., B.A. 1913, Stephen Carlton Clark, B.A. 1903, and Mabel Brady Garvan Funds
1968.38

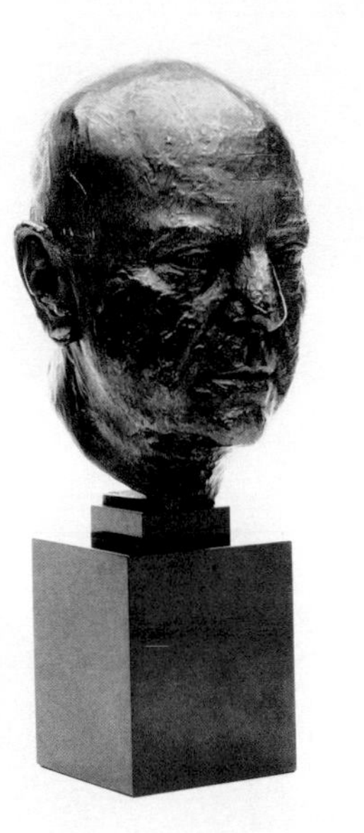

257

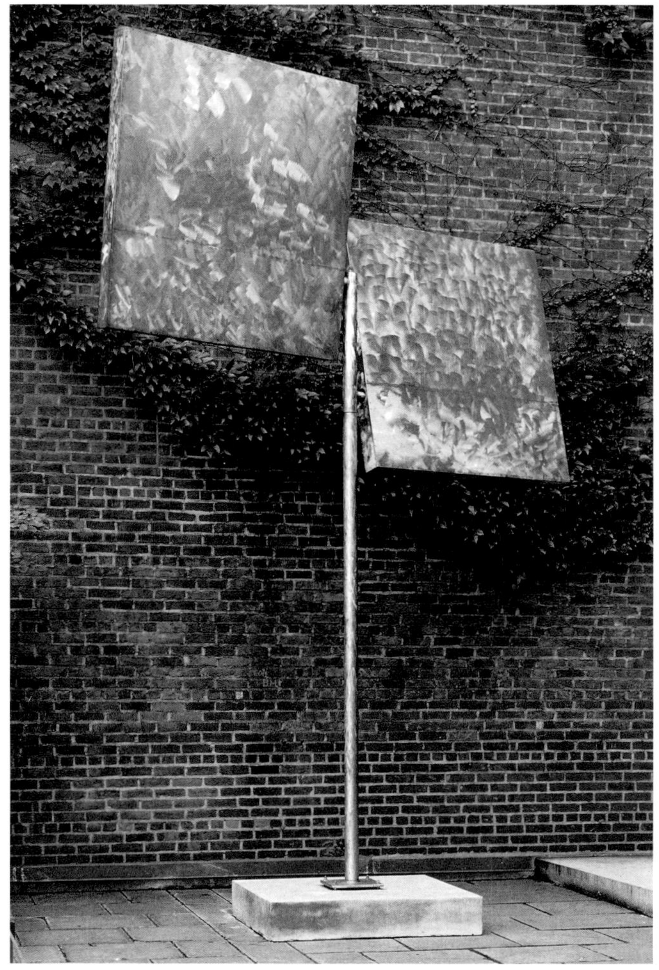

258

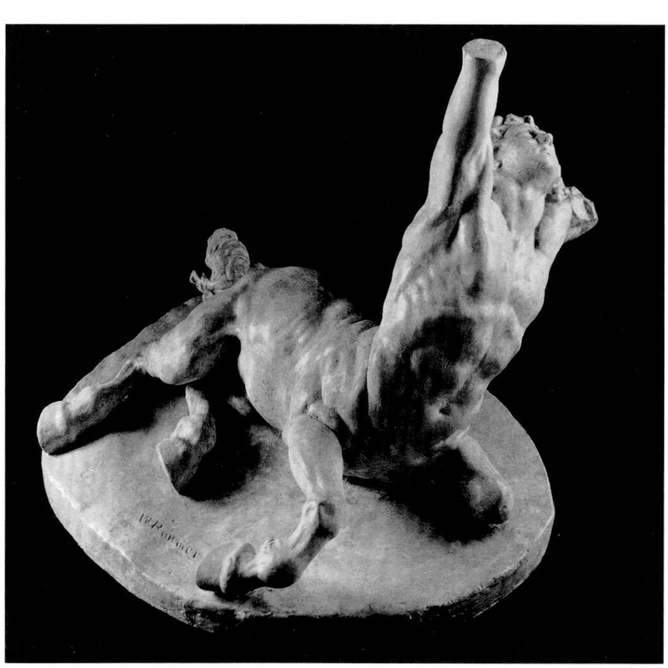

259

WILLIAM HENRY RINEHART

1825 Frederick, Maryland –
1874 near Rome, Italy

260 *Sleeping Children*

1869
Marble
15¾ x 37½ x 19 (40 x 95.3 x 48.3)

Signed, dated, and inscribed proper right side edge of base: W.m. H. RINEHART. SCVLP^{T} ROMA. 1869

Provenance unknown
1900.47

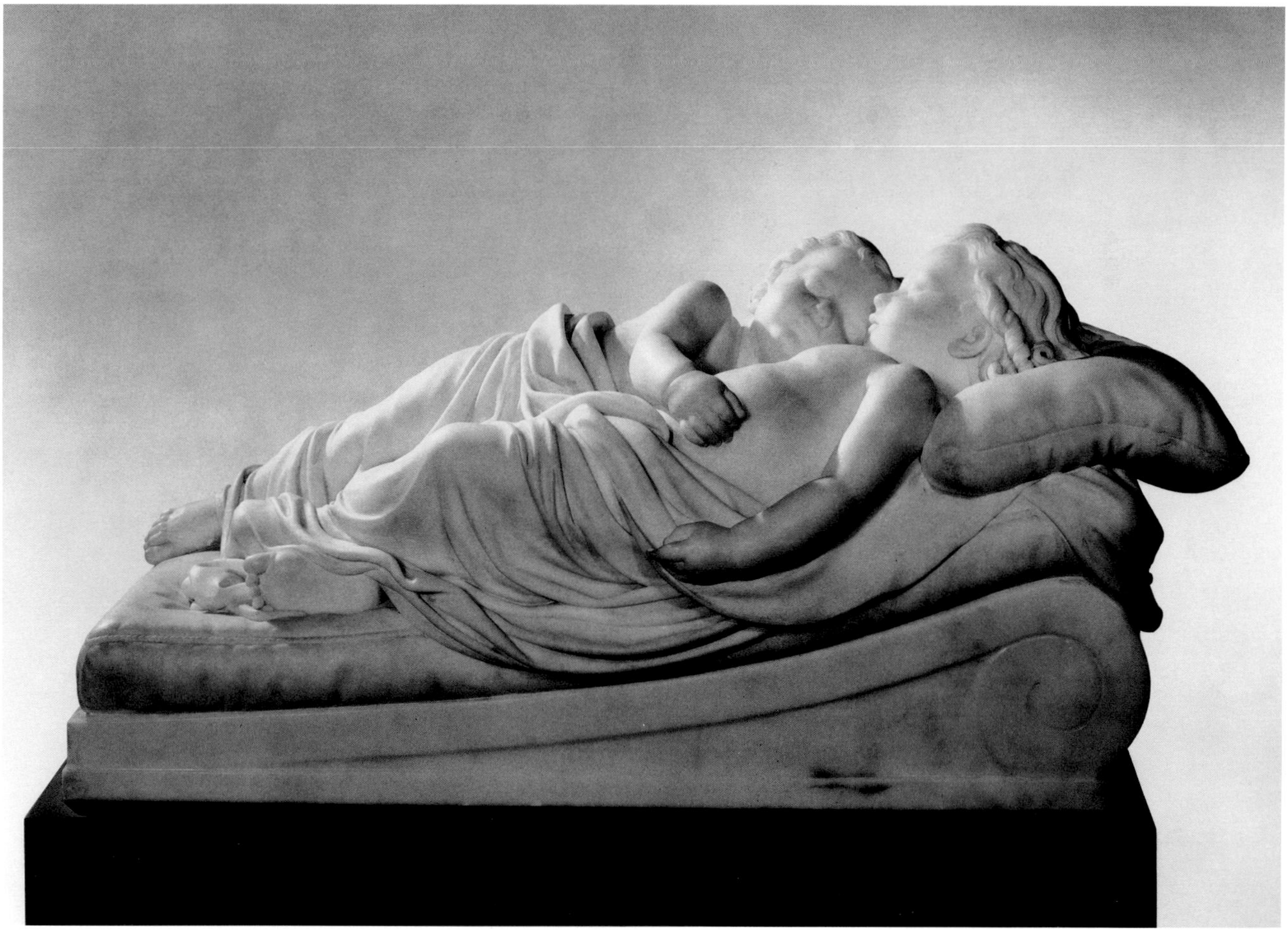

260

after
AUGUSTE RODIN

See Edmond Thomas Quinn, cat. 252

JOHN ROGERS

1829 Salem, Massachusetts –
1904 New Canaan, Connecticut

261 *The Picket Guard*

Patented April 1, 1862
Painted plaster
14½ x 10¼ x 8 (36.8 x 26 x 20.3)

Signed proper right top front of base: JOHN ROGERS / NEW YORK

Dated rear edge of base: PATENTED APRIL 1862

Inscribed front edge of base: THE PICKET GUARD

Mabel Brady Garvan Collection
1932.177

262 *The Town Pump*

Patented May 27, 1862
Painted plaster
13½ x 10½ x 7¾ (34.3 x 26.7 x 19.7)

Signed front of trough: JOHN ROGERS / NEW YORK

Inscribed front edge of base: THE TOWN PUMP

Mabel Brady Garvan Collection
1932.198

263 *Union Refugees*

Patented April 19, 1864
Painted plaster
22½ x 12¾ x 9 (57.2 x 32.4 x 22.9)

Signed proper right top front of base: JOHN ROGERS / NEW YORK

Dated rear edge of base: PATENTED APRIL 19 1864

Inscribed front edge of base: UNION REFUGEES

Mabel Brady Garvan Collection
1932.190

264 *Returned Volunteer – How the Fort Was Taken*

Patented May 17, 1864
Painted plaster
20 x 16 x 11½ (50.8 x 40.6 x 29.2)

Signed on anvil post, lower center front: JOHN ROGERS / NEW YORK

Inscribed front edge of base: RETURNED VOLUNTEER / HOW THE FORT WAS TAKEN

Mabel Brady Garvan Collection
1932.172

265 *The Wounded Scout – A Friend in the Swamp*

Patented June 28, 1864
Painted plaster
22¾ x 11 x 8¾ (57.8 x 27.9 x 22.2)

Dated rear edge of base: PATENTED JUNE 28 1864.

Inscribed front edge of base: THE WOUNDED SCOUT / A FRIEND IN THE SWAMP

Mabel Brady Garvan Collection
1932.157

266 *The Home Guard – Midnight on the Border*

Patented May 9, 1865
Painted plaster
23½ x 11 x 7¾ (59.7 x 27.9 x 19.7)

Signed proper left front top of base: JOHN ROGERS / NEW YORK

Dated rear edge of base: PATENTED MAY 9 1865

Inscribed front edge of base: THE HOME GUARD / MIDNIGHT ON THE BORDER

Mabel Brady Garvan Collection
1932.178

267 *Taking the Oath and Drawing Rations*

Patented January 30, 1866
Painted plaster
23 x 13 x 9 (58.4 x 33 x 22.9)

Signed top center front of base: JOHN ROGERS / NEW YORK

Dated rear edge of base: PATENTED / JAN 30 1866

Inscribed front edge of base: TAKING THE OATH / AND DRAWING RATIONS

Mabel Brady Garvan Collection
1932.171

268 *Uncle Ned's School*

Patented July 3, 1866
Painted plaster
20 x 14¼ x 9 (50.8 x 36.2 x 22.9)

Signed proper right front top of base: JOHN ROGE / NEW YORK

Dated on back of cupboard: PATENTED / JULY 3D / 1866.

Inscribed front edge of base: UNCLE NED'S SCHOOL

Mabel Brady Garvan Collection
1932.180

269 *The Charity Patient*

Patented December 4, 1866
Painted plaster
22¼ x 12 x 8¼ (56.5 x 30.5 x 21)

Signed front center top of base: JOHN ROGERS / NEW YORK

Dated on back of cabinet: PATENTED / DEC. 4 / 1866

Inscribed front edge of base: THE CHARITY PATIENT

Mabel Brady Garvan Collection
1932.181

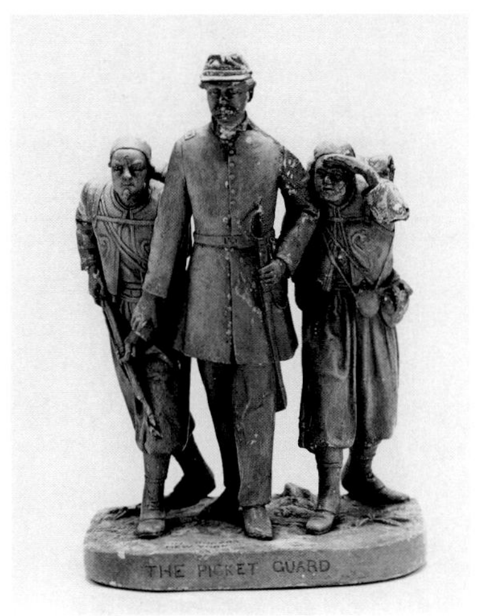

261

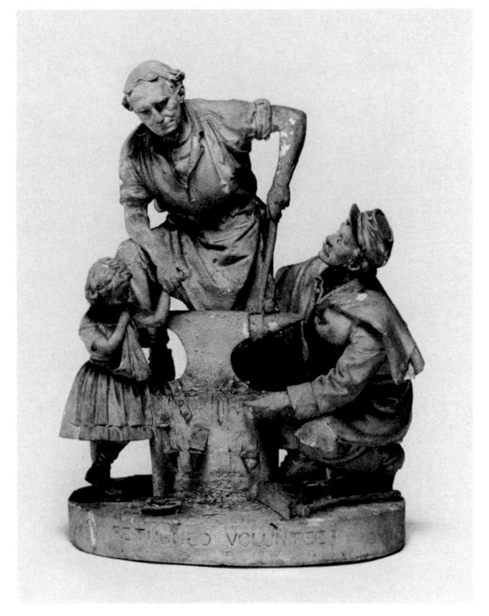

264

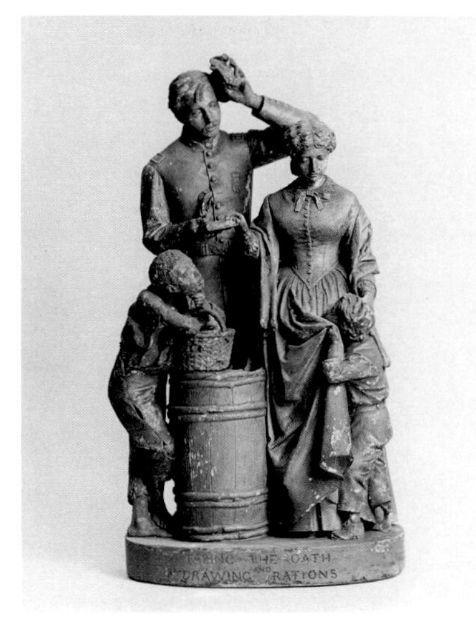

267

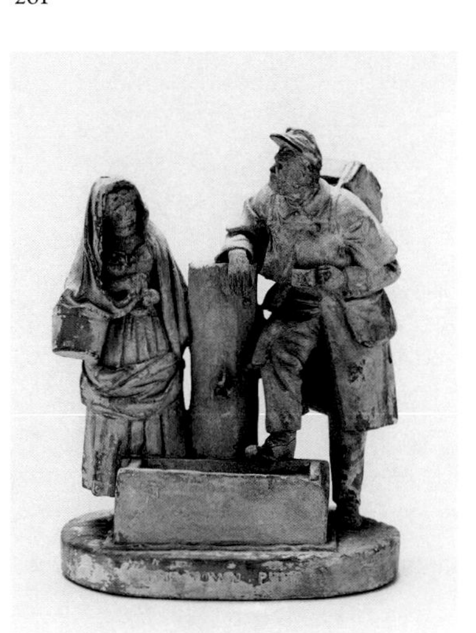

262

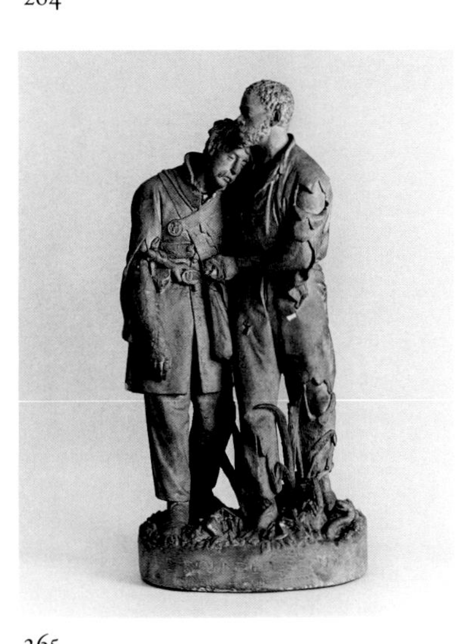

265

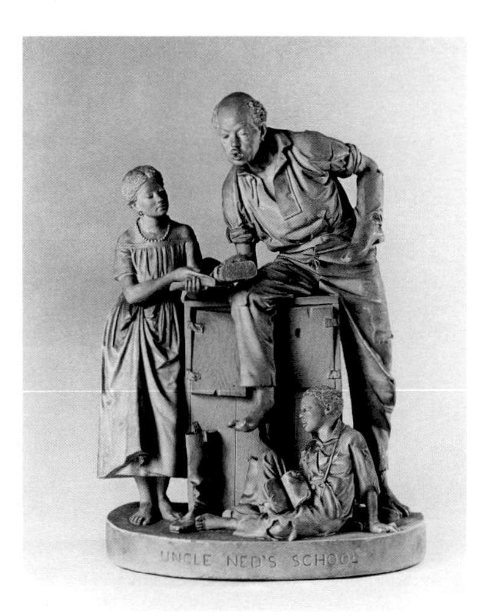

268

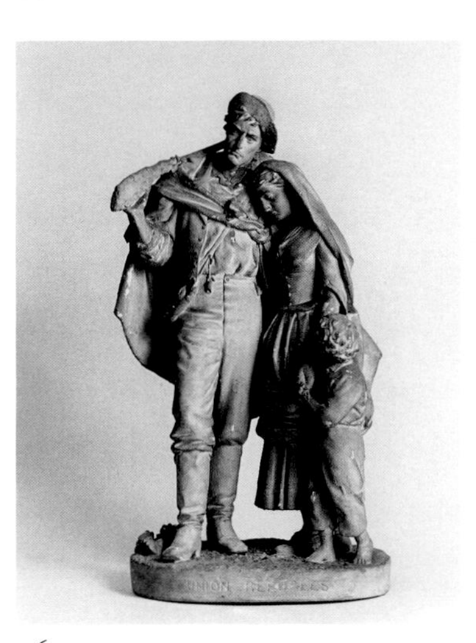

263

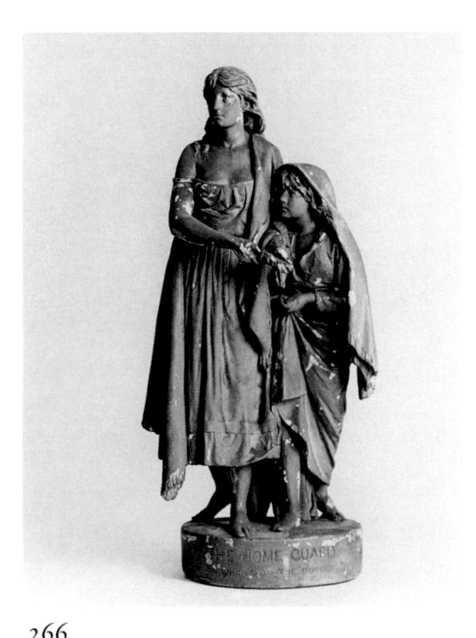

266

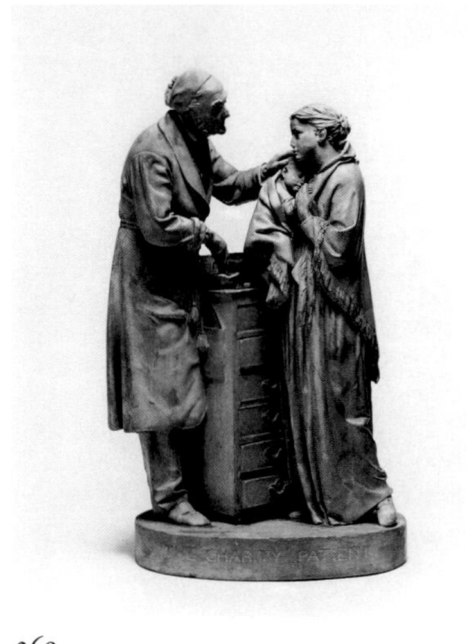

269

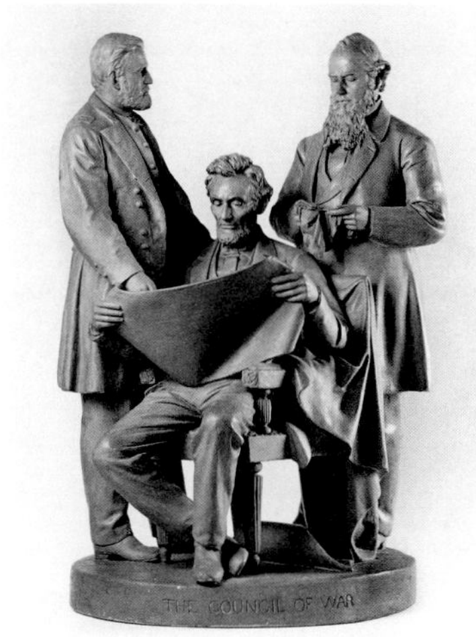

270

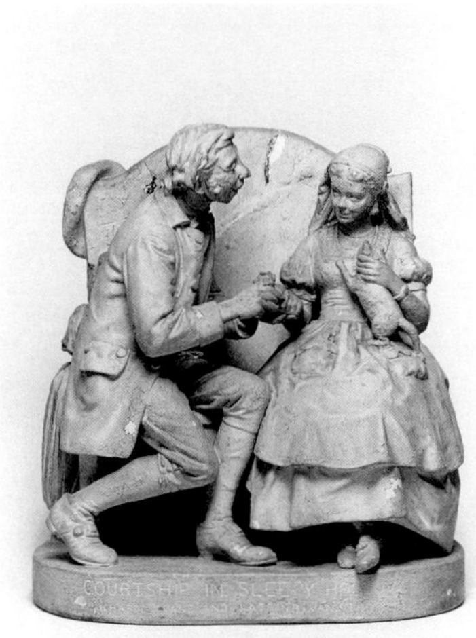

271

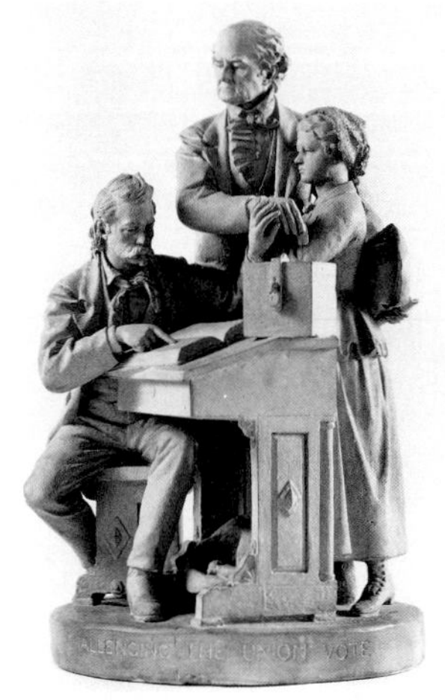

272

270 *The Council of War*

Patented March 31, 1868
Painted plaster
24 x 15½ x 12¼ (61 x 39.4 x 31.1)

Signed proper right front top of base: JOHN ROGERS / NEW YORK

Dated proper right rear top of base: PATENTED MARCH 31 · 1868

Inscribed front edge of base: THE COUNCIL OF WAR

Mabel Brady Garvan Collection
1932.162

271 *Courtship in Sleepy Hollow – Icabod Crane and Katrina Van Tassel*

Patented August 25, 1868
Painted plaster
16½ x 15½ x 9¼ (41.9 x 39.4 x 23.5)

Dated rear edge of base: PATENTED A[?]S[?] / 1868

Inscribed front edge of base: COURTSHIP IN SLEEPY HOLLOW / ICABOD CRANE AND KATRINA VAN TASSEL

Mabel Brady Garvan Collection
1932.188

272 *Challenging the Union Vote*

Patented February 9, 1869
Painted plaster
21 x 13 x 11 (53.3 x 33 x 27.9)

Signed proper right front top of base: JOHN ROGERS / NE YORK

Dated rear top of base: PATENTED / 1869

Inscribed front edge of base: CHALLENGING THE UNION VOTE; proper left: THE RIGHT TO PHOTOGRAPH THIS GROUP / IS NOT SOLD WITH IT

Mabel Brady Garvan Collection
1932.193

273 *The Fugitive's Story*

Patented September 7, 1869
Painted plaster
22 x 15¼ x 13½ (55.9 x 38.7 x 34.3)

Signed proper left front top of base: JOHN ROGERS / NEW YORK

Dated proper right rear top of base: PATENTED SEP. 7. 1869

Inscribed front edge of base: THE FUGITIVE'S STORY / JOHN C WHITTIER —— H.W. BEECHER WM LLOYD GARRISON

Mabel Brady Garvan Collection
1932.199

THE FUGITIVE'S STORY
JOHN G. WHITTIER _ H.W. BEECHER Wm LLOYD GARRISON

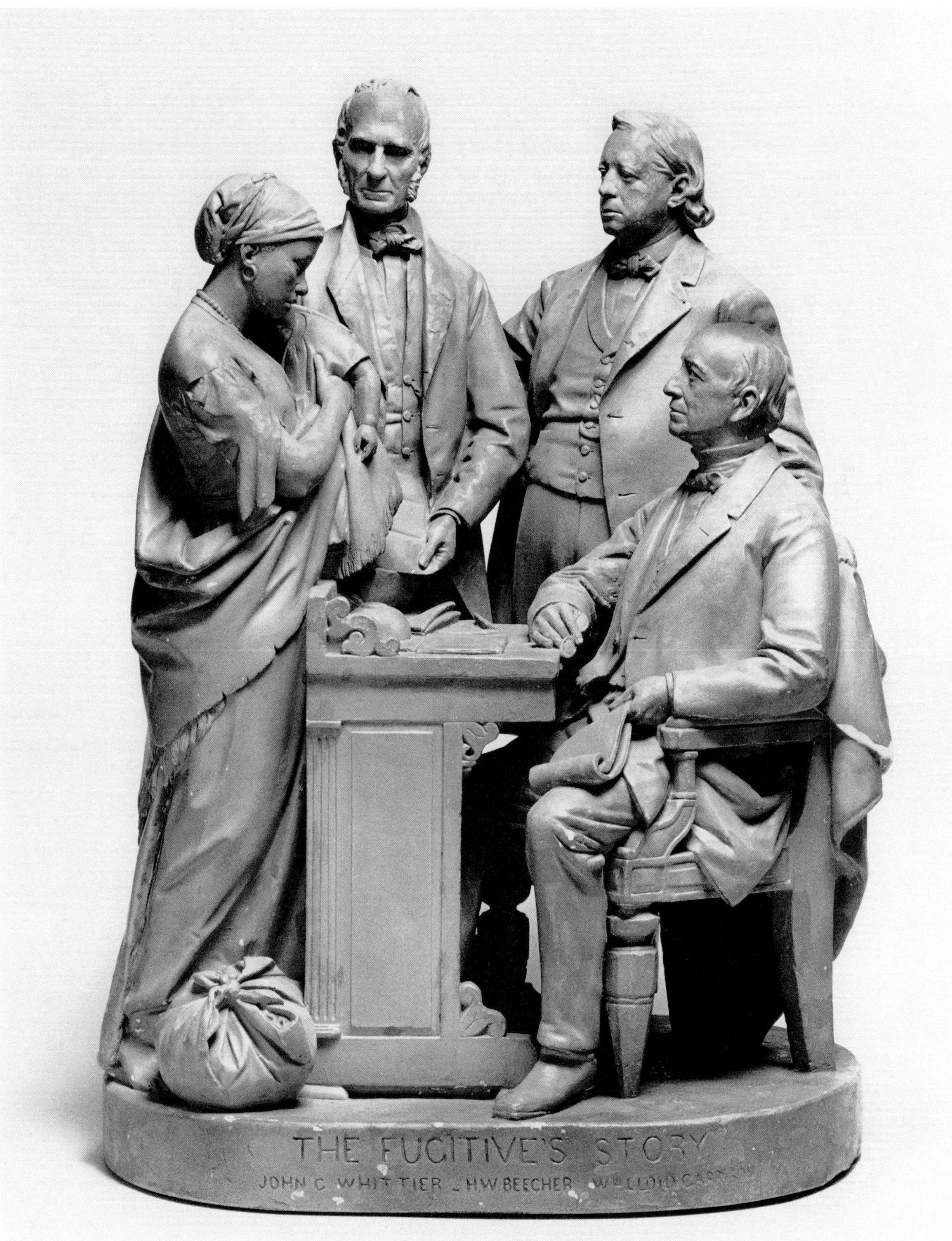

273

274 *Parting Promise*

Patented February 8, 1870
Painted plaster
21½ x 11 x 9 (54.6 x 27.9 x 22.9)

Signed proper left front top of base: JOHN ROGERS / NEW YORK

Inscribed front edge of base: PARTING PROMISE

Mabel Brady Garvan Collection
1932.185

275 *Coming to the Parson*

Patented August 9, 1870
Painted plaster
22 x 17½ x 10 (55.9 x 44.5 x 25.4)

Signed proper left front top of base: JOHN ROGERS / NEW YORK

Inscribed front edge of base: COMING TO THE PARSON

Mabel Brady Garvan Collection
1932.159

276 *The Foundling*

Patented November 22, 1870
Painted plaster
21 x 12½ x 10¾ (53.3 x 31.8 x 27.3)

Signed proper left front top of base: JOHN ROGERS / NEW YORK

Dated rear edge of base: NOV. 22. 1870.

Inscribed front edge of base: THE FOUNDLING

Mabel Brady Garvan Collection
1932.184

277 *Rip Van Winkle at Home*

Patented March 14, 1871
Painted plaster
18 x 10 x 9 (45.7 x 25.4 x 22.9)

Signed front top of base: JOHN ROGERS / NEW YORK

Inscribed front edge of base: RIP VAN WINKLE / AT HOME

Mabel Brady Garvan Collection
1932.168

278 *Rip Van Winkle on the Mountain*

Patented July 25, 1871
Painted plaster
21 x 12 x 9¾ (53.3 x 30.5 x 24.8)

Signed proper left top of base: JOHN ROGERS / NEW YORK

Inscribed front edge of base: RIP VAN WINKLE / ON THE MOUNTAIN

Mabel Brady Garvan Collection
1932.167

279 *Rip Van Winkle Returned*

Patented July 25, 1871
Painted plaster
21 x 9¾ x 8¾ (53.3 x 24.8 x 22.2)

Signed top center front of base: JOHN ROGERS / NEW YORK

Dated rear edge of base: PATENTED JULY 25 / 8[?]

Inscribed front edge of base: RIP VAN WINKLE / RETURNED

Mabel Brady Garvan Collection
1932.166

280 *We Boys*

Patented May 11, 1872
Painted plaster
17¼ x 15½ x 8¼ (43.8 x 39.4 x 21)

Signed proper left side of base: JOHN ROGERS / NEW YORK

Dated rear of base: PATENTED MAY 11 1872

Inscribed front edge of base: WE BOYS

Mabel Brady Garvan Collection
1932.192

281 *Playing Doctor*

Patented October 15, 1872
Painted plaster
15 x 15 x 11 (38.1 x 38.1 x 27.9)

Signed proper left front top of base: JOHN ROGERS / NEW YORK

Dated top rear of base: PATENTED / OCT · 15. 1872

Inscribed front edge of base: PLAYING DOCTOR

Mabel Brady Garvan Collection
1932.165

282 *The Favored Scholar*

Patented April 1, 1873
Painted plaster
21 x 16 x 12 (53.3 x 40.6 x 30.5)

Signed center front top of base: JOHN ROGERS / NEW YORK

Dated proper right rear top of base: PATENTED APRIL 1 1873.

Inscribed front edge of base: THE FAVORED SCHOLAR

Mabel Brady Garvan Collection
1932.158

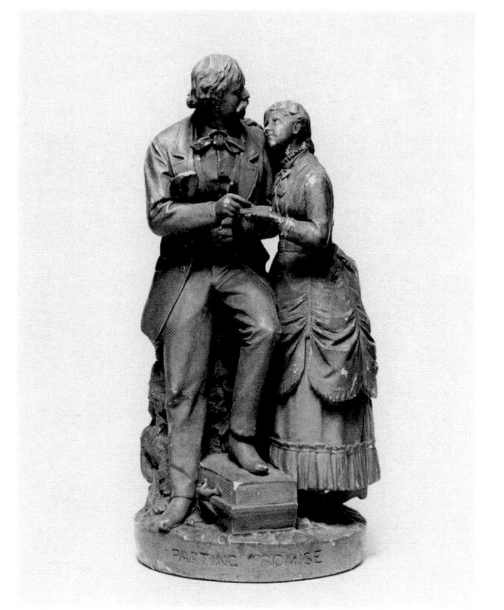
274

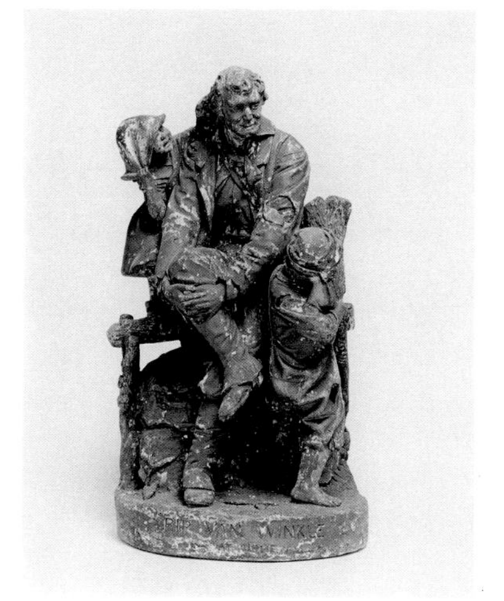
277

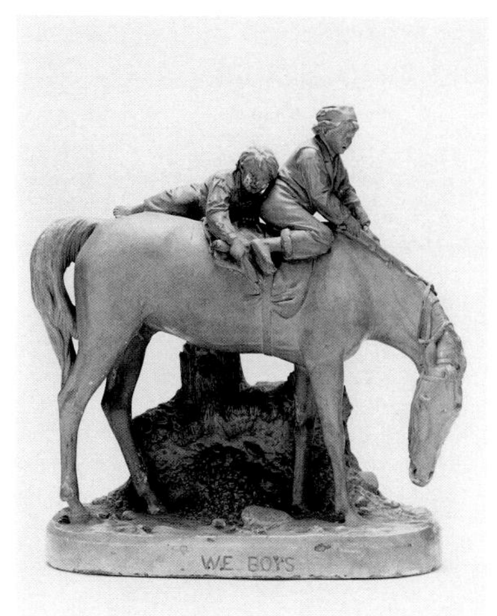

280

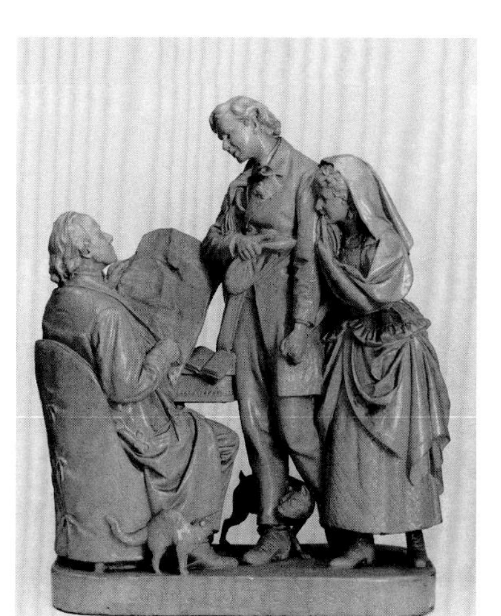
275

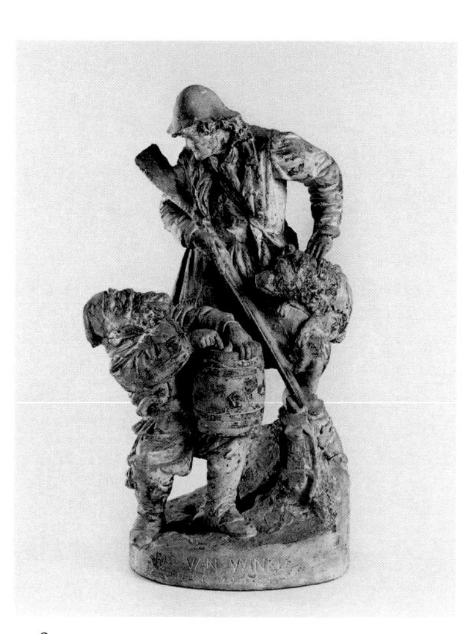
278

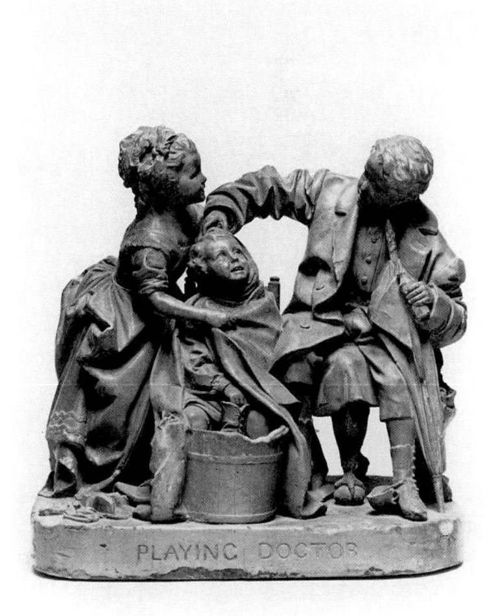

281

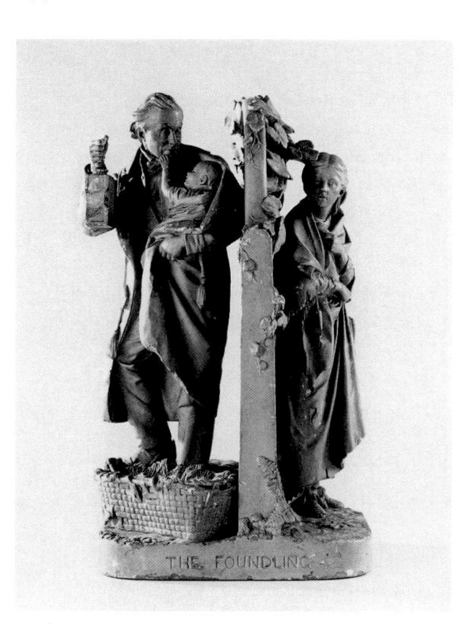

276

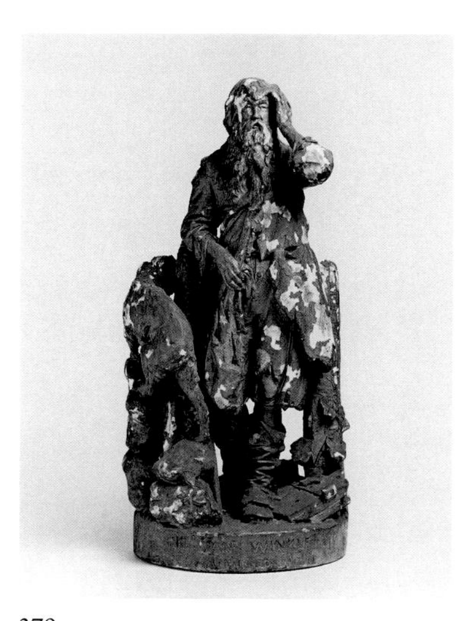
279

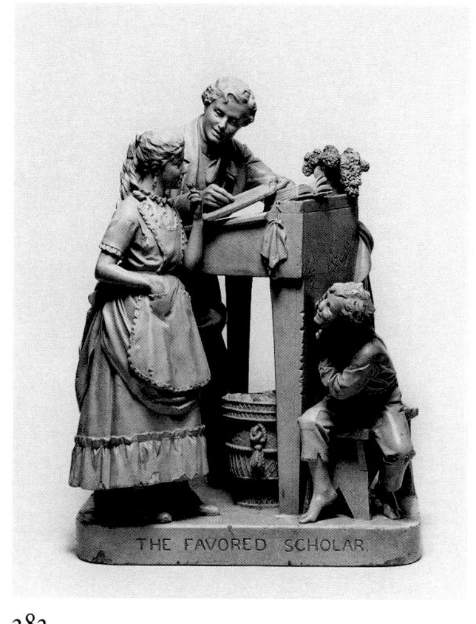

282

283 *Going for the Cows*

Patented December 2, 1873
Painted plaster
12 x 14½ x 9½ (30.5 x 36.8 x 24.1)

Signed proper left front top of base: JOHN ROGERS / NEW YORK

Dated rear top of fence post: PATENTED 1873.

Inscribed front edge of base: GOING FOR THE COWS

Mabel Brady Garvan Collection
1932.194

284 *The Tap on the Window*

Patented December 29, 1874
Painted plaster
19½ x 16 x 11½ (49.5 x 40.6 x 29.2)

Signed proper right front top of base: JOHN ROGERS / NEW YORK

Dated rear edge of base: PATENTED DEC 29 1874

Inscribed front edge of base: THE TAP ON THE WINDOW

Mabel Brady Garvan Collection
1932.169

285 *Checkers Up at the Farm*

Patented December 28, 1875
Painted plaster
20 x 16¾ x 12¾ (50.8 x 42.5 x 32.4)

Signed front center top of base: JOHN ROGERS / NEW YORK

Dated proper left rear top of base: PATENTED / DECEMBER 28 1875

Inscribed front edge of base: CHECKERS / UP AT THE FARM

Mabel Brady Garvan Collection
1932.186

286 *Weighing the Baby*

Patented November 21, 1876
Painted plaster
21 x 15½ x 14½ (53.3 x 39.4 x 36.8)

Signed and dated proper left front top of base: JOHN ROGERS / NEW YORK / 1876

Dated proper right front top of base: PATENTED / NOV. 21. 1876

Inscribed front edge of base: WEIGHING THE BABY

Mabel Brady Garvan Collection
1932.174

287 *The Mock Trial – Argument for the Prosecution*

Patented June 11, 1877
Painted plaster
22 x 21½ x 11¾ (55.9 x 54.6 x 29.8)

Signed and dated proper left front top of base: JOHN ROGERS / NEW YORK 187[7?]

Inscribed front edge of base: THE MOCK TRIAL / ARGUMENT FOR THE PROSECUTION

Mabel Brady Garvan Collection
1932.176

288 *School Days*

Patented June 26, 1877
Painted plaster
21½ x 14½ x 8½ (54.6 x 36.8 x 21.6)

Signed and dated front center top of base: JOHN ROGERS / NEW YORK / 1877

Inscribed front edge of base: SCHOOL DAYS

Mabel Brady Garvan Collection
1932.187

289 *The Traveling Magician*

Patented November 27, 1877
Painted plaster
22¾ x 15¼ x 14 (57.8 x 38.7 x 35.6)

Signed and dated proper left front top of base: OGERS / YORK / 1877

Inscribed front edge of base: THE TRAVELING MAGICIAN

Mabel Brady Garvan Collection
1932.197

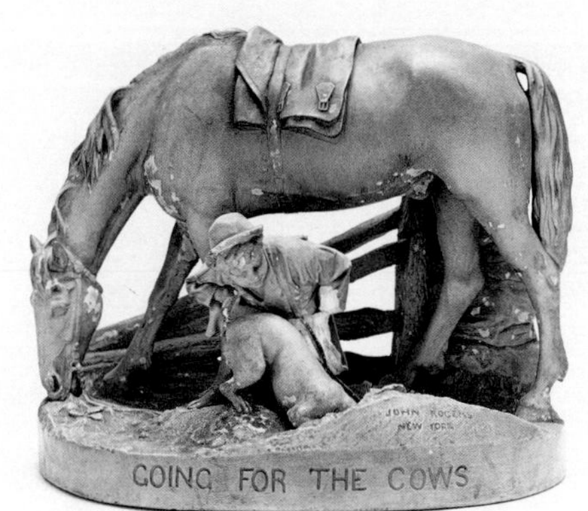

283

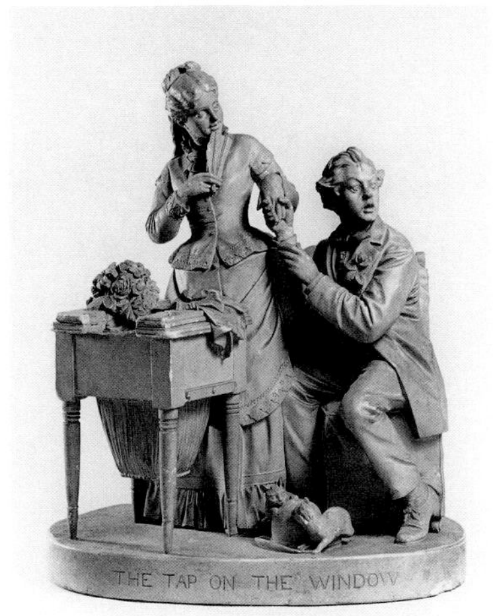

284

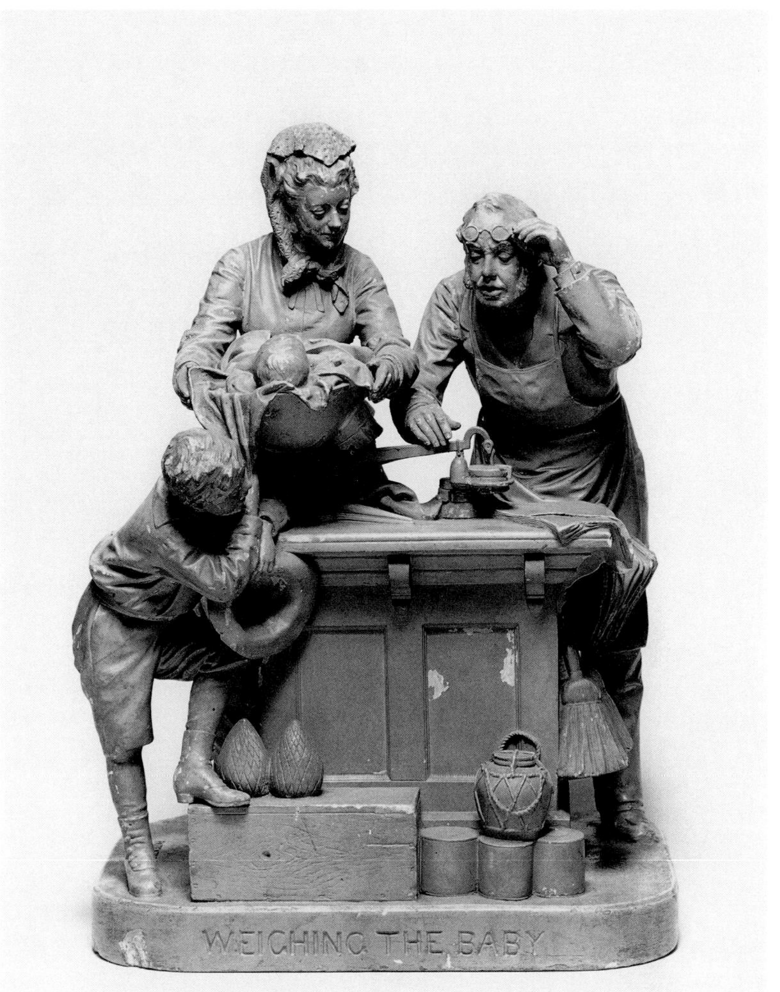

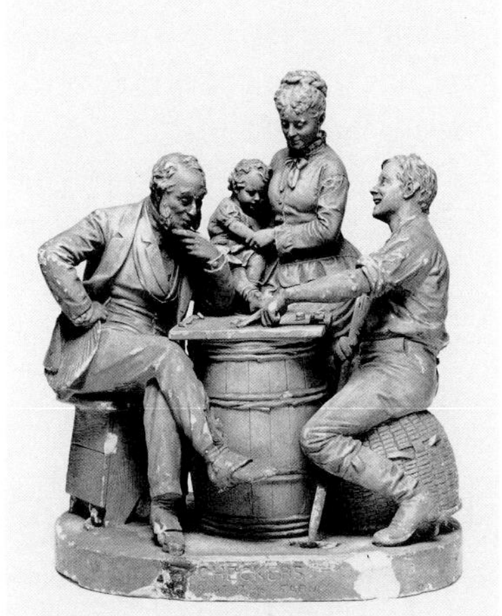

285

286

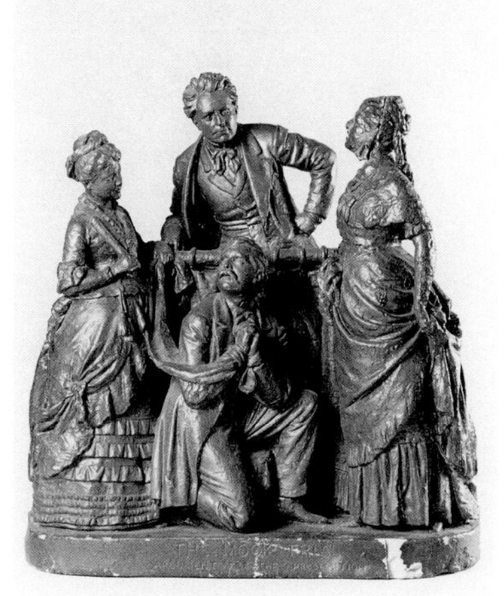

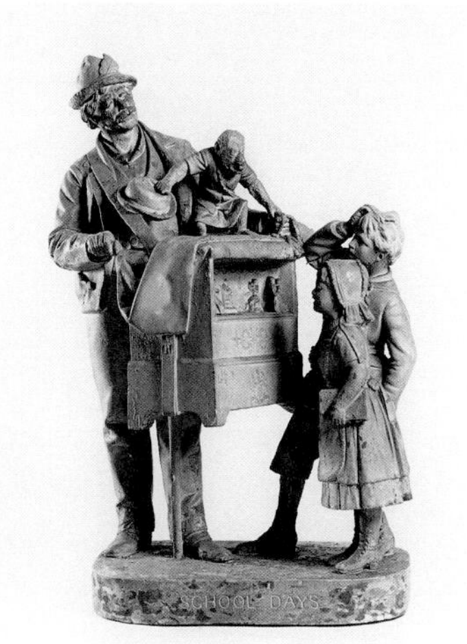

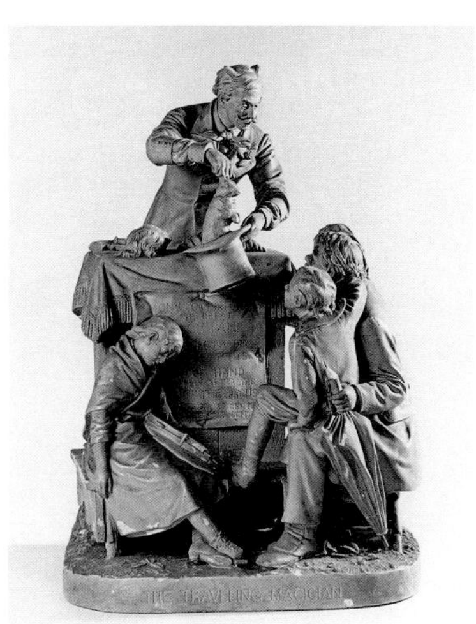

287

288

289

290 *Private Theatricals – Last Moments behind the Scenes*

Patented June 11, 1878
Painted plaster
24 x 20 x 12½ (61 x 50.8 x 31.8)

Signed and dated proper left front top of base: JOHN ROGERS / NEW YORK / 1878

Dated center rear top of base: PAT. JUNE

Inscribed front edge of base: PRIVATE THEATRICALS / LAST MOMENTS BEHIND THE SCENES

Mabel Brady Garvan Collection
1932.195

291 *The Peddler at the Fair*

Patented December 10, 1878
Painted plaster
20½ x 18 x 11 (52.1 x 45.7 x 27.9)

Inscribed front edge of base: THE PEDDLER AT THE FAIR

Mabel Brady Garvan Collection
1932.173

292 *Is It So Nominated in the Bond?*

Patented June 1, 1880
Painted plaster
23¼ x 20 x 12¼ (59.1 x 50.8 x 31.1)

Signed and dated proper right front top of base: JOHN ROGER / NEW. YORK / 1880

Dated at top of second step: PATENTED / JUNE 11, 1880

Inscribed front edge of base: ANTONIO BASSANIO PORTIA SHYLOCK / IS IT SO NOMINATED IN THE BOND?

Mabel Brady Garvan Collection
1932.163

293 *Ha! I Like Not That!*

1889, patented October 31, 1882
Painted plaster
22½ x 20½ x 13¾ (57.2 x 52.1 x 34.9)

Signed and dated center front top of base: JOHN ROGERS / NEW YORK / 1889

Dated proper right rear top of base: PATENTED OCT. 31. 1882.

Inscribed front edge of base: IAGO OTHELLO DESDEMONA CASSIO / HA! I LIKE NOT THAT!

Mabel Brady Garvan Collection
1932.160

294 *Neighboring Pews*

1883, patented January 29, 1884
Painted plaster
19 x 17 x 12¼ (48.3 x 43.2 x 31.1)

Signed and dated proper right front top of base: JOHN ROGERS / NEW YORK / 1883

Inscribed front edge of base: NEIGHBORING PEWS

Mabel Brady Garvan Collection
1932.179

295 *A Matter of Opinion*

Patented December 9, 1884
Painted plaster
21 x 18¼ x 13 (53.3 x 46.4 x 33)

Signed and dated proper left front top of base: JOHN ROGERS / NEW YORK / 1884

Inscribed front edge of base: A MATTER OF OPINION

Mabel Brady Garvan Collection
1932.164

296 *Why Don't You Speak for Yourself John?*

Patented February 10, 1885
Painted plaster
22 x 17 x 12 (55.9 x 43.2 x 30.5)

Signed proper right front top of base: JOHN ROGERS / NEW YORK

Dated proper left rear top of base: PATENTED. FEB. 10. 1885

Inscribed front edge of base: JOHN ALDEN PRISCILLA / WHY DON'T YOU SPEAK FOR YOURSELF JOHN?

Mabel Brady Garvan Collection
1932.156

297 *Madam, Your Mother Craves a Word with You*

Patented August 3, 1886
Painted plaster
20½ x 18½ x 10½ (52.1 x 47 x 26.7)

Signed proper right top of base: JOHN ROGERS / NEW YORK

Dated top center rear of base: PATENTED AUG 3, 1886

Inscribed front edge of base: ROMEO JULIET NURSE / MADAM, YOUR MOTHER CRAVES A WORD WITH YOU

Mabel Brady Garvan Collection
1932.170

298 *The Elder's Daughter*

Patented February 8, 1887
Painted plaster
22¼ x 19½ x 10 (56.5 x 49.5 x 25.4)

Signed proper right front top of base: JOHN ROGERS / NEW YORK

Inscribed front edge of base: THE ELDER'S DAUGHTER

Mabel Brady Garvan Collection
1932.196

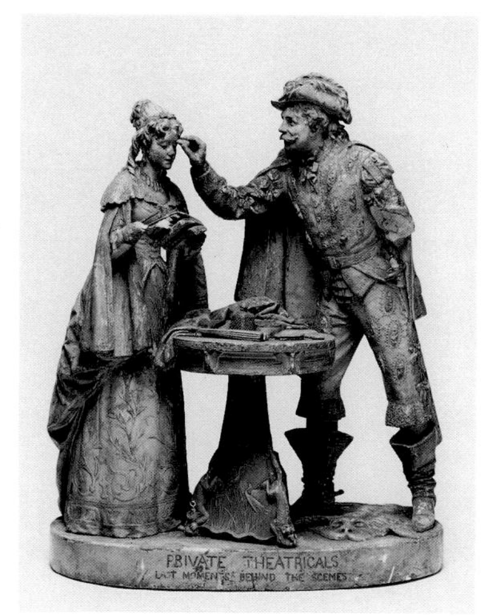

290

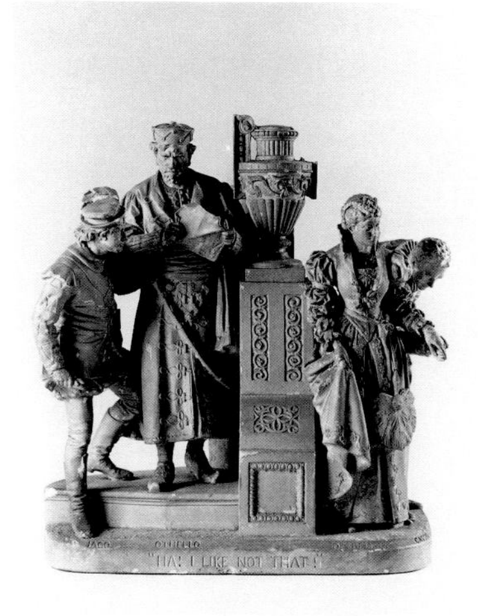

293

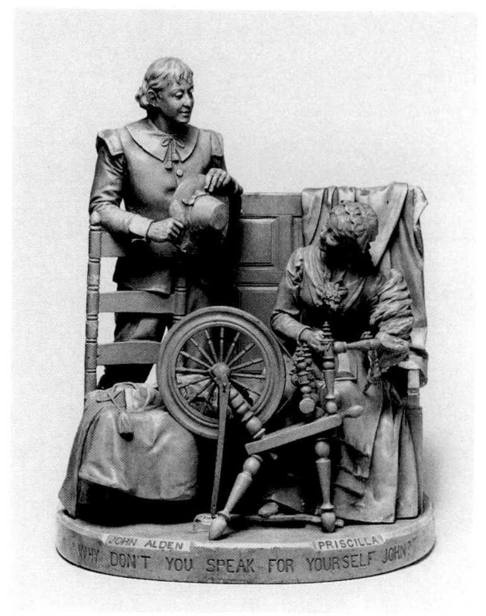

296

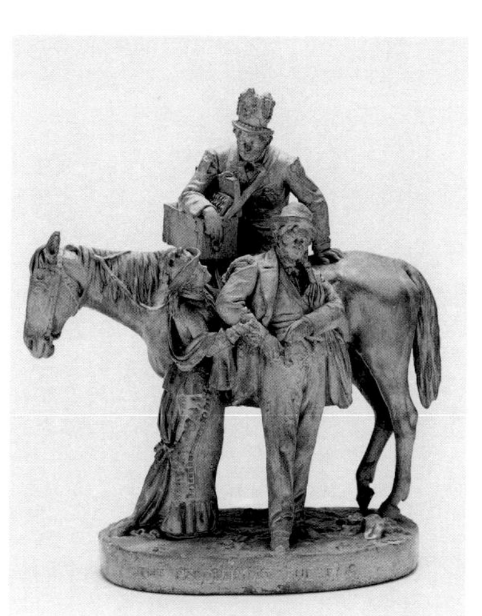

291

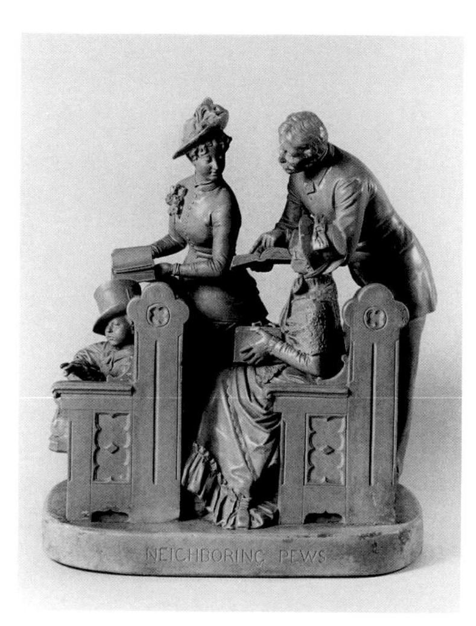

294

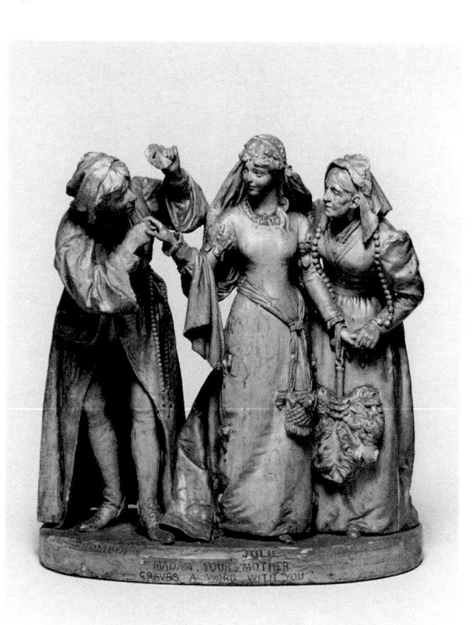

297

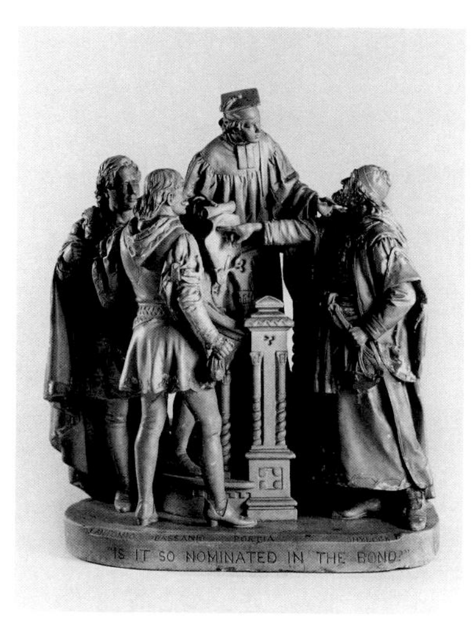

292

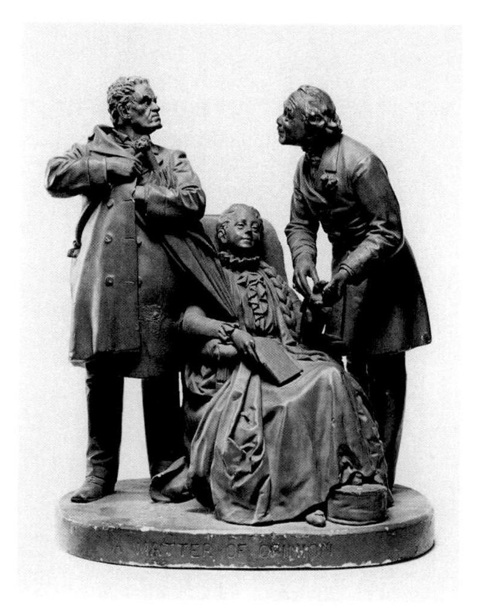

295

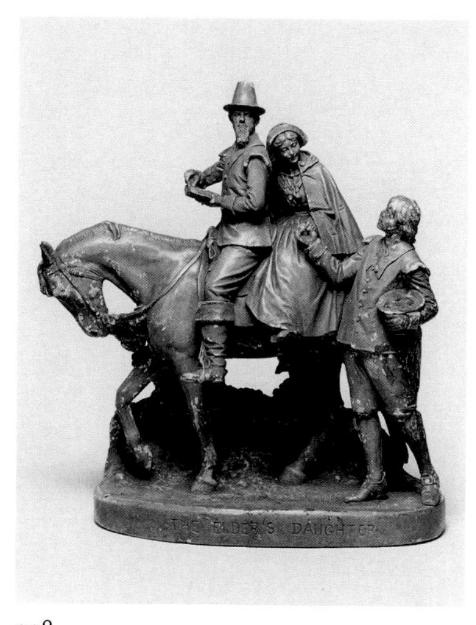

298

299 *A Frolic at the Old Homestead*

Patented May 31, 1887
Painted plaster
22¼ x 18 x 13¼ (56.5 x 45.7 x 33.7)

Signed and dated proper left front top of base: JOHN ROGERS / NEW YORK / 1887

Inscribed front edge of base: A FROLIC / AT THE / OLD HOMESTEAD

Mabel Brady Garvan Collection
1932.182

300 *Henry Ward Beecher 1813–1887*

Published 1887, no patent date
Painted plaster
30 x 17 x 12¾ (76.2 x 43.2 x 32.4)

Signed proper left front top of base: JOHN ROGERS / NEW YORK

Inscribed front edge of base: HENRY WARD BEECHER

Gift of Samuel A. Scoville, B.A. 1928, B.F.A. 1932, to the Yale University Library
1953.44.1

301 *Politics*

Patented November 13, 1888
Painted plaster
18½ x 17½ x 14 (47 x 44.5 x 35.6)

Signed proper left front top of base: JOHN ROGERS / NEW YORK

Inscribed front edge of base: POLITICS

Mabel Brady Garvan Collection
1932.191

302 *Fighting Bob*

Published October 1889, no patent date
Painted plaster
33¼ x 10¾ x 10 (84.5 x 27.3 x 25.4)

Signed proper left front top of base: JOHN ROGERS / NEW YORK

Inscribed front edge of base: FIGHTING BOB

Mabel Brady Garvan Collection
1932.161

303 *Football*

Published 1891, no patent date
Painted plaster
15¼ x 11¼ x 9¾ (38.7 x 28.6 x 24.8)

Signed and inscribed proper left front top of base: JOHN ROGERS / 14 WEST 12 ST / NEW YORK

Inscribed front edge of base: FOOTBALL

Gift of Malcolm P. Aldrich, B.A. 1922, to the Payne Whitney Gymnasium
1968.76

304 *Football*

Published 1891, no patent date
Painted plaster
16 x 12¾ x 10¼ (40.6 x 32.4 x 26)

Signed and inscribed proper left front top of base: JOHN ROGERS / 14 WEST 12 ST NEW YORK

Inscribed front edge of base: FOOTBALL

Yale University Library

305 *The Watch on the Santa Maria*

Published 1892, no patent date
Painted plaster
15 x 13 x 11½ (38.1 x 33 x 29.2)

Signed and inscribed proper left front top of base: JOHN ROGERS / 14 W 12 ST / NEW YORK

Inscribed front edge of base: THE WATCH ON THE SANTA MARIA

Mabel Brady Garvan Collection
1932.183

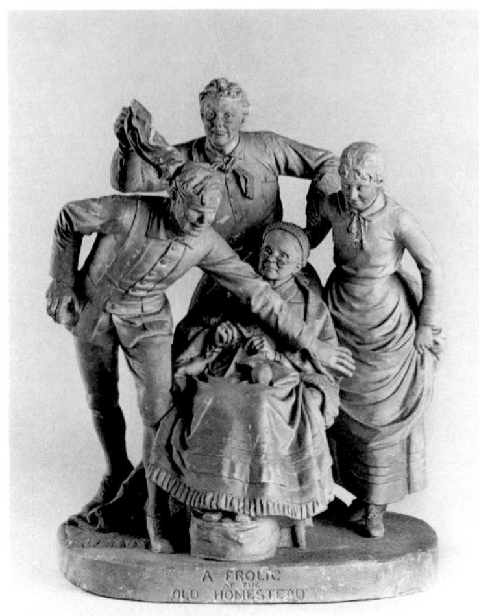

299

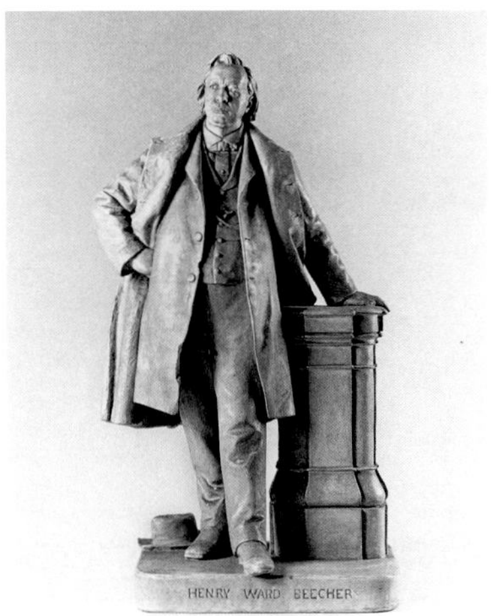

300

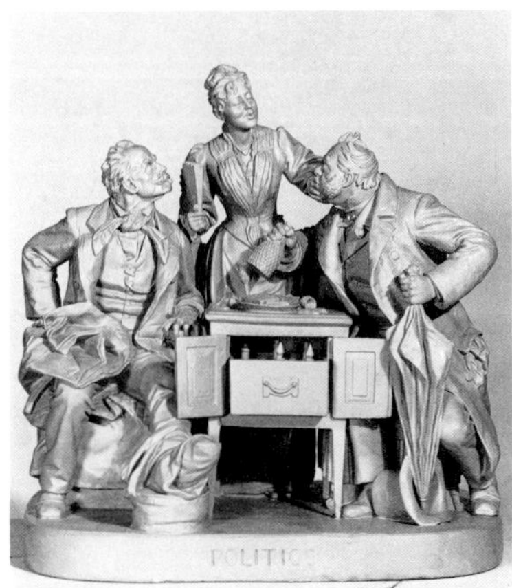

301

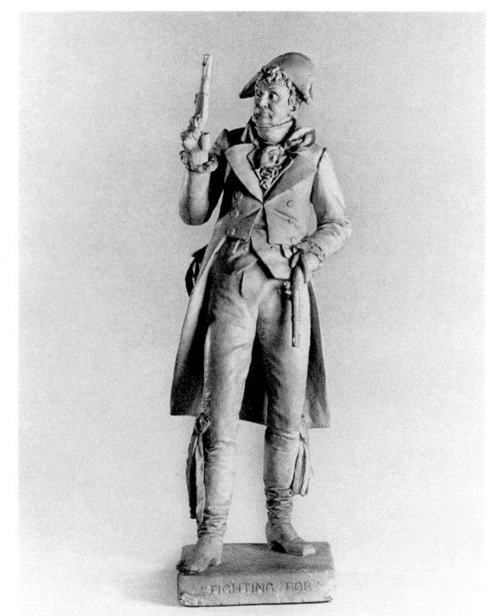

302

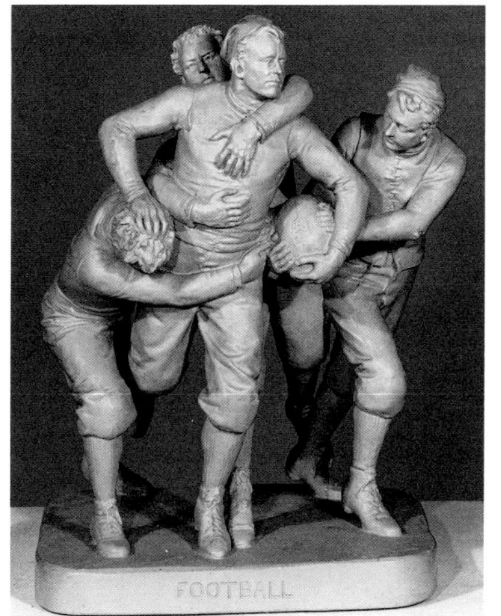

303

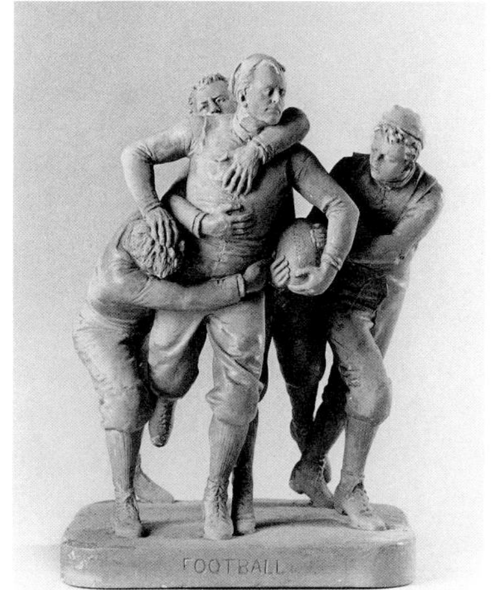

304

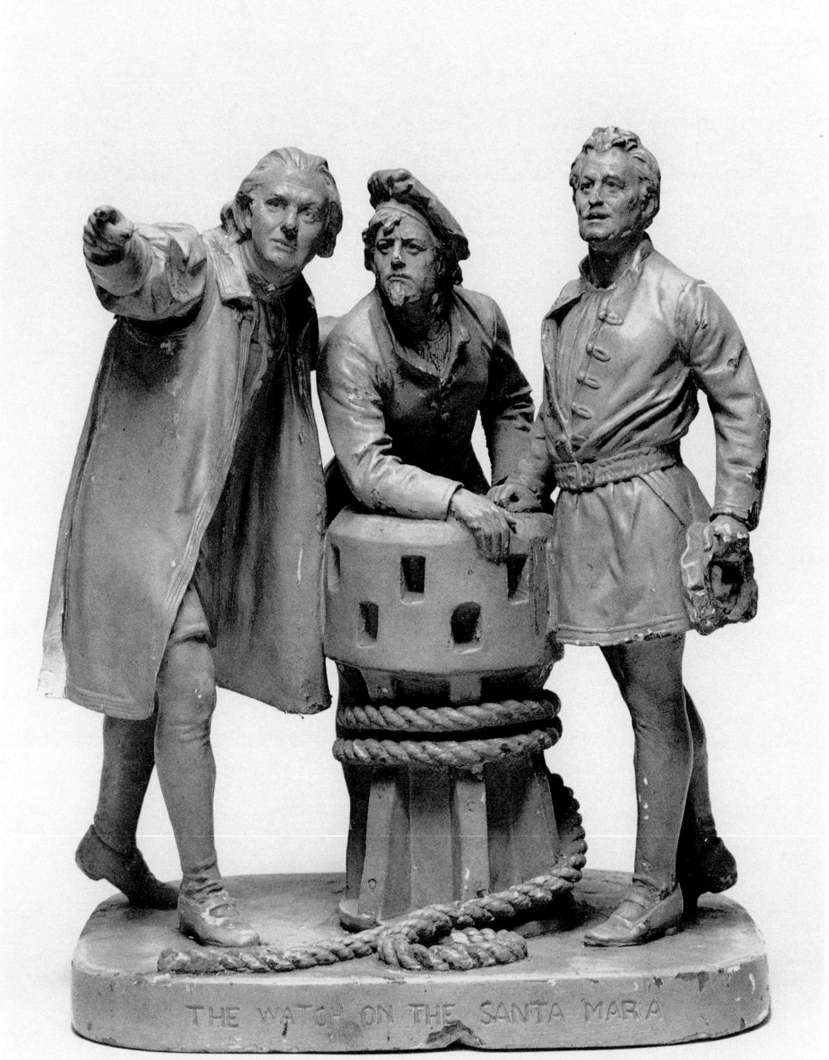

305

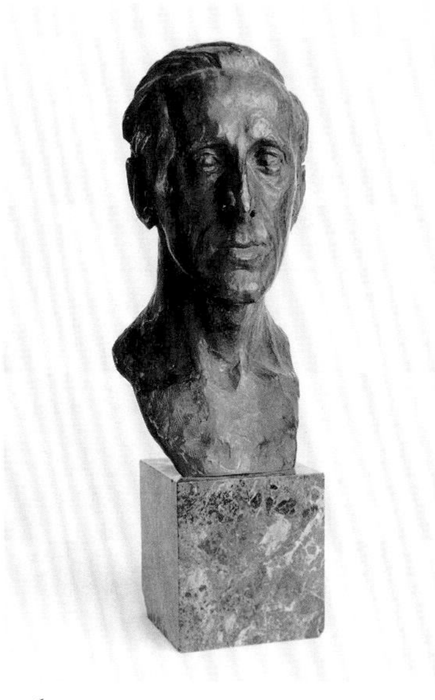
306

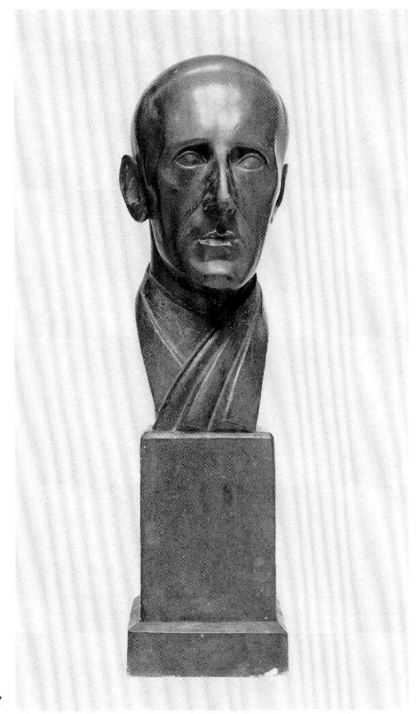
307

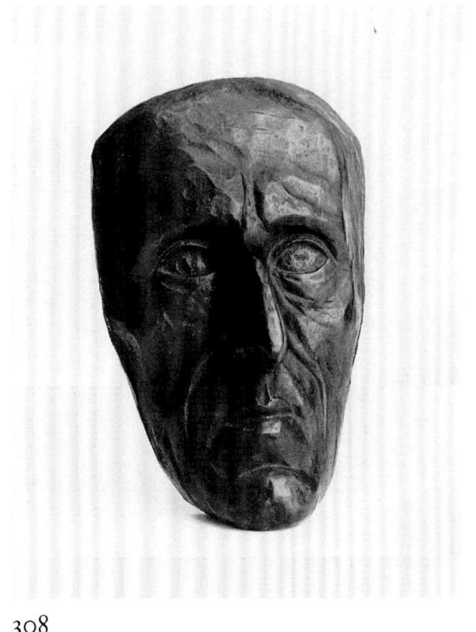
308

ARNOLD H. RÖNNEBECK

1885 Nassau, Germany –
1947 Denver, Colorado
Active U.S. after c.1928

306 *Marsden Hartley* 1887–1943

c.1913
Bronze, black patina
16¼ x 10¼ x 7½ (41.3 x 26 x 19.1)

Signed proper right lower rear:
A RONNEBECK

Foundry: P. Converset, Paris ; mark, proper left lower rear: P – CONVERSET / FONDEUR / PARIS

Gift of Mrs. Arnold Rönnebeck to the Collection of American Literature, Beinecke Rare Book and Manuscript Library
1952.26.1

307 *Marsden Hartley* 1887–1943

1923
Painted plaster
25¼ x 7 x 10¼ (64.1 x 17.8 x 26)

Gift of Mrs. Arnold Rönnebeck to the Collection of American Literature, Beinecke Rare Book and Manuscript Library
1952.26.2

308 *Marsden Hartley* 1887–1943

1923
Bronze, dark grey patina
8¾ x 5¾ x 3½ (22.2 x 14.6 x 8.9)

Signed and dated underneath chin:
19–A–23 / RÖNNEBECK

Gift of Mrs. Arnold Rönnebeck to the Collection of American Literature, Beinecke Rare Book and Manuscript Library
1952.26.3

309 *Self-Portrait in Monk's Costume*

1947
Painted plaster
22 x 22¾ x 16 (55.9 x 57.8 x 40.6)

Signed and dated lower proper right side: 19 AHR 47 (monogram)

Gift of Mrs. Arnold Rönnebeck to the Collection of American Literature, Beinecke Rare Book and Manuscript Library
1952.26.4

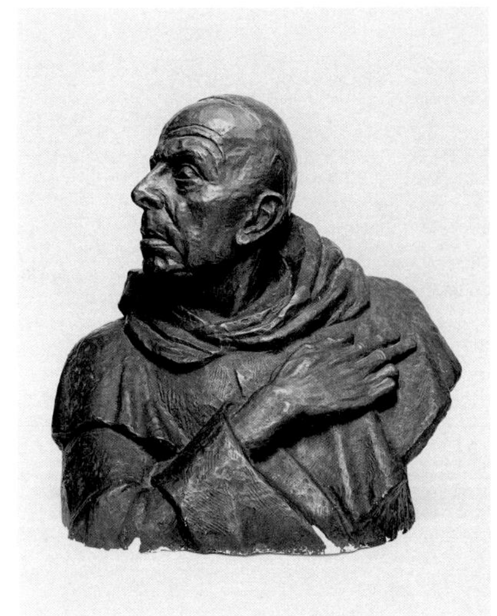
309

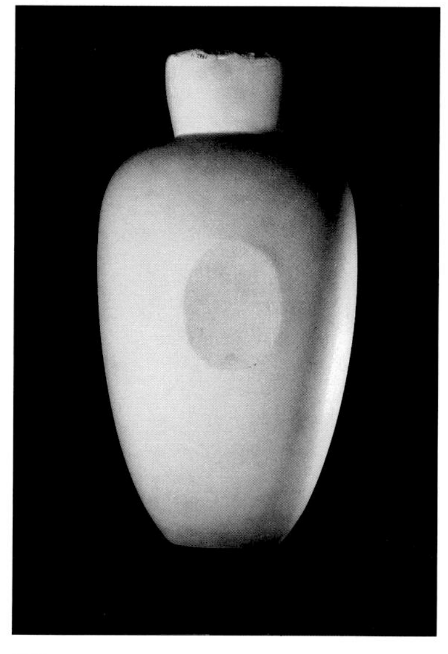

310

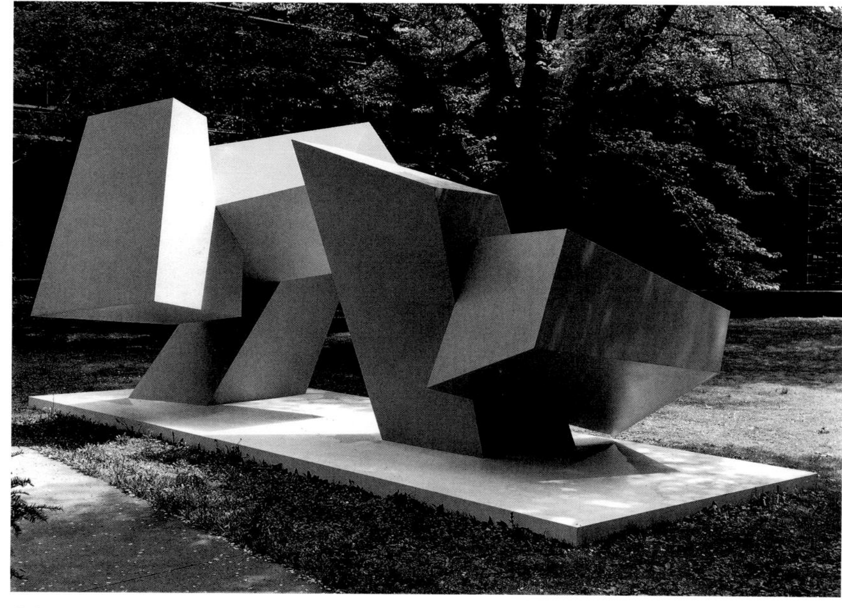

312

JAMES ROSATI

1912 Washington, Pennsylvania –
1988 New York City

310 *Interior — Castle*

1960
Marble
16 x 8¾ x 10¼ (40.6 x 22.2 x 26)

Gift of Frederick E. Ossorio, B.A. 1942
1962.11

311 *Study for Archimedes*

1963
Bronze, black and exposed bronze patina
12¾ x 10¾ x 7¾ (32.4 x 27.3 x 19.7)

Signed lower proper left front: JR (monogram)

Cast number lower proper left side: 1/3

Gift of the artist
1969.118

312 *Dialogue*

1964–69
Cor-ten steel, painted yellow
94 x 197 x 137 (238.8 x 500.4 x 348)

Cor-ten steel base, painted white
4¼ x 239¾ x 96¼ (10.8 x 609 x 244.5)

Signed and dated on plaque at top corner of base: *Rosati 64·69*

Fabricator's mark also stamped on plaque as inscription: WORK EXECUTED BY / Lippincott / NORTH HAVEN CONN

Metal fabricator: Lippincott, Inc., North Haven, Connecticut

Seymour H. Knox, B.A. 1920, Fund
1969.119

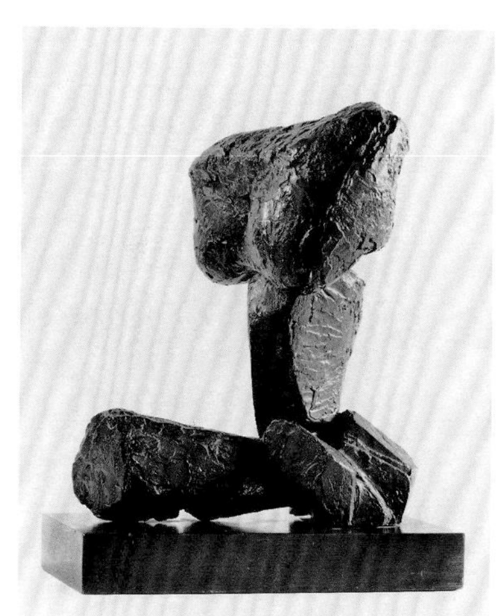

311

ANNETTE ROSENSHINE

1880 San Francisco – unknown

313 *Caricature of H.L. Mencken*
1880–1956

c.1930
Bronze, brown-black patina
4 x 2½ x 2½ (10.2 x 6.4 x 6.4)

Signed lower proper right rear: © AR

Gift of Bradford F. Swan to the Collection of American Literature, Beinecke Rare Book and Manuscript Library
1980.406

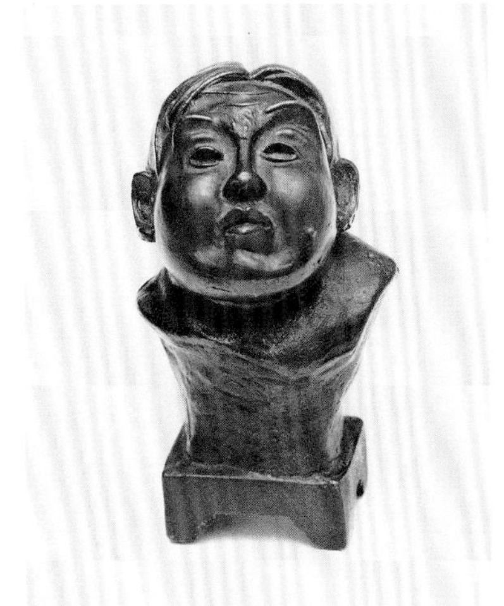

313

BERNARD J. ROSENTHAL

b. 1914 Chicago

314 *Odyssey II*

Designed 1968, executed 1973
Aluminum, painted red
84 x 67 x 102 (213.4 x 170.2 x 259.1)

Signed and dated on edge of one disk: ROSENTHAL 73

Gift of Susan Morse Hilles
1975.43

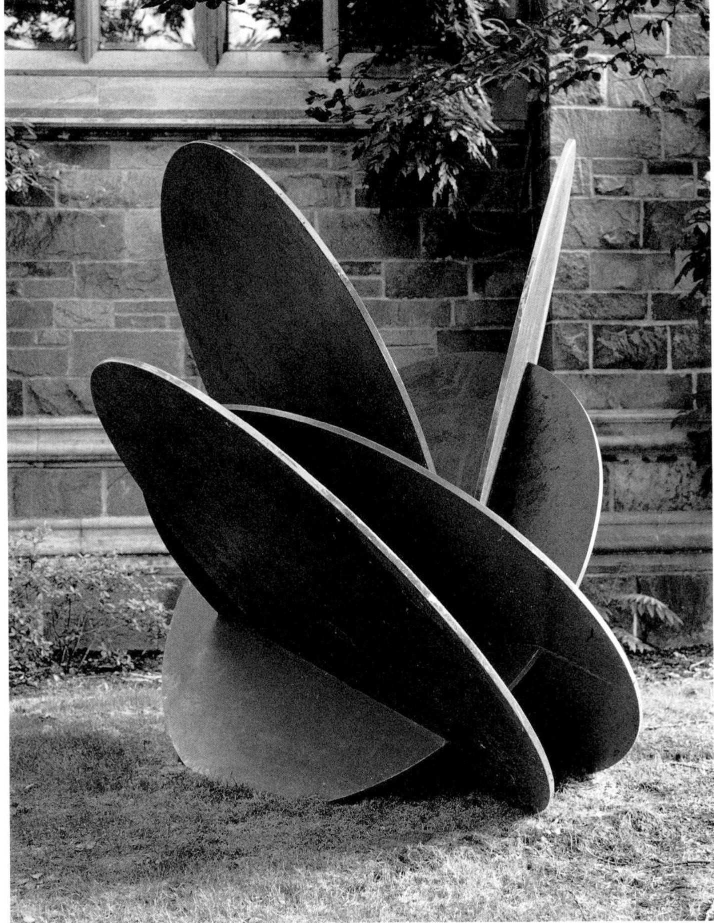

314

THEODORE J. ROSZAK

1907 Poznan, Poland –
1981 New York City
To U.S. 1909

315 *Skylark*

c.1950
Bronze, dark reddish-bronze patina, and steel base with dark reddish-bronze patina
34½ x 16 x 11½ (87.6 x 40.6 x 29.2)

Gift of Stephen Carlton Clark, B.A. 1903
1954.29.4

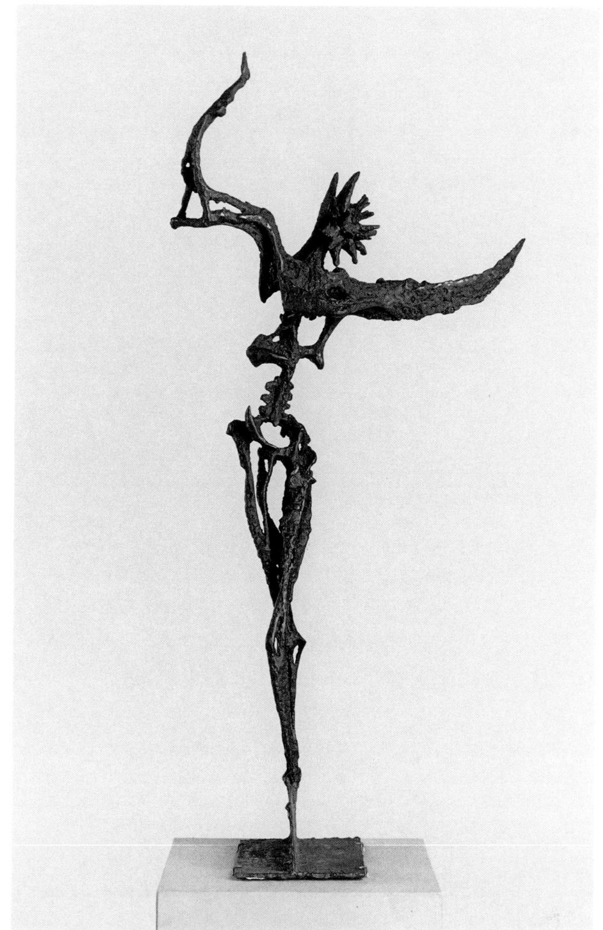

315

IRMA ROTHSTEIN

Dates unknown

316 *Hermann Broch* 1886–1951

Between 1939 and 1951
Bronze, black patina
14¼ x 8¼ x 10¼ (36.2 x 21 x 26)

Signed proper left rear: RMA / ROTHSTEIN

Founder's mark stamped lower rear edge: BE[?] BE[?] MAKKY

Bequest of Irma Rothstein for the Broch Archive, Collection of German Literature, Beinecke Rare Book and Manuscript Library
1980.339

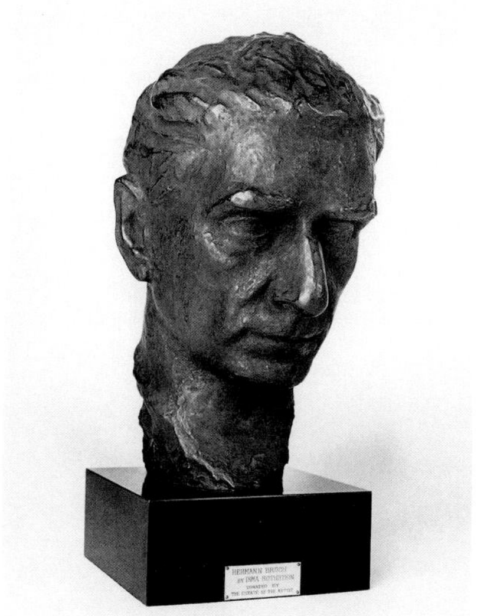

316

WILLIAM RUSH

1756 Philadelphia – 1833 Philadelphia

317 *Benjamin Franklin* 1706–1790
M.A.(hon.) 1753

1787
North American white pine
21½ x 15¾ x 15 (54.6 x 40 x 38.1)

Provenance unknown
1804.4

AUGUSTUS SAINT-GAUDENS

1848 Dublin, Ireland –
1907 Cornish, New Hampshire
To U.S. as an infant
LL.D.(hon.) 1905

318 *Theodore Dwight Woolsey*
1801–1889
B.A. 1820, M.A. 1823

1875–79
Marble
29½ x 24 x 15 (74.9 x 61 x 38.1)

Signed and dated proper right on coat sleeve band:
AVG · SAINT-GAVDENS · FECIT · / M·DCCCLXXV · M·DCCCLXXIX

Gift of Hon. Edwards Pierrepont, B.A. 1837, M.A. 1840, LL.D. 1873
1880.5

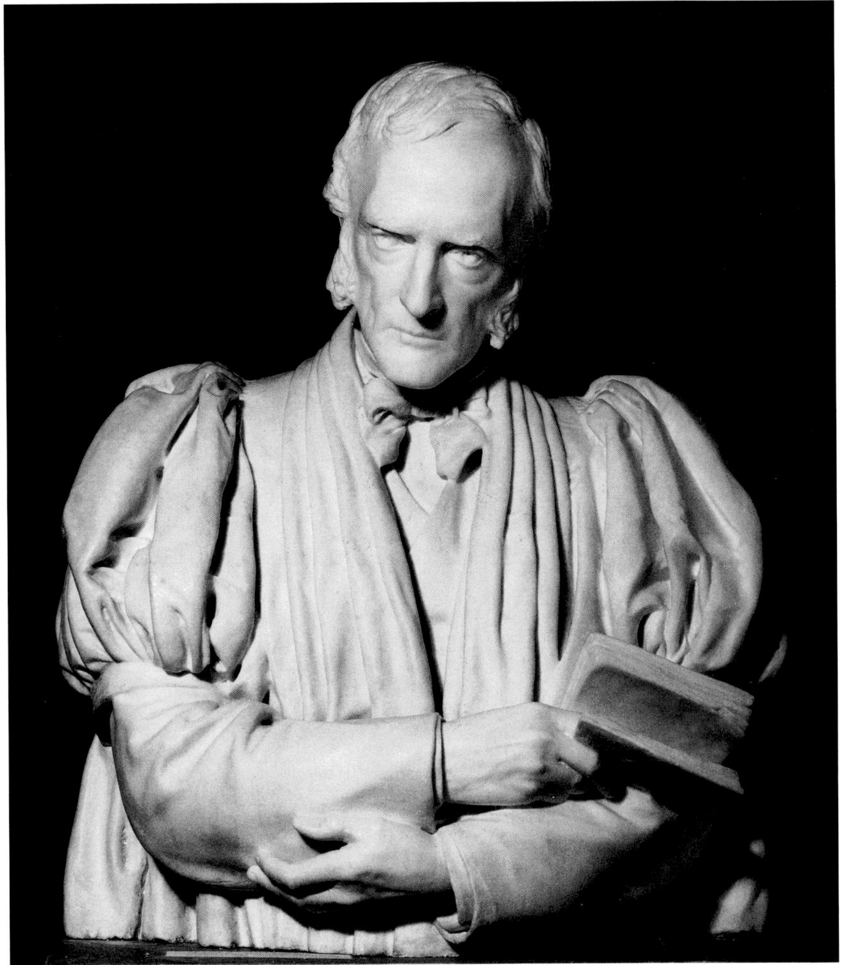

318

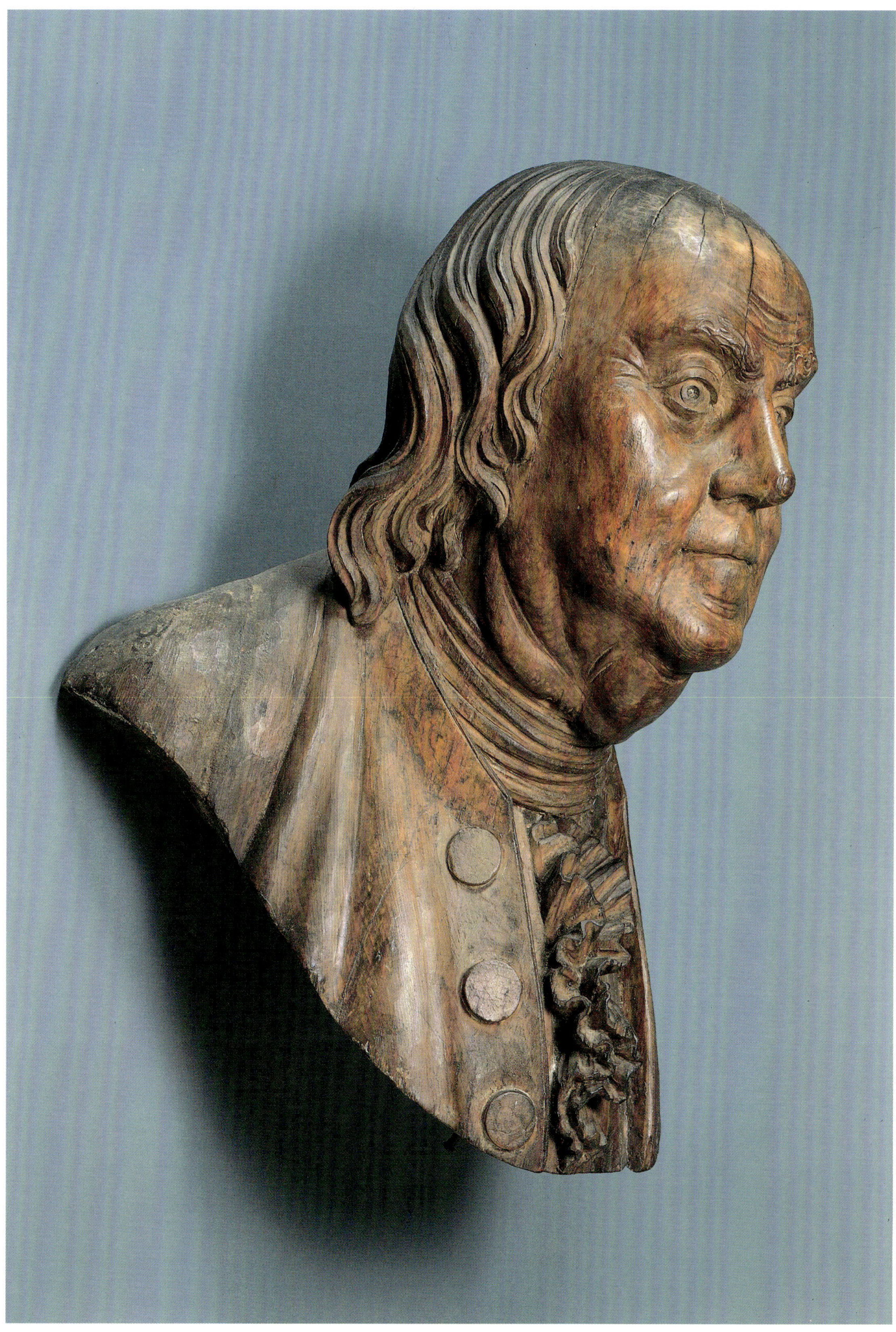

319 *Abraham Lincoln* 1809–1865

Reduction cast c. 1905, after the original monument of 1887
Bronze, dark reddish-brown patina
40 x 30½ x 16¼ (101.6 x 77.5 x 41.3)

Signed and dated lower front edge of proper left side in relief: AVGVSTVS · SAINT-GAVDENS · SCVLPTOR · M·DCCC·LXXXVII

Inscribed on front crest rail of chair in relief: PLVRIBVS

Gift of Allison V. Armour, B.A. 1884
1937.193

320 *Mary Gertrude Mead*
(Mrs. Edwin Austin Abbey) 1851–1931

1890
Bronze, black and bronze patina
14½ x 9 x ½ (36.8 x 22.9 x 1.3)

Signed, dated, and inscribed upper left front in relief: MARY·GERTRUDE MEAD / MARCH XX / M·D·C·C·C·LXXXX / ASG (monogram)

Edwin Austin Abbey Memorial Collection
1937.4003

321 *Mary Gertrude Mead*
(Mrs. Edwin Austin Abbey) 1851–1931

1890
Plaster
14¾ x 9 x ¾ (37.5 x 22.9 x 1.9)

Signed, dated, and inscribed upper left front in relief: MARY·GERTRUDE MEAD / MARCH XX / M·D·C·C·C·LXXX / ASG (monogram)

Edwin Austin Abbey Memorial Collection
1937.4004

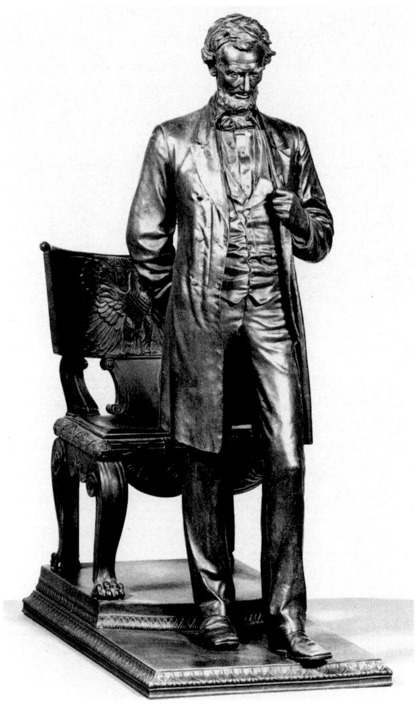

319

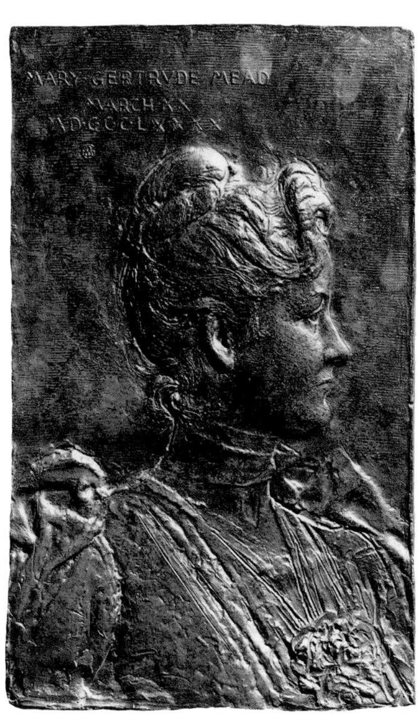

320

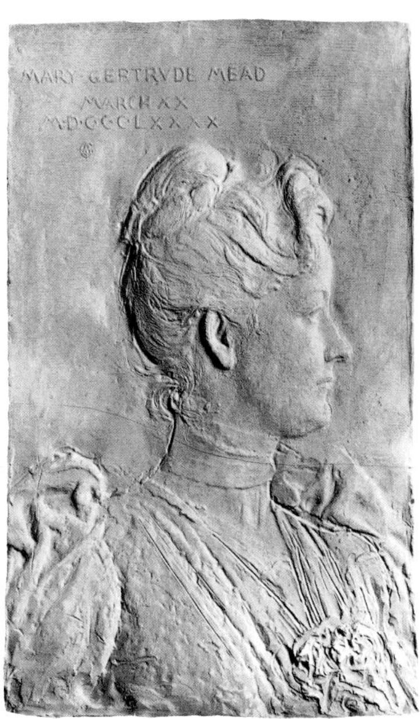

321

322 *Robert Louis Stevenson* 1850–1894

Cast after 1898, after original of 1887
Bronze, dark reddish-brown patina
DIAM. 18 x D. 1 (45.7 x 2.5)

Signed lower center in relief:
COPYRIGHT BY·AVGVSTVS SAINT-GAVDENS

Dated below poem in relief:
M·D·C·C·C·LXXXVII

Inscribed in relief upper left:
TO·ROBERT·LOVIS / STEVENSON; right: AVGVSTVS / SAINT-GAVDENS; upper center and left with stanzas from "Underwoods":

YOUTH·NOW·FLEES·ON·FEATHERED·FOOT·
·FAINT·AND·FAINTER·SOUNDS·THE·FLUTE·
RARER·SONGS·OF·GOD·AND·STILL·
SOMEWHERE·ON·THE·SUNNY·HILL
·OR·ALONG·THE·WINDING·STREAM·
THROUGH·THE·WILLOWS·FLITS·A·DREAM·
FLITS·BUT·SHOWS·A·SMILING·FACE·
FLEES·BUT·WITH·SO·QUAINT·A·GRACE·
NONE·CAN·CHOOSE·TO·STAY·AT·HOME·
ALL·MUST·FOLLOW·ALL·MUST·ROAM·

THIS·IS·UNBORN·BEAUTY·SHE·
NOW·IN·AIR·FLOATS·HIGH·AND·FREE·
TAKES·THE·SUN·AND·BREAKS·THE·BLUE·
LATE·WITH·STOPPING·PINION·FLEW·
RAKING·HEDGEROW·TREES·AND·WET·
HER·WING·IN·SILVER·STREAMS·AND·SET·
SHINING·FOOT·ON·TEMPLE·ROOF·
NOW·AGAIN·SHE·FLEES·ALOOF·
COASTING·MOUNTAIN·CLOUDS·AND·KISS'T·
BY·THE·EVENING'S·AMETHYST·
IN·WET·WOOD·AND·MIRY·LANE·
STILL·WE·PANT·AND·POUND·IN·VAIN·
STILL·WITH·LEADEN·FOOT·WE·CHASE·
WANING·PINION·FAINTING·FACE·
STILL·WITH·GREY·HAIR·WE·STUMBLE·ON·
TILL·BEHOLD·THE·VISION·GONE·
WHERE·HATH·FLEETING·BEAUTY·LED·
TO·THE·DOORWAY·OF·THE·DEAD·
LIFE·IS·OVER·LIFE·WAS·GAY·
WE·HAVE·COME·THE·PRIMROSE·WAY·

Gift of Edwin J. Beinecke, B.A. 1907, to the Robert Louis Stevenson Collection, Beinecke Rare Book and Manuscript Library
1952.36.6

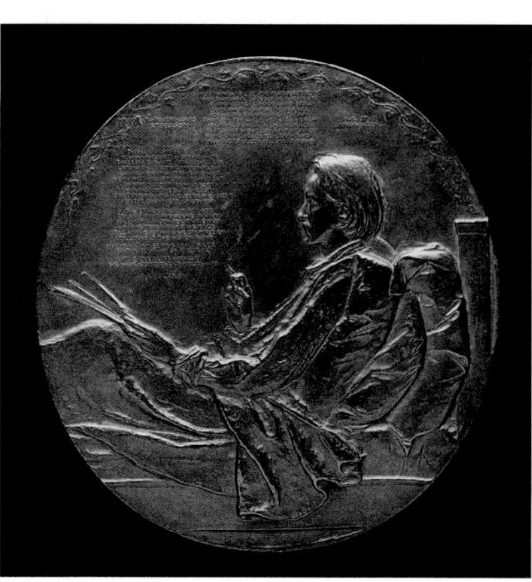

322

323 *Robert Louis Stevenson* 1850–1894

Cast after 1897, after original of 1887
Painted plaster
DIAM. 12 x D. 1 (30.5 x 2.5)

Signed upper right in relief:
AVGVSTVS / SAINT-GAVDENS

Dated center left in relief:
M·D·C·C·C·L·X·X·X·V·I·I; below poem: M·D·C·C·C·LXXXVII

Poem location and text same as cat. 322

Gift of Edwin J. Beinecke, B.A. 1907, to the Robert Louis Stevenson Collection, Beinecke Rare Book and Manuscript Library
1952.36.7

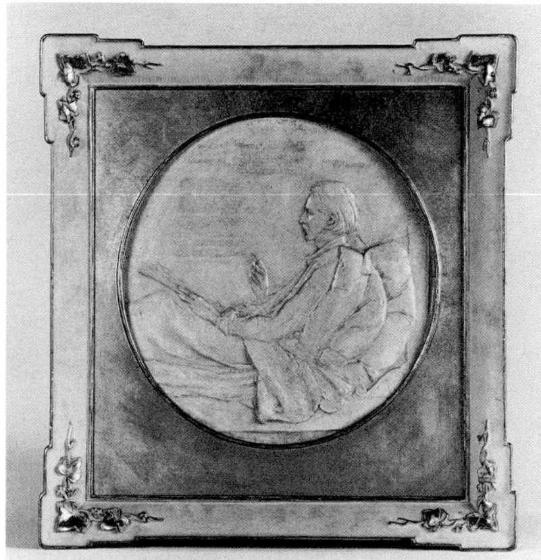

323

324 *Robert Louis Stevenson* 1850–1894

Cast after 1898, after original of 1887
Bronze, gold patina
DIAM. 18 x D. ¾ (45.7 x 1.9)

Signed lower center in relief:
COPYRIGHT AVGVSTVS · SAINT·GAVDENS

Dated below poem in relief:
M·D·C·C·C·LXXXVII

Inscribed in relief upper left: TO·ROBERT·LOVIS / STEVENSON; right: ·AVGVSTVS·SAINT·GAVDENS

Poem location and text same as cat. 322

Gift of Edwin J. Beinecke, B.A. 1907, to the Robert Louis Stevenson Collection, Beinecke Rare Book and Manuscript Library
1952.36.9

325 *Robert Louis Stevenson* 1850–1894

Cast after 1898, after original of 1887
Bronze, dark brown patina
DIAM. 11¾ x D. ½ (29.8 x 1.3)

Signed and inscribed in relief upper left: TO·ROBERT·LOVIS / ·STEVENSON·; right: ·AVGVSTVS· / ·SAINT·GAVDENS

Dated below poem in relief:
·M·D·C·C·C·LXXXVII

Poem location and text same as cat. 322

Gift of Miss Caroline Hunter
1965.123

326 *Robert Louis Stevenson* 1850–1894

1905
Painted plaster
17¾ x 25¼ x 1 (45.1 x 64.1 x 2.5)

Signed and dated lower right corner in relief: AVGVSTVS / SAINT GAVDENS / M·C·M·

Inscribed in relief upper right: TO·JEANNETTE·LEONARD / ·GILDER· / ·HOMER· SAINT-GAVDENS· / ·M·C·M·V·; left: ·ROBERT·LOVIS·STEVENSON· M·D·C·C·C·L·XXX·VII·; below with lines from "If This Were Faith":

·BRIGHT·IS·THE·RING·OF·
WORDS·WHEN·THE·RIGHT·
MAN·RINGS·THEM·

·FAIR·THE·FALL·OF·SONGS·
WHEN·THE·SINGER·SINGS·
THEM·

·STILL·THEY·ARE·CAROLLED·
AND·SAID·ON·WINGS·THEY·
ARE·CARRIED·

·AFTER·THE·SINGER·IS·DEAD·
AND·THE·MAKER·BVRIED·

Gift of Edwin J. Beinecke, B.A. 1907, to the Robert Louis Stevenson Collection, Beinecke Rare Book and Manuscript Library
1952.36.8

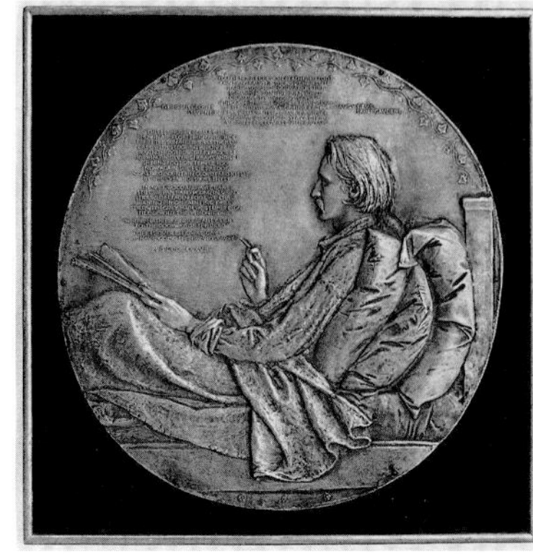

324

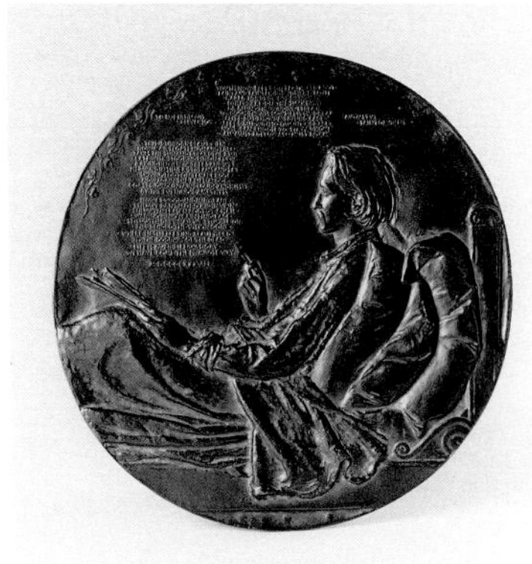

325

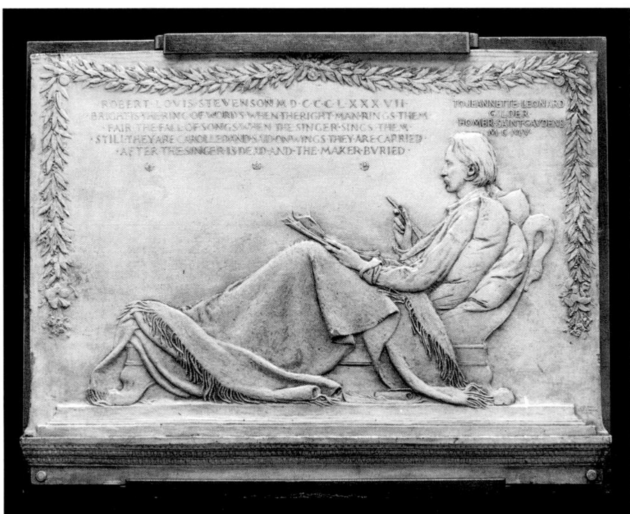

326

ANTONIO SALEMME

b. 1892 Gaeta, Italy
Active U.S. 1908–12, citizen

327 *Ethel Waters* 1900–1977

c.1925
Bronze, dark brown patina
14 x 6½ x 8½ (35.6 x 16.5 x 21.6)

Signed proper right lower rear: Antonio Salemme / ②

Foundry: Cellini Bronze Works, New York; mark, proper right lower side: CELLINI BRONZE WORKS / N–Y–

Gift of Fania Marinoff Van Vechten to the James Weldon Johnson Memorial Collection of Negro Arts and Letters, Beinecke Rare Book and Manuscript Library
1980.167

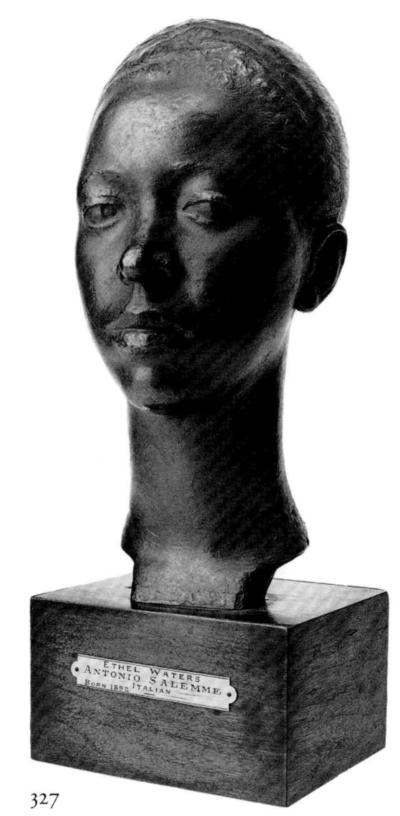

327

ALAN DANIEL SARET

b. 1944 New York City

328 *Silver Dispersion*

1969–70
Reprocessed wire
Three sections:
a) 22 x 62½ x 43 (55.9 x 158.8 x 109.2)
b) 36 x 53 x 30 (91.4 x 134.6 x 76.2)
c) 27 x 61 x 62 (68.6 x 154.9 x 157.5)

Gift of J. Frederic Byers III, B.A. 1962
1975.122

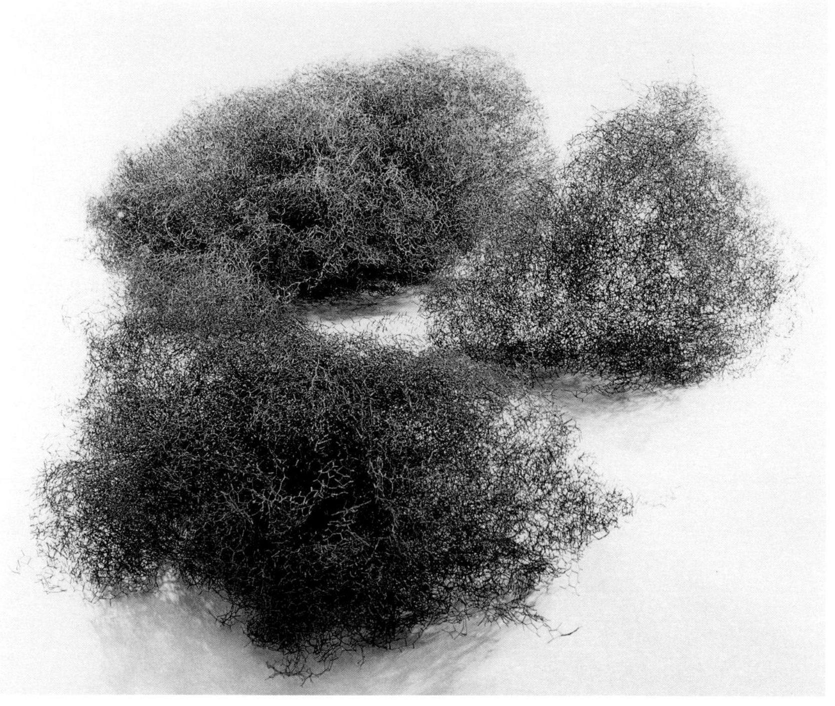

328

JOHN SINGER SARGENT

1856 Florence, Italy –
1925 London, England

Studies for decorations of the dome of the Rotunda, Museum of Fine Arts, Boston; cats. 329–62, bas-reliefs; cat. 363, freestanding

1916–18, final decorations completed 1921

Gift of Miss Emily Sargent and Mrs. Francis Ormond

329 *Architecture, Painting, and Sculpture Protected from the Ravages of Time by Minerva*
Plaster
16 x 13 x 3/4 (40.6 x 33 x 1.9)
1929.646.1a

330 *Architecture, Painting, and Sculpture Protected from the Ravages of Time by Minerva*
Plaster, gilded, shellacked, and mounted on cloth
16 x 12 3/4 x 3/4 (40.6 x 32.4 x 1.9)
1929.646.1b

331 *Architecture, Painting, and Sculpture Protected from the Ravages of Time by Minerva*
Plaster and wax, shellacked
16 x 13 x 3/4 (40.6 x 33 x 1.9)
1929.646.1c

332 *Classical and Romantic Art*
Plaster, gilded, shellacked, and mounted on cloth
14 x 21 x 3/4 (35.6 x 53.3 x 1.9)
1929.646.2a

333 *Classical and Romantic Art*
Plaster, painted, shellacked, and mounted on cloth
13 3/4 x 21 1/4 x 3/4 (34.9 x 54 x 1.9)
1929.646.2b

334 *Classical and Romantic Art*
Plaster
14 1/2 x 21 3/4 x 3/4 (36.8 x 55.2 x 1.9)
1929.646.2c

335 *Decorative Cartouche*
Plaster
12 1/4 x 11 x 1 3/4 (31.1 x 27.9 x 4.4)
Inscribed in graphite lower front center: R; upper right corner: 1
1929.646.3e

336 *Cartouche with Two Male Figures*
Plaster, wax, and clay, shellacked
13 1/2 x 11 x 1 3/4 (34.3 x 27.9 x 4.4)
Inscribed in graphite upper right front corner: 3
1929.646.3g

337 *Cartouche with Two Male Figures*
Plaster
14 x 11 x 1 1/2 (35.6 x 27.9 x 3.8)
Inscribed in graphite front corner upper left: 4; lower left: Over / Dancing Figures; right: Over / Dolphins; verso center: M [?] Dolphin
1929.646.3h

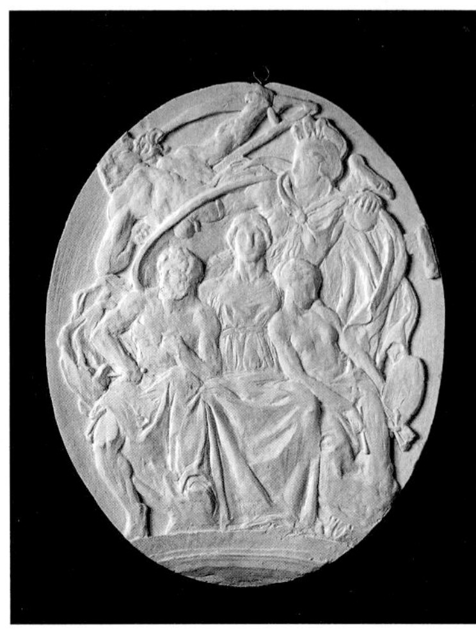
329

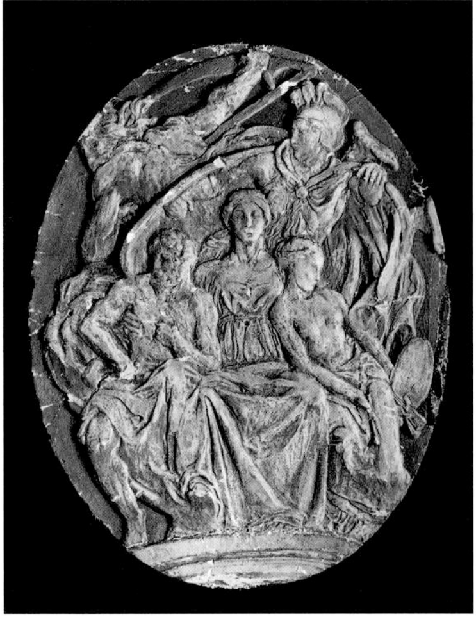
330

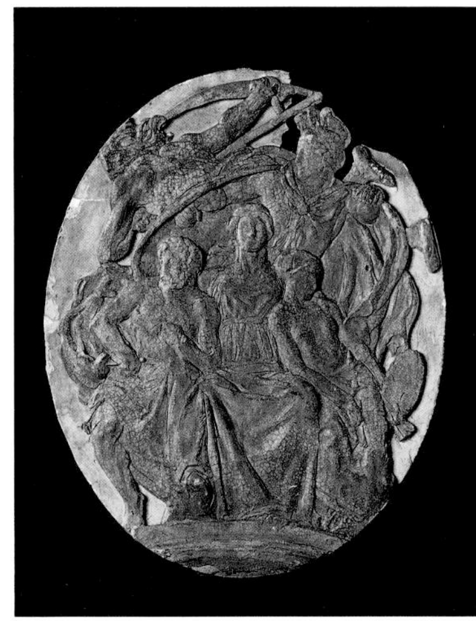
331

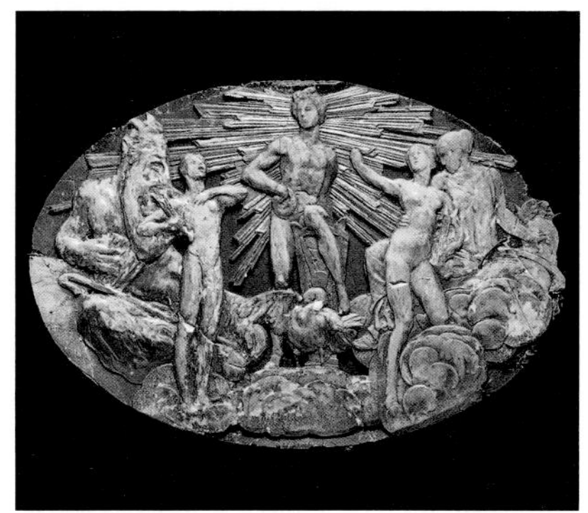

332

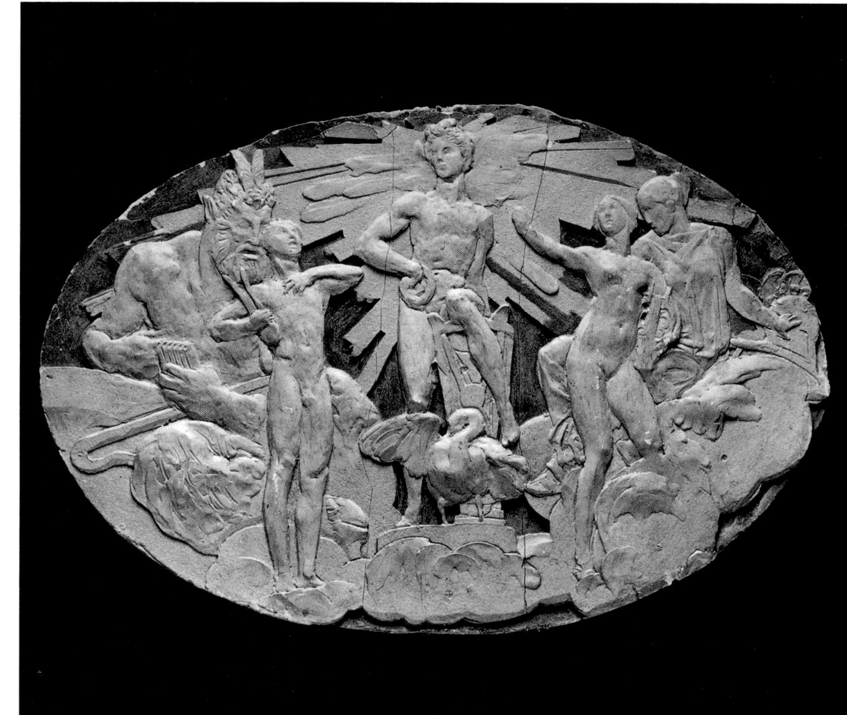

333

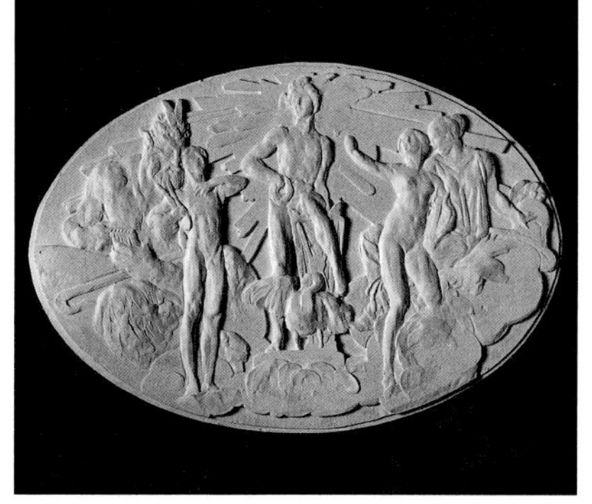

334

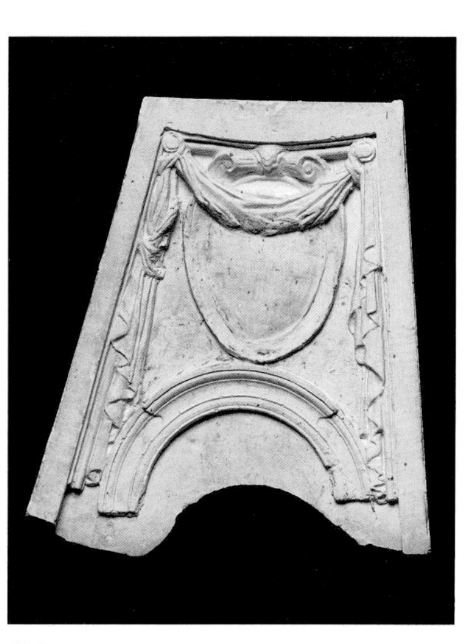

335

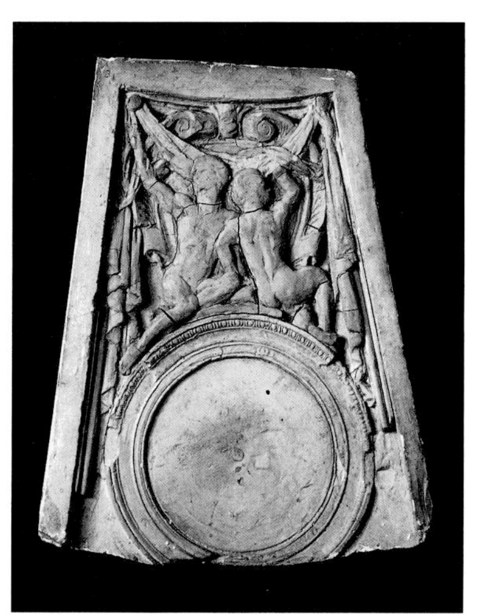

336

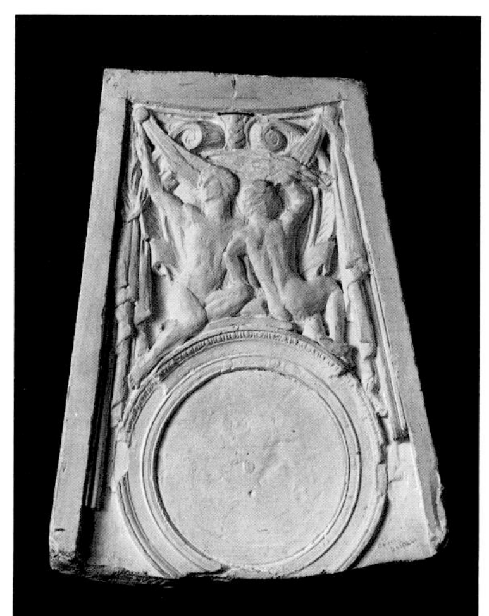

337

338 *Cartouche with Two Male Figures*
Plaster and wax, shellacked
15 x 11½ x ¾ (38.1 x 29.2 x 1.9)
Inscribed in graphite upper front right: B; center: B
1929.646.3c

339 *Cartouche with Two Male Figures*
Plaster and clay, shellacked
12 x 10½ x 1½ (30.5 x 26.7 x 3.8)
Inscribed in graphite front corner lower left: Southn end; upper left: 5; lower center: 3; verso center: Revised
1929.646.3a

340 *Cartouche with Two Male Figures*
Plaster
9½ x 9½ x ¾ (24.1 x 24.1 x 1.9)
Inscribed and dated in graphite verso center: Last Study, / May, 1918
1929.646.3f

341 *Cartouche with Two Male Figures*
Plaster, wax, and clay, shellacked
12 x 11 x 2 (30.5 x 27.9 x 5.1)
Inscribed in graphite front lower center under arch: A; upper left corner: 6; right corner: A
1929.646.3b

342 *Cartouche with Two Male Figures*
Plaster and clay, shellacked
12 x 11 x 2 (30.5 x 27.9 x 5.1)
Inscribed in graphite front lower center under arch: C; upper left corner: 8
1929.646.3d

343 *Tragic Mask*
Plaster and wax, shellacked
6¼ x 5¼ x ¾ (15.9 x 13.3 x 1.9)
1929.646.4c

344 *Tragic Mask*
Plaster
6¼ x 5¼ x ¾ (15.9 x 13.3 x 1.9)
Inscribed in graphite verso center: Su[?]rsided
1929.646.4e

345 *Tragic Mask*
Plaster
6¼ x 5¼ x ¾ (15.9 x 13.3 x 1.9)
Inscribed in graphite verso center: Su[?]rsider
1929.646.4f

346 *Comic Mask*
Plaster
6¼ x 5½ x ¾ (15.9 x 14 x 1.9)
1929.646.4g

347 *Tragic and Comic Masks*
Plaster
6 x 5¼ x ¾ (15.2 x 13.3 x 1.9)
1929.646.4d

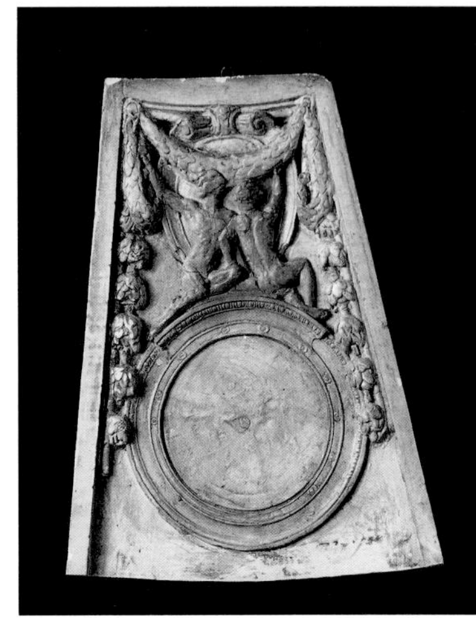
338

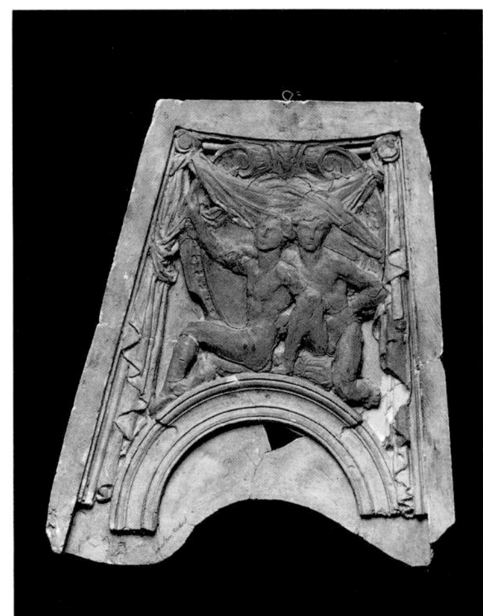
339

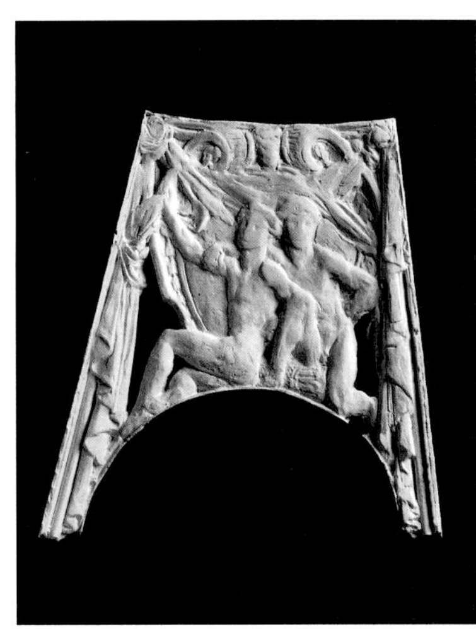
340

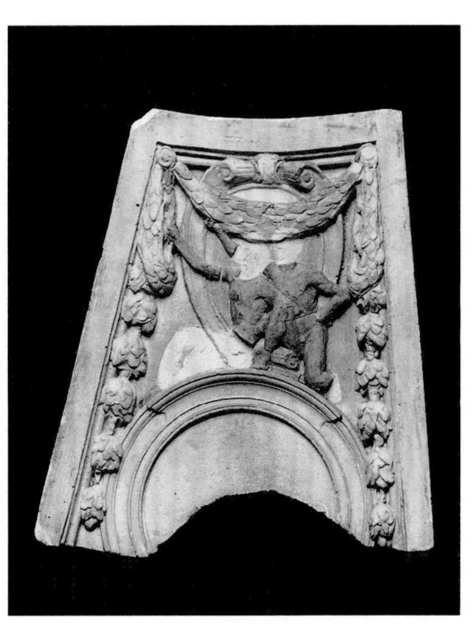

341

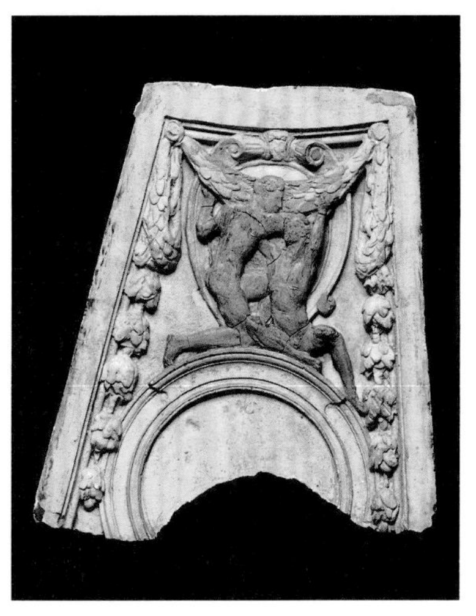

342

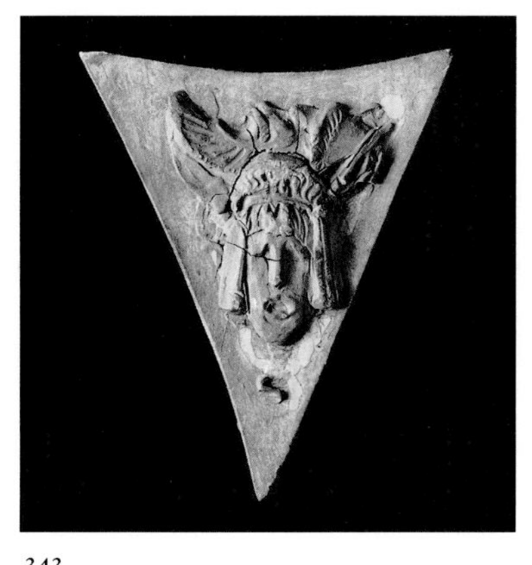

343

344

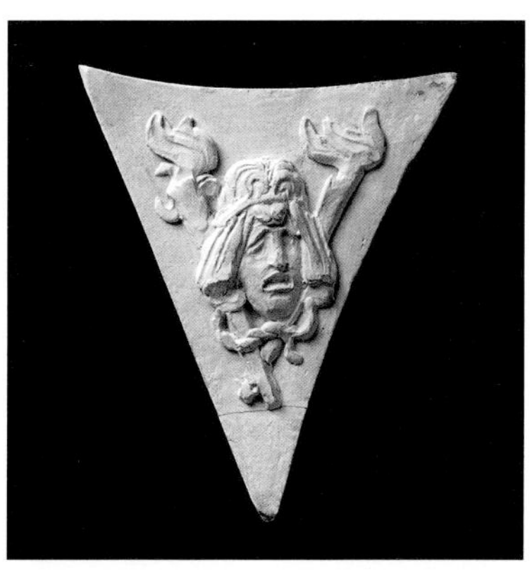

345

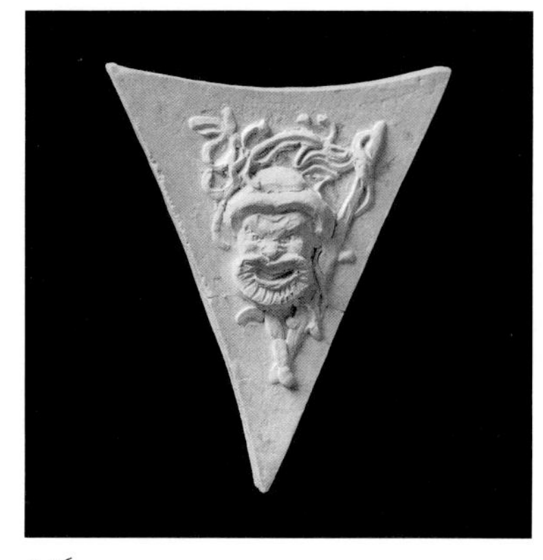

346

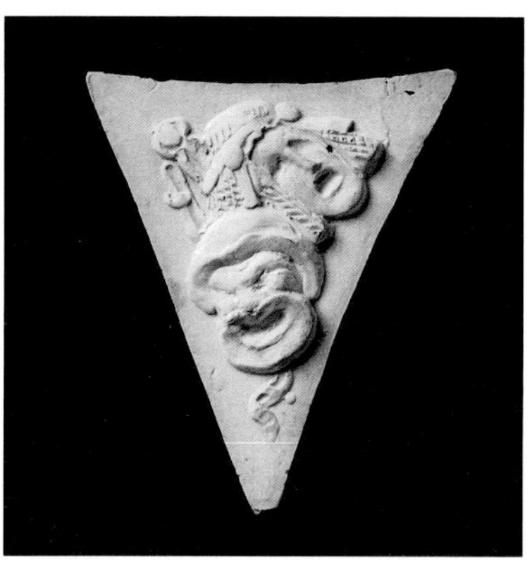

347

348 *Apollo and the Muses*

Plaster, painted, gilded, shellacked, and mounted on cloth
14 x 21¾ x ½ (35.6 x 55.2 x 1.3)

1929.646.5a

349 *Apollo and the Muses*

Plaster mounted on wood stretchers
17½ x 22¼ x 1¾ (44.5 x 56.5 x 4.4)

Wood stretchers
19 x 23¼ x 1 (48.3 x 59.1 x 2.5)

1929.646.5b

350 *Apollo and the Muses*

Plaster mounted on wood stretchers
17¼ x 22 x 1½ (43.8 x 55.9 x 3.8)

Wood stretchers
16½ x 23¾ x 1¼ (41.9 x 60.3 x 3.2)

1929.646.5c

351 *Birth of Venus*

Plaster and wax, gilded and shellacked
12½ x 7 x ¾ (31.8 x 17.8 x 1.9)

1929.646.6a

352 *Eros and Psyche*

Plaster
12½ x 7¼ x ¾ (31.8 x 18.4 x 1.9)

Inscribed in graphite verso: *Relief to be* [?] *line / Panel* [?] *Model ~*

1929.646.6b

353 *Eros and Psyche*

Plaster and wax, shellacked
12½ x 7¼ x ¾ (31.8 x 18.4 x 1.9)

1929.646.6c

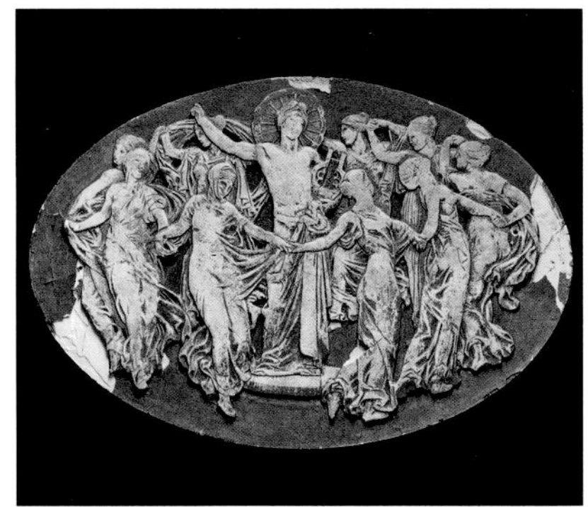
348

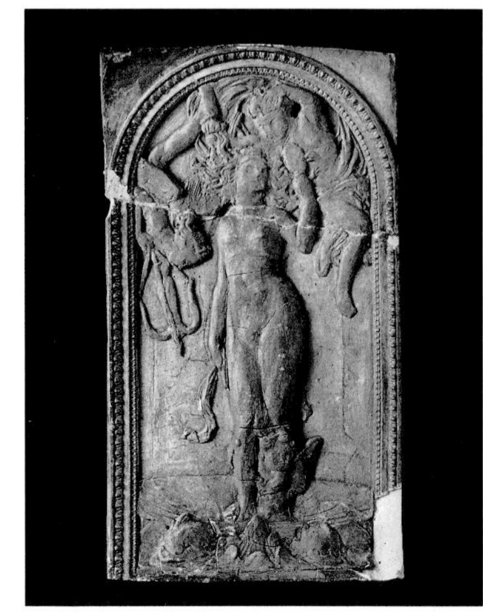
351

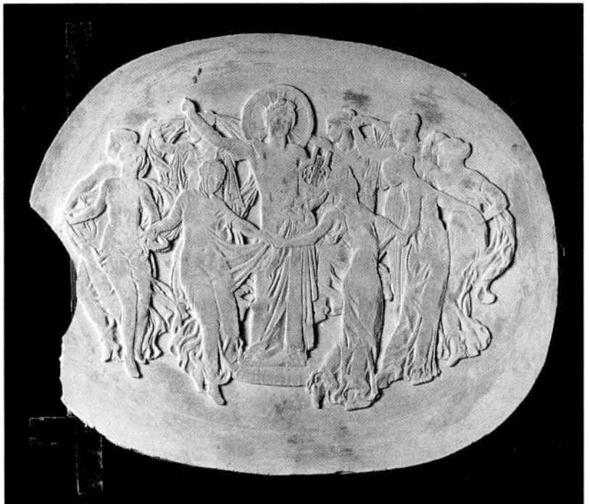
349

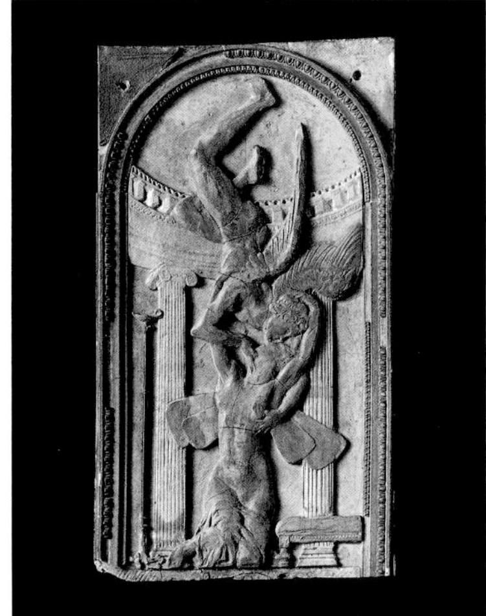
353

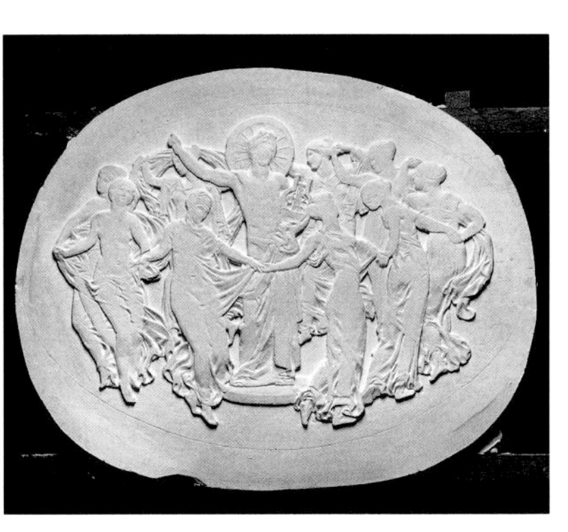
350

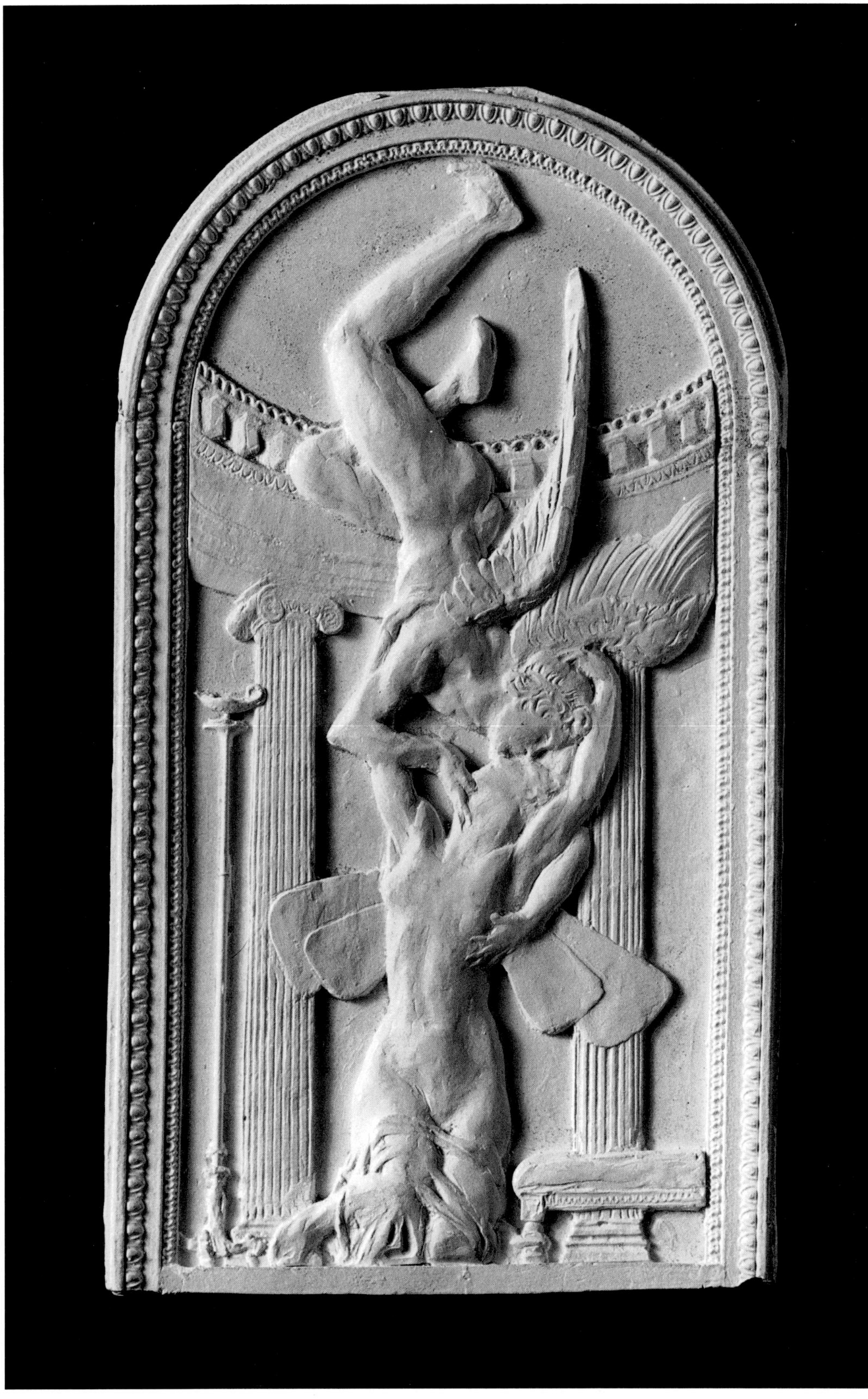

352

354 *Three Dancing Figures*

Plaster

10¾ x 6¾ x 1¼ (27.3 x 17.1 x 3.2)

1929.646.7a

355 *Three Dancing Figures*

Plaster and wax, shellacked

10½ x 6½ x 1¼ (26.7 x 16.5 x 3.2)

Inscribed in graphite center bottom edge: 2

1929.646.7b

356 *Three Dancing Figures*

Plaster

10 x 6¼ x ¾ (25.4 x 15.9 x 1.9)

Inscribed in graphite bottom left edge: 3

1929.646.7e

357 *Three Dancing Figures*

Plaster and wax, shellacked

10½ x 6½ x ¾ (26.7 x 16.5 x 1.9)

Inscribed in graphite bottom left edge: 4

1929.646.7d

358 *Three Dancing Figures*

Plaster

10½ x 6½ x 1⅛ (26.7 x 16.5 x 2.8)

Inscribed in graphite bottom left edge: 5

1929.646.7c

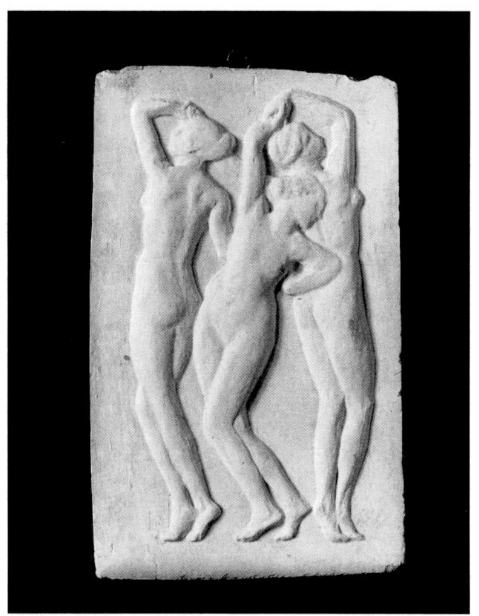

354

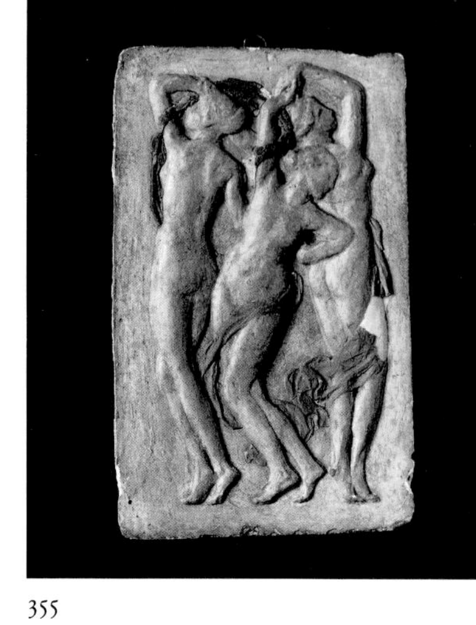

355

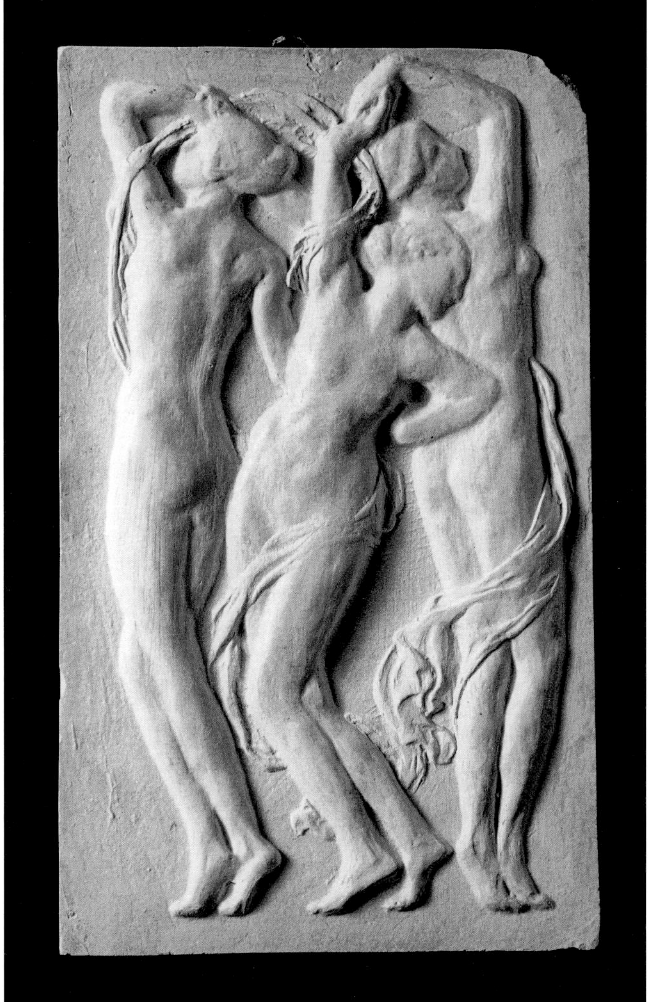

356

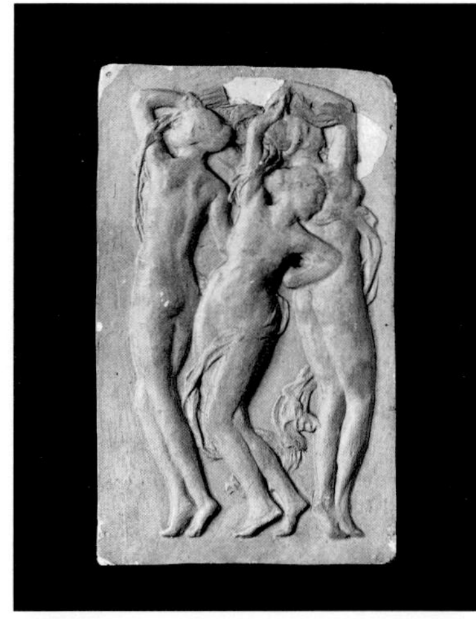

357

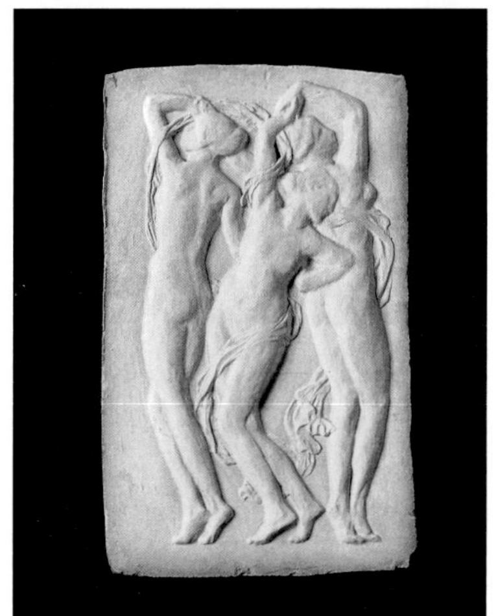

358

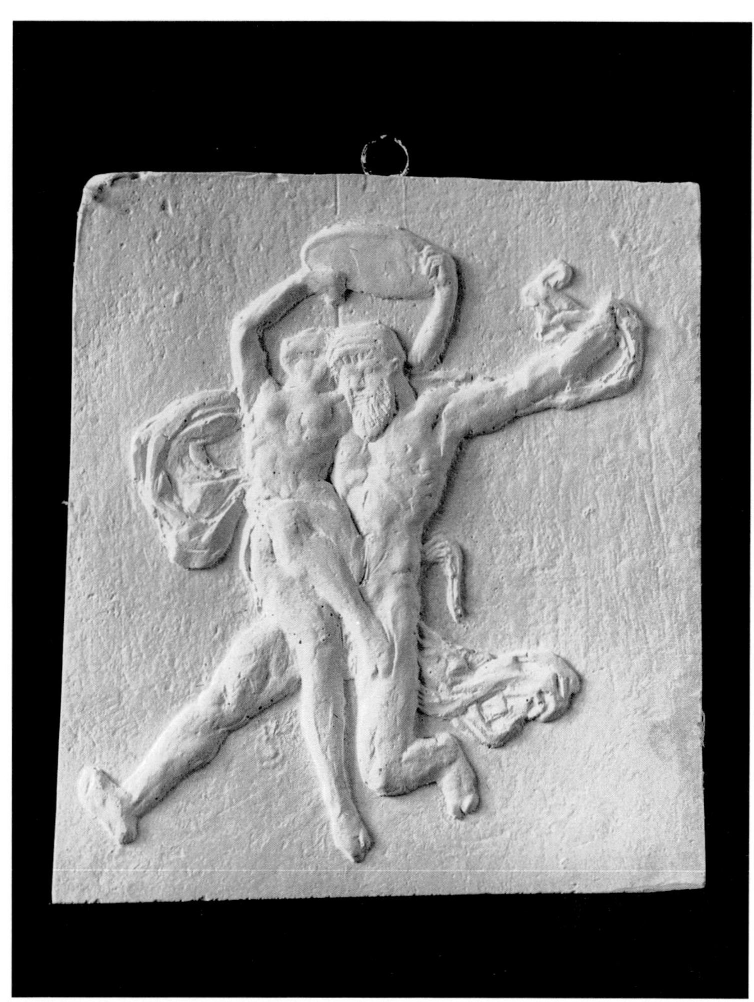

359

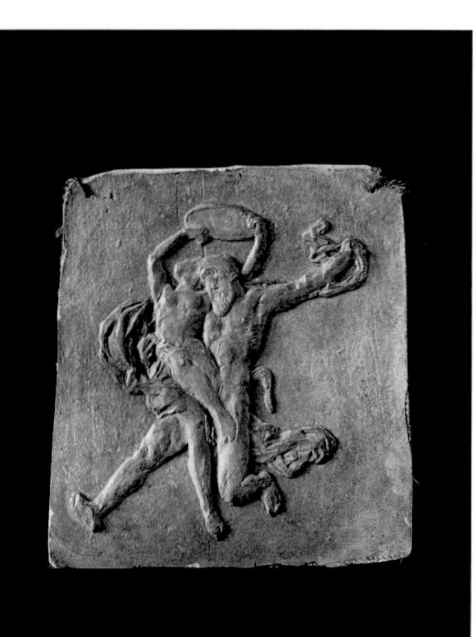

360

359 *Satyr and Maenad*

Plaster

7¼ x 6¾ x ¾ (18.4 x 17.1 x 1.9)

Inscribed in graphite bottom left edge: 2

1929.646.8a

360 *Satyr and Maenad*

Plaster and wax, shellacked

7½ x 7¼ x ½ (19.1 x 18.4 x 1.3)

Inscribed in graphite verso: 3

1929.646.8b

361 *Fame*

Plaster, painted and shellacked
9½ x 8 x ½ (24.1 x 20.3 x 1.3)

1929.646.4a

362 *The Centaur Chiron and His Pupil Achilles (Education of Achilles)*

Plaster
7¾ x 7 x ¾ (19.7 x 17.8 x 1.9)

1929.646.8c

363 *Urn with Two Sphinxes*

Plaster and wax on wood, shellacked
4½ x 4½ x 2¼ (11.4 x 11.4 x 5.7)

1929.646.4b

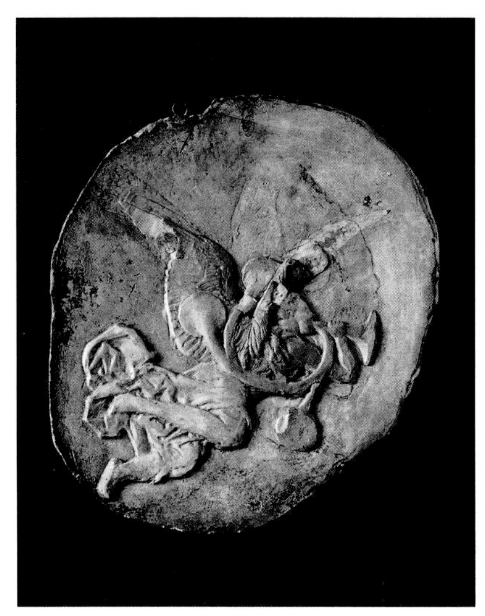

361

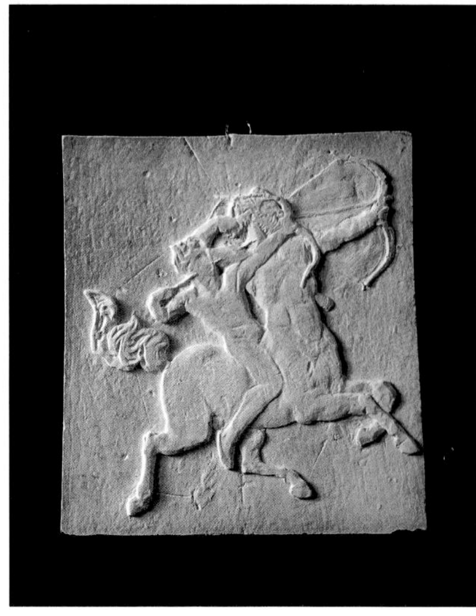

362

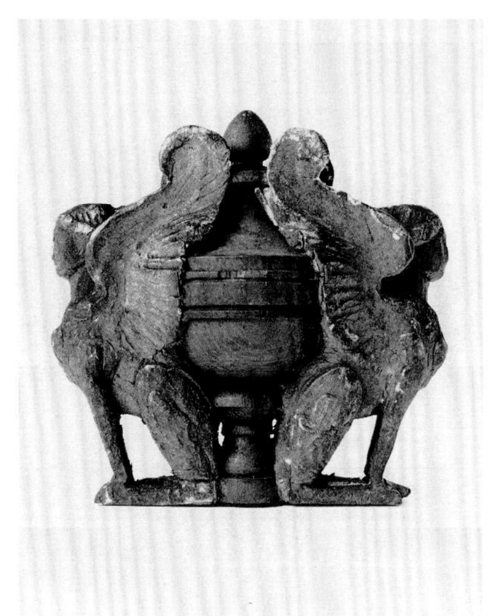

363

C. SATO

20th century

364 *Swimming Victor*

Probably 1950
Bronze, dark brown patina
22 x 7 x 6¾ (55.9 x 17.8 x 17.1)

Signed proper left top rear of base: C. SATO

Inscribed top front center of base: U.S.A. VS JAPAN / 3RD DUAL / SWIMMING MEET / TOKYO 1950

Payne Whitney Gymnasium

AUGUSTA CHRISTINE SAVAGE

1900 Green Cove Springs, Florida – 1962 Bronx, New York

365 *Green Apples*

1928
Bronze, black patina
15¾ x 7¼ x 5¾ (40 x 18.4 x 14.6)

Signed and dated proper left top of base: A SAVAGE 1928

Inscribed front edge of base: GREEN APPLES

Foundry: The Gorham Manufacturing Company, Providence, Rhode Island; mark, bottom rear edge of base: GORHAM CO. FOUNDERS OGBU

James Weldon Johnson Memorial Collection of Negro Arts and Letters, Beinecke Rare Book and Manuscript Library
1980.702

366 *Lift Every Voice and Sing*

1939
Metal, oxidized silver patina
10¾ x 9½ x 4 (27.3 x 24.1 x 10.2)

Signed and dated on edge of base proper left side: *Augusta Savage,* proper right side: WORLDS FAIR 1939

Inscribed in relief proper right side edge of base: COPYRIGHT; on plaque held by front figure: LIFT EVERY VOICE AND SING

Foundry: Possibly Augusta Savage Studios, Inc., New York, NY

Gift of Mrs. James Weldon Johnson to the James Weldon Johnson Memorial Collection of Negro Arts and Letters, Beinecke Rare Book and Manuscript Library
1980.133

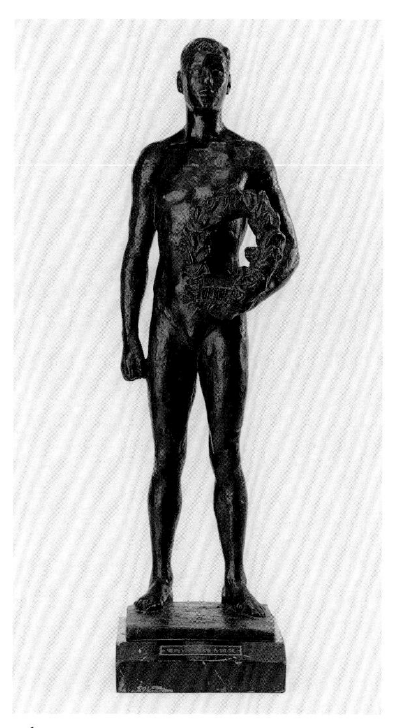

364

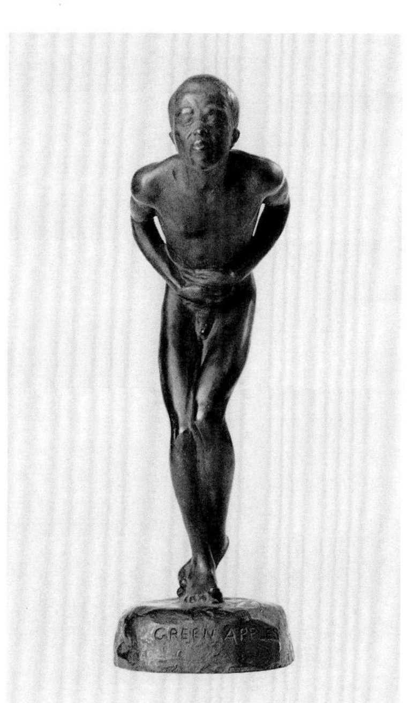

365

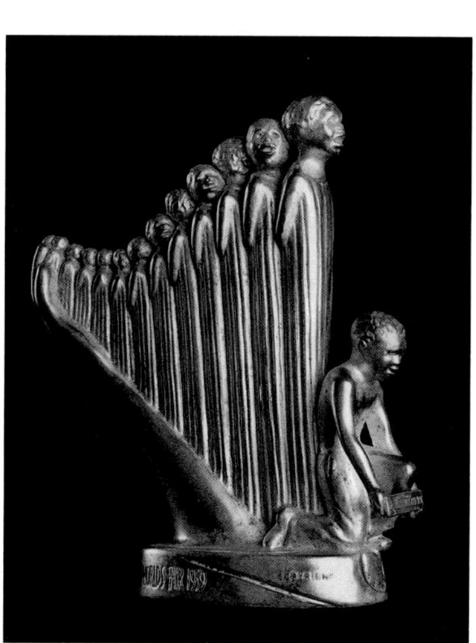

366

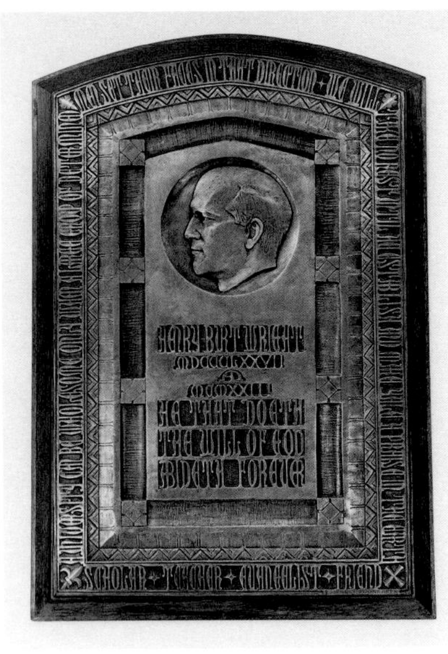

367

EUGENE SPALDING SCHOONMAKER

b. 1898 New York City

367 *Henry Burt Wright* 1877–1923
B.A. 1898, PH.D. 1903

1926
Bronze, bronze patina
31¼ x 21 x ½ (79.4 x 53.3 x 1.3)

Wood mount
34¼ x 23½ x 1 (87 x 59.7 x 2.5)

Signed and dated front lower proper left corner: EUGENE SCHOONMAKER; lower proper left: 1926

Inscribed in relief front center: HENRY BURT WRIGHT / MDCCCLXXVII / AD / MCMXXIII / HE THAT DOETH / THE WILL OF GOD / ABIDETH FOREVER; bottom: SCHOLAR + TEACHER + EVANGELIST + FRIEND; along perimeter: A UNIVERSITY CAN BE WHOLESOME ONLY WHEN A LARGE GROUP OF DETERMINED MEN SET THEIR FACES IN THAT DIRECTION + WE WILL TAKE NO REST UNTIL HE ESTABLISH AND MAKE YALE A PRAISE IN THE EARTH

Dwight Hall

RICHARD SERRA

b. 1939 San Francisco
B.F.A. 1962, M.F.A. 1964

368 *Stacks*

1990
Rolled steel
Two elements, each: 93 x 96 x 10 (236 x 244 x 25)

Foundry: Lukens Steel, Lukens, Pennsylvania

Katharine Ordway Fund
1990.2.1

SPENCER SIMPSON

Dates unknown

369 *George Pierce Baker* 1866–1935
M.A.(hon.) 1925

Probably 1908
Bronze, bronze patina
DIAM. 4½ x D. ¼ (11.4 x 0.64) sight

Signed, dated, and inscribed around front border in relief: GEORGE · PIERCE · BAKER· A·D MDCCCCVIII ·T·S–S ·FEC·

Gift of Mrs. George Pierce Baker

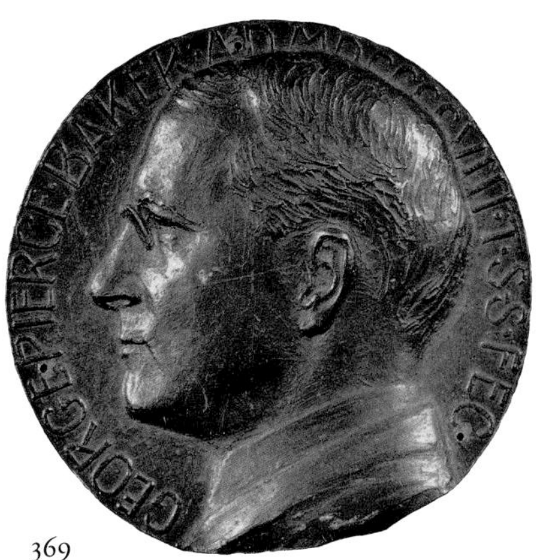

369

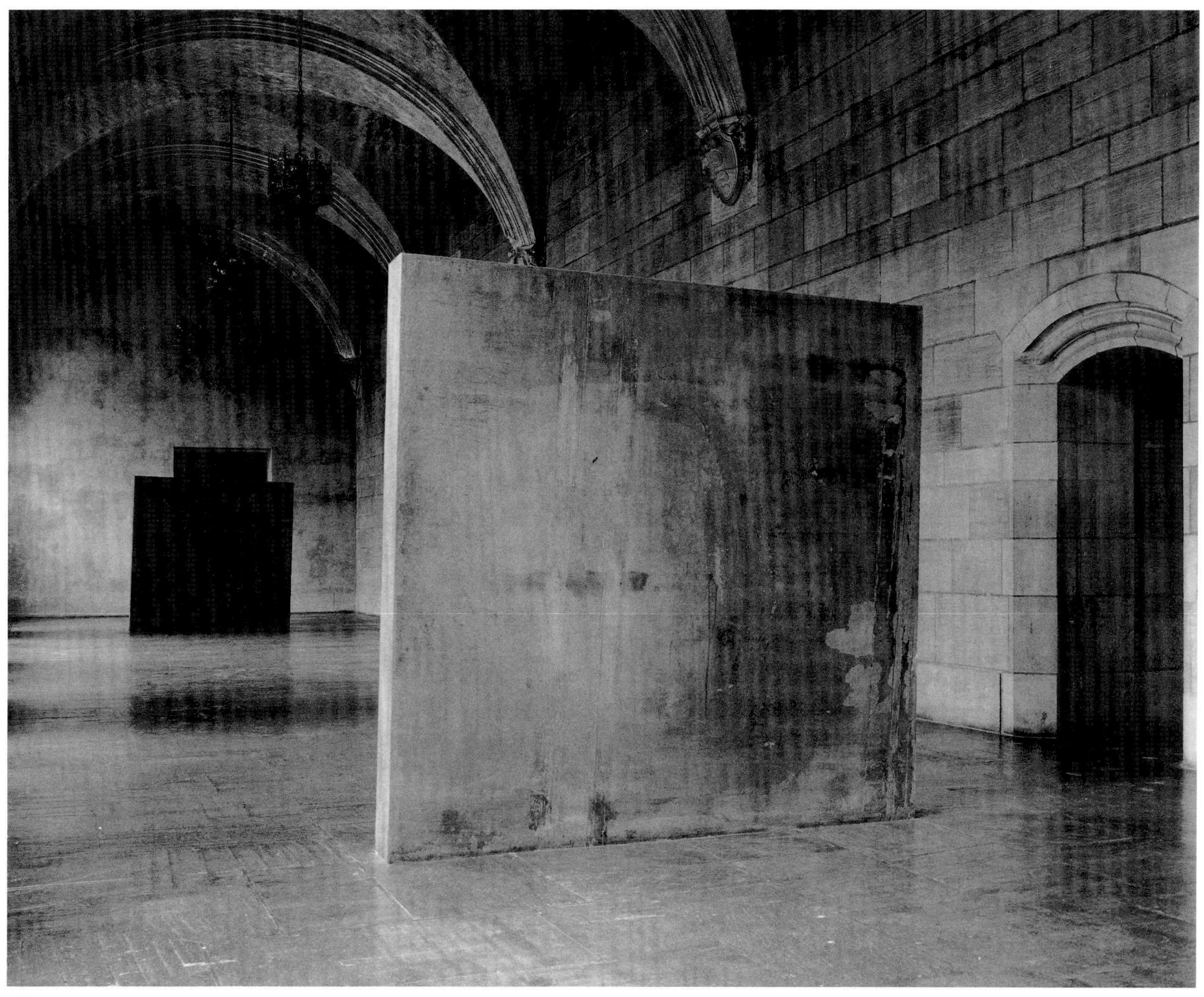

368

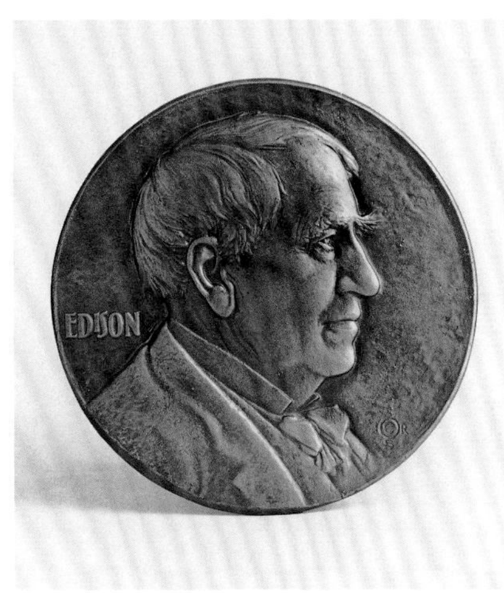

370

JOHN RAY SINNOCK

1888 Raton, New Mexico –
1947 Staten Island, New York

370 *Thomas Edison* 1847–1931

Probably 1936
Gilded bronze
DIAM. 16 X D. 1 (40.6 x 2.5)

Signed lower right front: © R / S

Inscribed left front center in relief:
EDISON

Foundry: Medallic Art Company, New York; mark, verso top center in relief:
MEDALLIC – ART – CO. / N.Y.

Becton Engineering and Applied Science Center

JOHN SKILLIN

1746 Boston – 1800 Boston

SIMEON SKILLIN, JR.

1756/57 Boston – 1806 Boston

371, 372, 373
Peace, Virtue, and Plenty
Also known as
Peace, Liberty, and Plenty

1791
Pediment figures on chest-on-chest by Stephen Badlam, 1751–1815
Mahogany
Peace: 5½ x 13½ x 3¼ (14 x 34.3 x 8.3)

Virtue: 14 x 9¼ x 3½ (35.6 x 23.5 x 8.9)

Plenty: 6 x 15½ x 2½ (15.2 x 39.4 x 6.4)

Mabel Brady Garvan Collection
1930.2003

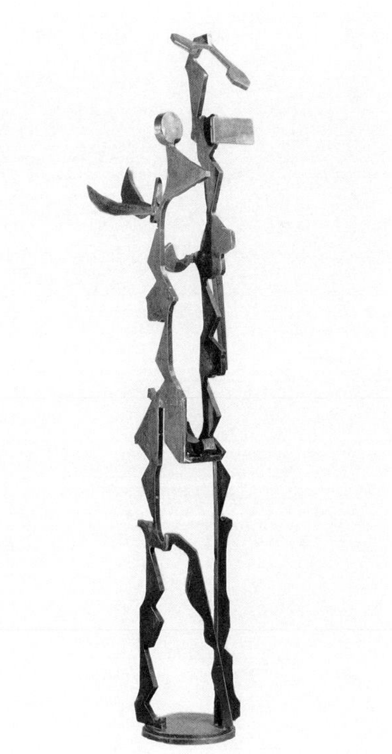

374

DAVID SMITH

1906 Decatur, Indiana –
1965 Bennington, Vermont

374 *Man and Woman in the Cathedral*

1956
Steel, dark reddish-brown patina
85½ x 18½ x 20½ (217.2 x 47 x 52.1)

Signed and dated on underside of base in relief: *David / Smith / 1 /31 1956*

Gift of Susan Morse Hilles
1957.39.1

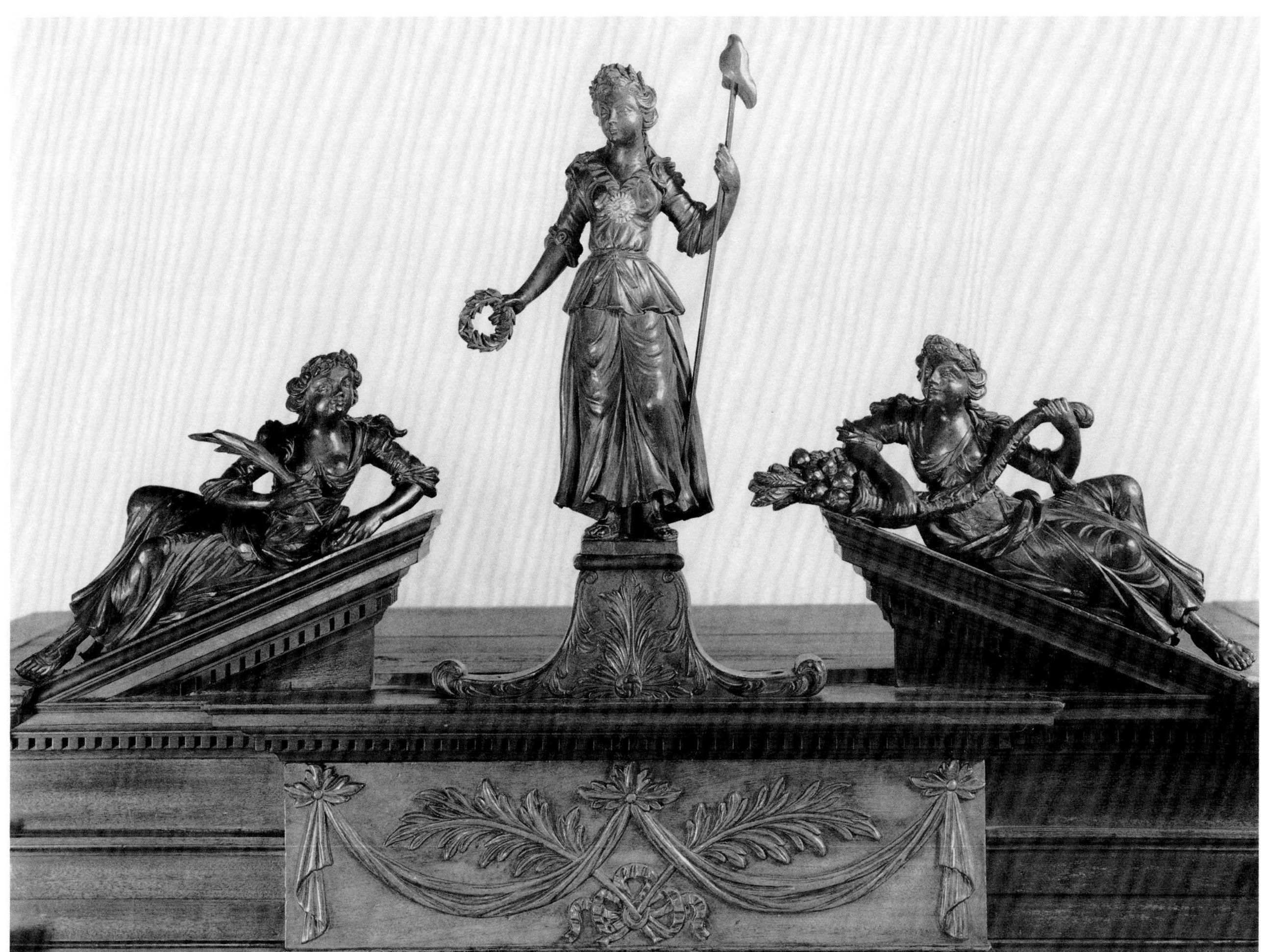

371, 372, 373

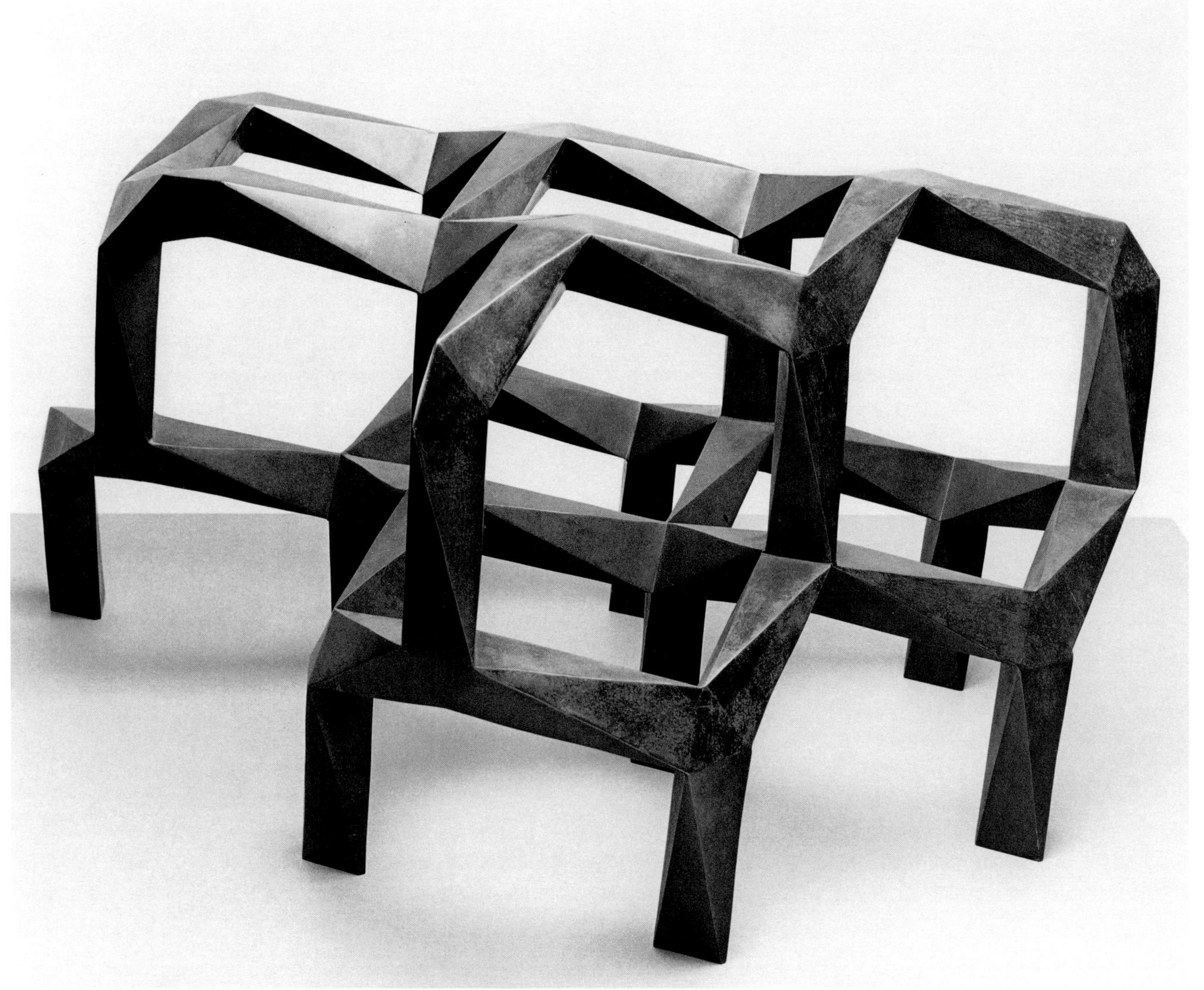

376

375 *Cubi XXII*

1964
Burnished stainless steel
103¾ x 72¾ x 35 (263.5 x 184.8 x 88.9)

Signed proper right top front of base in relief: *David Smith*

Dated proper left top front of base in relief: *June 5 1964*

Inscribed proper left top rear of base in relief: CUBI XXII

Stephen Carlton Clark, B.A. 1903, Fund
1968.31

TONY SMITH

1912 South Orange, New Jersey –
1980 New York City

376 *Untitled*

1967
Bronze, black patina
23½ x 47½ x 32 (59.7 x 120.7 x 81.3)

Gift of Susan Morse Hilles
1985.2.12

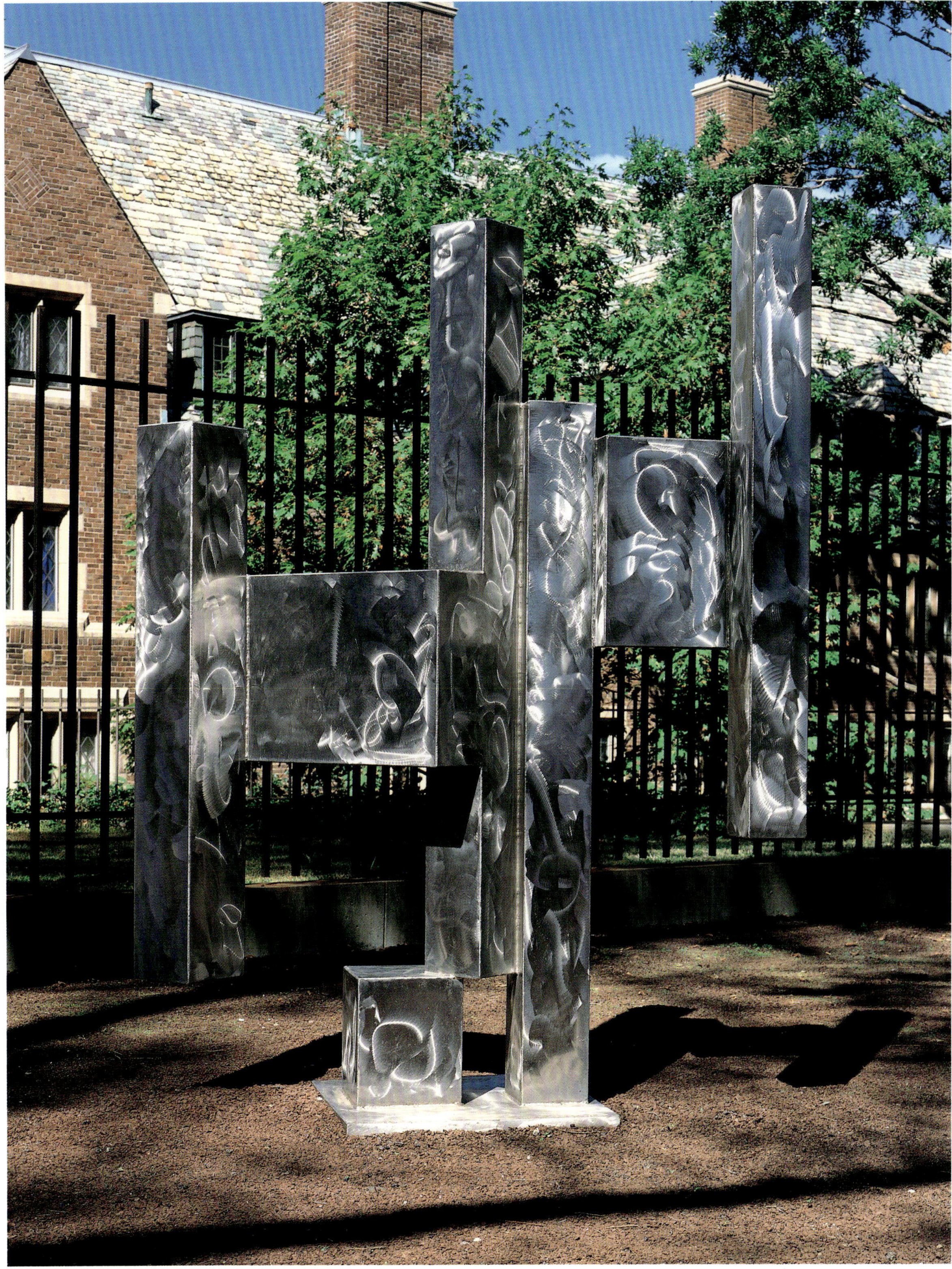

CARMELO SOBRINO

b. 1948 Manati, Puerto Rico

377 *Untitled*

c.1970
Plexiglas
21¾ x 21¾ x 8¼ (55.2 x 55.2 x 21)

Gift of Susan Morse Hilles
1985.2.11

GEORGE SPAVENTA

b. 1918 New York City

378 *Torso*

1958
Bronze, black patina
19½ x 7¾ x 10 (49.5 x 19.7 x 25.4)

Signed and dated proper left top rear of base: Spaventa / 58

Founder's mark and cast number proper left side of base: CAF 6/6

Gift of Mrs. David J. Randall
1967.79

EDGAR ZELL STEEVER IV

b. 1915 Pittsfield, Massachusetts
B.A. 1936, B.F.A. 1940, M.F.A. 1941

379 *Adolph Knopf* 1882–1966
M.A.(hon.) 1923

Unveiled May 13, 1951
Bronze, dark brown patina
27¼ x 17 x 1¾ (69.2 x 43.2 x 4.4)

Signed under collar: *Edgar Zell Steever*

Inscribed lower center of plaque in relief: ADOLPH KNOPF / Inspiring Teacher, Scholar, Friend / PRESENTED BY HIS STUDENTS / OF 1920–1951

Gift of the students of the sitter to the Department of Geology
1970.87

JOHN HENRY BRADLEY STORRS

1885 Chicago –
1956 Mer, Loire-et-Cher, France

380 *Untitled (The Dancer)*

1918–20
Polychromed terra cotta
4¾ x 4¼ x 3 (12.1 x 10.8 x 7.6)

Marble base
4 x 3¼ x 3¼ (10.2 x 8.3 x 8.3)

Bequest of Katherine S. Dreier to the Collection Société Anonyme
1952.30.3

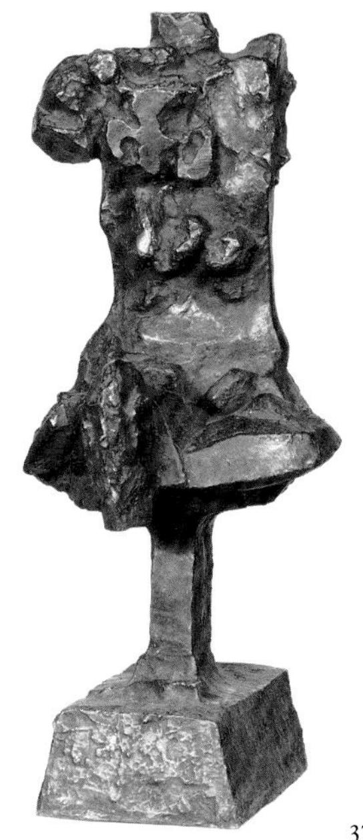

378

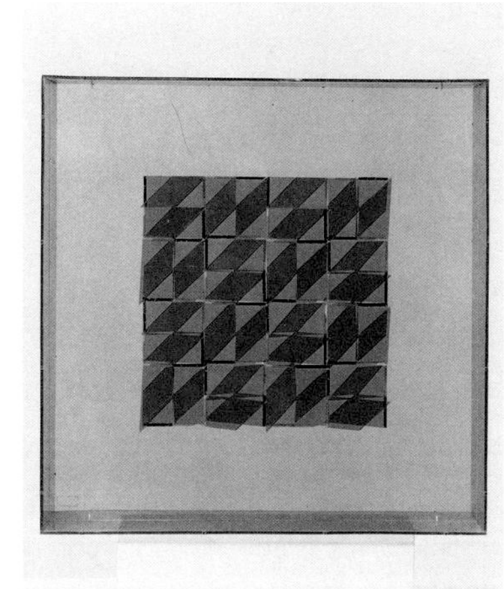

377

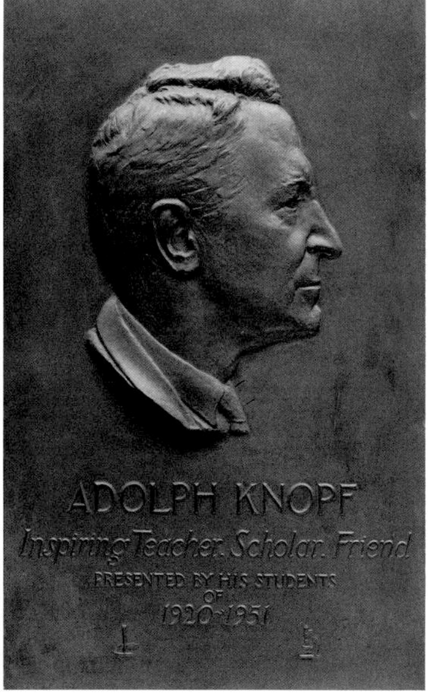

379

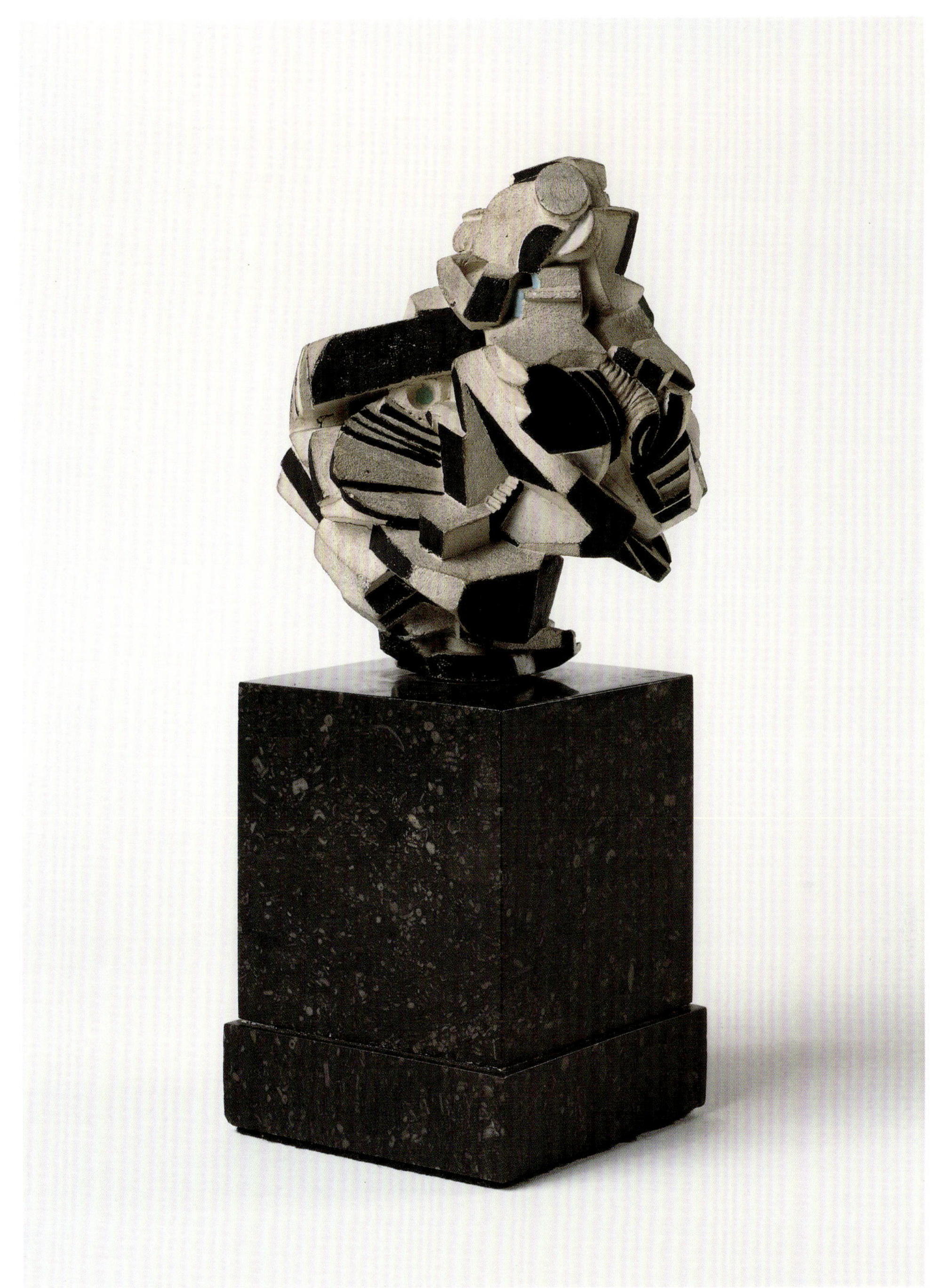

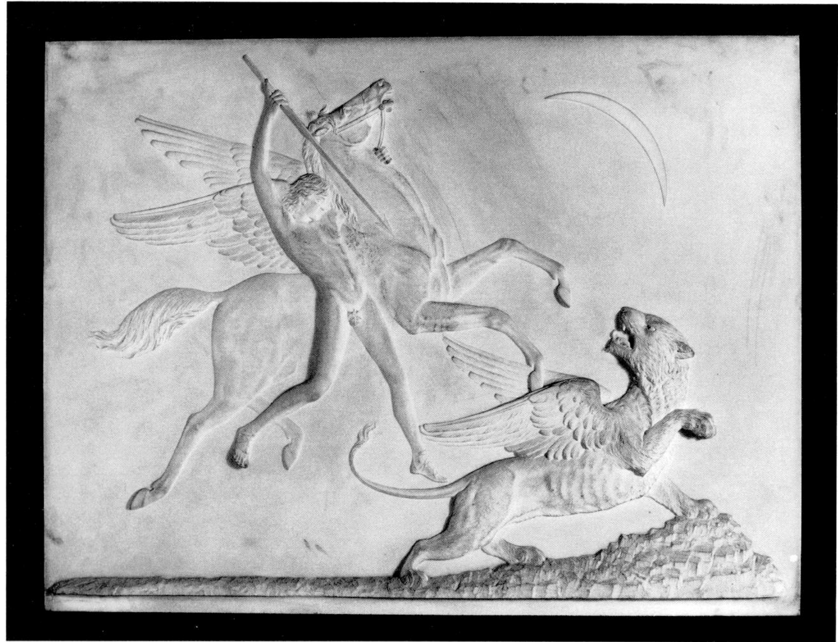

381

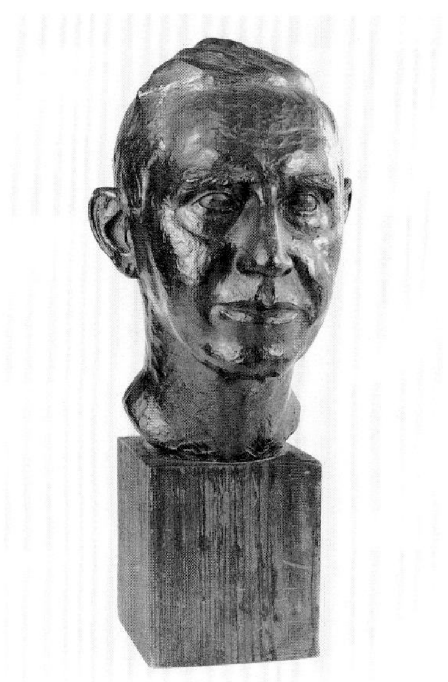

382

THOMAS WALDO STORY

1855 Rome, Italy – 1915 New York City

381 *Bellerophon Attacking the Chimera*

1884
Marble fireplace overmantel
26½ x 36½ x 2 (67.3 x 92.7 x 5.1)

Wood frame
39½ x 48½ x 4¼ (100.3 x 123.2 x 10.8)

Signed and dated lower right front: WALDO STORY / ROME 1884

Gift of John Davenport Wheeler, PH.B. 1858
1911.26

JUSTIN STURM

1899 Nehawka, Nebraska – 1967 Westport, Connecticut
B.A. 1922

382 *William McFee* 1881–1966
M.A.(hon.) 1936

c.1930
Bronze, brownish-black patina
12¼ x 8½ x 9½ (31.1 x 21.6 x 24.1)

Signed lower proper right rear: Justin Sturm

Foundry: Roman Bronze Works, New York; mark, lower center rear: ROMAN BRONZE WORKS. N.Y.

Gift of Mrs. James T. Babb to the Beinecke Rare Book and Manuscript Library
1980.369

383 *Ernest Hemingway*

1899–1961

1934
Bronze, dark brown patina

14½ x 10¼ x 11¼ (36.8 x 26 x 28.6)

Signed and dated lower proper right rear: Justin Sturm / Key West, 1934

Foundry: Roman Bronze Works, New York; mark, lower proper left rear: ROMAN BRONZE WORKS. N.Y.

Gift of Mrs. James T. Babb in memory of her husband to the Collection of American Literature, Beinecke Rare Book and Manuscript Library
1980.134

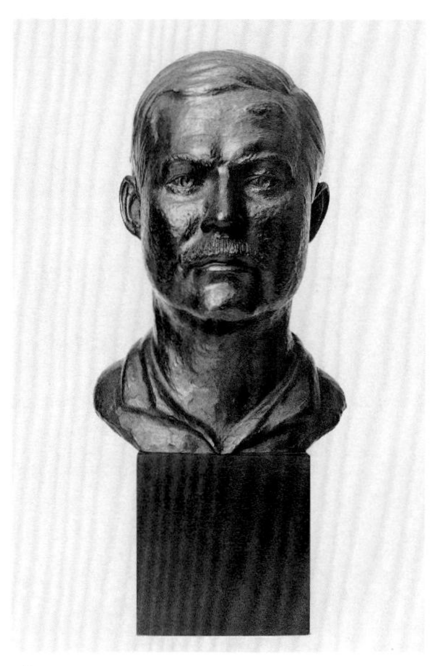

383

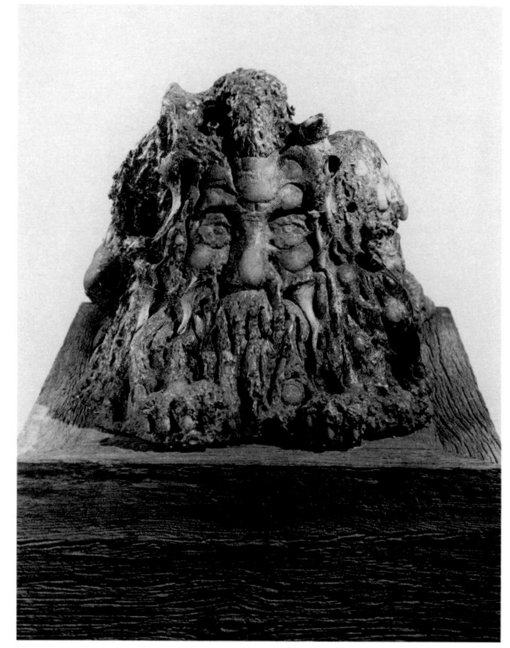

384

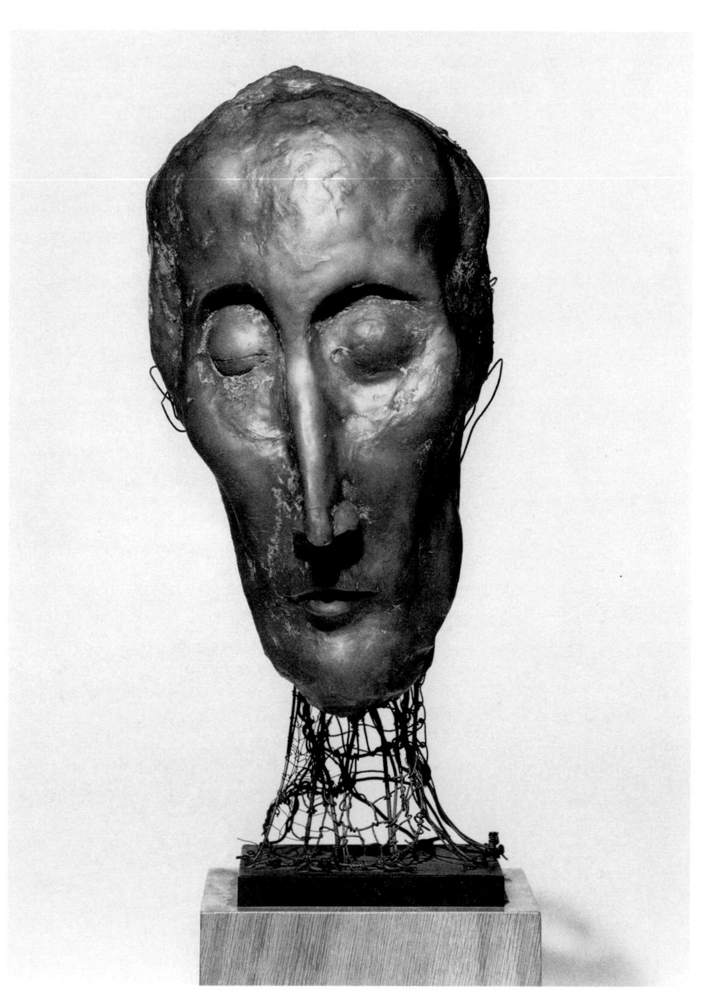

385

PAVEL TCHELITCHEW

1898 District of Kaluga, near Moscow, Russia – 1957 Rome, Italy
Active U.S. after 1934, citizen 1952

384 *Sleeper Awake*

c.1940
Plaster, stones, seashells, paint, and gilt
18¾ x 35½ x 22½ (47.6 x 90.2 x 57.2)

Barnwood base
22½ (24½ with casters) x 39½ x 25½
(57.2 [62.2 with casters] x 100.3 x 64.8)

Gift of Mr. and Mrs. James Thrall Soby
1945.33

385 *Dame Edith Sitwell* 1887–1964

n.d.
Wire, wax, sand, and nails
17 x 8 x 10 (43.2 x 20.3 x 25.4)

Wood base, painted black
¾ x 5½ x 5½ (1.9 x 14 x 14)

Bequest of Mr. R. Kirk Askew
1984.126.1

LAUNT THOMPSON

1833 Abbeyleix, County Queens, Ireland – 1894 Middletown, New York
To U.S. 1847
M.A.(hon.) 1874

386 *Joseph Parrish Thompson* 1819–1879
B.A. 1838, M.A. 1841

1872
Marble
24 x 12¾ x 10¾ (61 x 32.4 x 27.3)

Signed and dated proper left side: LAUNT·THOMPSON Sc / 1872.

Inscribed in paint on front of bust: Dr. J.P. Thompson. / Sc LAUNT THOMPSON.

Gift of the family of Joseph Parrish Thompson, B.A. 1838, M.A. 1841
1900.61

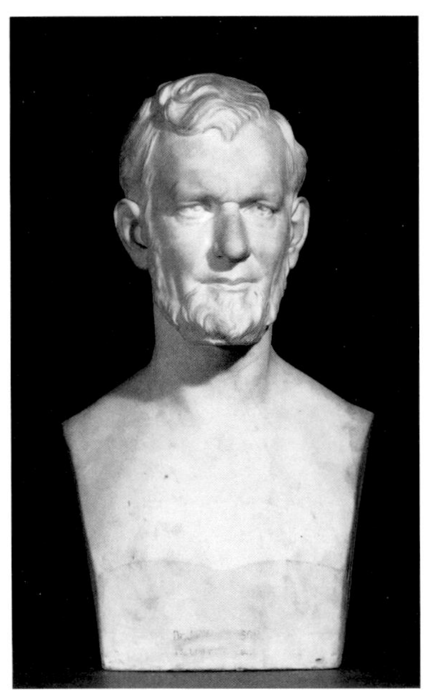

386

387 *Abraham Pierson* 1645–1707

1874
Bronze, original patina obscured by corrosion
77¾ x 29½ x 24 (197.5 x 74.9 x 61)

Granite base
77½ x 46 x 46 (196.9 x 116.8 x 116.8)

Signed and dated, proper left front of base: LAUNT. THOMPSON. / SCULPT. 1874

Inscribed front of pedestal: ABRAHAMUS PIERSON / PRIMUS / COLLEGIO YALENSI / PRAESEDIT / MDCCI–MDCCVII; rear of pedestal: HANC STATUAM / PONENDAM CURAVIT / CAROLUS MORGAN / NEO–EBORACENSIS / MDCCCLXXIV.

Foundry: Robert Wood & Company, Philadelphia; mark, proper right side of base toward rear: ROBERT WOOD & CO. / BRONZE FOUNDERS. / PHILA.

Gift of Charles Morgan to Yale University
1874.4

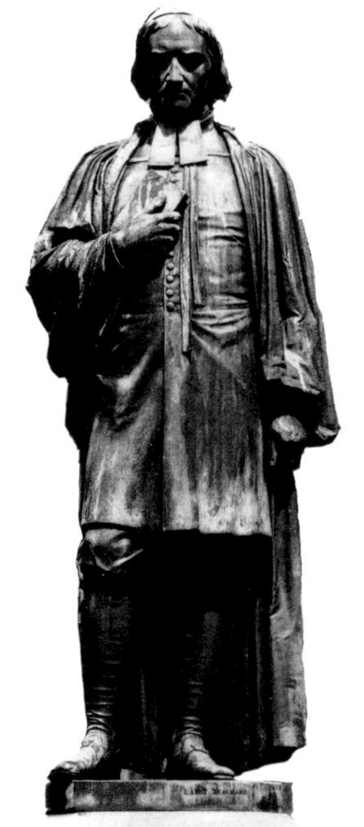

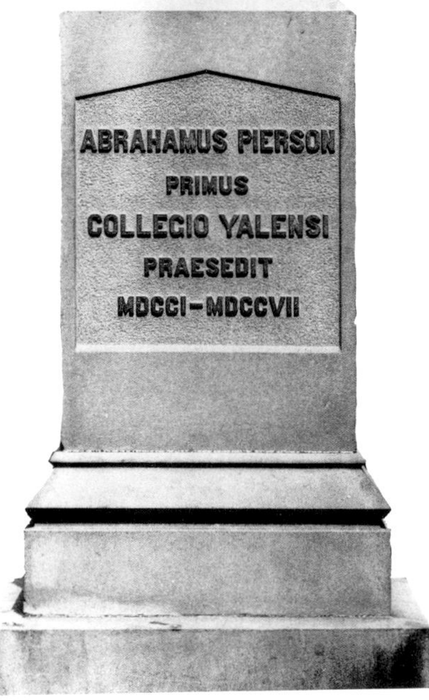

387

after
LAUNT THOMPSON

388 *Abraham Pierson* 1645–1707

Probably 19th century, after an original of 1874
Bronzed plaster
25½ x 9¼ x 7¼ (64.8 x 23.5 x 18.4)

Signed and dated proper left rear edge of base: *Launt Thompson / Sc Jan 1874*

Inscribed front edge of base: Rector Pierson: / Yale College

Woodbridge Hall

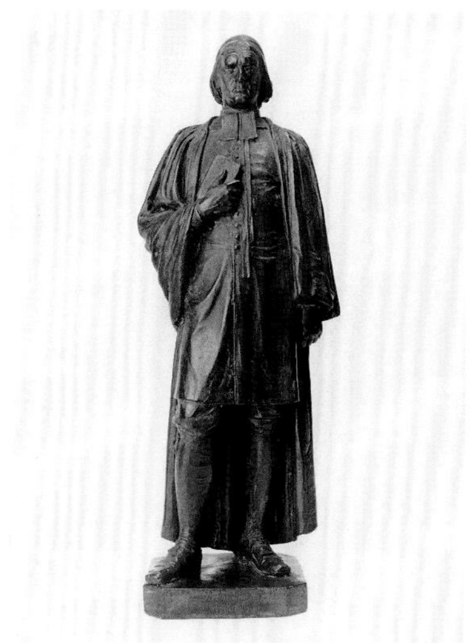

388

389 *Abraham Pierson* 1645–1707

Before 1938, after an original of 1874
Bronze, dark brown and bronze patina
24¾ x 9½ x 7¼ (62.9 x 24.1 x 18.4)

Signed and dated proper left side edge: LAUNT THOMPSON / JAN 1874

Inscribed front edge of base: Rector Pierson. / Yale College.

Gift of an associate fellow to Pierson College

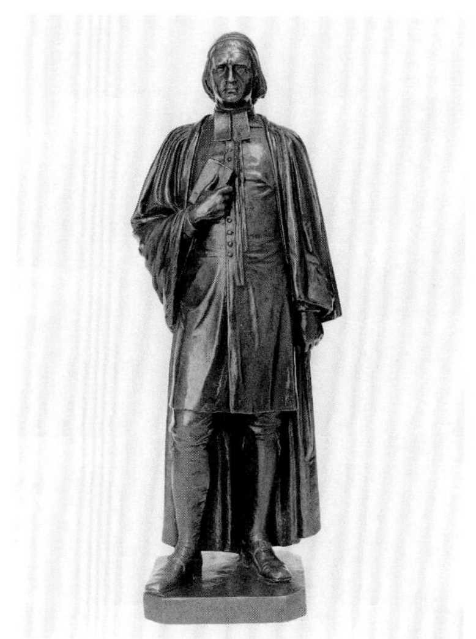

389

390 *Abraham Pierson* 1645–1707

Cast 1985, after an original of 1874
Bronze, dark brown and bronze patina
24½ x 9 x 6¾ (61.6 x 22.9 x 17.1)

Signed and dated proper left side edge of base: LAUNT THOMPSON / JAN 1874

Inscribed front edge of base: Rector Pierson / Yale college; proper left side: ON

Foundry: Cavalier Renaissance Foundry, Inc., Bridgeport, Connecticut

Pierson College

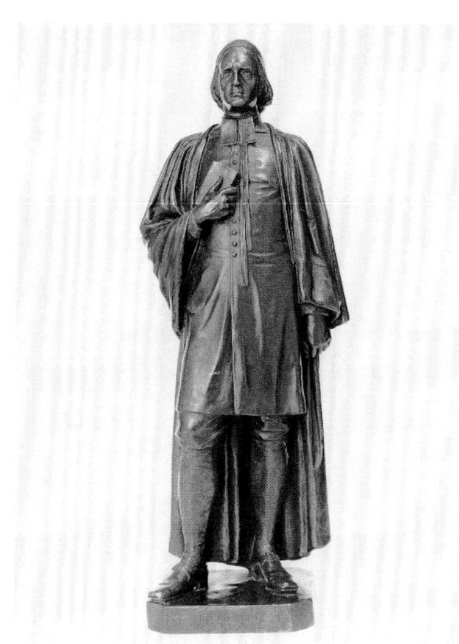

390

391 *Abraham Pierson*

Same as cat. 390

after
JOHN TRUMBULL
See cat. 440

RAOUL UBAC

b. 1910 Malmedy, Belgium
Active U.S. c.1960

392 *Untitled*

c.1960
Slate
55½ x 118½ x 1½ (141 x 301 x 3.8) approx.

Signed lower proper left corner: U

Kline Biology Tower
1968.49

HERK VAN TONGEREN

1943 Holland, Michigan – 1987 Hopewell, New Jersey

393 *Teatro IX*

1982
Bronze, mottled dark green and light green patina
17 x 25 x 12½ (43.2 x 63.5 x 31.8)

Wood base
2 x 27 x 14 (5.1 x 68.6 x 35.6)

Signed, dated, and numbered lower rear on edge: *Herk Van Tongeren 1/7 '82 / ©*

Cast at Johnson Atelier, Princeton, New Jersey

Stephen Carlton Clark, B.A. 1903, Fund
1983.14

DAVID VON SCHLEGELL

b. 1920 St. Louis, Missouri

394 *Untitled Steel Wedge #1*

1977
White coated steel
15½ x 90¾ x 45¼ (39.4 x 230.5 x 114.9)

Gift of the artist
1977.189

BESSIE ONAHOTEMA POTTER VONNOH

1872 St. Louis, Missouri – 1955 New York City

395 *Two Women (Daydreams)*

1902
Bronze, light green and exposed bronze patina
10 5/32 x 21 x 12 (25.8 x 53.3 x 30.5)

Signed, dated, and numbered lower proper left rear: Besse Potter Vonnoh / N. III Copyright 1902

Foundry: Roman Bronze Works, New York; mark, proper right rear edge of base: ROMAN BRONZE WORKS / N.Y.

John Hill Morgan, B.A. 1893, LL.B. 1896, Fund
1973.124

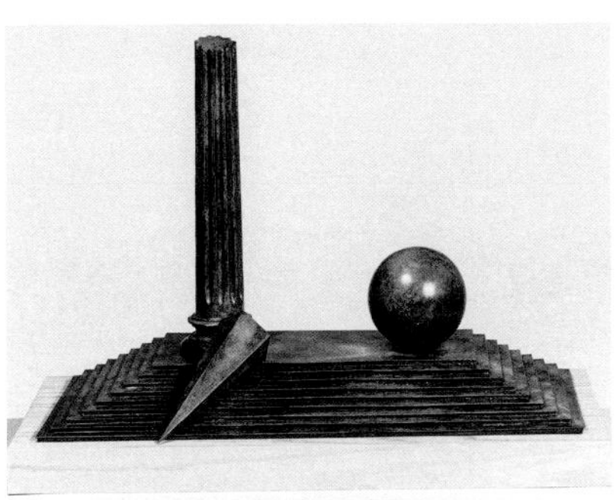

393

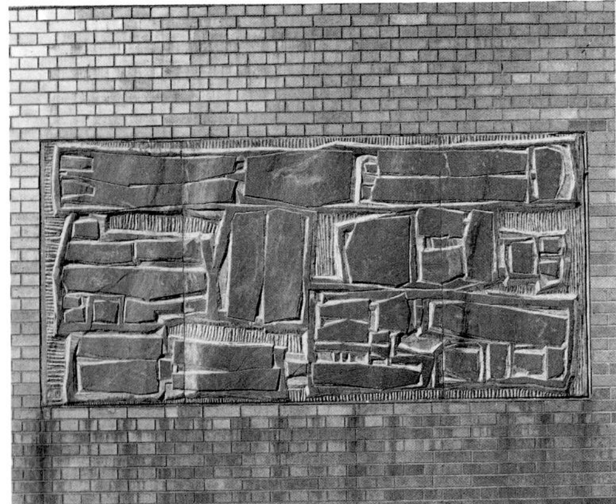

392

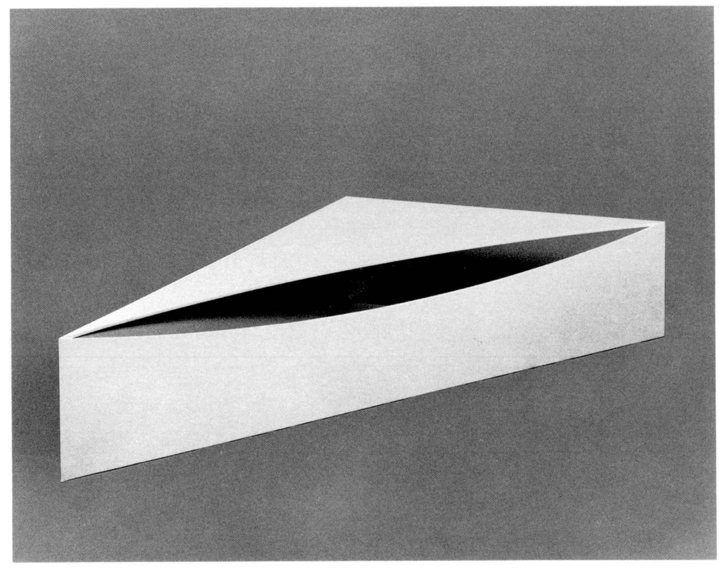

394

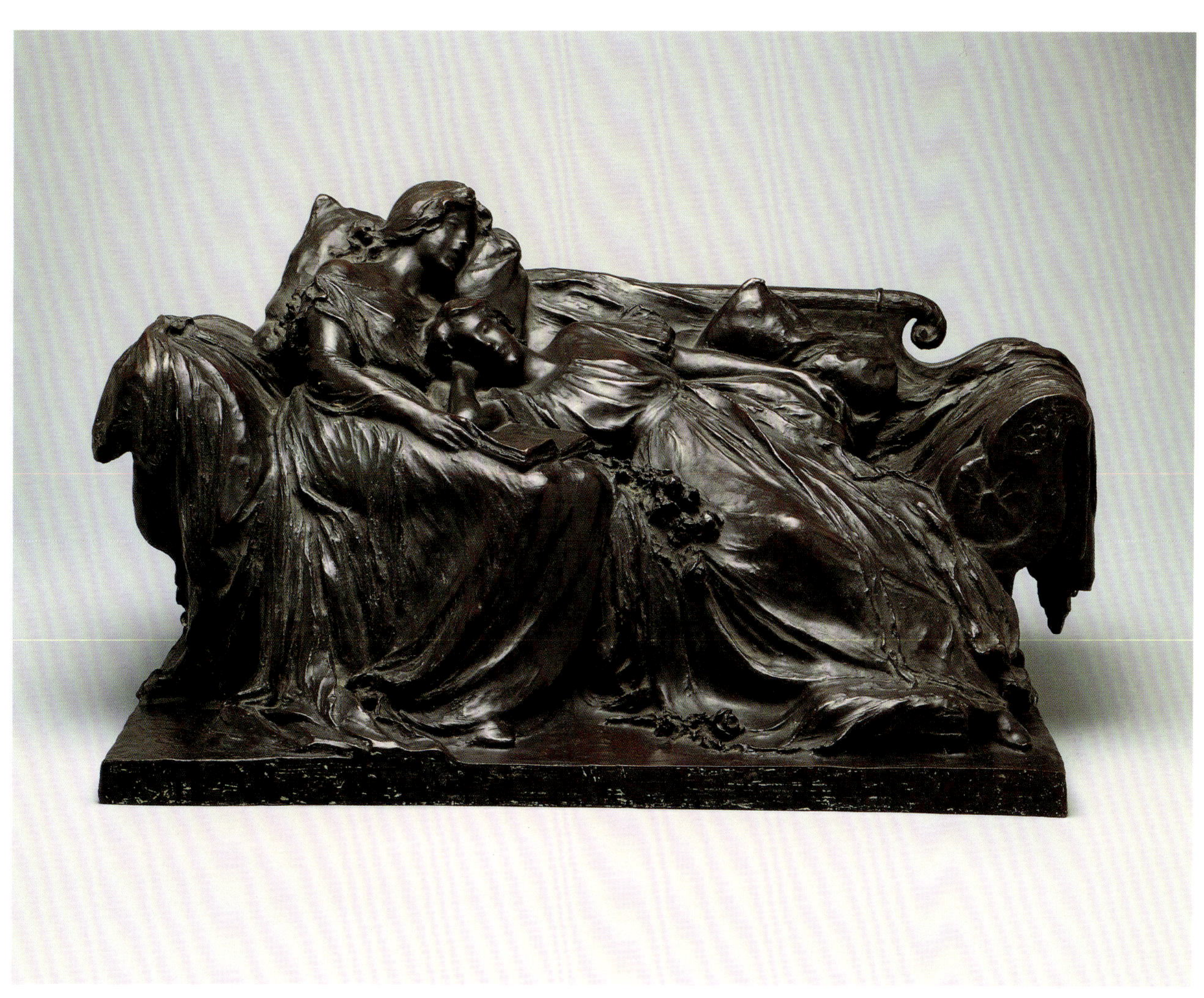

395

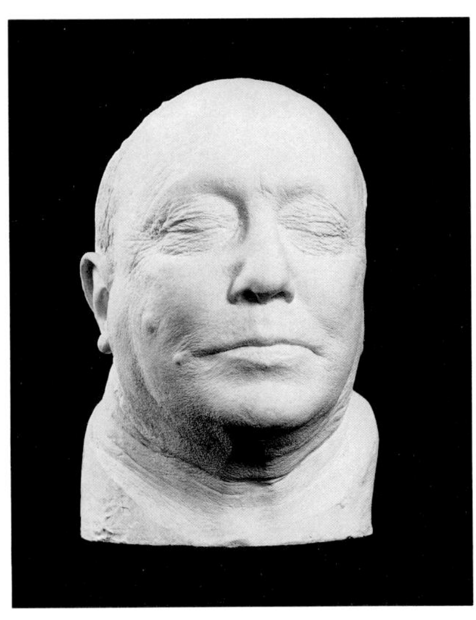

396

HERMAN WALTHAUSEN

Dates unknown

396 *William Rose Benét* 1886–1950
PH.B. 1907, M.A.(hon.) 1921

Probably 1950
Plaster
11¾ x 7½ x 9 (29.8 x 19.1 x 22.9)

Signed and inscribed in graphite lower rear: WILLIAM. BENÉT / By / H. WALTHAUSEN

Collection of American Literature, Beinecke Rare Book and Manuscript Library
1980.310

JOHN QUINCY ADAMS WARD

1830 near Urbana, Ohio – 1910 New York City

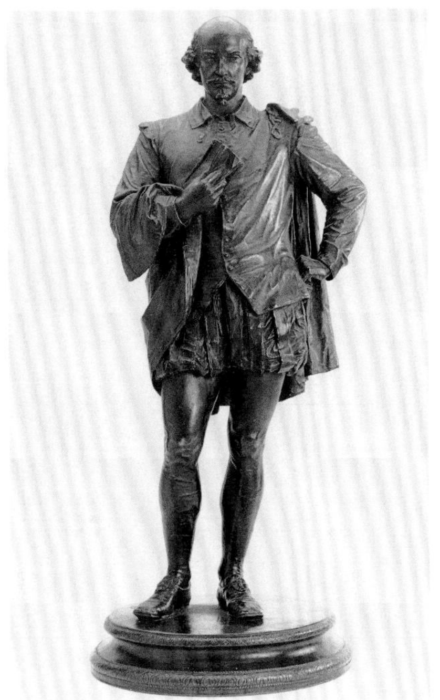

397

397 *William Shakespeare* 1564–1616

1894
Bronze, dark brown and bronze patina
27½ x 13 x 11 (69.9 x 33 x 27.9)

Signed and dated proper right top of base: J.Q.A. WARD / 1894

Foundry: The Henry-Bonnard Bronze Company, New York; mark, proper left top of base in relief: CAST BY THE HENRY BONNARD BRONZE CO / NEW YORK 1894

Collection of the Elizabethan Club

ANDY WARHOL

1928 Philadelphia – 1987 New York City

398 *Painted Shoe*

1958
Watercolor on wooden shoe form
5 x 8⅞ x 2¾ (12.7 x 22.5 x 7)

Signed in graphite in arch of shoe: Andy Warhol

Inscription on sole of shoe: Property of I. Miller & Sons Sep 11 1958 519 4B

Gift of Simeon Braguin
1988.94.1

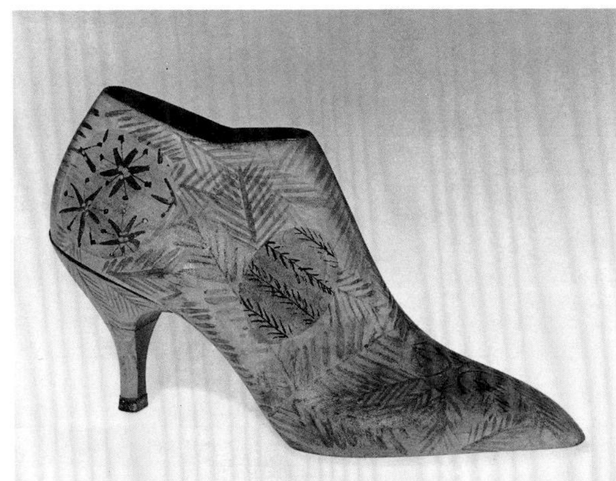

398

ELBERT WEINBERG

b. 1928 Hartford, Connecticut
M.F.A. 1955

399 *Angel*

1957–58
Bronze, dark greenish-black patina
61 x 28 x 22½ (154.9 x 71.1 x 57.2)

Signed top rear of base: E W (monogram)

Director's Purchase Fund
1958.84

JOHN FERGUSON WEIR

1841 West Point, New York –
1926 Providence, Rhode Island
M.A.(hon.) 1871

400 *Benjamin Silliman, Sr.* 1779–1864
B.A. 1796, M.A. 1799

1884
Bronze, original patina obscured by corrosion
96 x 40¼ x 31 (243.8 x 102.2 x 78.7)

Stone pedestal
66 x 46 x 46 (167.6 x 116.8 x 116.8)

Signature and date on proper right front of base: JOHN F. WEIR / SCULPT. 1884.

Inscribed front of pedestal: BENJAMIN SILLIMAN / PROFESSOR OF NATURAL SCIENCE / IN / YALE COLLEGE / FROM 1802–1853 / —— / BORN AUG. 8. 1779 / DIED NOV. 24. 1864 / ——

Foundry: The Henry-Bonnard Bronze Company, New York; mark, proper left edge of base: THE HENRY – BONNARD / BRONZE CO. N.Y.

Gift of the friends and students of the sitter
1884.3

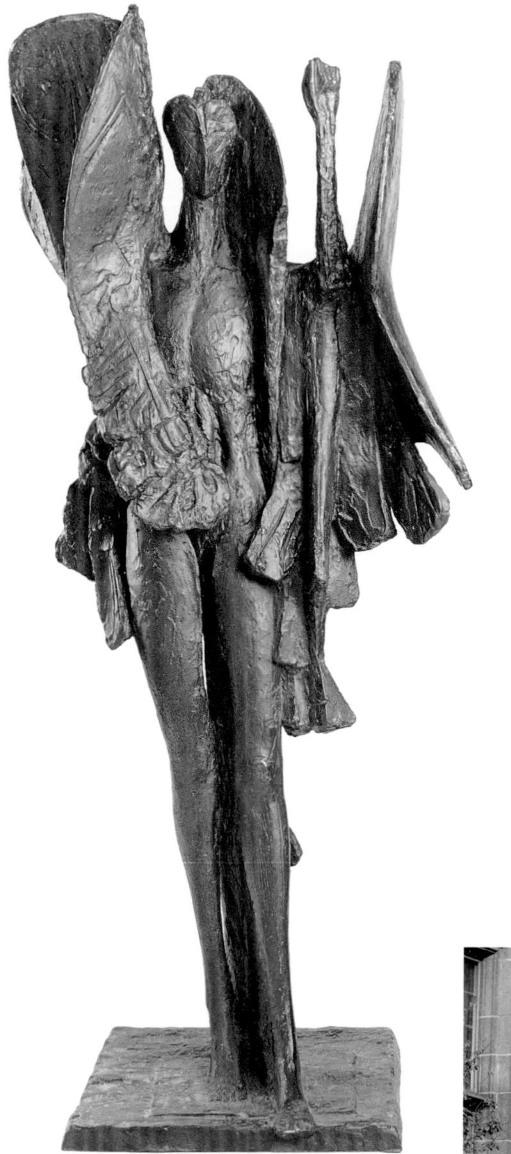

399

400

401 *Theodore Dwight Woolsey*
1801–1889
B.A. 1820, M.A. 1823

1896
Bronze, original patina obscured by corrosion
89¾ x 67¾ x 39¾ (228 x 172.1 x 101)

Marble pedestal
55 x 63½ x 90½ (139.7 x 161.3 x 229.9)

Signature proper right side of base: *Jno. F. Weir.* / Sculptor

Inscribed proper right side of pedestal: THEODORVS DWIGHT WOOLSEY; proper left side: PROFESSOR LINGVAE ET LITTERARVM GRAEGARVM MDCCCXXXI – MDCCCLI / PRAESES COLLEGII YALENSIS MDCCCXLVI – MDCCCLXXI

Foundry: The Henry-Bonnard Bronze Company, New York; mark, proper left rear of base: CAST BY THE HENRY – BONNARD BRONZE CO N.Y. 1896

Anonymous gift
1896.5

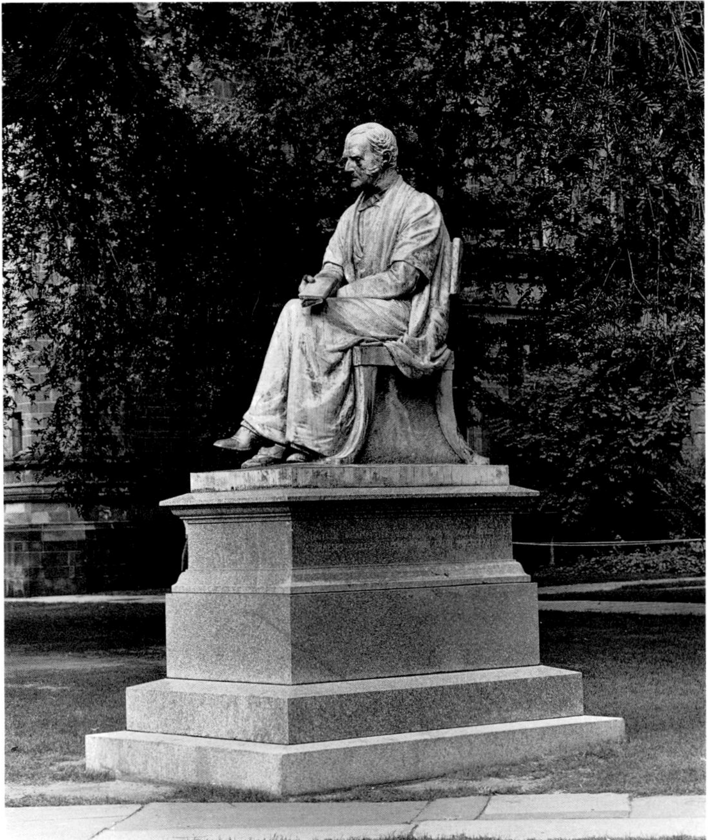

401

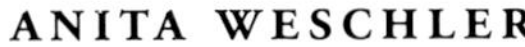

ANITA WESCHLER

b. New York City

402 *Frances Frost* 1905–1959

c.1935
Plaster, painted to simulate terra cotta
15 x 6¾ x 9 (38.1 x 17.1 x 22.9)

Signed lower proper right rear: ANITA WESCHLER

Inscribed lower proper right rear: ER

Gift of Jack A. Goldfarb to the Collection of American Literature, Beinecke Rare Book and Manuscript Library
1980.370

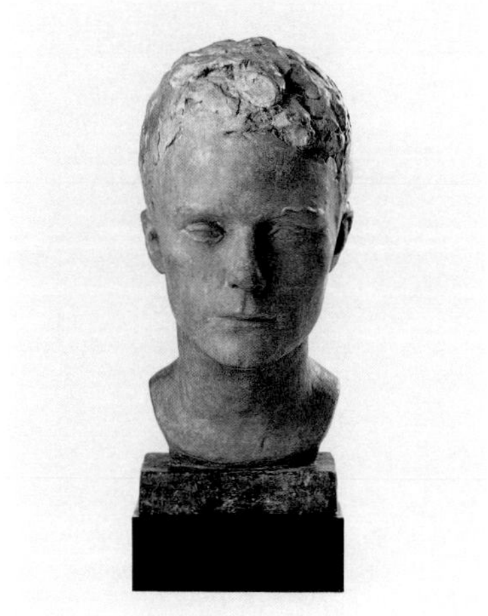

402

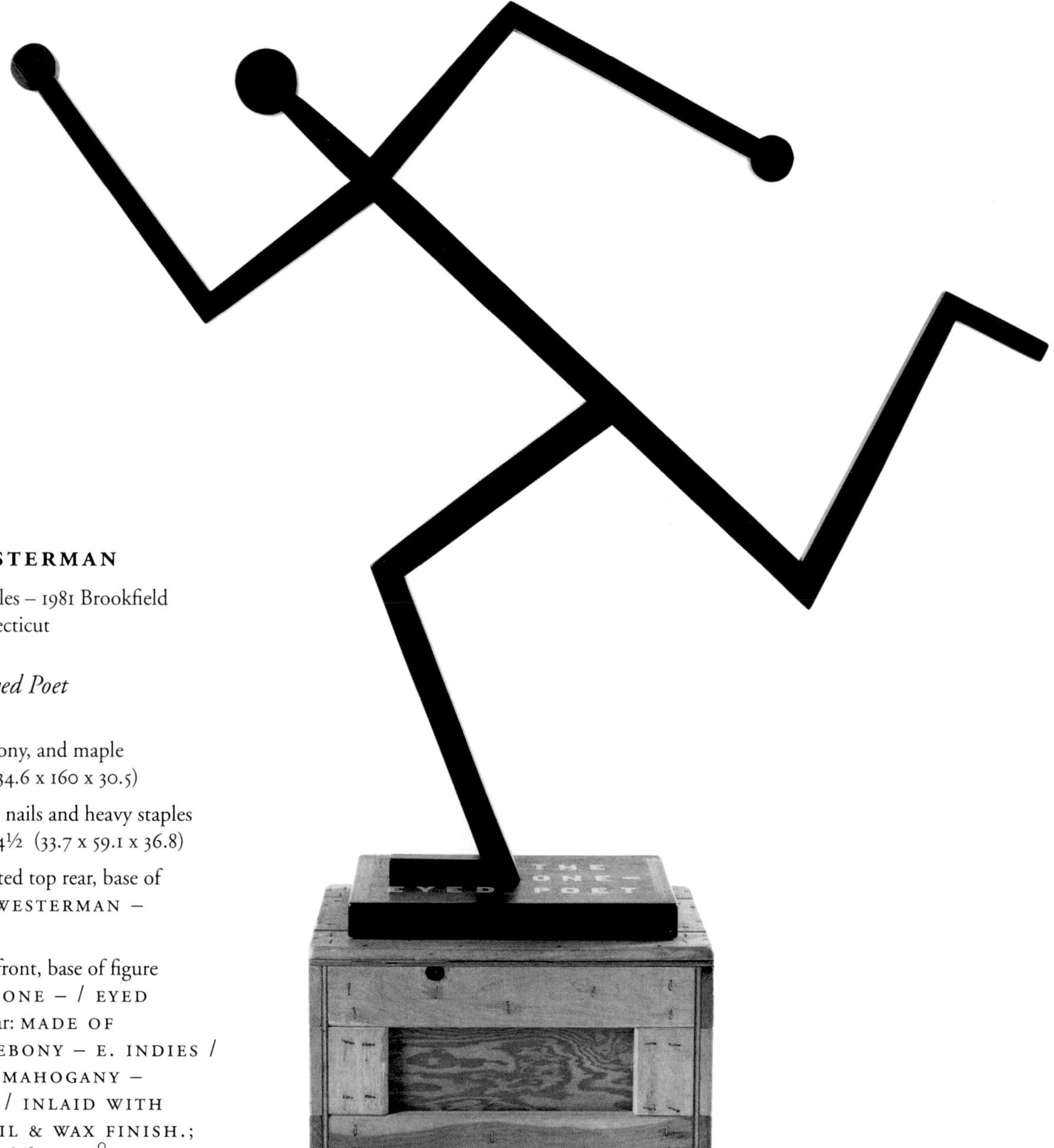

403

H.C. WESTERMAN

1922 Los Angeles – 1981 Brookfield Center, Connecticut

403 *The One–Eyed Poet*

1979
Mahogany, ebony, and maple
53 x 63 x 12 (134.6 x 160 x 30.5)

Pine base with nails and heavy staples
13¼ x 23¼ x 14½ (33.7 x 59.1 x 36.8)

Signed and dated top rear, base of figure: H.C. WESTERMAN – 1979 –294

Inscribed top front, base of figure (inlaid): THE ONE – / EYED POET; top rear: MADE OF MAGASSAR EBONY – E. INDIES / BLISTERED MAHOGANY – HONDURAS / INLAID WITH MAPLE. / OIL & WAX FINISH.; front of figure's left arm: ⚓ BORN / TO / LOSE; on right arm: MOTHER.

Gift of Susan Morse Hilles
1984.75.27

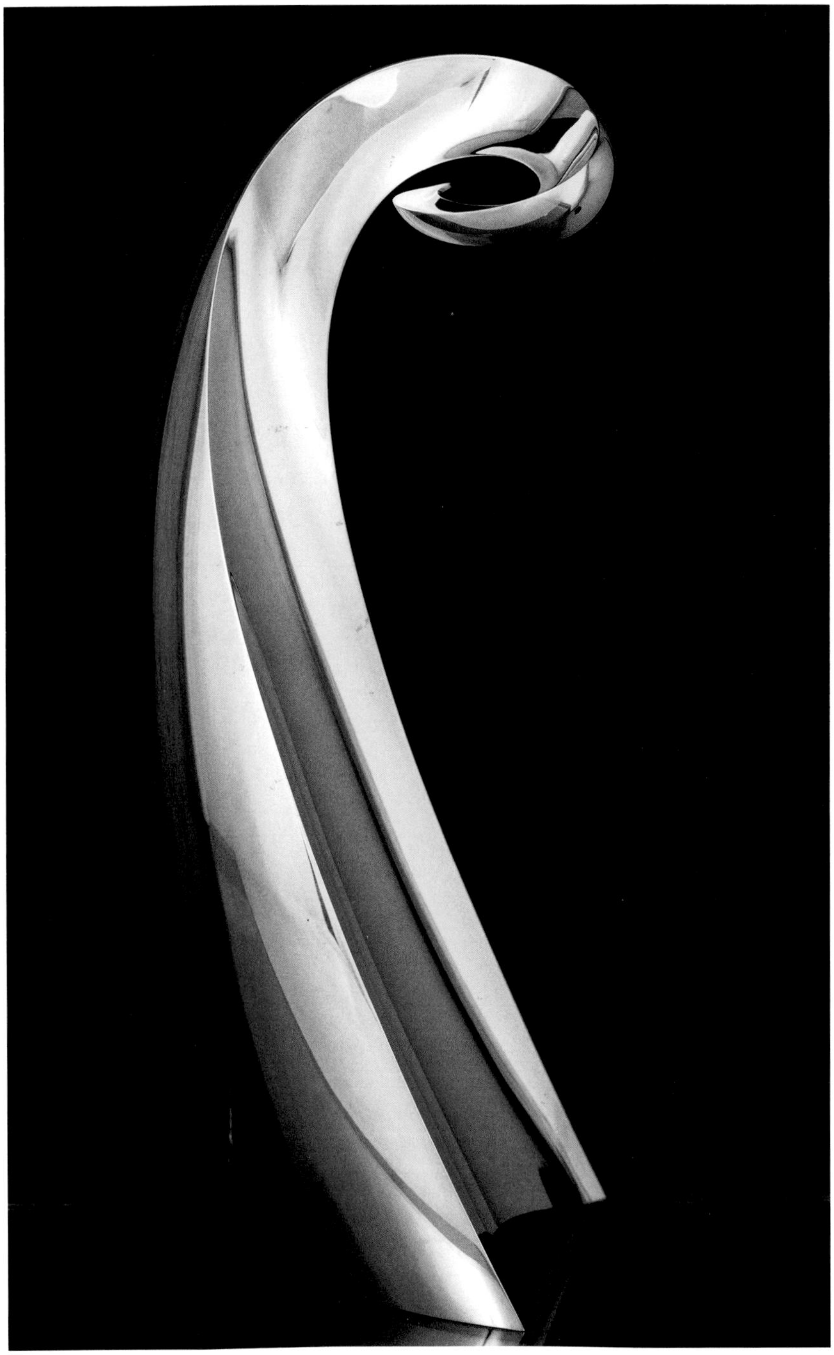

404

BYRON LEE WHITEHURST

b. 1950

404 *Spiral Form Number 1*

1973
Sterling silver
16 x 6¾ x 6¾ (40.6 x 17.1 x 17.1)

Mabel Brady Garvan Collection
1973.98

THOMAS WILFRED

(Richard Edgar Løvstrøm)

1889 Naestved, Denmark –
1968 West Nyack, New York
Active U.S. after 1916, citizen 1922

405 *#50: Elliptical Prelude and Chalice*

1928
Maple table, metal, fabric, glass, electrical and lighting elements
41 x 32½ x 18¾ (44 leaves open)
(104.1 x 82.6 x 47.6 [111.8 leaves open])

Gift of Thomas C. Wilfred
1983.66.1

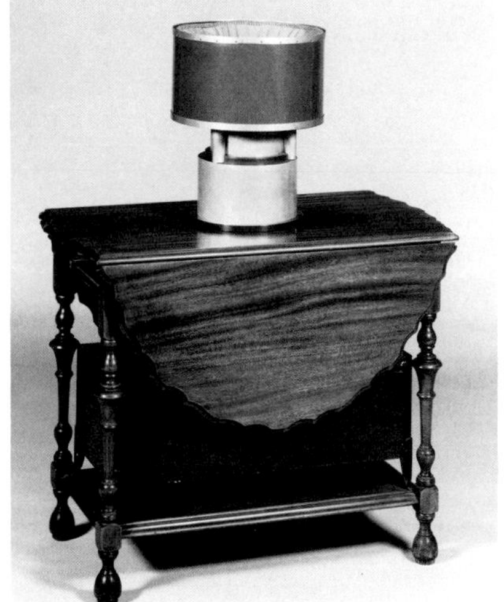

405

406 *The Firebird, Op. 91 (Abstract)*

1934
Wood, metal, glass, electrical and lighting elements
35½ x 41 x 10¼ (90.2 x 104.1 x 26)

Signed and dated in chalk upper right rear: *July 23 1934 / Thomas Wilfred*

Inscribed in chalk upper right rear: ABSTRACT, OP.91; lower right rear: MAKE BASE / 35½" HIGH!; lower left: 150 W

Gift of Thomas C. Wilfred
1983.66.2

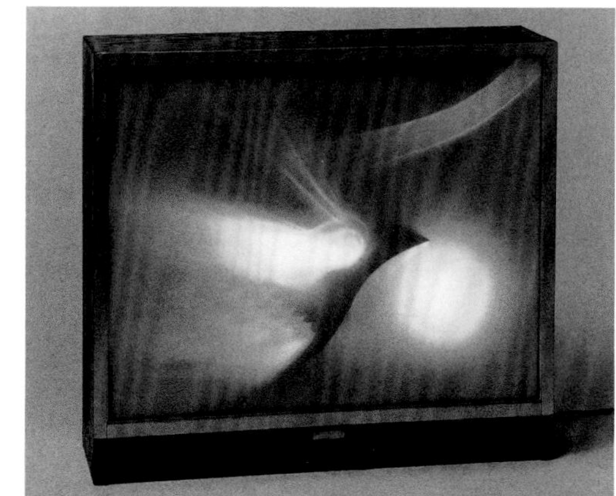

406

407 *Tranquil Study, Op. 92*

1934
Wood, metal, paint, glass, electrical and lighting elements
37 x 41 x 10¼ (94 x 104.1 x 26)

Signed and dated in chalk upper right rear: June 4, 1934 / *Thomas Wilfred*

Inscribed in chalk upper right rear: TRANQUIL STUDY / OP 92; lower center: 150 W

Gift of Thomas C. Wilfred
1983.66.3

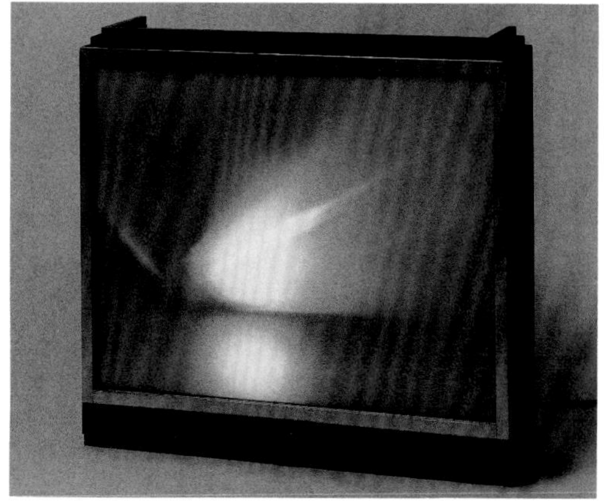

407

FREDERIC ALLEN WILLIAMS

1898 West Newton, Massachusetts – 1958 New York City

408 *Lee de Forest* 1873–1961
PH.B. 1896, PH.D. 1899, SC.D.(hon.) 1926

1952
Bronze, brown and bronze patina
19¼ x 9¾ x 10¼ (48.9 x 24.8 x 26)

Signed and dated proper left side edge: © *Frederic Allen Williams Sculptor / 1952*

Inscribed front edge of base: *Lee de Forest;* proper right: YALE 1896

Gift of the de Forest Pioneers to the Becton Engineering and Applied Science Library

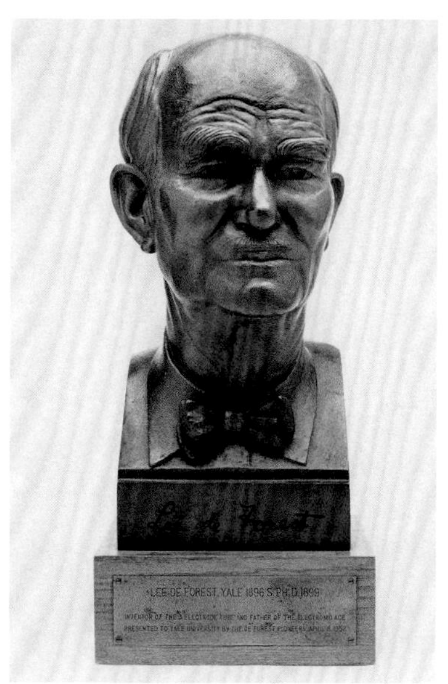

408

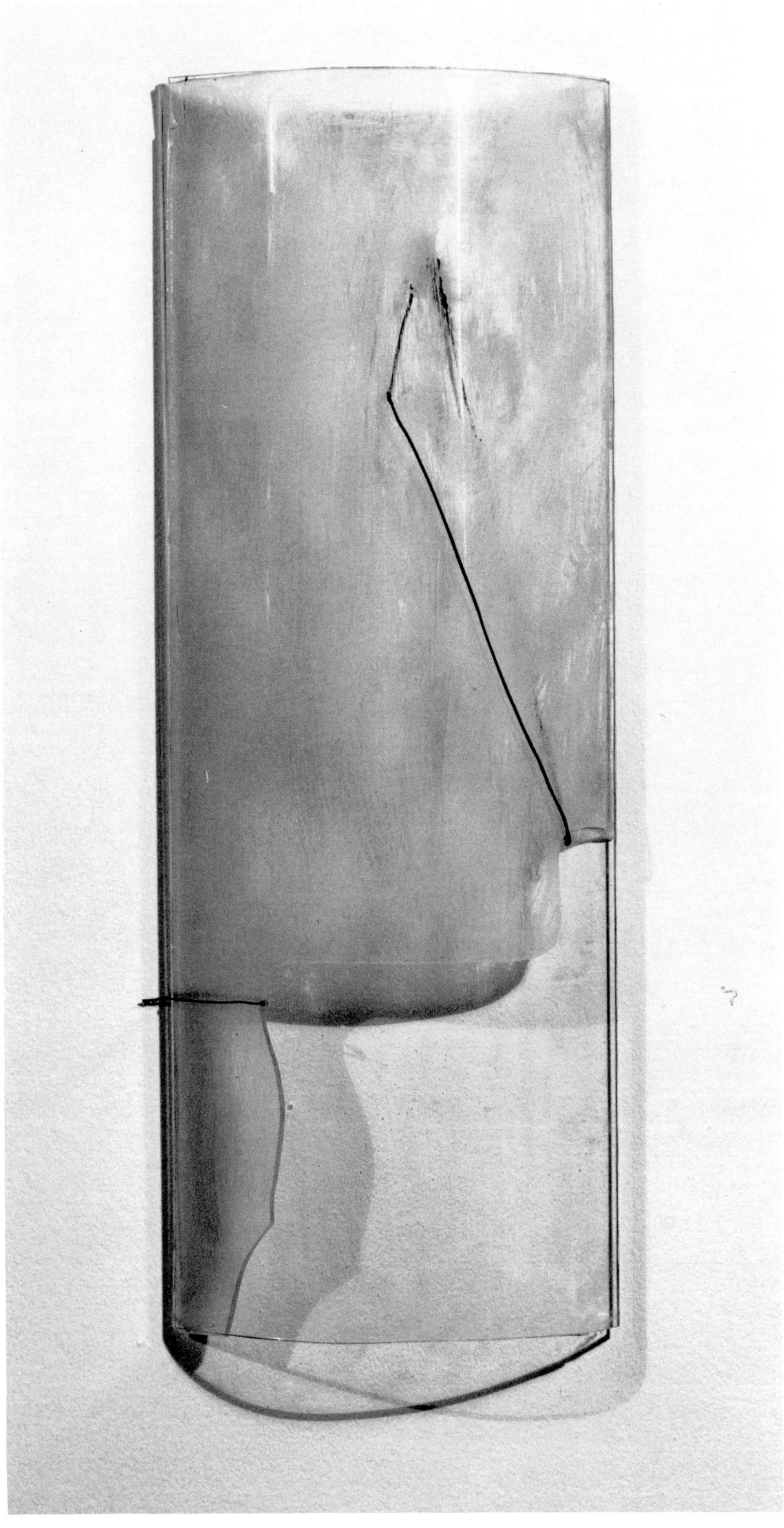

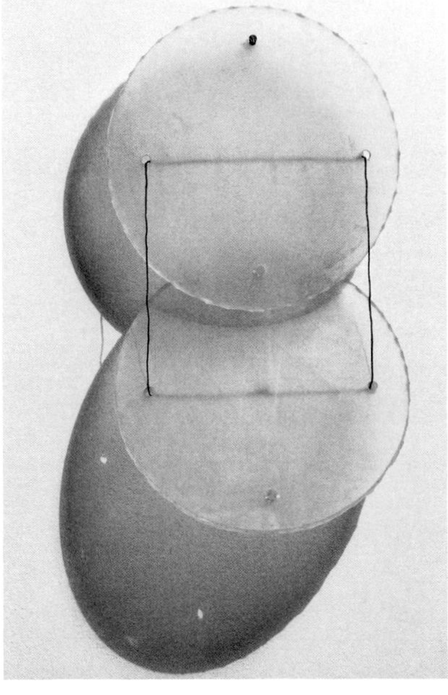

410

CHRISTOPHER WILMARTH

1943 Sonoma, California –
1987 Brooklyn, New York

409 *Clear Patch*

1970
Etched and clear glass, and wire
30 x 11 x 3 (76.2 x 27.9 x 7.6)

Signature, date, and inscription etched on lower proper left front near edge: *Clear Patch Christopher Wilmarth '70*

Gift of the Woodward Foundation
1977.49.29

410 *Fontella*

1970
Etched glass and wire
21 x 12 x 1 (53.3 x 30.5 x 2.5)

Signature, date, and inscription etched on bottom front of lower plate, near edge: *Fontella Christopher Wilmarth 1970*

Gift of the Woodward Foundation
1977.49.28

409

411 *Half Open Drawing*

1970
Etched and clear glass, and wire
17 x 17 x 1 (43.2 x 43.2 x 2.5)

Signature, date, and inscription etched on lower proper left front near edge: *Half Open Drawing Christopher Wilmarth 1970*

Gift of the Woodward Foundation
1977.49.30

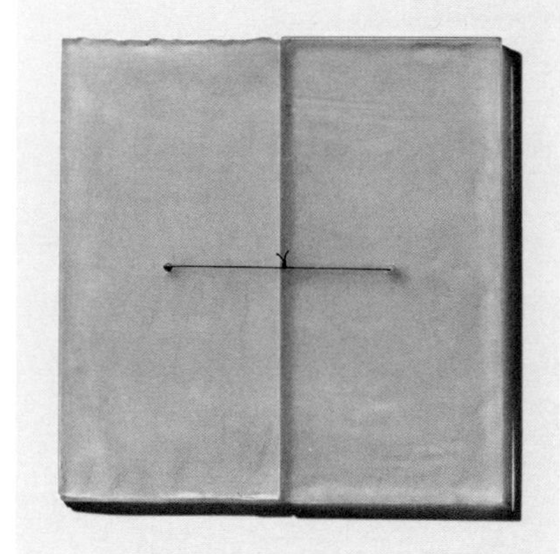

411

412 *Given #1*

1974, glass element replaced by the artist 1987
Etched glass, steel, and wire
41 x 40 x 4⅜ (104.1 x 101.6 x 11.1)

Signature, date and inscription etched on lower proper right corner of glass: *Given C.M.W. 1974*; lower proper right corner of metal: *Given C.M.W. 74*

Gift of Catherine Cahill and William L. Bernhard, B.A. 1954
1984.99

412

CHARLES H. WILSON

b. 1937
B.F.A. 1962, M.F.A. 1963

413 *Untitled Sculpture*

1961
Marble
27¼ x 12 x 11¾ (69.2 x 30.5 x 29.8)

Given to the Yale Schools of Art and Architecture in memory of Miss Mary Ann Florio from her family and friends

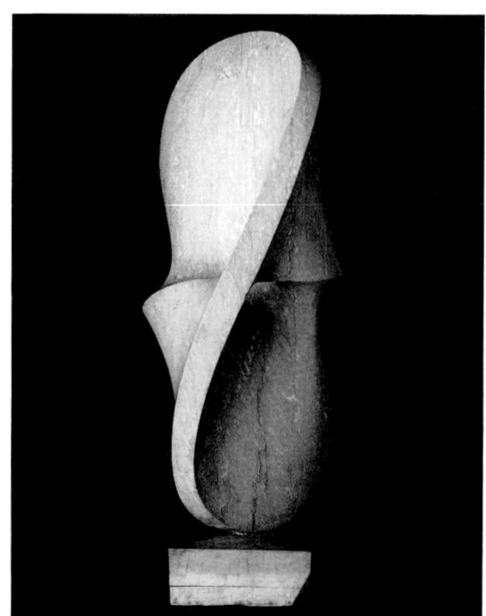

413

414 *Bird*

c.1962
Plaster on plastic webbing
H. 26¼ x DIAM. 10¾ (66.7 x 27.3)

Metal base
H. 1¼ x DIAM. 5 (3.2 x 12.7)

Morse College Purchase Fund
1975.83

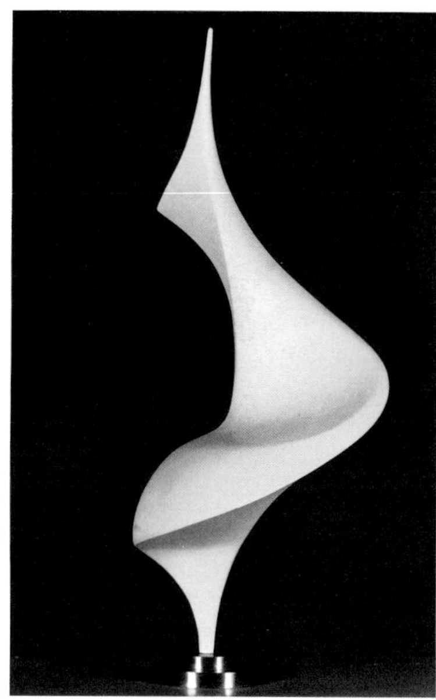

414

after
JOSEPH WRIGHT

See cats. 417, 420

OLAFS ZEIDENBERGS

b. 1936 Latvia
M.F.A. 1963

415 *Hanging Moebius Strip*

c.1962
Stainless steel and plaster on plastic webbing
H. 21½ x DIAM. 14¾ (54.6 x 37.5)

Morse College Purchase Fund
1975.82

WILLIAM ZORACH

1887 Eurburg, Lithuania –
1966 Bath, Maine
To U.S. 1891

416 *Ushas (Dawn)*

1962
Stone
13 x 8¾ x 6 (33 x 22.2 x 15.2)

Metal support post
Length 2¼ (5.7) sight

Signed and dated lower rear: *Zorach / 1962*

Gift of Susan Morse Hilles
1984.75.6

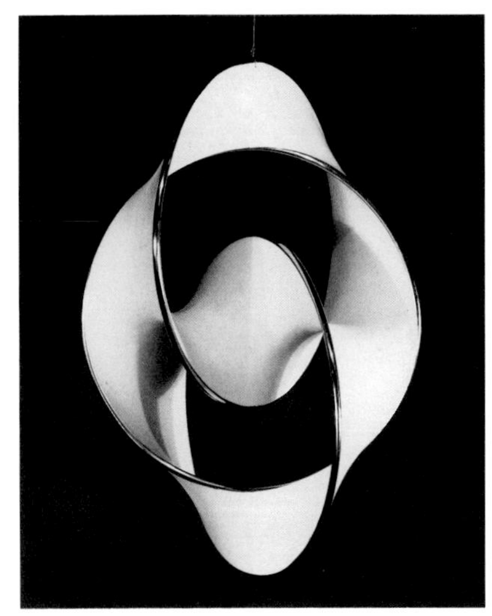

415

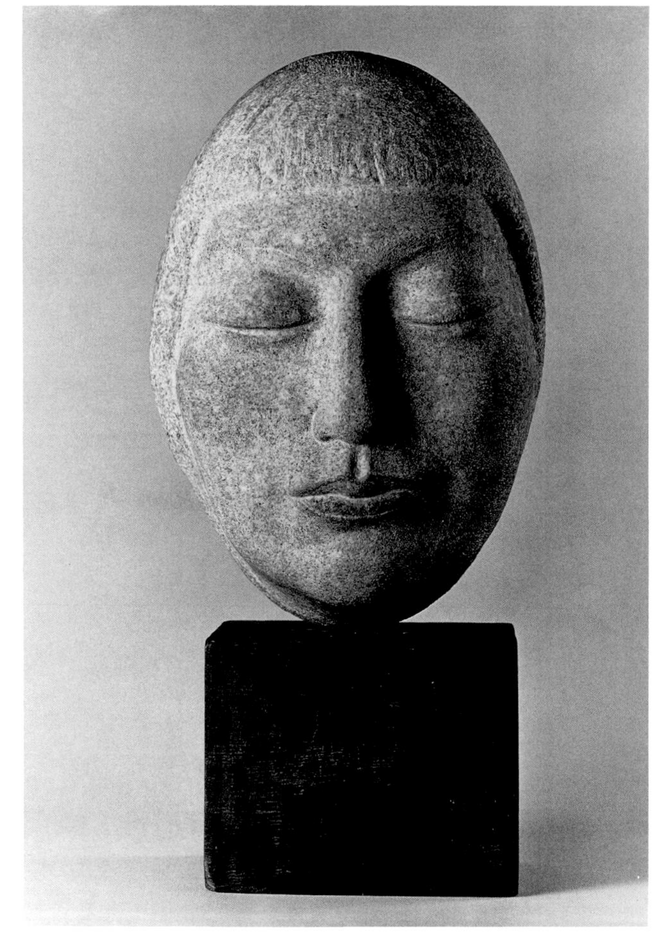

416

UNKNOWN EIGHTEENTH CENTURY

417 *Benjamin Franklin* 1706–1790
Possibly after Joseph Wright, 1756–1793
M.A.(hon.) 1753

c.1784
Alabaster
8½ x 8 x 4 (21.6 x 20.3 x 10.2)

Inscribed center rear of base: FW(?)F (monogram)

Gift of William Smith Mason, PH.B. 1888, M.A.(hon.) 1924, to the Benjamin Franklin Collection, Yale University Library

418 *David Humphreys* 1752–1818
B.A. 1771, M.A. 1774

c.1780
Marble
22½ x 18½ x 12 (57.2 x 47 x 30.5)

Gift of Mrs. David Humphreys
1820.1

419 *Indian Weather Vane*

Late 18th – early 19th century
Iron
80¼ x 25¾ x 1¼ (203.8 x 65.4 x 3.2)

Mabel Brady Garvan Collection
1930.831

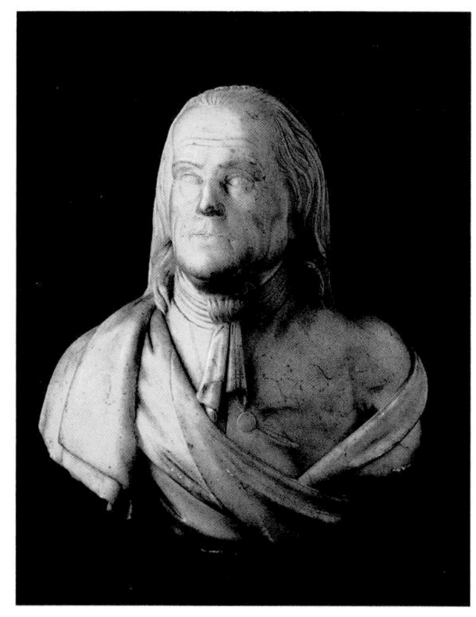
417

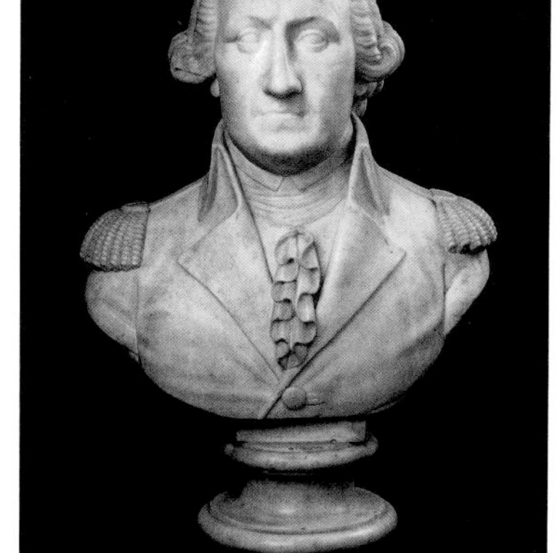
418

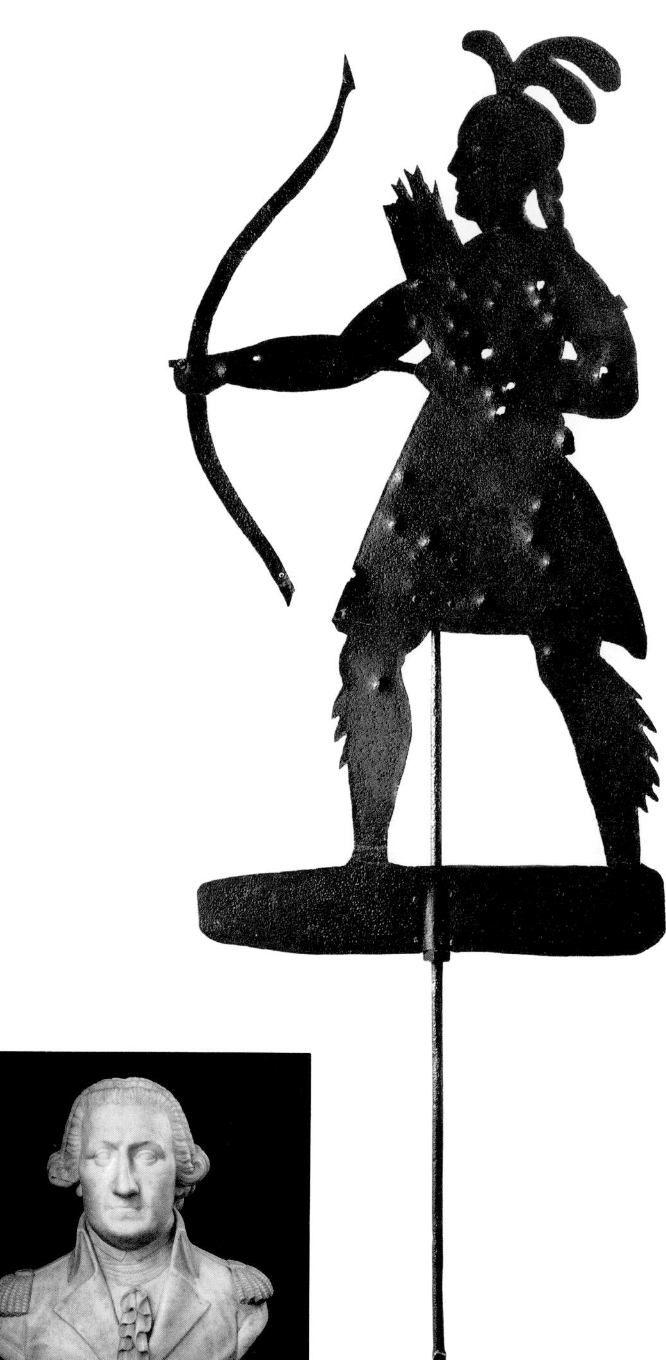
419

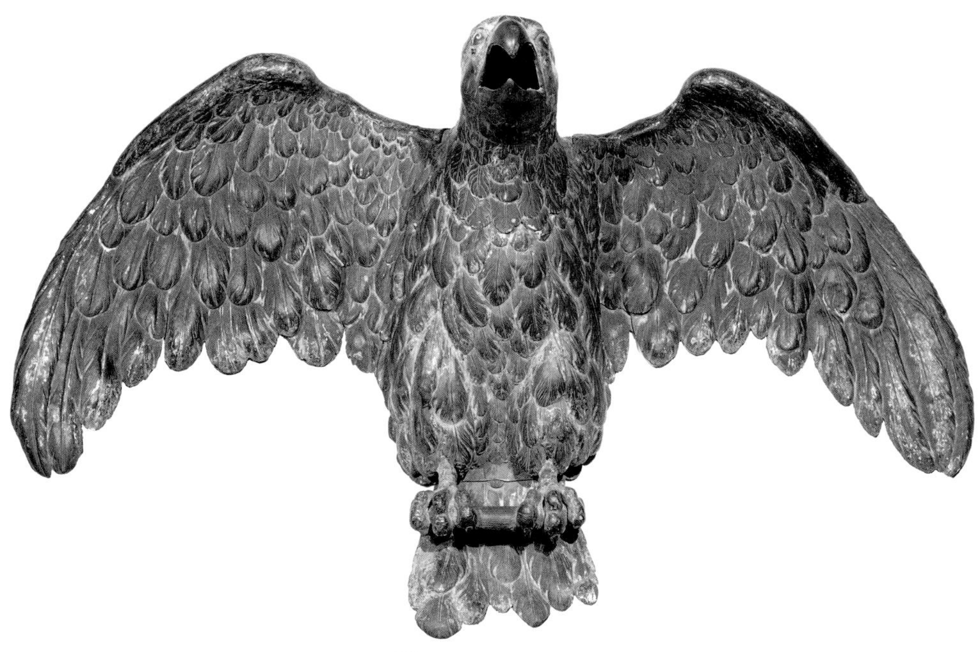

422

420 *George Washington* 1732–1799
Possibly after Joseph Wright, 1756–1793
LL.D. 1781

Late 18th – early 19th century
Colored wax mounted on paper board
6 x 5 x ¼ (15.2 x 12.7 x .64)

Wood frame
6½ x 5½ x 1 (16.5 x 14 x 2.5)

Gift of Mrs. John Hill Morgan
1945.258

421 *Steven Williams of Massachusetts*

Late 18th century
Colored wax mounted on glass
5⅝ x 4 5/16 x ½ (14.3 x 10.9 x 1.3)

Wood frame
7 x 6½ x 1 (17.8 x 16.5 x 2.5)

Gift of Mrs. Paul Moore
1956.2.2

UNKNOWN NINETEENTH CENTURY

422 *American Eagle*

n.d.
Gilded bronze
24 x 42 x 15 (61 x 106.7 x 38.1)

Mabel Brady Garvan Collection
1930.832

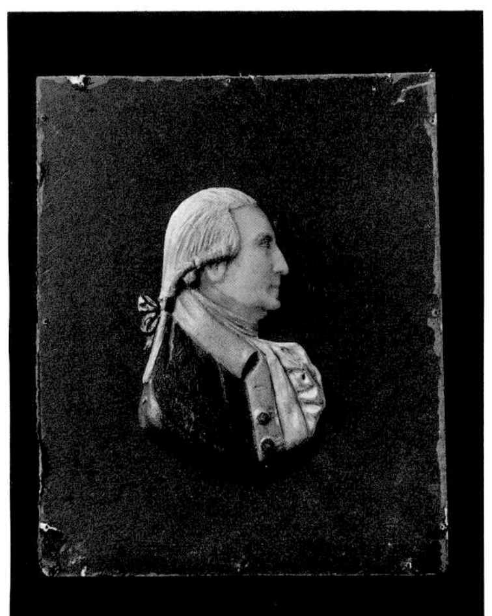

420

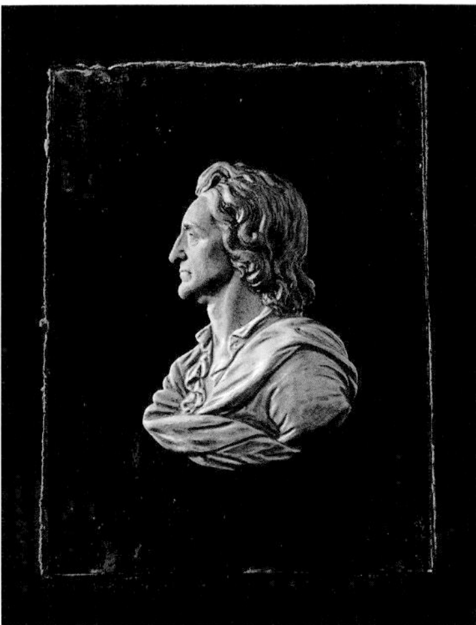

421

423 *Aeschines,* probably after Greenough, see cat. 110

n.d.
Marble
22 x 10 x 6½ (55.9 x 25.4 x 16.5)

Inscribed in ink on bottom of base: Homer / by T. Crawford / Edward [?] Salisbury [?] 186[?]

Gift of Professor Edward E. Salisbury, B.A. 1832, M.A. 1835, LL.D. 1869 to the Yale University Library

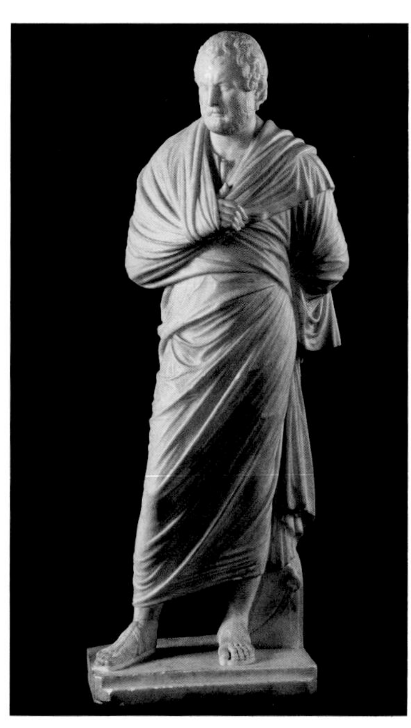

423

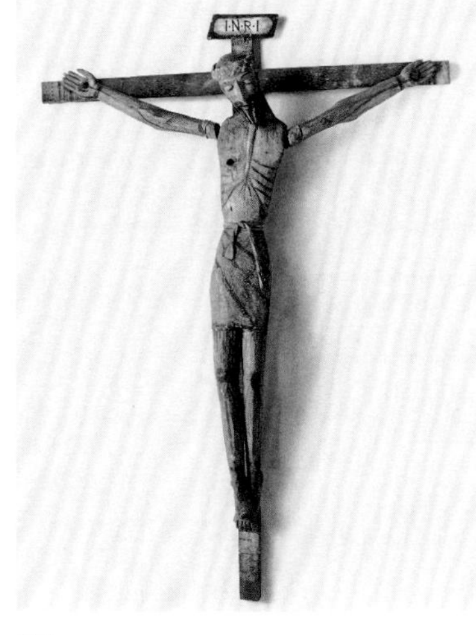

424

424 *Bulto Crucifix,* possibly by José Benito Ortega, 1858–1941

Late 19th – early 20th century
Polychromed wood, leather, fabric
60 x 42½ x 10 (152.4 x 108 x 25.4)

Gift of Adam Bianchi
1957.29

425 *Caricature Head of a Negro Male*

n.d.
Polychromed wood
12½ x 9 x 8¼ (31.8 x 22.9 x 21)

Wood base
3¼ x 10 x 9 (8.3 x 25.4 x 22.9)

James Weldon Johnson Memorial Collection of Negro Arts and Letters, Beinecke Rare Book and Manuscript Library
1980.701

426 *Carved Fish*

n.d.
Whalebone
¾ x 3½ x ¼ (1.9 x 8.9 x 0.6)

Bequest of Bradford F. Swan, B.A. 1929
1976.105.14

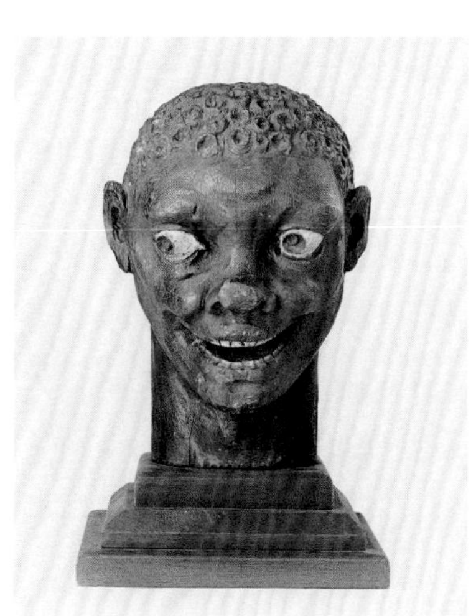

425

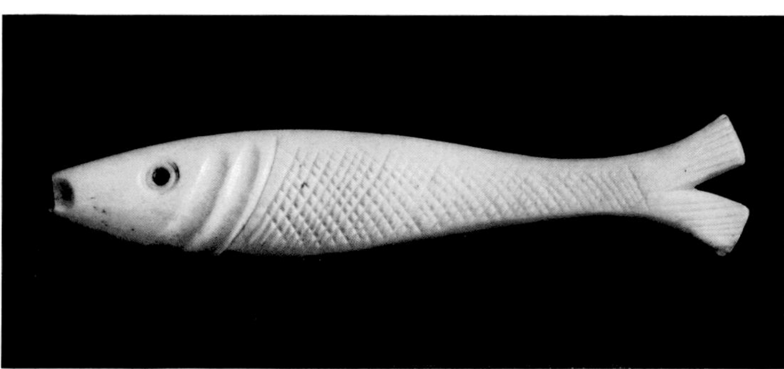

426

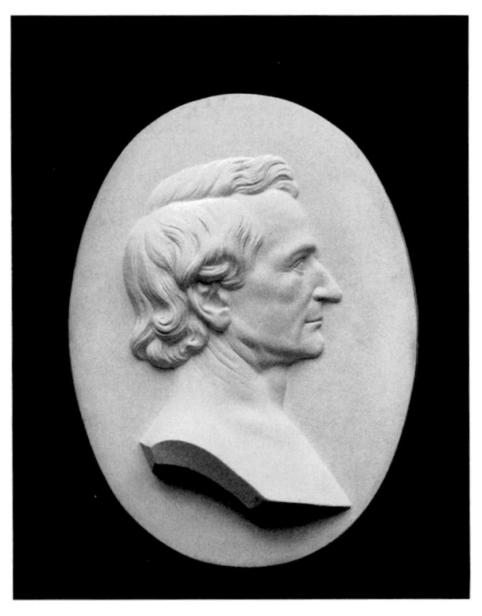

427

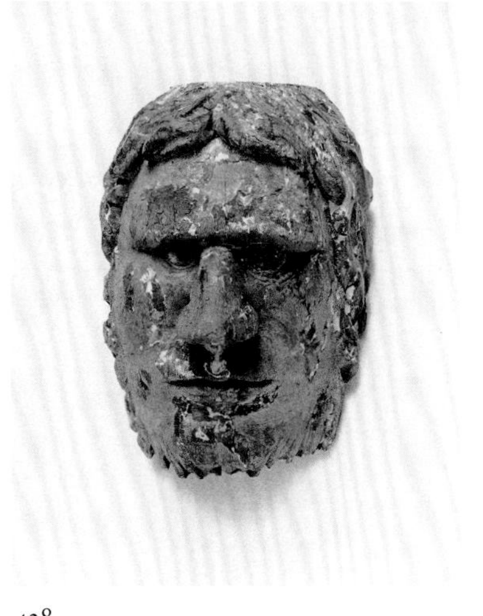

428

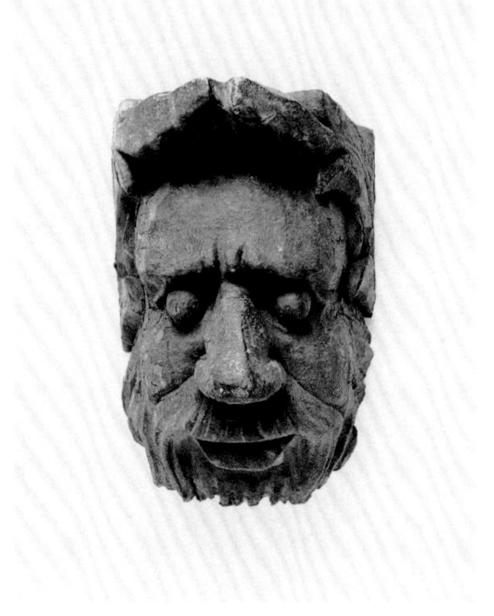

429

427 *James Dwight Dana* 1813–1895
B.A. 1833, M.A. 1836

c.1870
Plaster
20¼ x 15¼ x 2 (51.4 x 38.7 x 5.1)
Wood frame
29½ x 25 x 4½ (74.9 x 63.5 x 11.4)

Provenance unknown
1973.116

428 *Grotesque Head*

c.1842
Painted wood
12 x 8½ x 9 (30.5 x 21.6 x 22.9)

Inscribed (in chalk by a later hand?) center rear: GRISWOLD

Provenance unknown
1990.18.1

429 *Grotesque Head*

c.1842
Painted wood
12 x 8½ x 9 (30.5 x 21.6 x 22.9)

Provenance unknown
1990.18.2

430 *Hermes of Praxiteles Found in the Temple of Hera*

c.1900
Bronze, dark reddish-brown patina
31 x 22¾ x 13 (78.7 x 57.8 x 33)

Inscribed on socle at base of bust center front: COPY OF THE HERMES OF PRAXITELES / FOUND IN THE TEMPLE OF HERA. / OLYMPIA, 1878.; rear: *A gift from / Jonathan Ackerman Coles, A.M., M.D., / and Emilie S. Coles, / from the Estate of their father / Abraham Coles, M.D., PH.D., LL.D.*

Foundry: Tiffany & Company, New York; mark, top rear of proper left shoulder: TIFFANY & CO

Gift of Jonathan Ackerman Coles, A.M., M.D., and Emilie S. Coles from the estate of their Father, Abraham Coles, M.D., PH.D., LL.D., to the Yale University Library

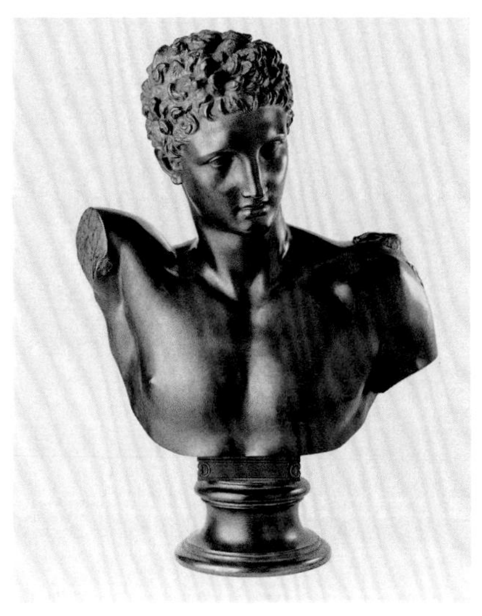

430

431 *Edward Claudius Herrick*
1811–1862
M.A.(hon.) 1838

c.1865
Plaster
11½ x 8¼ x 1¾ (29.2 x 21 x 4.4) sight

Yale University Library

432 *James Abraham Hillhouse*
1789–1841
B.A. 1808, M.A. 1811

Probably 1841
Plaster
13 x 9¼ x 7 (33 x 23.5 x 17.8)

Inscribed in ink on front of base: Hillhouse of New Haven / Poet; proper right side: LNF

Beinecke Rare Book and Manuscript Library
1980.305

433 *Horse and Rider Weather Vane*
n.d.
Wrought iron
16 x 13¾ x ¾ (40.6 x 34.9 x 1.9)

Detachable wrought iron support rod
21¼ x 2 x ¾ (54 x 5.1 x 1.9)

Mabel Brady Garvan Collection
1930.5027

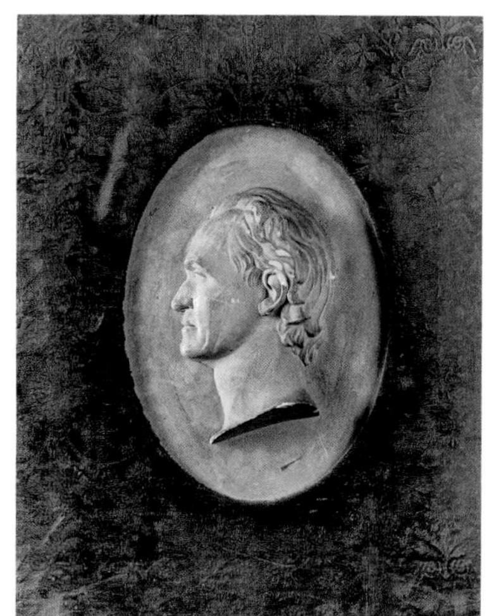
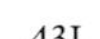

431

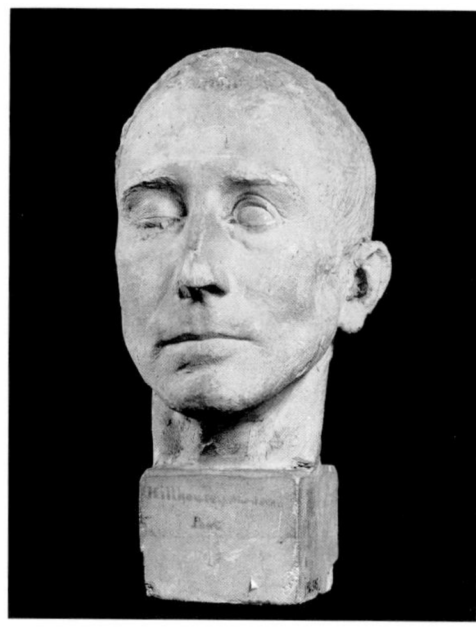

432

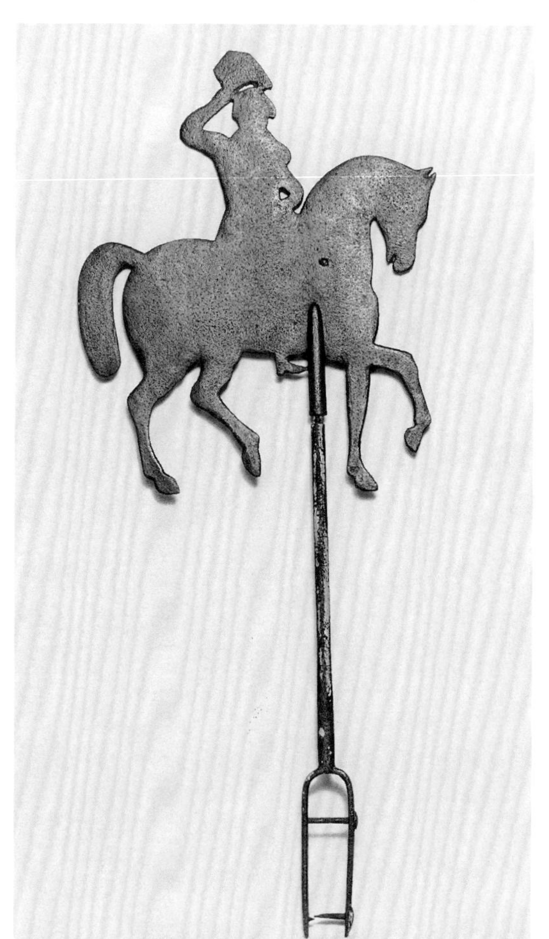

433

434, 435
Lion with Shield

1897
Bronze, original patina obscured by corrosion
Pair: 57 x 20½ x 17¾ (144.8 x 52.1 x 45.1); and 57 x 19¾ x 21 (144.8 x 50.2 x 53.3)

Foundry: John Williams, New York; mark, proper left front of base: JNO. WILLIAMS. FOUNDER. / NEW YORK. 1897

Old Campus, Wright Courtyard

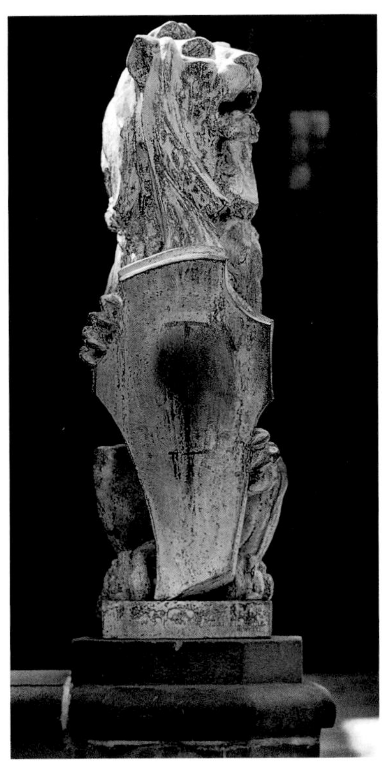

434

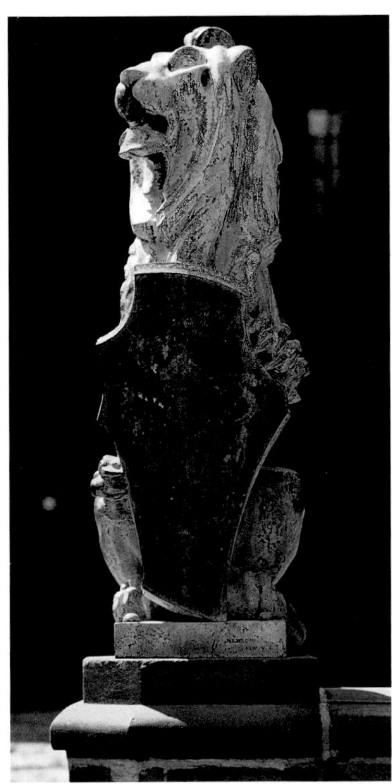

435

436 *John Marshall* 1755–1835

c.1893
Bronze, dark brownish-black patina
11¾ x 8¾ x 2½ (29.8 x 22.2 x 6.4)

Wood support
18 x 15 x 1 (45.7 x 38.1 x 2.5)

Inscribed upper left front in relief: JOHN MARSHALL / 1755–1835; in paint on upper front of wood support: THE JOHN MARSHALL PRIZE OF THE / JOHNS HOPKINS UNIVERSITY.; lower front: AWARDED TO / CHARLES McLEAN ANDREWS. / 1893

Gift of Charles McLean Andrews, M.A.(hon.) 1910, to the Yale University Library

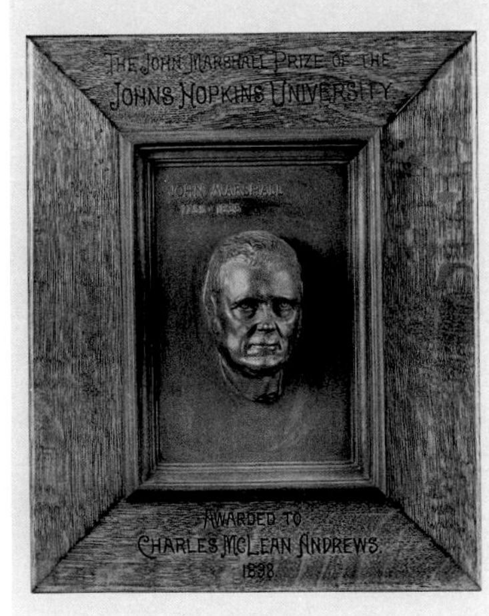

436

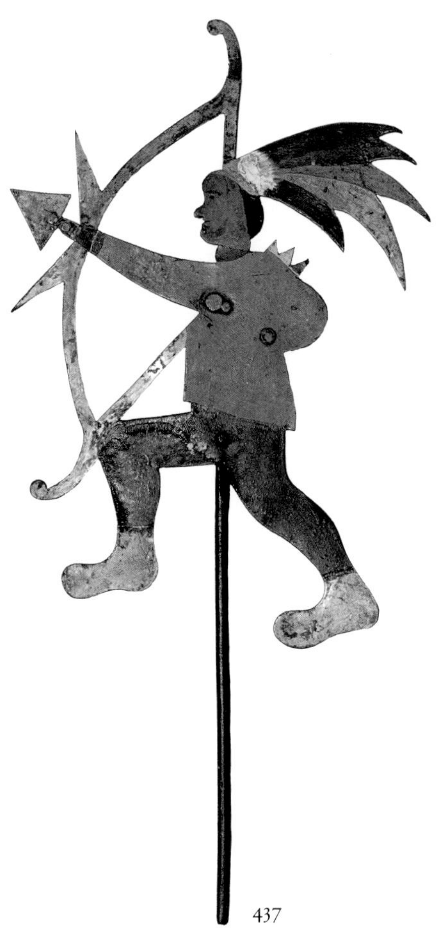
437

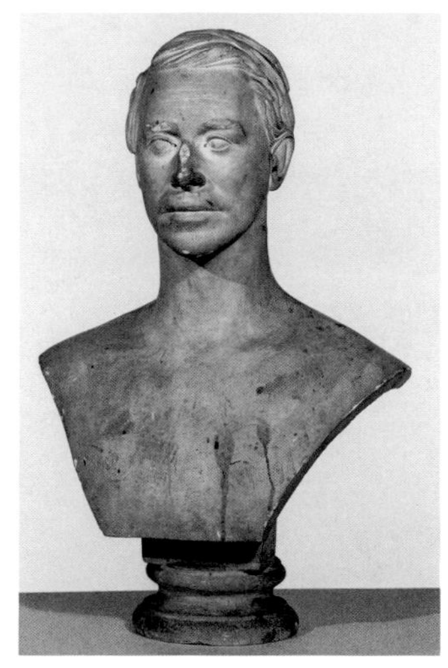
438

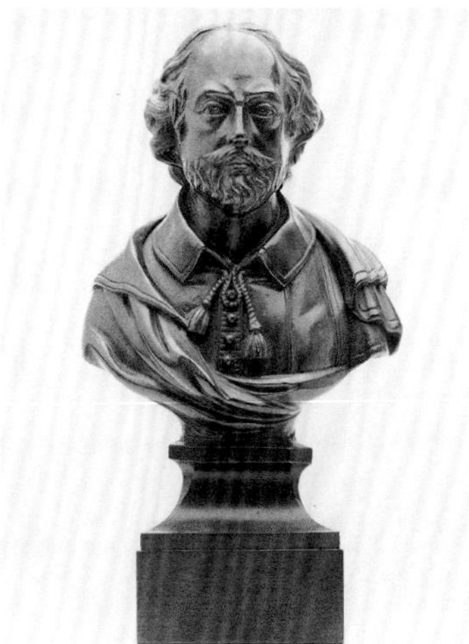
439

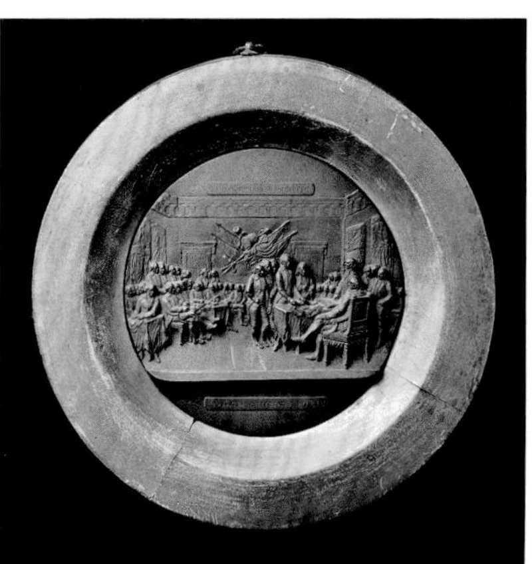
440

437 *Painted Indian Weather Vane*

n.d.
Painted wrought iron
23¾ x 11½ x ½ (60.3 x 29.2 x 1.3)

Mabel Brady Garvan Collection
1930.5026

438 *Portrait of an Unidentified Man*

n.d.
Plaster
26½ x 17 x 9½ (67.3 x 43.2 x 24.1)

Provenance unknown
1989.3.1

439 *William Shakespeare* 1564–1616

n.d.
Wood
13½ x 7¼ x 3¾ (34.3 x 18.4 x 9.5)

Collection of the Elizabethan Club

440 *Signing of the Declaration of Independence,* after John Trumbull, 1756–1843

c.1858
Metal, possibly copper, with black patina
DIAM. 6⅛ x D. ½ (15.5 x 1.3) sight

Gilded wood frame
DIAM. 10 x D. 1 (25.4 x 2.5)

Inscribed on front lower center: *Entered according to act of Congress in the year 1858 by Charles Kippel in the* [illegible] *Office of the / District Court of Maryland;* upper center: THE DECLARATION OF INDEPENDENCE.; lower center: CONGRESS, 4th JULY 1776 PHILADELPHIA.

Benjamin Franklin Collection,
Yale University Library

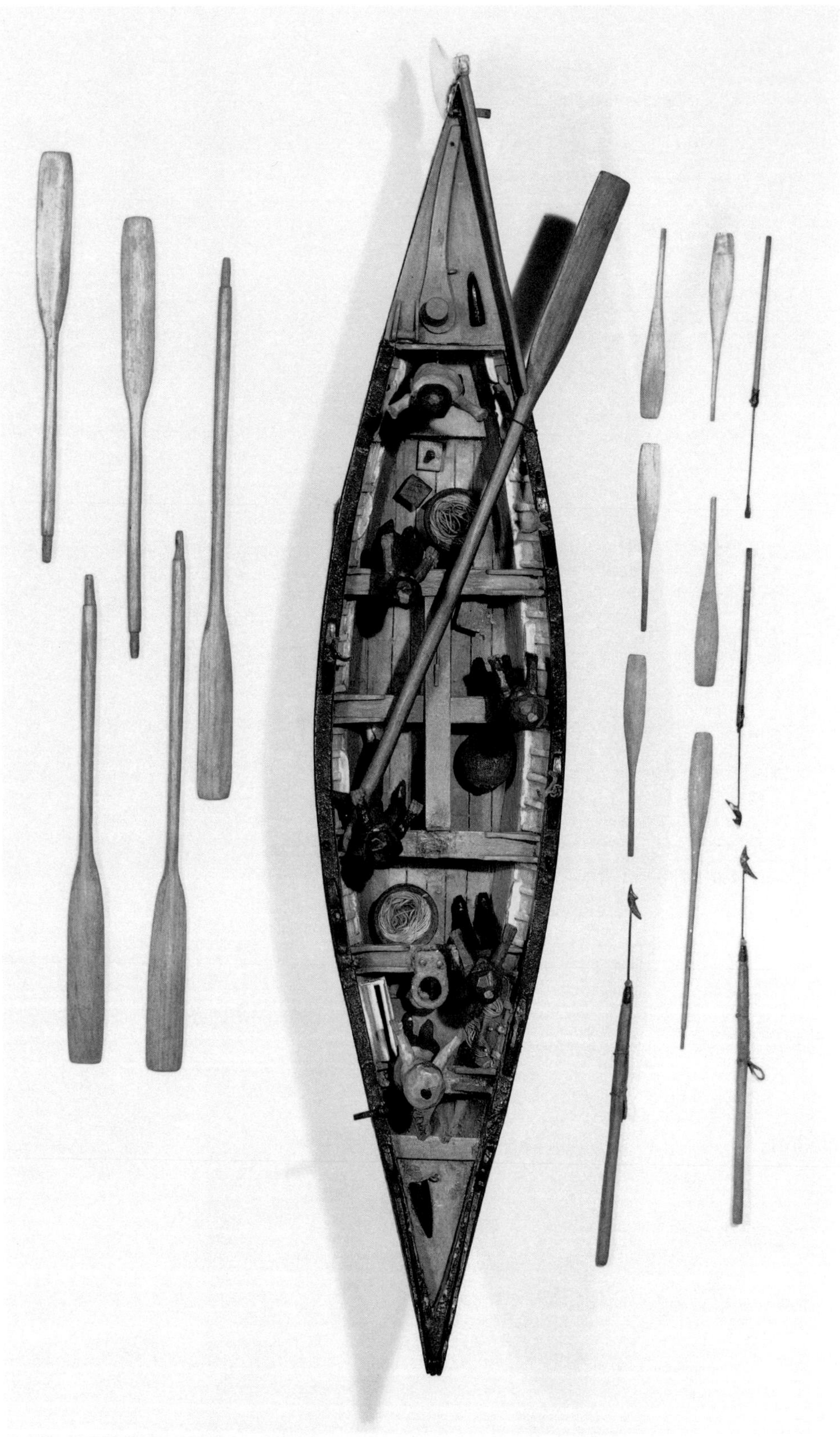

441

441 *Whaleboat*

Late 19th – early 20th century
Polychromed wood, string, beads, metal
5 x 17 x 3¾ (12.7 x 43.2 x 9.5)

Bequest of Bradford F. Swan, B.A. 1929
1976.105.9

442 *Oliver Wolcott* 1760–1833
B.A. 1778, LL.D. 1819

c.1830
Plaster
28 x 17¼ x 10¼ (71.1 x 43.8 x 26)

Provenance unknown
1900.27

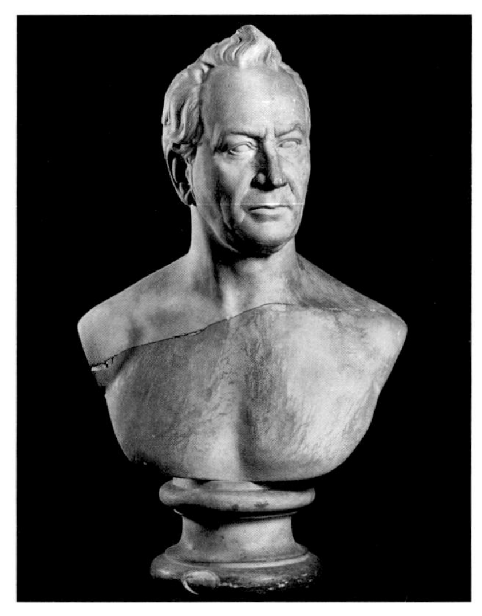

442

UNKNOWN TWENTIETH CENTURY

443 *Simeon Eben Baldwin* 1840–1927
B.A. 1861, M.A. 1864, LL.D. 1916

1912
Bronze, dark green patina
13 x 9¾ x 1½ (33 x 24.8 x 3.8)

Wood support
24 x 17¾ x 1¼ (61 x 45.1 x 3.2)

Yale University Library

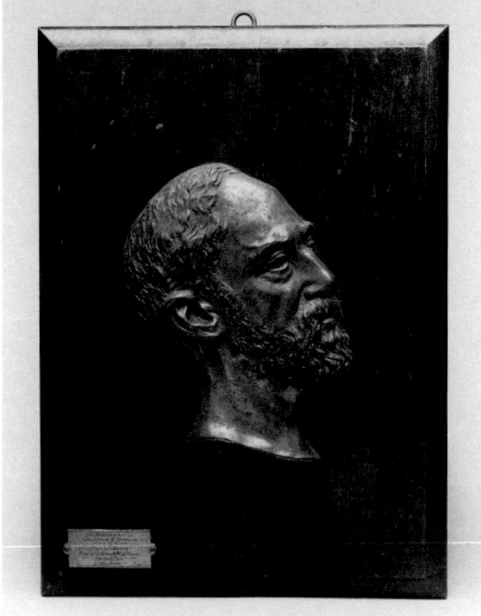

443

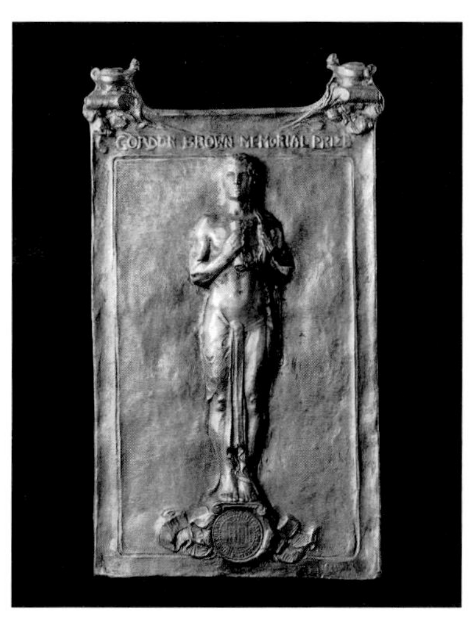

444

444 *Gordon Brown Memorial Prize*

c.1910
Bronze, gold patina or gilt
14½ x 8¾ x 1½ (36.8 x 22.2 x 3.8)

Inscribed in relief on upper front: GORDON BROWN MEMORIAL PRIZE; lower: Yale University seal; below and to right of seal: ⊕

Foundry: Roman Bronze Works, New York; mark, lower right edge: ROMAN BRONZE WORKS, N–Y–

Yale University Library

445 *Buffalo Bill* (William Frederick Cody) 1846–1917

n.d.
Painted plaster
DIAM. 14 x D. 2½ (35.6 x 6.4)

Inscribed front right in relief: BUFFALO BILL

Gift of William Robertson Coe, M.A.(hon.) 1947, to the Collection of Western Americana, Beinecke Rare Book and Manuscript Library
1980.375

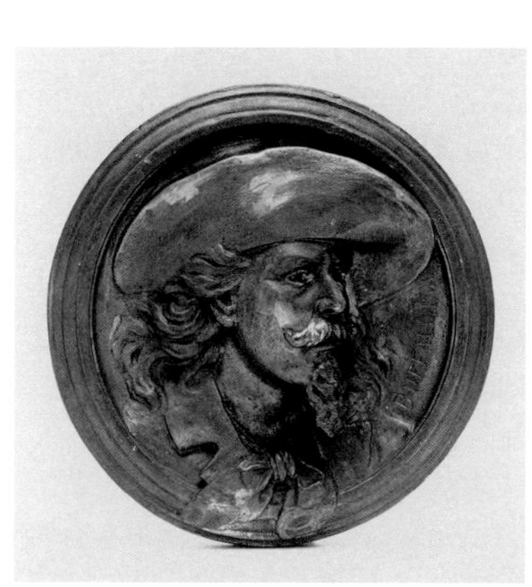

445

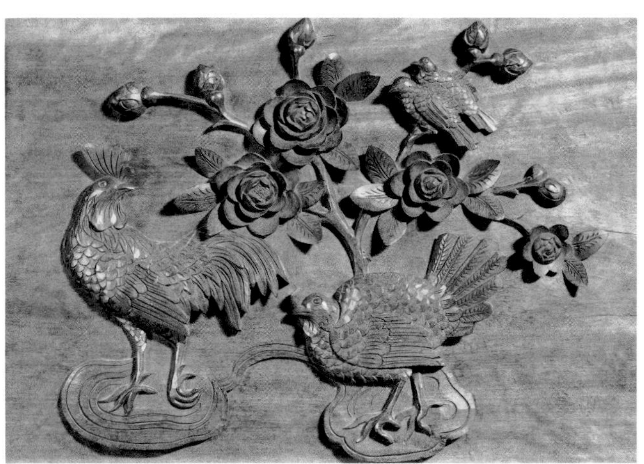

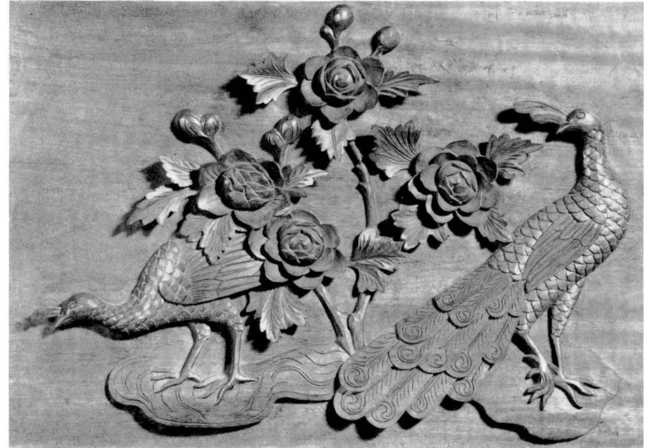

446

446 *Cock and Chicken with Flowers,* and *Peacock and Flowers*

n.d.
Walnut
Each panel: 12½ x 18¾ x 1
(31.8 x 47.6 x 2.5) sight

Each frame: 14½ x 20½ x 1¼
(36.8 x 52.1 x 3.2)

Bequest of Marie-Antoinette Slade
to Berkeley College
1970.49.11

447 *Timothy Dwight* 1752–1817
B.A. 1769, M.A. 1772

c.1925
Bronze, dark reddish-brown patina
DIAM. 17 x D. 1 (43.2 x 2.5)

Inscribed on front in relief along perimeter: 1752 · TIMOTHY DWIGHT · S·T·D·LLD·1817; right center: EDUCATOR

Timothy Dwight College

448 *Figure of a Renaissance Man*

c.1920
Painted plaster
23¼ x 8½ x 7½ (59.1 x 21.6 x 19.1)

Fabricator's mark on metal seal impressed into bottom of base in relief:
P.P. CAPRONI & BRO.
BOSTON / PLASTIC ARTS

Fabricator: P.P. Caproni & Brothers, Plastic Arts, Boston

Presented by Nellie Cotter Gager in memory of her husband Edwin Baker Gager, B.A. 1877, M.A.(hon.) 1907, to the Yale University Library

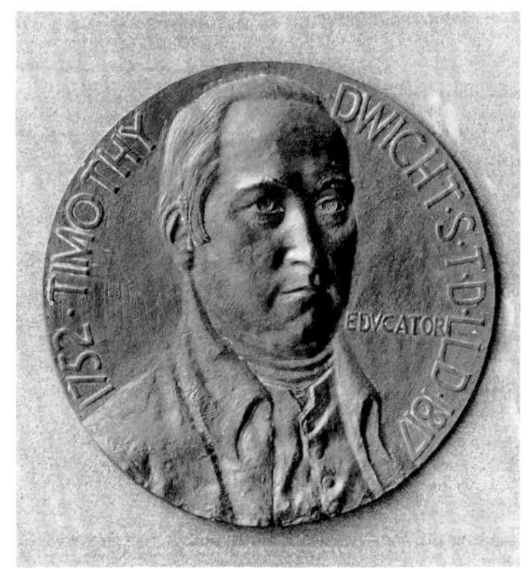

447

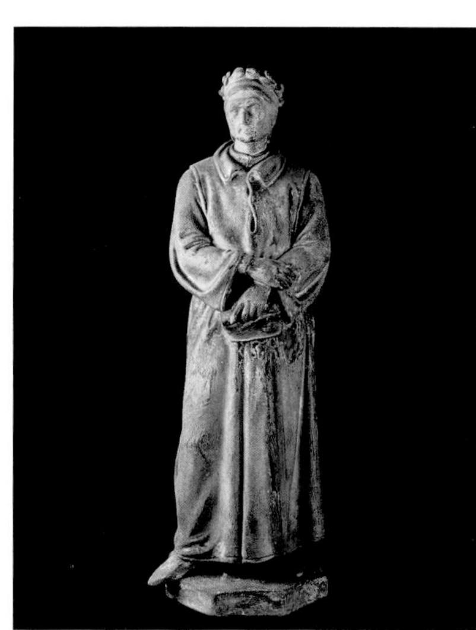

448

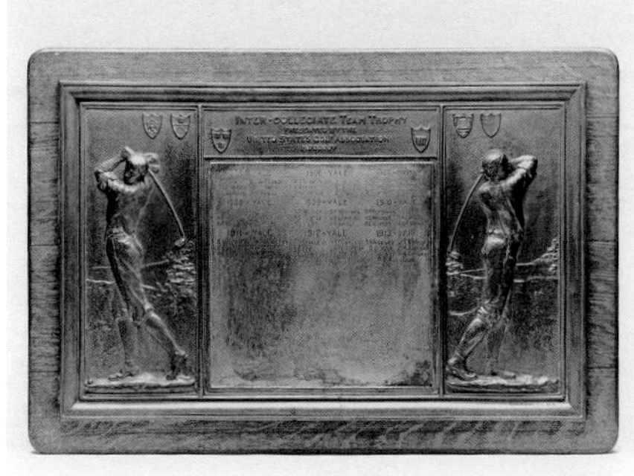

449

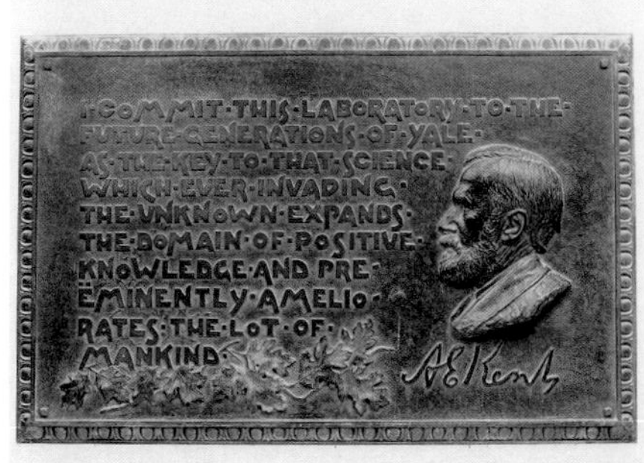

450

449 *Golf (Inter-Collegiate Team Trophy)*

1905
Bronze, light golden bronze patina and silver plate
19¼ x 30¾ x 1½ (48.9 x 78.1 x 3.8)

Wood mount
23 x 34¾ x 1 (58.4 x 88.3 x 2.5)

Inscribed upper center front in relief: INTER–COLLEGIATE TEAM TROPHY / PRESENTED BY THE / UNITED STATES GOLF ASSOCIATION / MDCCCCV

Foundry: The Gorham Manufacturing Company, New York; mark, lower right: Gorham Co. N.Y.

Payne Whitney Gymnasium

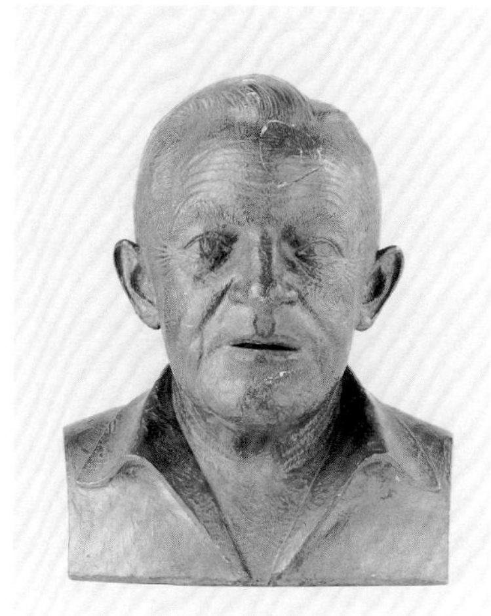

451

450 *Albert Emmett Kent* 1830–1901
B.A. 1853

c.1920
Bronze, dark brownish-black and exposed bronze patina
35¼ x 56 x 4¼ (89.5 x 142.2 x 10.8)

Inscribed in relief lower proper left corner: *A E Kent;* across the front: I · COMMIT · THIS · LABORATORY · TO · THE · / FUTURE · GENERATIONS · OF · YALE · / AS · THE · KEY · TO · THAT · SCIENCE · / WHICH · EVER · INVADING · / THE · UNKNOWN · EXPANDS · / THE · DOMAIN · OF · POSITIVE · / KNOWLEDGE · AND · PRE– / ËMINENTLY · AMELIO– / RATES · THE · LOT · OF · / MANKIND ·

Sterling Chemistry Laboratory

451 *Robert J.H. Kiphuth* 1890–1967
M.A.(hon.) 1950

c.1950
Painted plaster
15½ x 12 x 10½ (39.4 x 30.5 x 26.7)

Payne Whitney Gymnasium

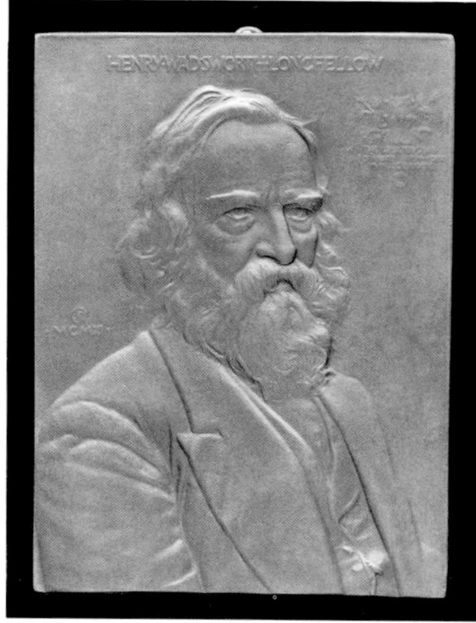

452

452 *Henry Wadsworth Longfellow*
1807–1882

1911
Bronze, dark greenish-grey patina
7½ x 5¾ x ½ (19.1 x 14.6 x 1.3)

Inscribed in relief left center front: (JF) (monogram) / ·MCMXI·; upper front: HENRY·WADSWORTH·LONGFELLOW; upper right beneath Grolier Club seal: THE GROLIER CLUB / FOUNDED·NEW–YORK / MDCCCLXXXIV / ©

Foundry: possibly Griffoul et Lores, Founders, France; mark, verso center right: GRIFFOUL FOUNDERS

Gift of Adrian Van Sinderen, B.A. 1910, to the Collection of American Literature, Beinecke Rare Book and Manuscript Library
1980.307

453 *Henry Wadsworth Longfellow*
Bronze, dark brown patina

1980.325
Same as cat. 452 except for patina and location of founder's mark, which in this version appears on verso upper center left.

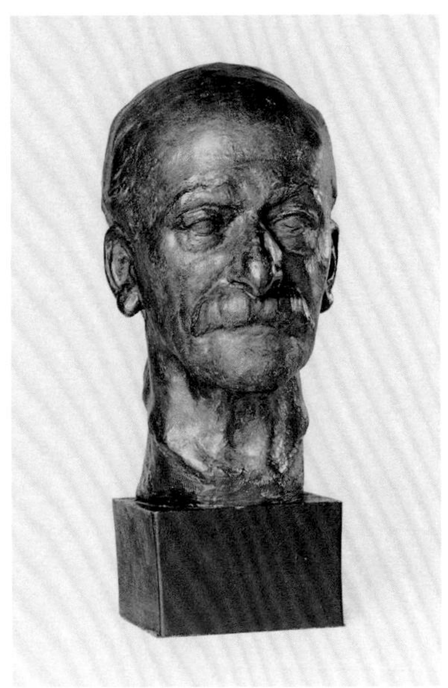

454

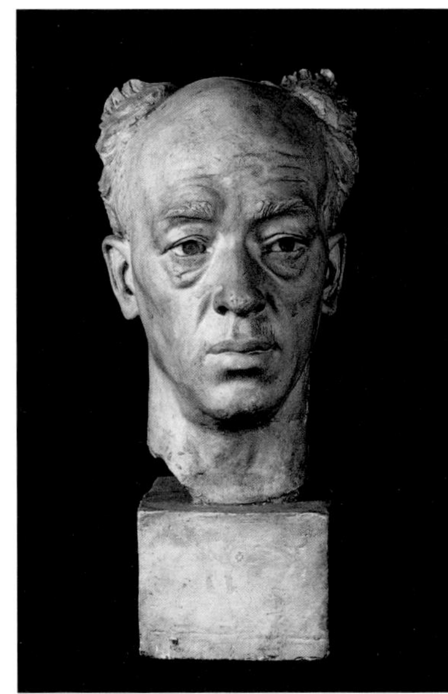
456

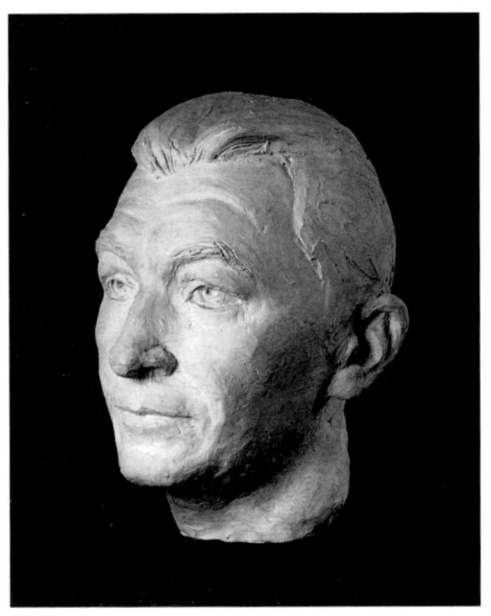
455

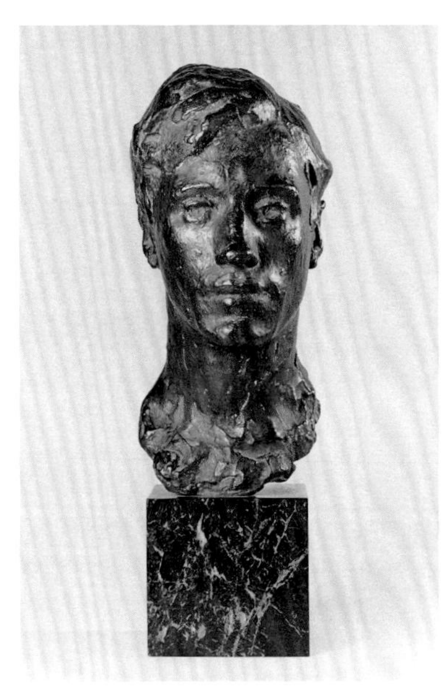
457

454 *Max Neuberger* 1865–1955

1935
Painted plaster
12½ x 10 x 7½ (31.8 x 25.4 x 19.1)

Wood base
3½ x 5¾ x 5½ (8.9 x 14.6 x 14)

Inscribed proper left rear on neck:
W.E.N FEC. 1935

Yale University School of Medicine
Historical Library

455 *John Spangler Nicholas* 1895–1963
PH.D. 1921

n.d.
Plaster
10½ x 6¾ x 8 (26.7 x 17.1 x 20.3)

Yale University Library

456 *Portrait of an Unidentified Man*

n.d.
Painted plaster and plastic
15¾ x 8 x 10 (40 x 20.3 x 25.4)

Yale University Library

457 *Portrait of an Unidentified Man*

Early 20th century
Bronze, dark brown patina
14 x 7 x 8¾ (35.6 x 17.8 x 22.2)

Foundry: C. Valsuani, Paris; mark, impressed in relief at bottom of neck:
CIRE / C. VALSUAN / PERDUE

Provenance unknown
1969.88.3

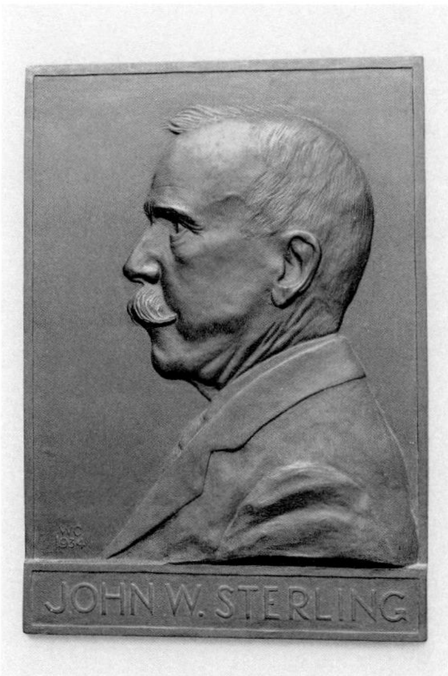

458

458 *John William Sterling* 1844–1918
B.A. 1864, M.A. 1869, LL.D. 1893

1934
Bronze, dark brown patina
14½ x 10¾ x ¾ (36.8 x 27.3 x 1.9)

Inscribed on front in relief lower left: WC / 1934; lower center: JOHN W. STERLING

Yale University Divinity School
Purchase
1951.45.1

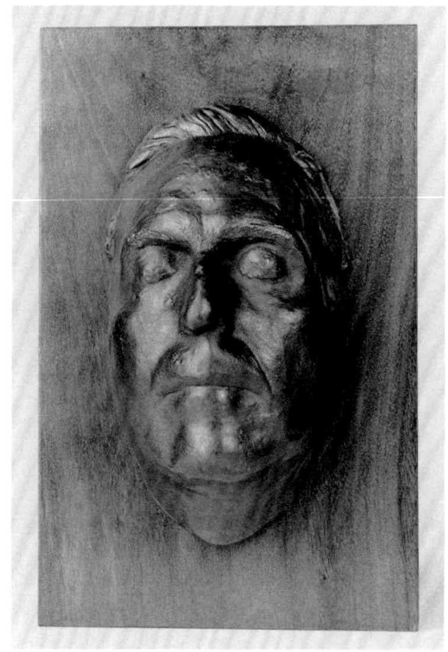

459

459 *Dr. Edward Clark Streeter*
1874–1947
B.A. 1898

1947
Bronze, brown and exposed bronze patina
10 x 5¾ x 4 (25.4 x 14.6 x 10.2)

Wood mount
13¾ x 9 x ⅝ (34.9 x 22.9 x 1.6)

Foundry: The Gorham Manufacturing Company, Providence, Rhode Island; mark beneath chin: GORHAM CO. FOUNDERS OJLF

Gift of Mrs. Edward C. Streeter to the Yale University School of Medicine Historical Library
1948.312

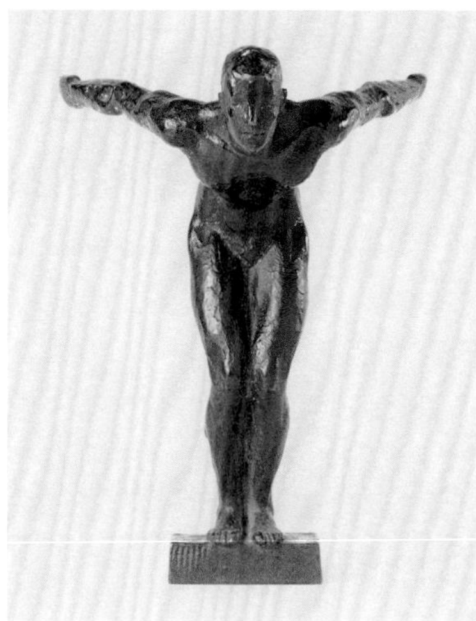

460

460 *The Swimmer*

c.1920
Bronze, black patina
9½ x 7 x 7 (24.1 x 17.8 x 17.8)

Inscribed proper left rear edge of base: 2E

Payne Whitney Gymnasium

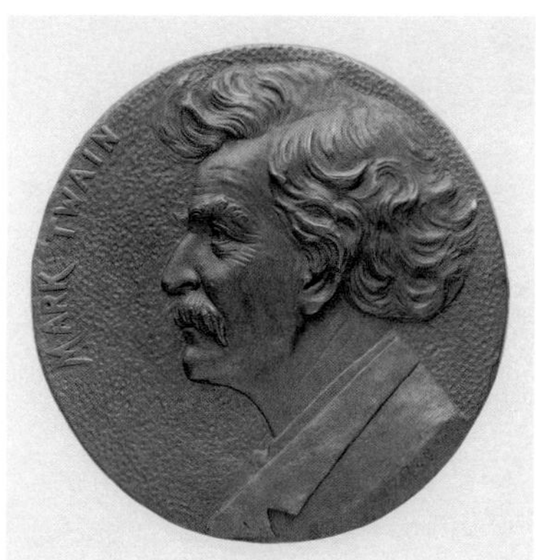

461

461 *Mark Twain* (Samuel Langhorne Clemens) 1835–1910
M.A.(hon.) 1888, LITT.D. 1901

n.d.
Plaster with black foil covering
DIAM. 9½ x D. 1 (24.1 x 2.5)

Inscribed on front lower right: F.E.G. Sept; upper left in relief: MARK TWAIN

Gift of Willard S. Morse to the Collection of American Literature, Beinecke Rare Book and Manuscript Library
1980.309

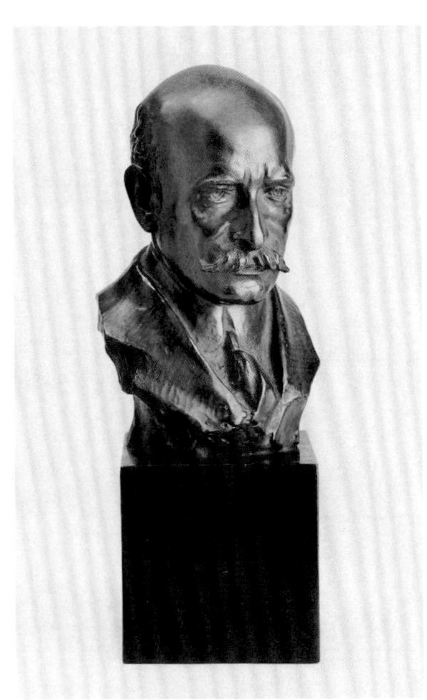

462

462 *Paul M. Warburg* 1868–1932

1933
Bronze, golden brown patina
8 x 5 x 5 (20.3 x 12.7 x 12.7)

Wood base
4 x 4 x 4¾ (10.2 x 10.2 x 12.1)

Signed, dated, and inscribed on side of proper left shoulder: DMN 1933 / M II

Foundry: Roman Bronze Works, New York; mark, on lower proper right rear, near bottom edge: ROMAN BRONZE WORKS N.Y.

Gift of James P. Warburg to the Yale University Library

463 *War Memorial*

1926
Stone, slate, gilt
149¾ x 165 x 113½
(380.4 x 419.1 x 288.3)

Inscribed front center: In Memory of THE MEN of YALE / who, true to Her Traditions, / gave THEIR LIVES that FREEDOM / might not perish from the Earth / 1914 ~ ANNO DOMINI ~ 1918; center rear: ERECTED BY THE GRADUATES OF / YALE UNIVERSITY / A.D. MDCCCCXXVI

Erected by the Graduates of Yale University in 1926

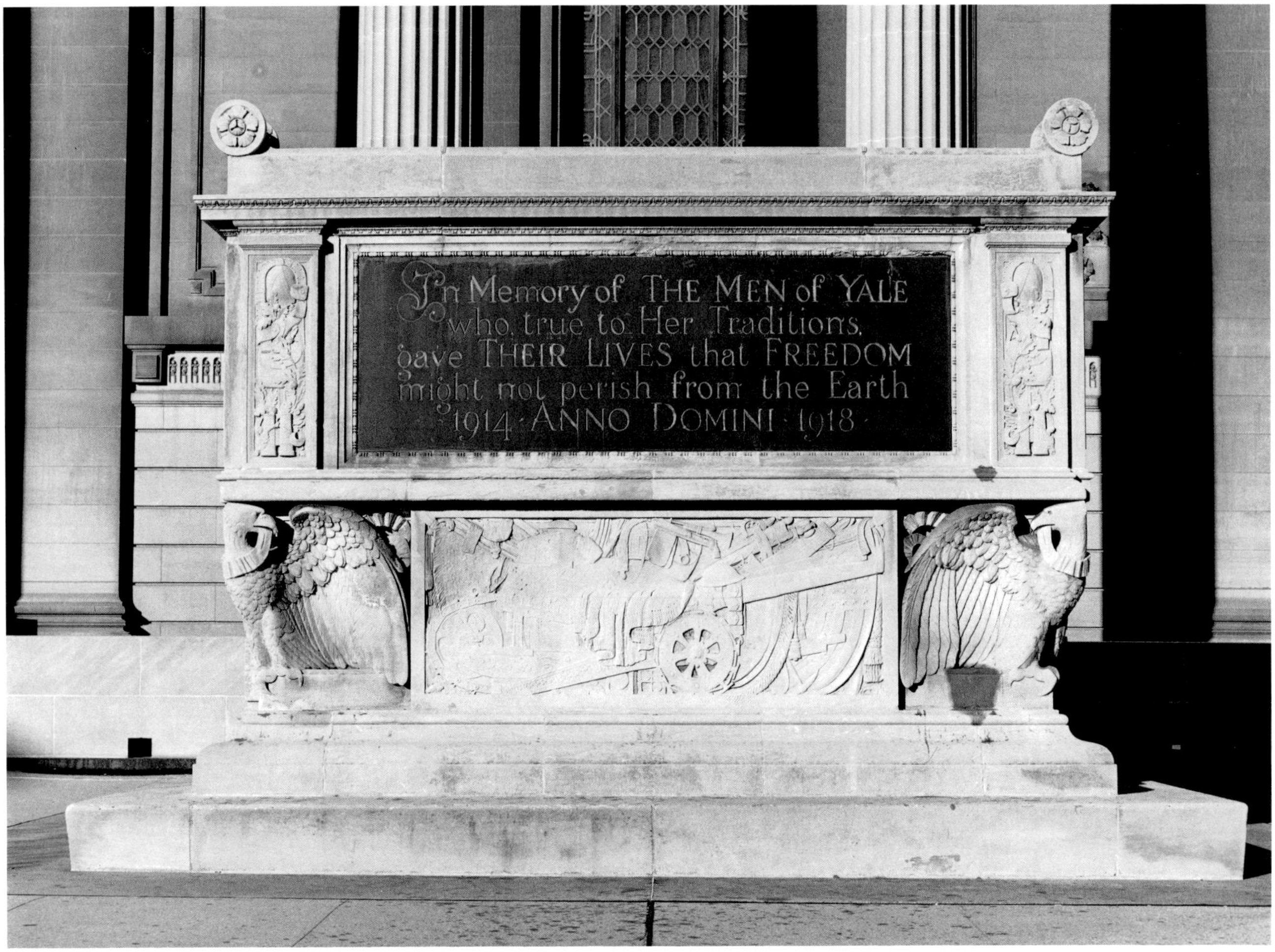

463

464 *Thornton Niven Wilder* 1897–1975

B.A. 1920, LITT.D. 1947

n.d.
Painted plaster
9 x 6 x 4 (22.9 x 15.2 x 10.2)

Gift of Miss Isabel Wilder to the Collection of American Literature, Beinecke Rare Book and Manuscript Library
1980.327

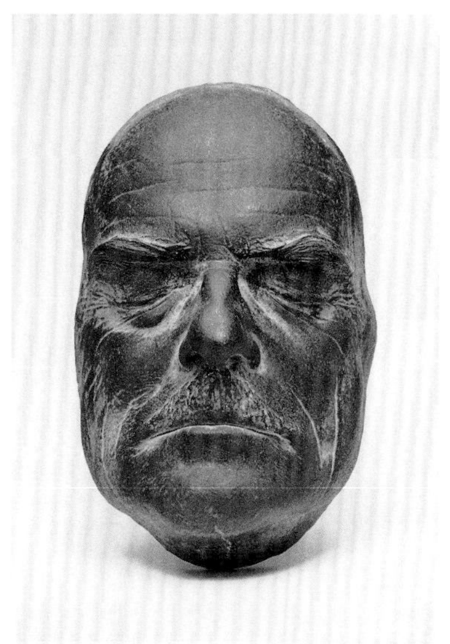

464

465 *Elinor Hoyt Wylie* 1886–1928

1923
Clay
DIAM. 3½ x D. ¼ (8.9 x 0.64)

Wood mount
4⅜ x 5 x ¾ (11.1 x 12.7 x 1.9)

Inscribed lower left front: 1923 / E[?]; along perimeter, only partially legible: EL WYLIE

Gift of Mrs. William Rose Benét to the Collection of American Literature, Beinecke Rare Book and Manuscript Library
1980.504

466 *Yale Varsity Wrestling Trophy*

c.1933
Bronze, green patina
15 x 18 x 12 (38.1 x 45.7 x 30.5)
Wood base, painted black
11½ x 25 x 17¼ (29.2 x 63.5 x 43.8)

Inscribed on cast and metal labels affixed to front of wood base in relief: YALE VARSITY WRESTLING TROPHY / PRESENTED BY / JAMES R. GETZ / CLASS OF 1933 / "IN MEMORY OF HIS MOTHER" / A RECOGNITION OF THE WRESTLER / WHO IS OF THE MOST VALUE / TO THE TEAM EACH YEAR

Gift of James R. Getz, B.A. 1933, in memory of his mother, to Payne Whitney Gymnasium

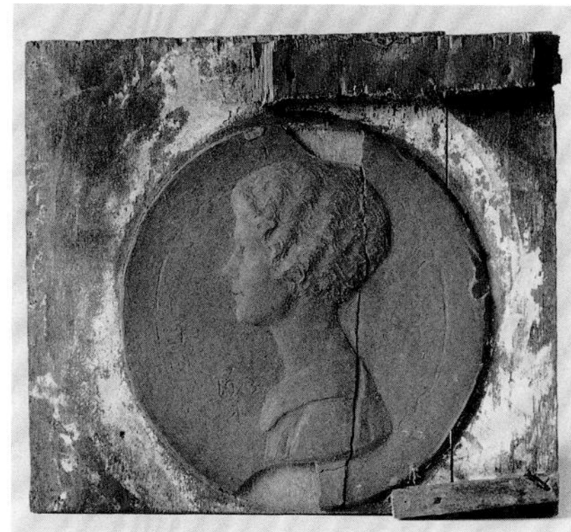

465

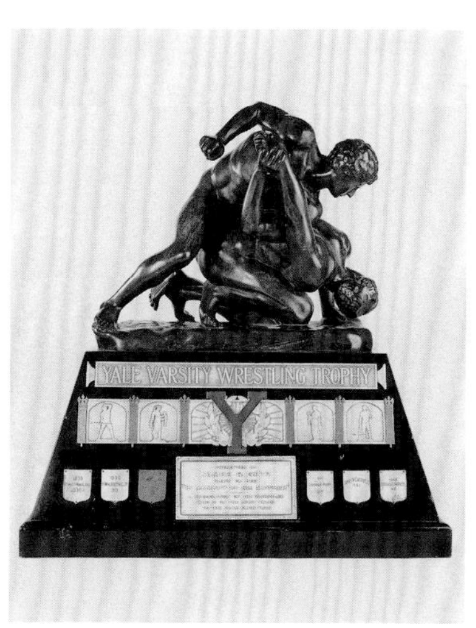

466

ACCESSION NUMBER INDEX

TITLE INDEX

DONOR INDEX

PHOTOGRAPHY CREDITS

All photography is by Marianne Bernstein, except as listed below. Numbers refer to catalogue entries.

Beinecke Rare Book and Manuscript Library, Yale University 15

Courtesy of Richard Lippold 179

Office of Public Information, Yale University (Michael Marsland) 228, 368

Oil and Steel Gallery 70

Robert Hennessey 169

Yale University Art Gallery (Michael Agee) 317; (Joseph Szaszfai) 5–7, 11–13, 22, 25, 30, 37, 40, 44, 53, 55, 56, 62, 65–68, 71–75, 80, 87, 90, 92–94, 99, 107–09, 112, 113, 118–20, 128, 132, 138, 141, 146, 149, 152–54, 174, 175, 177, 180, 181, 202, 204, 207, 214, 216, 220, 221, 224, 225, 229, 233, 234, 245, 246, 256, 258, 260, 301, 303, 310, 312, 318–20, 371–75, 377, 378, 380, 384–87, 393–95, 398, 401, 404–07, 409–11, 414, 415, 422, 438, 441, 446

Copyedited by Elise K. Kenney

Composition in Adobe Garamond types by Hoblitzelle Graphics

Printed by The Stinehour Press • Bound by Mueller Trade Bindery

Production Supervision by Yale University Printing Service

Design & Typography by John Gambell and Jeanne Spencer